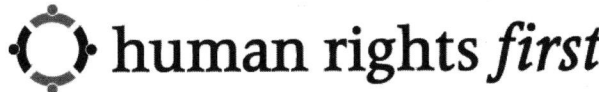 

In Pursuit of Justice
Prosecuting Terrorism Cases in the Federal Courts

A White Paper

Richard B. Zabel
James J. Benjamin, Jr.
May 2008

About Us

Human Rights First believes that building respect for human rights and the rule of law will help ensure the dignity to which every individual is entitled and will stem tyranny, extremism, intolerance, and violence.

Human Rights First protects people at risk: refugees who flee persecution, victims of crimes against humanity or other mass human rights violations, victims of discrimination, those whose rights are eroded in the name of national security, and human rights advocates who are targeted for defending the rights of others. These groups are often the first victims of societal instability and breakdown; their treatment is a harbinger of wider-scale repression. Human Rights First works to prevent violations against these groups and to seek justice and accountability for violations against them.

Human Rights First is practical and effective. We advocate for change at the highest levels of national and international policymaking. We seek justice through the courts. We raise awareness and understanding through the media. We build coalitions among those with divergent views. And we mobilize people to act.

Human Rights First is a non-profit, nonpartisan international human rights organization based in New York and Washington D.C. To maintain our independence, we accept no government funding.

This report is available for free online at www.humanrightsfirst.org

© 2008 Human Rights First. All Rights Reserved.

human rights first

Headquarters

333 Seventh Avenue
13th Floor
New York, NY 10001-5108

Tel.: 212.845.5200
Fax: 212.845.5299

Washington D.C. Office

100 Maryland Avenue, NE
Suite 500
Washington, DC 20002-5625

Tel: 202.547.5692
Fax: 202.543.5999

www.humanrightsfirst.org

Preface

The primary authors of this White Paper are Richard B. Zabel and James J. Benjamin, Jr., partners in the New York office of Akin Gump Strauss Hauer & Feld LLP. They, along with a terrific team at Akin Gump, devoted much hard work and many long hours to prepare this Paper on a pro bono basis. Members of the Akin Gump team include Michael Lockard and Joseph Sorkin, who provided indispensable leadership and assistance throughout the process, as well as Jessica Budoff, Daniel Chau, Russell Collins, Kirk Conway, Rachel Gerstein, Samidh Guha, Christopher Kercher, Natasha Kohne, Amit Kurlekar, Leslie Lanphear, Sherene Lewis, Kathleen Leicht, Alana Martell, Jessica Mason, Robert Pees, Elizabeth Peterson, Charles Riely, Jamie Sheldon and Ashley Waters. Although Akin Gump is proud of the firm's commitment to pro bono work, the views expressed in this White Paper include those of the primary authors and Human Rights First; they are not the views of Akin Gump as a firm or of other Akin Gump attorneys.

As former Assistant United States Attorneys in the Southern District of New York, Rich and Jim brought to this project their deep and accomplished experiences, perspectives, and understanding of the inner workings of the federal criminal justice system in the United States. This White Paper benefits from their appreciation and understanding of the range of tools that prosecutors can and will use to prosecute individuals whom the government believes to be complicit in international terrorism. This perspective is extraordinarily valuable to Human Rights First and to the broader debate on these issues. In publishing this Paper, we hope that it will inform the vitally important public discussion of these matters and provide some much-needed practical information on how the U.S. criminal justice system has worked in the past and should work in the future.

Human Rights First is a non-profit, nonpartisan international human rights organization based in New York and Washington D.C. To maintain its independence, it accepts no government funding. Human Rights First believes that building respect for human rights and the rule of law will help ensure the dignity to which every individual is entitled and will stem tyranny, extremism, intolerance, and violence. Human Rights First protects people at risk: refugees who flee persecution, victims of crimes against humanity or other mass human rights violations, victims of discrimination, those whose rights are eroded in the name of national security, and human rights advocates who are targeted for defending the rights of others. These groups are often the first victims of societal instability and breakdown; their treatment is a harbinger of wider-scale repression. Human Rights First works to prevent violations against these groups and to seek justice and accountability for violations against them. Human Rights First is practical and effective. It advocates for change at the highest levels of national and international policymaking. It seeks justice through the courts. It raises awareness and understanding through the media. It builds coalitions among those with divergent views. And it mobilizes people to act.

Human Rights First staff who contributed to this White Paper include Devon Chaffee, Associate Attorney; Deborah Colson, Senior Associate, Law and Security Program; Neil Hicks, International Policy Advisor; Anwen Hughes, Senior Counsel, Refugee Protection Program; Kevin Lanigan, Director, Law and Security Program; Sahr MuhammedAlly, Senior Associate, Law and Security Program; and Gabor Rona, International Legal Director.

From our own institutional perspective, we at Human Rights First are very proud to publish this White Paper, which reflects enormous time and effort by these experienced prosecutors and their Akin Gump colleagues. It is part of Human Rights First's continuing effort to work collaboratively with those on the front lines of protecting U.S. national security. Such collaborations are both very valuable and at times challenging. This is a Human Rights First report, and although it was at times challenging to fully harmonize Human Rights

First's views with those of Rich and Jim, we take full responsibility for the Paper's contents and conclusions. Going forward, we expect and have encouraged Rich and Jim to express their own perspectives on this important set of issues in various venues. We welcome their active participation in the public debate, not just as the primary authors of this Paper but more broadly as respected former prosecutors.

In the end, what will be most useful about this White Paper is its detailed demonstration of the strengths and capacities of the federal criminal justice system to try individuals accused of terrorism and other threats to national security. And on this central conclusion we could not be in closer agreement.

Table of Contents

I. **Introduction** 1

II. **Executive Summary** 5
    A. Discussion of Data Collection 5
    B. Substantive Law 6
    C. Securing the Defendant's Presence in Court 6
    D. Detention of Individuals Suspected of Involvement in Terrorism 7
    E. The Challenge of Dealing with Sensitive Evidence that Implicates National Security 8
    F. *Brady* and the Government's Other Discovery Obligations 9
    G. *Miranda* and the Right to Remain Silent 10
    H. Evidentiary and Speedy Trial Issues 10
    I. Sentencing 11
    J. Safety and Security of Trial Participants and Others 11

III. **A Brief History of Terrorist Attacks Against United States Interests and an Introduction to the Law Enforcement Response** 13
    A. The Beginnings of Modern International Terrorism 13
    B. The New Era 14
        1. The First Attack on the World Trade Center and the Exposure of the Conspiracy Led by Sheikh Abdel Rahman 14
        2. The Khobar Towers Bombing 15
        3. The East Africa Embassy Bombings 15
        4. The Millennium Plot 16
        5. The Attack on the USS *Cole* 16
        6. The 9/11 Attacks 16
    C. The Criminal Justice Response to International Terrorism 17
        1. The Airline Hijacking Cases of the 1980s 17
        2. World Trade Center I and Related Conspiracies in the Early 1990s 17
        3. The Embassy Bombings Trial 17
        4. Zacarias Moussaoui 18
        5. "Sleeper Cell" Cases 18
        6. Material Support Cases 19
        7. Prosecuting Those Who Incite Terrorism 19
        8. Material Witness and "Enemy Combatant" Cases 20

IV. **The Data on Cases Prosecuted in Federal Court** 21

Table of Contents

V. Existing Criminal Statutes Cover a Broad Spectrum of the Crimes Committed by International Terrorists 31

    A. Material Support of Terrorist Organizations 31

        1. Providing Material Support in Furtherance of a Terrorist Act (18 U.S.C. § 2339A) 32

        2. Providing Material Support to Designated Terrorist Organizations (18 U.S.C. § 2339B) 34

        3. Providing or Collecting Funds to Be Used in an Act of Terrorism (18 U.S.C. § 2339C) 38

        4. Receiving Military Training from a Designated Foreign Terrorist Organization (18 U.S.C. § 2339D) 38

    B. Other Terrorism Statutes Under Chapter 113B of the Federal Criminal Code 39

        1. Homicide or Serious Assault Against U.S. Nationals Outside the United States with Intent to Conduct Terrorism (18 U.S.C. § 2332) 39

        2. Use of Weapons of Mass Destruction (18 U.S.C. § 2332a) 40

        3. Acts of Terrorism Within the United States that Transcend National Boundaries (18 U.S.C. § 2332b) 41

        4. Financial Transactions with Countries Supporting International Terrorism (18 U.S.C. § 2332d) 43

        5. Bombings of Places of Public Use (18 U.S.C. § 2332f) 43

        6. Missile Systems Designed to Destroy Aircraft and Radiological Dispersal Devices (18 U.S.C. §§ 2332g and 2332h) 44

        7. Harboring or Concealing Terrorists (18 U.S.C. § 2339) 45

    C. Treason (18 U.S.C. § 2381) 45

        1. Levying War Against the United States 46

        2. Adhering to Enemies, Giving Them Aid and Comfort 47

    D. Seditious Conspiracy (18 U.S.C. § 2384) 48

    E. Recruitment of and Enlistment for Hostile Force (18 U.S.C. §§ 2389-90) 50

    F. Use of Alternative Statutes to Prosecute Defendants Believed to Be Complicit in Terrorism 51

    G. Use of Generally Applicable Statutes Aimed at Violence or Conspiracy 54

    H. Biological Weapons (18 U.S.C. §§ 175-78) 56

    I. Criminal Incitement Offenses: The Smith Act (18 U.S.C. § 2385) and Criminal Solicitation (18 U.S.C. § 373) 57

        1. The Smith Act 58

        2. Criminal Solicitation 59

        3. Considerations of Extraterritorial Application 60

VI. Courts Have Consistently Exercised Jurisdiction Over Defendants Brought Before Them, Even if the Defendant Was Subjected to Forcible Treatment Outside the Scope of Normal Arrest or Extradition Proceedings 61

VII. In the Overwhelming Majority of Cases, Existing Law Provides an Adequate Basis to Detain or Appropriately Monitor Terrorism Suspects 65

    A. Detention of Persons Charged with a Federal Crime 66

    B. Detention of Aliens Subject to Removal 67

    C. The Material Witness Statute 69

    D. Evaluating the Detention of Terrorism Suspects Under Existing Law 71

        1. The *Padilla* Case 72

        2. The *al-Marri* Case 73

        3. Assessing *Padilla* and *al-Marri* 74

VIII. Using Statutes Such as FISA and CIPA, Courts Have Effectively Managed the Challenge of Dealing with Classified or Sensitive Evidence that Implicates National Security **77**
   A. The Foreign Intelligence Surveillance Act 77
      1. Overview of FISA Procedures 79
      2. The Use of FISA Evidence in Criminal Cases—The Creation and Demise of the FISA "Wall" 79
   B. The Classified Information Procedures Act 81
      1. Overview of CIPA's Provisions 82
      2. The Use of CIPA Procedures in Terrorism Cases 84
      3. Assessing CIPA's Effectiveness in Terrorism Cases 87

IX. Courts Have Effectively Applied the *Brady* Rule and the Government's Other Disclosure Obligations in Terrorism Cases **91**
   A. Balancing the Government's *Brady* Obligations Against the Need to Protect Sensitive National-Security Information 93
   B. Managing Problems Presented by Voluminous FISA Materials and Overclassification 95
   C. The Scope of the Prosecution's Obligation to Search for *Brady* Material...96

X. The *Miranda* Rule: Applying the Fifth Amendment Protections Against Coerced Confessions in a Practical Manner in Terrorism Cases **101**
   A. Application of the *Miranda* Rule in International Terrorism Cases Where the Defendant Is Subject to Custodial Interrogation Outside the United States 101
   B. The Implications of Judge Sand's Ruling in *Bin Laden* 103

XI. Courts Have Generally Applied the Federal Rules of Evidence in a Common-Sense, Practical Manner in Terrorism Cases **107**

XII. Terrorism Trials Have Not Presented Novel Speedy Trial Problems **111**

XIII. In Many Terrorism Cases, Federal Sentencing Laws Result in Severe Sentences and Sometimes Lead to Cooperation and Guilty Pleas **115**

XIV. The Court System Generally Is Able to Assure the Safety and Security of Trial Participants and Others **121**
   A. Courtroom and Juror Security 122
   B. Security Within the Bureau of Prisons 124

XV. Conclusion **129**

Appendices **131**
   A. Terrorism Prosecution Cases 133
   B. Historical Timeline of Significant Terrorism Statutes Enacted by Congress 137

Endnotes **143**

I.
Introduction

This White Paper examines the capability of the federal courts to handle criminal cases arising from international terrorism. In the Paper, we focus on terrorism that is associated—organizationally, financially, or ideologically—with self-described "jihadist" or Islamist extremist terrorist groups like al Qaeda.[1] Many observers have expressed views on this important subject.[2] Some have argued for prosecuting terrorist criminals outside of the civilian court system; others have called for the establishment of an entirely new "national security court."[3] A premise of such arguments is that the traditional court system is not well-equipped to handle international terrorism cases. We aim to explore that premise.

As we first approached this White Paper, we began with the proposition that the adequacy of the criminal justice system in this area is not an abstract or academic question. Over the years, and especially since the early 1990s, the government has brought scores of criminal prosecutions against defendants who are alleged to have been involved in international terrorism. The cases range from epic mega-trials, mainly brought before 9/11 in the Southern District of New York, to a broad range of cases of varying size in more recent years. The roster of prosecutions encompasses retrospective cases arising from completed acts of terrorism (e.g., the August 1998 Embassy Bombings in Africa) and preemptive prosecutions that are focused on prevention (e.g., numerous prosecutions since 9/11 for material support of terrorist organizations). In preparing this White Paper, we have set out to identify, examine, and analyze each of the terrorism cases that have been prosecuted in federal courts since the early 1990s. Although we may have missed some cases, we have amassed a considerable set of data that, we believe, is valuable in examining the adequacy of the court system to cope with terrorism cases.

Following an executive summary, this White Paper begins with a brief historical overview of terrorism by Islamist extremists in the United States and against U.S. interests abroad, followed by an introduction to certain federal court prosecutions illustrating some of the major issues in terrorism cases. We then discuss our approach to collecting information on terrorism cases, followed by a summary of, and some observations about, the data.

The White Paper then moves on to a discussion of the key legal and practical issues that are commonly presented in international terrorism cases and an examination of how the court system has dealt with these issues. Our focus is not only on legal issues addressed in court decisions and statutes passed by Congress, but also on practical issues that confront courts and law enforcement. We address the adequacy and scope of criminal statutes to prosecute alleged terrorists and examine a host of substantive, procedural, and practical issues that have arisen in real-world terrorism prosecutions. For example, we examine how courts have balanced defendants' rights to be informed of the relevant evidence with the need to preserve the secrecy of information that could compromise national security if disclosed. We also examine issues as diverse as pre-trial detention, the *Miranda* rule, speedy trial issues, sentencing proceedings, and ensuring the safety of judges, jurors, and other trial participants.[4]

In preparing this White Paper, we have relied not only on legal authorities such as judicial decisions and statutes, but also on docket sheets, indictments, and motion papers filed in numerous terrorism prosecutions around the country. We have also studied the views of academics and journalists and have sought out the personal perspectives of people who have firsthand experience in the litigation of international terrorism cases.[5] Our conclusion, based on the data we have examined and our review of the key legal and practical issues, is that the criminal justice system is reasonably well-equipped to handle most international terrorism cases. Specifically, prosecuting terrorism defendants in the court system appears as a general matter to lead to just, reliable results and not to cause serious security breaches or other problems that threaten the nation's security. Of course, challenges arise from time to time—sometimes serious ones—but most of these challenges are not unique to international terrorism cases. One implication of our conclusion that the criminal justice system serves as an effective means of convicting and incapacitating terrorists is that the need for a "national security court" that would displace the criminal justice system is not apparent. However, there are several important qualifications on our conclusion.

First, we firmly agree with those who say that the criminal justice system, by itself, is not "the answer" to the problem of international terrorism. Given the magnitude and complexity of the international terrorism threat, it is plain that the government must employ a multifaceted approach involving the use of military, intelligence, diplomatic, economic, and law enforcement resources in order to address the threat of international terrorism. Managing these different efforts is a challenging task that requires flexibility and creativity on the part of the government.

Second, we also agree with those who note that major terrorism cases pose strains and burdens on the criminal justice system. Some of the cases have presented challenges—both legal and practical—that are virtually unprecedented. The blockbuster international terrorism cases are extraordinarily complex. Managing them successfully requires navigating through thorny legal issues as well as challenging practical problems.

Third, we agree with those who argue that the criminal justice system sometimes stumbles. It is susceptible to errors of all kinds and may fairly be criticized, in different cases, as being too slow, too fast, too harsh, too lenient, too subtle, too blunt, too opaque, and too transparent. Yet for all of these well-justified criticisms, experience has shown that the justice system has generally remained a workable and credible system. Indeed, the justice system has shown a key characteristic in dealing with criminal terrorism cases: adaptability. The evolution of statutes, courtroom procedures, and efforts to balance security issues with the rights of the parties reveals a challenged but flexible justice system that generally has been able to address its shortcomings. Where appropriate, we have offered our constructive criticisms of the court system and our views on still-unsettled legal questions.

A few important words about the scope of our White Paper. In approaching this project, we have confined our analysis to the legal and practical issues associated with handling international terrorism cases in the criminal justice system. While we have covered a broad array of issues presented in terrorism cases, we recognize that we have not covered every one. Further, because it is beyond the scope of this White Paper, we have not sought to examine related issues such as the legality of capture, detention, interrogation, and trial of prisoners by the military or the CIA outside the civilian courts. Nor have we undertaken any comparative analysis of jurisdiction or procedure in civilian courts versus courts martial versus military commissions. Likewise, comparative analysis of other countries' legal systems lies outside our scope. Finally, we have avoided more abstract "policy" arguments such as whether terrorism prosecutions serve as an effective deterrent and whether open and fair civilian trials promote public confidence in the United States around the world. Although these arguments are provocative and important, they are difficult to resolve based on legal research or authority.

We are of course keenly aware that the U.S. armed forces are presently fighting on multiple fronts against al Qaeda and other Islamist extremist terrorist groups that intend to commit acts of violence against the United States. As part of ongoing military operations, soldiers and sailors will capture and detain enemy fighters, without punishing them, in order to disable them from fighting against the United States. This is both lawful and fundamental to the effective prosecution of war, and it does not generally implicate the criminal justice system. In some cases, however, the government may wish to go further and actually try and punish captured enemy fighters. Consistent with the law of war and the traditional role of military justice, military courts have a crucial role to play in the prosecution of individuals who are subject to trial under the law of war. We do not suggest that it would be wise or remotely possible for the civilian justice system to supplant the military justice system in this area: far from it. However, in some cases it is not obvious where alleged terrorists who are captured by the military should be tried for their alleged crimes—in a federal court, a court martial, or a military tribunal—and it may be the case that the government could lawfully choose among several different forums. The analysis in this White Paper suggests that in many cases, the criminal justice system may be a suitable venue for prosecution.

In this White Paper, we do not respond directly to the proposals of those who have advocated a "national security court." Although thoughtful proposals have been circulated and deserve consideration, our focus is on assessing the adequacy of the civilian justice system that already exists, not on attempting to foresee and assess how an alternative system could work. We note, however, that one significant downside of a new national security court would be the need to create from scratch the procedures, precedents, and body of law that would govern such a court. The disarray that has plagued the military commissions at Guantánamo—with abundant litigation as well as internal dissension within the military command structure but not a single completed trial some six years after the presidential order authorizing military commissions—does not bode well for those who envision creating a brand new system from scratch.[6] By contrast, a significant advantage of the criminal justice system is the fact that the federal courts have amassed many years of experience and a reservoir of judicial wisdom as well as a broadly experienced bar—both prosecutors and defense attorneys—to guide the course of particular cases.

We recognize that the project we have undertaken is large and that views on this subject are charged and will vary. We do not profess to have found definitive answers, only to have undertaken a serious and objective review of the subject. We hope that our findings and analysis are of value in the ongoing debate about how best to reconcile our national commitment to the rule of law with the imperative of assuring security for all Americans.

II. Executive Summary

In attempting to eradicate the threat of international terrorism by Islamist extremists, our country faces enormous challenges. Among the more difficult problems is what to do with individuals who come into the custody of the U.S. government and who are suspected of complicity in terrorist acts. Some detainees may properly be held under the law of war for the duration of active hostilities to prevent them from returning to the field of battle, and without any effort by the government to file charges or impose punishment. However, for some suspected terrorists, military detention is not appropriate and, even if it is, the government may find it both desirable and necessary, at some point, to bring formal charges in the civilian court system with a view toward imposing punishment.

Recently, some commentators have proposed an entirely new "national security court" to handle some or all international terrorism prosecutions. Although proposals vary, many offer novel features that would give the government more power and make it easier for the government to secure convictions. However, creating a brand new court system from scratch would be expensive, uncertain, and almost certainly controversial. Indeed, there is the risk that the very same issues now debated simply would be transferred to a new arena for resolution. In our view, before dramatic changes are imposed—such as the creation of an entirely new court or new detention scheme—it is important to take a step back and evaluate the capability of the existing federal courts and the existing body of federal law to handle criminal cases arising from international terrorism. Given the strength and vitality of our existing court system—and the fact that it reflects in many ways the best aspects of our legal and cultural traditions—there are obvious advantages to relying on the existing system, provided that it is up to the job.

Our analysis of the capability of the federal courts to handle criminal cases arising from international terrorism is based heavily on the actual experience of more than 100 international terrorism cases that have been prosecuted in federal courts over the past fifteen years. Based on our review of that data and our other research and analysis, we conclude that, contrary to the views of some critics, the court system is generally well-equipped to handle most terrorism cases. We reach this conclusion based on the broad analysis conducted in this White Paper. A high-level summary of that analysis follows immediately below.

A. Discussion of Data Collection

In preparing this White Paper, we have sought to avoid abstract or academic approaches, focusing instead on the rich body of actual experience with terrorism cases in the federal courts. We have sought to identify all cases arising from terrorism that is associated—organizationally, financially, or ideologically—with Islamist extremist terrorist groups like al Qaeda. With that as our focus, we have combed through a number of sources in an effort to identify all such cases that have been brought in federal courts since 9/11, as well as the most significant cases from the 1990s. To the extent that materials were publicly available, we have obtained docket sheets, motion papers, and judicial opinions from these cases, as well as press accounts and other information, in an effort to understand the major issues that were presented in each case. Although our data collection effort is not foolproof and, indeed, is almost certainly incomplete, we believe that we have gathered a reasonable set of data that permits us to draw reasonable conclusions about the way the court system has dealt with a whole array of substantive and procedural issues in terrorism cases. In Appendix A of this Paper, we include a list of all of the terrorism cases that we have identified and examined.

B. Substantive Law

Over the years, and especially since 1996, Congress has enacted a host of anti-terrorism laws. Prosecutors have successfully invoked many of these specially tailored terrorism laws to obtain convictions in all manner of criminal terrorism cases. In addition, prosecutors have relied on the large body of generally applicable criminal statutes in cases against accused terrorists, including statutes that criminalize murder, bombings, conspiracy, money laundering, and other unlawful conduct. Experience has shown that the existing array of federal criminal statutes contains a more-than-adequate set of tools for prosecutors to invoke against accused terrorists.

Some of the most important criminal statutes in terrorism cases are those prohibiting "material support" of terrorist organizations. Under these statutes, it is unlawful for a person to provide money, personnel, or any other support to an organization if the person knows or intends that the organization is planning to commit a terrorist act or if the person knows that the organization has engaged in terrorism or has been designated, by the U.S. government, as a terrorist organization. The material support statutes initially were drafted very broadly, causing concerns that they could be used to penalize individuals for exercising legitimate First and Fifth Amendment rights, but over the years the courts have construed and Congress has amended the statutes so that they are less susceptible to abuse.

Because material support prosecutions do not require that any act of terrorism actually occured, they have been a pillar of the government's post-9/11 strategy of preventive prosecutions. Material support cases have been brought against persons who enrolled at terrorist training camps, who acted as messengers for terrorist leaders, who intended to act as doctors to terrorist groups, or who raised money to support terrorist organizations. Although these cases can potentially result in overreaching, and although not all material support cases have resulted in convictions, the government's overall record of success in this area is impressive, and most if not all of the convictions seem sound.

Another key approach, since 9/11, has been for law enforcement to charge terrorism defendants with violations of "alternative statutes"—i.e., generally applicable crimes that are not directly related to terrorism such as immigration violations, false statements, credit card fraud, and the like.

Prosecutors have used a similar strategy for many years in other areas of criminal law, and we believe that it is both appropriate and effective to deploy it against terrorists. Individuals who are involved in terrorism will often violate a number of generally applicable criminal laws—for example, by traveling with a forged passport or using stolen credit cards—and prosecutors have been able to bring successful and largely uncontroversial cases against them for engaging in these violations.

Other statutes, such as those prohibiting seditious conspiracy and terrorism-related homicide, have been used in important cases such as the prosecutions of Sheikh Omar Abdel Rahman and the Embassy Bombers. The government rarely has charged terrorism defendants with treason but that statute, too, offers a powerful tool in certain cases. Other statutes, such as detailed criminal laws regarding biological weapons and radiological dispersal devices, have not yet been used, one hopes because those weapons are still not easy for terrorists to obtain. Finally, the government has brought several important cases against authority figures who have engaged in criminal incitement by urging their followers to commit acts of violence against the United States. Although such cases need to be carefully considered in light of the First Amendment implications, to date, courts and prosecutors have ensured that incitement cases are brought within proper constitutional boundaries and in appropriate cases. In Appendix B of this Paper, we include an historical timeline of significant statutes that have been enacted to address terrorism-related offenses.

C. Securing the Defendant's Presence in Court

In many terrorism cases, the defendant is brought to court to face criminal charges after being arrested by a federal law enforcement officer or after traditional extradition proceedings. These cases present no novel issues. In some cases, however, defendants have been brought into the justice system by unconventional means, including transfer by U.S. military authorities or informal "rendition" by foreign officials outside the extradition process. In some scenarios, the circumstances surrounding the defendant's apprehension may be murky, and the defendant may allege that he was subjected to forcible treatment or prolonged detention.

Under longstanding Supreme Court precedent embodied in the so-called *Ker-Frisbie* doctrine, irregularities in the manner in which a defendant was captured and brought to court do not generally prevent federal courts from exercising jurisdiction over the case. Over the years, lower courts have identified two narrow circumstances in which a defendant's irregular abduction might cause a federal court to lose jurisdiction over a criminal case—(i) if the abduction violates an explicit term in an extradition treaty or (ii) if it is accompanied by torture or other extreme conduct that "shocks the conscience" of the court. However, to our knowledge the courts have never dismissed a case under either of these exceptions, and case law indicates that both exceptions are narrow. Indeed, the first exception is so narrow as to be virtually invisible given the manner in which U.S. extradition treaties generally are drafted. There is a possibility that a federal court might decline to exercise jurisdiction under the second exception if U.S. officials were shown to have participated in torture, but no court has ever dismissed a case on this basis.

D. Detention of Individuals Suspected of Involvement in Terrorism

Some commentators have argued that the existing legal system does not give the government enough authority to detain individuals who are suspected of terrorism, but we believe that this criticism is overstated. There are at least four well-established and lawful means by which the government can detain persons whom it suspects of participating in terrorism. Three of these approaches do not require the government to file criminal charges:

- Under the law of war, the government has ample authority to detain enemy fighters who are captured during hostilities in order to prevent them from rejoining the battle. More aggressive and controversial theories of military detention are outside the scope of this White Paper.

- Away from the battlefield, the government has broad latitude to arrest and seek detention of suspected terrorists as soon as it is prepared to file criminal charges against them. After arresting a defendant, the government must promptly bring the defendant before a magistrate judge, who decides whether the defendant should be detained or released on bail. But the government is entitled to a presumption that terrorism defendants should be detained, and judges have often ordered detention of defendants charged in such cases.

- In cases involving aliens who are alleged to have violated the immigration laws, the government has broad latitude to arrest and detain aliens pending a decision on whether they should be removed from the country. Thus, under the immigration laws, the government can arrest and detain many suspected terrorists (excluding U.S. citizens, of course) without filing criminal charges. Under the immigration statutes, the courts have no power to review the Executive Branch's discretionary decision to detain an alien charged with immigration violations.

- When a grand jury investigation is under way, the government may apply to a federal judge for authority to arrest an individual who is deemed to be a "material witness" in the investigation. This provision allows the government to arrest and seek detention of individuals who are charged neither with crimes nor with immigration violations. However, the material witness procedure is subject to close judicial oversight, carries a number of procedural protections, and may only be used for a limited period of time.

As experience shows, each of these procedures has at times been put to widespread use in the years since 9/11. In general, detention in criminal and immigration cases is uncontroversial and based on well-settled principles. There has been some controversy surrounding the use of the material witness statute, but the procedure is well-established in our existing legal system and is subject to close judicial oversight. Together, these various tools have given the government the authority to detain the overwhelming majority of individuals whom it has arrested in connection with terrorism.

We acknowledge the possibility that, on rare occasions, the government may believe that an individual is dangerous and is closely associated with terrorism, but may lack the legal authority to detain the person. For example, consider the hypothetical possibility of a U.S. citizen where the government has valid intelligence information suggesting a link to terrorism but insufficient admissible evidence to bring criminal charges, and where the material witness procedure has expired or is otherwise unavailable. In such a case, the government would face a dilemma and existing legal tools would probably not afford a means of detaining the individual.

However, we believe that this hypothetical scenario is an unlikely one. Given the breadth of the federal criminal code, the energy and resourcefulness of law enforcement agents and federal prosecutors, and the fact that terrorists, by definition, are criminals who often violate many laws, we believe that it would be the rare case indeed where the government could not muster sufficient evidence to bring a criminal charge against a person it believes is culpable. And experience bears out this conclusion. The empirical data we have reviewed from actual terrorism cases reveals only a tiny handful of cases where, potentially, existing tools may have been insufficient to secure the detention of a suspected terrorist. Those exceptional cases, *Padilla* and *al-Marri*, merit discussion and analysis, but we believe that they are anomalous and provide a poor basis to draw broader conclusions about the efficacy of the justice system. To the contrary, the overall body of cases strongly suggests that existing tools provide an adequate basis for the lawful detention of suspected terrorists.

We recognize further that the public record may not fully reflect all the occasions during which prosecutors could not charge and detain a dangerous individual. While it is not possible for us to assess the magnitude of the non-public record of this problem, there are likely to be those who will invoke it to argue for additional means of detaining individuals even where they cannot be charged, as is done in certain European jurisdictions. Putting aside as beyond the scope of this White Paper the very serious constitutional questions such an administrative detention scheme would raise, two practical considerations bear mentioning. First, even where law enforcement cannot charge and detain an individual, it is not powerless. It may confront the individual and disrupt and/or monitor in a variety of ways that individual's conduct. Second, in our experience, most prosecutors with whom we have discussed the issue agree that the ability to administratively detain an individual for several days or even weeks, as can be done in some European jurisdictions, would not materially help them beyond the available tools in developing a case against an individual who posed the problems Jose Padilla did. Therefore, anyone who is arguing for an administrative detention scheme to address the dilemma of a defendant like Padilla, will likely be arguing for a long-term scheme that would mark a dramatic departure from our country's longstanding ideals and practices.

E. The Challenge of Dealing with Sensitive Evidence that Implicates National Security

In many terrorism cases, the government seeks to rely on evidence that is probative of the defendant's guilt but which implicates sensitive national security interests, particularly intelligence sources, means of intelligence gathering, and even the state of our intelligence on other subjects or intelligence priorities. Dealing with classified or sensitive evidence can be one of the most important challenges in terrorism cases. Over the years, however, courts have proved, again and again, that they are up to the task of balancing the defendant's right to a fair trial, the government's desire to offer relevant evidence, and the imperative of protecting national security.

The Foreign Intelligence Surveillance Act ("FISA"), provides a lawful means for the government to conduct wiretaps and physical searches within the United States in terrorism investigations without satisfying the normal Fourth Amendment requirement of probable cause that a crime was committed. Under FISA, the government must make an ex parte application to a special FISA court, composed of a select group of federal judges, and must satisfy a number of technical requirements before the FISA court can give authority to conduct a FISA wiretap or a FISA search. The FISA procedures are very different from those used in normal criminal investigations.

In the years before 9/11, the Department of Justice ("DOJ") imposed an internal "wall" that made it difficult for FISA evidence to be used in court. Under the "wall" procedures, the government erected barriers between intelligence gathering, on one hand, and criminal prosecution on the other. As a result, it was difficult for the government to use FISA evidence in court, since it was deemed to be the province of the intelligence community. FISA itself, however, did not require the "wall"; to the contrary, from its inception the statute envisioned that FISA evidence could be used in court. After 9/11, Congress amended FISA to make it clear that the "wall" should be dismantled and FISA evidence could be shared with criminal investigators and prosecutors. Courts have found the amendments constitutional, and in the years since 9/11, FISA evidence has been used without incident in many criminal terrorism cases.

Errata Sheet

In Pursuit of Justice: Prosecuting Terrorism Cases in the Federal Courts

June 3, 2008

Please find the following modifications to the text of the report, which are provided in order to clarify and make more precise the discussion of the particular issue set forth below.

On page 9 of the report, the second sentence of the fourth full paragraph should be replaced with the following:

> We are aware of two reported incidents in which sensitive information was supposedly disclosed in terrorism cases, but we have not been able to confirm one of those incidents, and in the other it is our understanding that the government did not try to invoke non-disclosure protections.

On pages 88-89 of the report, the last full paragraph on page 88 and the carryover paragraph on pages 88-89 should be replaced with the following:

> We have not been able to confirm the other example most commonly cited for the proposition that terrorism trials have led to security breaches. It has been reported that during the trial of Ramzi Yousef, testimony about the delivery of a cell phone battery alerted terrorists that a communications link had been compromised and caused them to stop using that link, depriving the government of valuable intelligence. See Mukasey, *Jose Padilla Makes Bad Law*. Based on publicly available information, we have not been able to confirm this incident. Moreover, the trial record from the Embassy Bombings case suggests the possibility that Judge Mukasey may have intended to refer not to the *Yousef* trial, but rather to evidence in the Embassy Bombings case regarding Bin Laden's satellite phone records and the delivery of a satellite phone battery pack to Bin Laden, which is discussed below. However, assuming that the report is accurate, it bears noting that, as with the co-conspirator list from the *Rahman* trial, there is no indication that the government sought to invoke non-disclosure protections. Further, it seems at least plausible that the government could have avoided the risk of disclosure by tailoring the evidence it offered to avoid mention of sensitive communications links. In our experience, such tactics are often used, and properly so, to avoid disclosure of sensitive evidence such as information about confidential informants.
>
> To be clear, and in the event that Judge Mukasey intended to refer to the Embassy Bombings trial, we are not aware of any security breach that occurred as a result of that trial. In the Embassy Bombings case, phone records believed to be from Bin Laden's satellite phone and documents and other evidence regarding a satellite phone battery pack delivered to Bin Laden were introduced into evidence, but this did not affect the government's ability to monitor the phone. As the record makes clear, Bin Laden had stopped using the phone years before the records and testimony were offered in evidence at trial.[275]
>
> Documents regarding the satellite phone were seized in the September 23, 1998, search by New Scotland Yard of the London home of Khalid al-Fawwaz, an alleged al Qaeda associate who handled public relations.[276] Subsequently obtained records indicated that the phone was not used at all after October 9, 1998, and that the phone's use had dropped off dramatically after August 21, 1998, which was the day after the U.S. cruise missile attack on Bin Laden.[277] There are at least two reasons why neither the presentation of the phone records evidence or testimony in the Embassy Bombings trial, nor even the disclosure of those records to the defense in discovery, could possibly have caused Bin Laden to stop using the monitored phone: (1) the phone records and the delivery of the satellite phone battery pack to Bin Laden were not first the subject of trial testimony until March 20, 2001, almost two-and-a-half years after the phone went dead,[278] and (2) discovery regarding the phone records was not turned over to the defense until well after the phone had gone dead.[279] Therefore, while there is no doubt that terrorism trials can pose risks for the disclosure of sensitive information and put strain on all the participants to take great care, we are not aware of any security breaches in cases where the government has sought to invoke CIPA or devices such as protective orders.

Endnotes

[275] The 9/11 Commission Report pointed to a "leak" to *The Washington Times* and the ensuing article discussing Bin Laden's use of a satellite phone as the cause of Bin Laden abandoning the use of the phone, compromising U.S. intelligence efforts. See Nat'l Comm'n on Terrorist Attacks Upon the U.S., *The 9/11 Commission Report* 127 (2004) (hereafter "*9/11 Commission Report*") ("Worst of all, al Qaeda's senior leadership had stopped using a particular means of communication almost immediately after a leak to the *Washington Times*") & n. 105. The 9/11 Commission

Report cites to an August 21, 1998 article in *The Washington Times* as the public disclosure of the leak and also cites to two interviews as support. While we have not had access to those interviews, it seems questionable whether the article caused Bin Laden to cease using his phone. First, it had been reported since 1996 that Bin Laden used a satellite phone. *See* Glenn Kessler, *File the Bin Laden Phone Leak Under 'Urban Myths'*, Wash. Post, Dec. 22, 2005, at A02. Second, the United States had launched a cruise missile attack on Bin Laden the day before the article appeared and just missed him, reportedly, by hours. *See id.* This would have likely have caused him to be more circumspect about using the phone. *See generally id.* (discussing reasons why the August 21, 1998 article probably would not have been the cause of Bin Laden ceasing to use the phone).

276 Al-Fawwaz was ultimately named as a defendant in the Embassy Bombings indictment, which charged him with setting up "a media information office in London, England . . . which was designed both to publicize the statements of USAMA BIN LADEN and to provide a cover in support of al Qaeda's 'military' activities, including . . . the procurement of necessary equipment (including satellite telephones).'" *See* Superseding Indictment at ¶ 9, *United States v. el-Hage*, No. 98-cr-01023 (S.D.N.Y. Mar. 12, 2001) (Dkt. No. 550). On March 26, 2001, during the Embassy Bombings trial, Detective Constable Paul Webber testified that on September 23, 1998, while he was assigned to work with the antiterrorism branch of New Scotland Yard in London, he participated in the search of a residence in London that he understood to be the home of al-Fawwaz, during which New Scotland Yard recovered a large number of documents relating to Bin Laden and al Qaeda, including correspondence bearing names and telephone numbers. *See* Tr. of Record Proceedings at 3349-73, *el-Hage* (S.D.N.Y. Mar. 26, 2001) (Dkt. No. 606) (trial testimony of Det. Constable Paul Webber). The following day, the government displayed documents seized by Detective Constable Webber, including a number of documents relating to a satellite phone. *See* Tr. of Record Proceedings at 3478-81, *el-Hage* (S.D.N.Y. Mar. 27, 2001) (Dkt. No. 606). *See also* Sean O'Neill, *The Worldwide Trail of Bloodshed that Leads to a Semi in Suburban London*, Daily Telegraph (U.K.), Sept. 19, 2001, at 3.

277 *See* Tr. of Record Proceedings at 3035 & Gov't Ex. 594, *el-Hage* (S.D.N.Y. Mar. 20, 2001) (Dkt. No. 605) (trial testimony of Marilyn Morelli of O'Gara Satellite Networks and exhibit establishing that the last activity for the satellite phone was October 9, 1998). The phone records reflect some 450 phone calls between January 1, 1998 and August 21, 1998, including seventy-seven calls between August 1, 1998 and August 21, 1998. *See id.* After August 21, 1998, however—which was the day after the cruise missile strikes against al Qaeda sites in Afghanistan and a pharmaceutical factory in Sudan, *see 9/11 Commission Report*, at 116-17, the phone went dead for the rest of the month of August. *See* Gov't Ex. 594, *el-Hage* (S.D.N.Y. Mar. 20, 2001) (Dkt. No. 605). Thereafter, the records show insignificant activity—a total of four calls in September 1998 and nine calls in October 1998. The last call was at 13:28 Greenwich Mean Time on October 9, 1998. *See id.*

278 *See* Tr. of Record Proceedings at 3033-35, *el-Hage* (S.D.N.Y. Mar. 20, 2001) (Dkt. No. 605) (trial testimony of Marilyn Morelli of O'Gara Satellite Networks including testimony regarding phone records from satellite phone provider). *See also* Tr. of Record Proceedings at 3478-81, *el-Hage* (S.D.N.Y. Mar. 27, 2001) (Dkt. No. 606) (additional documents and testimony showing that the satellite phone battery was shipped to an individual who accompanied ABC news reporters to interview of Bin Laden in Afghanistan on May 28, 1998); Tr. of Record Proceedings at 5292-94, *el-Hage* (S.D.N.Y. May 1, 2001) (Dkt. No. 600) (government's closing argument tying exhibits and testimony together and discussing delivery of satellite phone battery pack to Bin Laden at the time of the ABC news interview).

279 The first defendant to be arrested in the Embassy Bombings case, Wadih el-Hage, was arrested on September 16, 1998. *See* Minute Entry, *el-Hage* (S.D.N.Y. Sept. 16, 1998). On October 7, 1998, just two days before the satellite phone went dead entirely, prosecutors and el-Hage's defense counsel appeared for an initial pretrial conference before Judge Sand and the government stated that it would need another month even to assess how long it would take to make discovery. *See* Minute Entry, *el-Hage* (S.D.N.Y. Oct. 7, 1998). Further, the protective order that governed discovery was not entered until December 17, 1998. *See* Protective Order, *el-Hage* (S.D.N.Y. Dec. 17, 1998) (Dkt. No. 27). Although the actual date of the government's first discovery production is not listed in the docket, based on our experience it is inconceivable that the government made discovery of the phone records within two days of the initial pretrial conference, especially when it had requested a month to even formulate an initial timetable for discovery and when the protective order governing discovery was not entered for more than two months after the initial pretrial conference.

A separate statute, the Classified Information Procedures Act ("CIPA"), outlines a comprehensive process for dealing with instances in which either the defendant or the government seeks to use evidence that is classified. Before CIPA was adopted in 1980, some criminal defendants, mainly in espionage cases, sought to engage in "graymail," the practice of threatening to disclose classified information in open court in an effort to force the government to dismiss the charges. CIPA was intended to eliminate this tactic and, more broadly, to establish regularized procedures and heavy involvement by the presiding judge, so that the defendant's right to a fair trial would be protected while national security would not be jeopardized by the release of classified information.

Under CIPA's detailed procedures, classified evidence need not be disclosed to the defense in discovery unless the court finds, based on an in camera review, that it is relevant under traditional evidentiary standards. If the government still objects to the disclosure after a finding that the information is relevant, then the court enters a non-disclosure order and determines an appropriate sanction for the government's failure to disclose. Absent a non-disclosure order, the judge enters a protective order and the information is disclosed only to defense counsel, who must obtain a security clearance, but not to the defendant. Alternatively, the judge may find that the information can be provided directly to the defendant in a sanitized form—e.g., through a summary or redacted documents.

As trial draws near, if either the government or the defense seeks to use classified information at trial, a separate proceeding occurs, in private, in which the judge and the lawyers for both sides (but not the defendant himself) attempt to craft substitutions for the classified evidence—using pseudonyms, paraphrasing, and the like—which must afford the defendant substantially the same ability to make his defense as if the original evidence were used. If it proves impossible to craft an adequate substitution, then the court must consider an appropriate sanction against the government, ranging from the exclusion of evidence to findings against the government on particular issues to dismissal of the indictment in extreme cases. Under CIPA, all of these proceedings are conducted in secure facilities within the courthouse, and sensitive documents are carefully safeguarded pursuant to written security procedures.

CIPA repeatedly has been upheld as constitutional, and it has been used successfully in scores of terrorism prosecutions.

We are aware of two reported incidents in which sensitive information was supposedly disclosed in terrorism cases, but as this White Paper makes clear, one of these incidents simply did not occur and in the other the government did not try to invoke non-disclosure protections. Based on our review of the case law, we are not aware of a single terrorism case in which CIPA procedures have failed and a serious security breach has occurred. This is not to say that CIPA is perfect, and in this White Paper we note some potentially problematic situations—e.g., where a defendant seeks to proceed pro se such as Zacarias Moussaoui—as well as some areas for possible improvement in the statute.

F. *Brady* and the Government's Other Discovery Obligations

One of the core elements of our criminal justice system is the requirement, under *Brady v. Maryland*, that the government disclose exculpatory information to the defense so that it can be effectively used at trial. The government also must comply with other discovery obligations, including the requirement that it turn over prior statements of government witnesses before those witnesses testify during trial. The government's *Brady* and discovery obligations are fundamental, and violations, such as those which occurred in the Detroit Sleeper Cell case, can have disastrous consequences for the effectiveness and reputation of the criminal justice system.

In the *Moussaoui* case, the courts wrestled with a difficult *Brady* problem when Moussaoui demanded to interview notorious terrorism figures who were detained in U.S. custody outside the criminal justice system. The government understandably objected, on grounds that allowing Moussaoui or his counsel to interview these individuals would disrupt intelligence-gathering and jeopardize national security. At the same time, the defense reasonably contended that these individuals could potentially have evidence that would help Moussaoui show that his involvement in al Qaeda activities with which he was charged was limited. After extensive litigation, the Fourth Circuit devised a CIPA-like compromise under which Moussaoui would not be given direct access to the detained individuals, but his counsel would be able to propose summaries from intelligence reports that would be read to the jury, conveying the essence of the exculpatory information. Although Moussaoui ultimately decided to plead guilty, this procedure was employed on his behalf in his sentencing trial. In addition, in a subsequent case in the Southern District of New York, the presiding judge adopted essentially the same approach, and defense counsel consented to the procedure. We believe that the Fourth Circuit's creative approach demonstrates the adaptability of the court system to handle difficult challenges presented by terrorism cases.

Other terrorism cases have presented different *Brady* problems. For example, in some cases the defense has been deluged by thousands of hours of un-transcribed FISA recordings and has been forced to wade through the evidence to see if it contains anything exculpatory. Although it is indeed a challenge to handle a case with voluminous evidence, courts have generally afforded adequate time for defense counsel to do the job. Another issue is the scope of the government's obligation to search for *Brady* material. In a multi-agency, and sometimes multi-government, investigation involving intelligence and military authorities, how widely must the prosecutors search in order to discharge their *Brady* obligations? These situations are sometimes challenging because of the complicated record-keeping systems and far-flung operations of intelligence and military agencies. And previously unknown problems sometimes emerge, as exemplified by the recent disclosure in the *Moussaoui* case of three CIA recordings which were not previously known to the prosecutors or the defense. Nevertheless, courts have generally adopted common-sense approaches to these problems, and there is no indication that prosecutors experience major or recurring obstacles to conducting proper review of the evidence for *Brady* material.

G. *Miranda* and the Right to Remain Silent

The famous *Miranda* warnings—"You have the right to remain silent" and so on—are deeply ingrained in domestic law enforcement and, more broadly, in our national culture. In general, if a law enforcement officer procures a confession from a defendant who is being questioned while in custody, the confession is admissible in court only if the officer read the *Miranda* warning at the beginning of the interrogation and the defendant agreed to waive his *Miranda* rights. Where a terrorism defendant is arrested in the United States by law enforcement, compliance with the *Miranda* warnings is easy. But what happens when an individual is arrested overseas?

If the questioning is conducted by foreign officials, then under well-settled case law, *Miranda* does not apply, and a defendant's post-arrest confession is admissible so long as it was voluntarily given. However, in the Embassy Bombings case, the presiding judge broke new ground by holding that when U.S. law enforcement questions a detained suspect overseas, the U.S. officers must administer a variant of the *Miranda* warnings even though the questioning is occurring outside the United States.

Some have criticized this holding, invoking the absurdity of soldiers administering *Miranda* warnings to fighters who are captured on the battlefield. We agree that soldiers need not and should not administer *Miranda* warnings in the heat of battle, but we do not believe that this scenario has significant implications for criminal terrorism prosecutions. As an initial matter, few individuals have been placed on trial following a battlefield capture; the vast majority of confessions in terrorism cases have resulted from traditional interrogation by law enforcement officers rather than soldiers. (The case of John Walker Lindh is an interesting exception that we discuss in this Paper.) Further, we believe in a battlefield situation, the courts would likely find that *Miranda* does not apply.

H. Evidentiary and Speedy Trial Issues

Some commentators have posited that the Federal Rules of Evidence, which are applied in criminal cases, would somehow make it difficult or impossible for the government to present probative evidence in terrorism cases. Among the alleged problems are those surrounding the authentication of physical evidence, sometimes referred to as "chain of custody problems," and the alleged unavailability of witnesses who are deployed around the world. We believe that these objections are significantly overstated. The Federal Rules of Evidence, including the rules that govern authentication of physical evidence, generally provide a common-sense, flexible framework to guide the decision whether evidence is admissible in court. We are not aware of any terrorism case in which an important piece of evidence has been excluded on authentication or other grounds. Further, the government generally can arrange for its personnel to travel long distances to court to testify if needed, and has done so in some important cases, including the *al-Moayad* case in Brooklyn.

Terrorism cases also do not present unique or insuperable speedy trial problems. It is true that some of the larger terrorism cases can drag on for years before they are resolved, but courts have repeatedly recognized that delays are permissible in complex cases. Indeed, in one important terrorism case, the *al-Arian* material support prosecution in Florida, the presiding judge overruled the defendant's speedy trial objections and established a reasonable schedule for the case.

I. Sentencing

In the federal criminal system, the presiding judge has the job of imposing the sentence except in capital cases. The judge possesses significant discretion, but that discretion is guided by a series of legal provisions including the Federal Sentencing Guidelines. The applicable legal principles prescribe severe sentences for many terrorism crimes, and experience has shown that terrorism defendants have generally received very stiff sentences. In general, the sentencing of terrorism defendants has not presented unique or unusual problems.

One important feature of the federal sentencing regime is that it offers leniency to defendants who choose to cooperate with the government and assist in the investigation and prosecution of others. The cooperation process is extremely well-defined in federal criminal practice; judges and lawyers are familiar, on an everyday basis, with the proper method for approaching cooperation and for the process that a prospective cooperator must go through before he is accepted by the government. Some significant terrorism defendants have decided to cooperate, after consulting with their lawyers, in an effort to achieve leniency. This is yet another benefit of using the existing court system.

J. Safety and Security of Trial Participants and Others

Finally, some terrorism prosecutions present real security risks for judges, jurors, witnesses, prison guards, and others. As exemplified by a horrible attack on a prison guard in the Embassy Bombings case, some terrorism defendants are violent killers who will not hesitate to harm others if given the chance. As a result, court officers, judges, and prison officials face a challenge in maintaining a secure and safe environment for terrorism cases to proceed.

However, the challenges of maintaining security are hardly unique to terrorism cases. For many years the court system has dealt with all manner of violent individuals, including gang members and others. There are well-recognized tools, such as extra security screening, anonymous juries, shackling the defendants, and out-of-court protection by the Marshals Service, that can be used to ensure security. These methods are costly and disruptive, and they are certainly not foolproof, but in general they work reasonably well in terrorism cases and many other cases where trial participants present a risk of violence.

Within the prison system, the Bureau of Prisons, upon direction of the Attorney General, has authority to impose Special Administrative Measures, or SAMs, to ensure security for highly dangerous defendants. SAMs are intended to prevent acts of violence within the prison system and also to prevent defendants from communicating with others outside of prison in a manner that may lead to death or serious injury. SAMs are inmate-specific and may be imposed only pursuant to special procedures. They generally encompass housing a prisoner in segregation and denying him privileges such as correspondence, visits with persons other than his counsel or close family members, and use of the telephone. Courts have generally upheld the use of SAMs, although they have tended to modify the SAMs to make sure that the prisoner is able to communicate effectively with counsel. In the highly publicized Lynne Stewart case, Stewart was convicted of serious crimes after the jury found that she had violated the SAMs by helping her client, Sheikh Abdel Rahman, deliver terrorism-related messages to the news media. The Stewart case stands as a stark reminder of the government's determination to ensure strict compliance with SAMs.

III.
A Brief History of Terrorist Attacks Against United States Interests and an Introduction to the Law Enforcement Response

Although of a magnitude never before experienced, 9/11 was not the first time our nation was targeted for a terrorist attack. The United States Senate, for example, has been bombed twice: during the summer recess in 1915, a German sympathizer, angered by American support for Britain in World War I, exploded three sticks of dynamite in the Senate Reception Room; and late one night in 1983, an organization known as the Armed Resistance Unit set off a bomb that damaged a conference room near the Senate Chamber to protest American military action in Grenada and in Lebanon.[7] Wall Street was attacked by unknown persons in 1920 when, just past noon on September 16, a horse-cart full of dynamite and sash weights exploded outside the headquarters of J.P. Morgan & Company, killing dozens and wounding hundreds. The blast shattered windows up to half-a-mile away and etched scars into the stone façade of 23 Wall Street that are still visible today.[8] And in 1965, several members of the Black Liberation Front were arrested and later convicted for their part in the "Monumental Plot," a plan to dynamite the Statue of Liberty, the Liberty Bell, and the Washington Monument with dynamite supplied by Québécois separatists.[9]

These incidents, however, were notable as much for their rarity as for the scale of their actual or intended destruction. Particularly in the post-World War II era, a number of extremist groups around the world have employed the tactics of terrorism, including among others the Shining Path in Peru, the Irish Republican Army in Northern Ireland, and the Tamil Tigers in Sri Lanka.[10] But while Latin America, Southeast Asia, the Middle East, and Europe suffered the effects of increasingly varied, sophisticated, and destructive terrorist activity, the United States remained relatively insulated from foreign terrorists, and attacks against American interests were rare until the 1980s.

This section offers a brief overview of the rise of international terrorism in recent years. The discussion begins with the development of organized, systematic terrorist attacks by Arab nationalist groups, the historical precursors to modern Islamist extremist terrorism. It briefly describes the increasing focus on American interests as targets, the rise of religious and Islamist extremist influences, and the recent efforts to target the United States within our own borders. Finally, we discuss the criminal law enforcement response to some of the recent attacks by transnational terrorist groups and the evolution of law enforcement priorities and prosecutorial efforts in the wake of 9/11.

A. The Beginnings of Modern International Terrorism

After Israel's decisive military victory in the Six Day War in 1967, some Arab nationalist groups turned to terrorism as a means of opposition to Israel. In the late 1960s and 1970s, groups like the Abu Nidal Organization ("ANO"), al-Fatah, the Popular Front for the Liberation of Palestine ("PFLP"), Black September, and others engaged in an international campaign of bombings, assassinations, hijackings, and hostage-taking directed against Israeli diplomatic, military, and economic interests; the interests of Israel's allies; rival organizations; and even Arab governments perceived as insufficiently supportive of the groups' goals or tactics, or insufficiently hostile to rapprochement with Israel.[11] The PFLP infamously pioneered airline hijackings and bombings as a tactic to draw international media attention, to protest actions by Israel or countries sympathetic to Israel, and to demand the release of Arab prisoners held by Israel or Western law enforcement authorities. Some of these attacks explicitly targeted U.S. interests, like the PFLP's 1969 hijacking of TWA flight 840 and its September 1970 coordinated hijackings of three flights en route from Europe to New York.[12]

The 1980s saw three important developments in international terrorism. The first was the rise of Islamist extremism. New Islamist organizations like Hezbollah and Hamas grew in prominence relative to older, more secular groups like Fatah, PFLP, and the Democratic Front for the Liberation of Palestine ("DFLP").[13] Second, and related, was the new use of suicide bombings as a terrorist tactic, introduced by Hezbollah to the Middle East region and later adopted by a number of Islamist and other extremist groups.[14] Third was the first wave of direct attacks on U.S. military and diplomatic resources abroad. These three developments coalesced catastrophically in a string of attacks against U.S. interests by Hezbollah over a seventeen-month period in the mid-1980s. Between April 1983 and September 1984, Hezbollah suicide bombers drove explosives-filled trucks into the U.S. embassy in Beirut, a U.S. Marine barracks in Beirut, the U.S. and French embassies in Kuwait, and the U.S. embassy annex in Beirut. These attacks killed nearly 400 people and wounded hundreds more,[15] and generally are credited with influencing the decision to withdraw American forces from Lebanon in 1984.[16] In November 1984, Italian law enforcement arrested six Lebanese men allegedly plotting a similar attack on the U.S. embassy in Rome.[17]

The 1980s also witnessed another key event in the evolution of Islamist extremism: the mujahideen resistance to the Soviet occupation of Afghanistan. In that conflict, which lasted approximately from the 1979 Soviet invasion to their 1989 withdrawal, Osama bin Laden and his associates created international recruiting and financing structures that Bin Laden would convert to al Qaeda's use after the Soviet withdrawal.[18] Al Qaeda's international recruiting and training efforts brought it into contact with other Islamist extremist organizations and gave it the ability to cooperate and coordinate with other groups. Indeed, al Qaeda eventually merged with the Egyptian Islamic Jihad.[19] Al Qaeda pursues a fantastic international goal: the establishment of a pan-Islamic caliphate and the eradication of Western cultural and political influence. It sees the United States as a primary enemy and target.[20] During the 1990s, al Qaeda was involved, directly or indirectly, in most of the significant attacks on U.S. interests abroad and at home, and over the course of the decade its role evolved to a point where it directed and executed large-scale attacks.

B. The New Era

The late 1990s were marked by a trend away from secular groups toward organizations with explicit international Islamist extremist goals. As groups like al Qaeda grew in funding, sophistication, and ambition, their attention focused increasingly on the United States. These groups have also demonstrated increasing willingness to target civilians directly, relying on mass murder as a terrorist weapon. Attacks and attempted attacks on U.S. political, economic, and military interests overseas and at home have come with greater frequency, more sophisticated planning, deeper commitment of resources and, correspondingly, with graver effect.

1. The First Attack on the World Trade Center and the Exposure of the Conspiracy Led by Sheikh Abdel Rahman[21]

On February 26, 1993, a Ryder rental van filled with homemade explosives detonated in the parking garage beneath one of the towers at the World Trade Center in downtown New York City. The blast tore through seven stories, killing six and injuring more than 1,000 people. Within days, the investigation led to Mohammed Salameh, who had rented the Ryder van and reported it stolen. Salameh was arrested at the rental office, where he had returned to seek a refund of his $400 rental deposit. The investigation soon identified Salameh's co-conspirators as Ramzi Yousef, the nephew of Khalid Sheikh Mohammed, and Ahmad Mohammad Ajaj, a Palestinian who lived in Houston. Yousef and Ajaj were accused of training together at Camp Khaldan on the Afghanistan/Pakistan border, a terrorist training camp allegedly run by a Bin Laden associate, Abu Zubaydah. The conspirators also included Eyad Ismoil, a Jordanian who moved from Dallas to New York to aid the plot; Nidal Ayyad, an Allied Signal engineer; Mahmoud Abouhalima, an Egyptian and one-time New York City cab driver who also had attended terrorist training at Camp Khaldan; and Abdul Rahman Yasin, an Iraqi man with U.S. citizenship. All six men were indicted, though Yasin fled to Iraq, Abouhalima to Egypt, and Yousef and Ismoil to Jordan. Abouhalima, Yousef, and

Ismoil eventually were apprehended by foreign authorities and transported to the United States for trial.[22]

After the World Trade Center bombing, the FBI intensified an ongoing investigation of a related terrorist cell operating in New York. The driver's license Salameh used to rent the Ryder van bore the address of an apartment in Brooklyn occupied by Ibrahim el-Gabrowny, the cousin of El Sayyid Nosair. At the time of the bombing, Nosair was serving time in Attica, a state correctional facility in New York, for his involvement in the 1990 assassination of Meir Kahane, the founder of the Jewish Defense League, who was gunned down after a speech at a Marriott hotel in midtown Manhattan. El-Gabrowny and Nosair were followers of Sheikh Omar Ahmad Ali Abdel Rahman, a blind Egyptian cleric and spiritual leader of al-Gama'a al-Islamiyya (the Islamic Group), a radical Islamist Egyptian organization. Abdel Rahman had been living in the United States since 1990 after several years spent in an Egyptian prison on suspicion that he was involved in the assassination of Egyptian President Anwar Sadat. Abdel Rahman preached at mosques in Jersey City and Brooklyn, and was known for his violent oratory against the United States and Israel. Abdel Rahman and his associates had been infiltrated by Emad Saleh, a former Egyptian soldier and FBI informant.

The FBI learned that, with Abdel Rahman's encouragement, el-Gabrowny, Siddig Ibrahim Siddig Ali (a Sudanese immigrant and Rahman's translator), and several other associates were planning a number of terrorist attacks, including assassinating Hosni Mubarak, the President of Egypt, bombing the Holland and Lincoln Tunnels, and the United Nations building using stolen cars filled with explosives. On June 24, 1993, the FBI arrested five of the men while they were mixing 200 gallons of gasoline with fertilizer in a garage in Queens and in the following weeks arrested eight more men, including Abdel Rahman. All those arrested pled guilty or were convicted at trial and many received sentences ranging from thirty years to life plus an additional term of years.

2. The Khobar Towers Bombing[23]

After Operation Desert Storm, the U.S. Air Force was deployed in the Middle East to enforce the terms of the cease-fire and to patrol the no-fly zone. A fighter wing was stationed in Dhahran, Saudi Arabia, where about 3,000 Air Force personnel lived in a large housing complex called the Khobar Towers, along with several hundred Army personnel and British and French forces. After a car bomb exploded outside Saudi government offices in Riyadh in 1995, the Air Force increased security around the Towers, including heightening security at the entry gates and reinforcing the perimeter fence with a barrier of Jersey walls.

Shortly before 10:00 p.m. on June 25, 1996, two cars and a sewage tanker truck pulled into a parking lot north of the Khobar complex. After the tanker truck backed up against the perimeter fence, directly across from one of the residential towers, the truck's driver and a passenger jumped into one of the cars. As the two cars sped off, security radioed in an evacuation alert to the tower. Moments later, the tanker detonated with the force of more than 20,000 pounds of TNT. The cylindrical shape of the tank funneled the blast directly at the residential tower eighty feet away. The outer walls of the lower floors imploded into the exterior rooms, and the rest of the façade was torn off the building. Nineteen airmen and women died in the attack and over 300 more were injured. The blast left a crater in the parking lot eighty-five feet wide and thirty-five feet deep.

In 2001, thirteen members of Saudi Hezbollah were indicted for the attack, along with an unidentified member of Lebanese Hezbollah. The defendants have not been apprehended and the charges are still pending.[24]

3. The East Africa Embassy Bombings[25]

Truck bombs, which had proven so deadly in Beirut, New York, and Dhahran, were used again in 1998 against U.S. embassies in Nairobi, Kenya, and Dar es Salaam, Tanzania. Shortly before 10:30 a.m. on Friday, August 7, 1998, a truck pulled up to the rear gate of the U.S. embassy in Nairobi, Kenya. When security guards refused the occupants' demands to open the gate, the occupants opened fire and threw a flash grenade at the guards. The guards scattered. Occupants of the embassy, drawn by the sound of gunfire and the flash grenade, went to the windows to see what was happening. The truck drove toward the embassy while a passenger who had been riding in it, Mohamed Rashed Daoud al-'Owhali, ran for cover. Seconds later, one ton of explosives loaded in the truck detonated, reducing much of the interior of the five-story building to rubble, causing a neighboring building to collapse and setting the tar-covered street ablaze. The blast killed 213 and wounded some 4,000. About five minutes after the explosion in Nairobi, a second truck bomb exploded outside the U.S. Embassy in Dar es Salaam, killing eleven and wounding eighty-five. A water tanker truck between the truck bomb and the embassy kept the truck bomb from getting closer to the embassy and partially shielded the building, although the tanker itself was blown three stories into the air.

The United States responded to the Embassy Bombings with an aggressive criminal investigation and a limited military response. On August 20, 1998, Navy vessels in the Arabian Sea fired Tomahawk cruise missiles at eight known al Qaeda camps in Afghanistan near the town of Khost and at a pharmaceutical plant in al Shifa, Sudan, that American authorities suspected was used by al Qaeda to produce VX gas precursors.[26] By mid-September, Wadih el-Hage had been arrested and charged in connection with the bombings, and an arrest warrant was issued for Mamdouh Mahmud Salim. Eventually, twenty-five defendants, including Osama bin Laden, Mohammed Atef, and Ayman al-Zawahiri were charged, and five defendants were convicted and sentenced to prison terms ranging from ten years to life. One other defendant currently is being held in military custody in Guantánamo[27] and three more were taken into custody in the United Kingdom.[28]

4. The Millennium Plot[29]

On December 14, 1999, customs officials guarding the U.S.-Canadian border at the ferry station in Port Angeles, Washington, stopped a young man driving a green Chrysler sedan. The man nervously answered questions about his destination and the purpose of his trip. He agreed to open the trunk for the officers, where they found the spare tire compartment filled with over 100 pounds of explosives.

The driver was Ahmed Ressam, an Algerian emigrant who had lived illegally in Montreal for several years before traveling to Afghanistan for approximately eight months of training at al Qaeda-run terrorist camps, including Camp Khaldan, in 1998 and 1999. While there, and with the encouragement of Abu Zubaydah, Ressam and four other trainees plotted to attack the United States on the millennium New Year. Ressam's four co-conspirators were apprehended on their way back to Montreal, so Ressam recruited new compatriots, obtained explosives ingredients and components for home-made timing devices, and hatched a plan to detonate a suitcase full of nitroglycerin in the Los Angeles International Airport. Ressam was en route to Los Angeles from Vancouver, where he and a co-conspirator had mixed the explosives in a motel room, when he was arrested.

After his arrest, Ressam was tried on charges of smuggling, transporting explosives, international terrorism, and related crimes. He was convicted by a jury in April 2001 and then began cooperating with authorities, providing intelligence and testifying in the trial of Mokhtar Haouri.[30] Ressam stopped cooperating in 2002 and in 2005 was sentenced to twenty-two years' imprisonment.[31]

5. The Attack on the USS *Cole*[32]

In 1999, al Qaeda began plans to adapt the truck bomb tactic to the marine setting. Al Qaeda agents in Yemen searched for targets in the port of Aden, a city on the southern tip of the Arabian Peninsula across the Strait of Mandeb from Djibouti. The al Qaeda operatives leading the operation were Abdul Rahim al-Nashiri, whose cousin had been the suicide bomber behind the wheel of the truck bomb in Nairobi, and Tawfiq bin Attash (also called Khallad). The team originally targeted an oil tanker, but Bin Laden urged them to go after a U.S. warship. In January of 2000, as part of the Millennium Plot, Khallad's and Nashiri's group sought to approach the USS *The Sullivans* in a small skiff packed with explosives, but the overloaded vessel got mired in the shallows.

The group tried again on October 12, 2000, when the USS *Cole*, a guided-missile destroyer, docked in Aden for refueling. This time the skiff, piloted by two suicide bombers, drew alongside the *Cole* near lunchtime and detonated its payload. The blast ripped a forty-foot-wide hole in the *Cole*'s armored hull, killing seventeen sailors and wounding thirty-nine. People two miles away reportedly thought there had been an earthquake. The *Cole* required fourteen months of repairs at a cost of approximately $250 million before it returned to service.[33]

Nashiri and Khallad were arrested in 2002 and 2003, respectively, and turned over to the United States. Both men are in U.S. custody at Guantánamo.[34]

6. The 9/11 Attacks

The devastating attacks on targets in New York and Washington, D.C., on 9/11, the preparations leading up to them, and the U.S. response have been analyzed extensively by others.[35] We will not attempt to retrace that thoughtful body of work. The 9/11 attacks reflected a frightening degree of sophistication and coordination and resulted in catastrophic damage. The plot involved coordinated attacks among nineteen suicide hijackers on four different airplanes and followed more than two years of planning. The attacks killed 2,974 innocent victims plus the nineteen hijackers. Both towers of the World Trade Center in New York were completely destroyed, along with four other World Trade Center buildings, a hotel, and a church; two adjacent buildings suffered such extensive damage that they were condemned. The Pentagon sustained major damage in a separate attack and the fourth hijacked airplane crashed in a field in rural Pennsylvania, killing all on board. Khalid Sheikh Mohammed, Mohammed al-Qahtani, Ramzi bin al-Shibh, Ali Abd al-Aziz Ali, Mustafa Ahmed al-Hawsawi, and Walid bin Attash are detained at Guantánamo for their roles in the 9/11 attacks.[36] On February 4, 2008, military prosecutors filed capital charges against each of these five individuals and announced that they would face trial in the military commission system.[37]

C. The Criminal Justice Response to International Terrorism

The U.S. criminal justice system started gaining significant experience with international terrorism cases in the 1980s, with the prosecutions of airline hijackers. In the early 1990s, blockbuster trials arising out of the first World Trade Center bombing and related conspiracies resulted in lengthy prison terms for the high-profile defendants. Following the 9/11 attacks, law enforcement and prosecutorial priorities shifted more intently toward prevention. Post-9/11 prosecutions show increased focus on bringing charges for inchoate crimes such as conspiracy, on charging individuals or organizations that provide financial or other material support to terrorist organizations, and on charging individuals who solicit or incite others to commit terrorist attacks.

1. The Airline Hijacking Cases of the 1980s

Some of the earliest international terrorism prosecutions arose from airplane hijackings in the 1980s. *United States v. Rashed*, *United States v. Yunis*, and *United States v. Rezaq* all were prosecutions of terrorists who were apprehended abroad after they hijacked international flights originating in Tokyo, Beirut, and Athens, respectively.[38] This trio of cases provided a preview of several issues that would recur in later international terrorism prosecutions, including challenges to the manner in which the defendant was apprehended;[39] challenges to the extraterritorial reach of domestic laws criminalizing acts of terrorism;[40] and disputes over the defendant's right to review, or the admissibility of, classified materials under the Classified Information Procedures Act ("CIPA").[41]

2. World Trade Center I and Related Conspiracies in the Early 1990s

The prosecution of those involved in the first World Trade Center bombing actually involved three separate criminal cases and at least three major criminal conspiracies: the actual bombing of the World Trade Center led by Ramzi Yousef; a foiled conspiracy to simultaneously bomb multiple U.S. commercial airliners flying routes out of Southeast Asia (the "Bojinka Plot"), also masterminded by Yousef; and another conspiracy to support the World Trade Center bombers and to bomb major New York landmarks, led by Sheikh Abdel Rahman and Siddig Ali.

These cases involved approximately twenty-five defendants, a total of seventeen months of trial before anonymous juries,[42] and resulted in a guilty plea or conviction for every defendant brought to trial. All of the cases were brought in the Southern District of New York. The presiding judges, Kevin Thomas Duffy and Michael B. Mukasey, addressed, among many issues, disclosure requirements under CIPA;[43] the admissibility of evidence obtained pursuant to warrants issued under the Foreign Intelligence Surveillance Act ("FISA");[44] the scope of discovery from foreign jurisdictions;[45] the extraterritorial scope of criminal anti-terrorism statutes;[46] the admissibility of statements to law enforcement officers during the defendant's transit from an overseas location to the trial location;[47] and the admissibility of expert testimony on the Quran and the Arabic language.[48] In the words of the 9/11 Commission, the cases represented a "superb investigative and prosecutorial effort."[49]

3. The Embassy Bombings Trial

Hours after the August 7, 1998 bombings of the U.S. embassies in Nairobi, Kenya and Dar es Salaam, Tanzania, dozens of FBI investigators were dispatched to East Africa.[50] The FBI and federal prosecutors interviewed numerous witnesses and suspects. Later, after extensive litigation regarding *Miranda* warnings, important inculpatory statements of two defendants were received in evidence.[51] By October 1998, the government had obtained indictments against several alleged participants in the conspiracy that led to the attacks, and eventually twenty-five individuals were charged, including Osama bin Laden, Mohammed Atef, and Ayman al-Zawahiri, though many have never been brought into custody.

After a five-month trial that began in January 2001, defendants Wadih el-Hage, Mohamed Sadeek Odeh, Mohamed Rashed Daoud al-'Owhali, and Khalfan Khamis Mohamed were convicted of charges including murder, conspiracy, and perjury. Each was sentenced to life imprisonment.[52] Another defendant, Mamdouh Mahmud Salim, was sentenced to thirty-two years' imprisonment on charges arising out of an attempted murder of a prison guard while he was awaiting trial for the embassy attacks;[53] charges arising out of the bombings are still pending against him. Two other defendants pled guilty.[54] In March 2008, the Department of Defense announced that Ahmed Khalfan Ghailani, a Tanzanian charged but not tried in the embassy bombings case, would be prosecuted before a military commission.[55]

Like the earlier trials of Abdel Rahman, Yousef and their co-conspirators, the embassy bombing trial involved extensive jury security measures, including the closed voir dire of a 1,500-member jury pool and an anonymous jury.[56] The trial involved significant issues under CIPA and evidence gathered through foreign intelligence efforts.[57] The defendants' appeals are still pending before the Second Circuit.

4. Zacarias Moussaoui

In December 2001, the United States brought the only criminal prosecution directly related to the 9/11 attacks against Zacarias Moussaoui, an al Qaeda-trained operative who was arrested by immigration authorities in August 2001 when his Minnesota flight-school instructor reported his suspicious behavior.[58] Moussaoui had enrolled in flight lessons for 747s, but lacked significant experience on smaller aircraft and was not interested in getting licensed.[59] After the 9/11 attacks, Moussaoui was charged with conspiring with other al Qaeda members in connection with the attacks.[60] Moussaoui proved a difficult defendant, arguing with the court and with his attorneys, refusing to enter a plea, and using the courtroom as a forum for diatribes against the United States.

The trial court initially granted Moussaoui's request to be allowed to depose detainees held in custody by the United States outside the criminal justice system.[61] After the Fourth Circuit reversed, holding that written summaries of those individuals' testimony could be produced instead,[62] Moussaoui pled guilty.[63] Following a two-month death penalty trial, the jury returned a verdict of life imprisonment.[64]

5. "Sleeper Cell" Cases

In the years since 9/11, a number of criminal cases have targeted individuals who have sought to bring the al Qaeda model into the United States. Prosecutors have charged conspiracies in New York City, Detroit, Virginia, Oregon, New Jersey, Seattle, Buffalo, and Miami. Some of these cases have involved individuals who trained in camps in Afghanistan or Pakistan, while others have inspiration as their primary link to al Qaeda. The cases have ranged from groups who had engaged in training, but without a specific terrorist plot, to those that had begun planning attacks against specific targets.

In some cases, evidence showed that individuals were engaged in training and other preparations for some kind of attack, but had not selected a target or engaged in specific preparations. In the case of the Lackawanna Six,[65] for example, several men from a Yemeni-American community outside of Buffalo were recruited by Kamal Derwish, an al Qaeda recruiter, to enroll in al Qaeda's al Farooq training camp in Afghanistan in the summer of 2001, but the evidence is unclear whether the men planned any particular acts of terrorism.[66] They were arrested and prosecuted in the fall of 2002, and all six men pled guilty.[67]

Similarly, a Seattle resident was charged in 2002 with plotting to establish a terrorist training camp on a farm in rural Oregon, modeled on al Qaeda training camps, and to prepare trainees for jihad against the United States and other countries.[68] He pled guilty to charges of providing material support to the Taliban.[69] An alleged co-conspirator recently was extradited from Sweden to stand trial.[70] In a separate case, eleven men in northern Virginia were indicted in 2004 on charges that they stockpiled weapons and engaged in tactical training in preparation to fight with the al Qaeda-associated organization Lakshar-e-Taiba in Kashmir.[71] Six of the men pled guilty. Following a bench trial three were convicted of some charges[72] and two were acquitted.[73] One of the acquitted men was re-indicted on charges of lying to the grand jury about his participation in a jihadist training camp in Pakistan or Afghanistan in 1999.[74]

In other cases, the evidence showed that the defendants had selected targets and had begun preparations to carry out an attack. Six men in New Jersey were charged in May 2007 with plotting to attack the Fort Dix Army base, thirty miles west of Philadelphia, with semi-automatic assault weapons.[75] The men are alleged to have engaged in tactical and weapons training at paintball facilities and firing ranges and to have surveilled Fort Dix as well as four other Army, Air Force, and Coast Guard bases in New Jersey, Delaware, and Pennsylvania.[76] At the time of writing, one of the men had pled guilty to weapons charges in connection with the conspiracy and was sentenced to twenty months in prison[77] and the others were scheduled to proceed to trial in September 2008.[78] Two other men have been convicted of separate plots to bomb targets in New York City. Iyman Faris pled guilty in 2003 to charges of providing material support to al Qaeda by casing the Brooklyn Bridge as a potential target for a terrorist attack.[79] Shahawar Siraj, a clerk at an Arabic bookstore in Brooklyn, was convicted of conspiring with individuals whom he believed were associated with al Qaeda to bomb the subway station at Herald Square.[80] Recently, four men were indicted for plotting to bomb New York's John F. Kennedy International Airport.[81] One of the men is in custody and the other three are in Trinidad awaiting a decision on their challenges to the government's approval of their extradition.[82]

Two "sleeper cell" cases in Michigan and Florida, however, have resulted in acquittals or the dismissal of terrorism charges. Days after 9/11, three former employees of the Detroit Metropolitan Airport and a Chicago resident were arrested on document fraud charges and were later charged with operating as a sleeper cell with schemes to attack American airbases abroad and landmarks in the United States, including Disneyland and the MGM Grand Hotel in Las Vegas.[83] One individual pled guilty, one was acquitted by the jury, and convictions of the other two men were reversed when the government conceded, after trial, that the prosecution team had withheld exculpatory evidence.[84] Document fraud charges have been refiled against two defendants.[85] In another case brought in Miami, a jury acquitted one of seven men accused of plotting with an individual they believed to be an al Qaeda operative to destroy targets in the United States, including the Sears Tower and government buildings; the jury deadlocked on charges against the other six men, resulting in a mistrial.[86] A second trial against the six men also resulted in a mistrial when the jury deadlocked.[87]

6. Material Support Cases

In the years since 9/11, investigations and prosecutions have focused intensely on sources of funding and support for terrorist organizations abroad. In 2003, Mohammed Ali Hasan al-Moayad, a Yemeni cleric who raised money that ultimately was provided to al Qaeda and Hamas, was arrested in Germany and brought to the United States for trial on charges of providing material support to terrorist organizations. Al-Moayad was convicted in 2005 and sentenced to seventy-five years' imprisonment and a $1.25 million fine.

The Holy Land Foundation for Peace and its officers were charged with using its charity status as a front for funneling money to Hamas, while the Benevolence International Foundation and its founder were charged with lying about sending money raised ostensibly for humanitarian purposes to al Qaeda-affiliated individuals and groups in Bosnia and Chechnya. The founder of Benevolence International, Enaam Arnaout, pled guilty to a single count of racketeering, and was sentenced to more than eleven years' imprisonment.[88] The Holy Land Foundation case, on the other hand, resulted in acquittals or deadlock on all charges, resulting in a mistrial.[89]

7. Prosecuting Those Who Incite Terrorism

Prosecutors have focused their efforts not only on individuals and organizations who plan and carry out attacks and those who provide them material support, but also on those individuals who incite others to violent, jihadist attacks—particularly religious leaders who, through fatwas and exhortatory rhetoric, encourage young Muslim men to engage in terrorist attacks.[90] Sheikh Omar Abdel Rahman, for example, famously issued a fatwa to kill Americans wherever they may be found: "Muslims everywhere, dismember their nation, tear them apart, ruin their economy, provoke their corporations, destroy their embassies, attack their interests, sink their ships, and shoot down their planes, kill them on land, at sea, and in the air. Kill them wherever you find them."[91] In 1993, Sheikh Rahman was indicted and subsequently convicted for taking part in conspiracies to attack the United States because "he was looked to as a leader, and ... he accepted that role and encouraged his co-conspirators to engage in violent acts against the United States."[92] His conduct included issuing fatwas that called for assassinations and bombings and suggesting particular targets for attacks.[93]

In 2005, Ali al-Timimi, a Muslim scholar in Fairfax, Virginia was convicted of inducing and soliciting others to levy war against the United States and to aid the Taliban, and was sentenced to life imprisonment.[94] The government alleged that al-Timimi was a spiritual and intellectual leader of the men charged in *United States v. Royer*[95] with conspiring to fight with the Taliban against U.S. forces in Afghanistan, and that he encouraged and incited them to take up arms against the United States.[96] The one-armed cleric Abu Hamza al-Masri has been indicted in New York on charges relating to operation of a Bly, Oregon, training camp and other conspiracies to aid al Qaeda and the Taliban.[97] Al-Masri has been imprisoned in the United Kingdom for inciting violence and presently is awaiting extradition to the United States.[98]

8. Material Witness and "Enemy Combatant" Cases

In the years since 9/11, the government has also invoked novel approaches to detention of suspected terrorists, including the use of material witness warrants and novel theories of military detention of "enemy combatants." While this paper will not address the military detention regime, that regime has intersected with the criminal justice system in a few cases.

Jose Padilla, a U.S. citizen, was arrested at Chicago's O'Hare International Airport in May 8, 2002, and held as a material witness until June 9, 2002, when he was designated an "enemy combatant," removed from prison, and placed in military custody at the Consolidated Naval Brig in Charleston, South Carolina.[99] Padilla's court-appointed counsel commenced habeas corpus proceedings in New York[100] that would be litigated over the course of the next three-and-a-half years, reaching two Courts of Appeals[101] and the Supreme Court.[102] After the Fourth Circuit upheld Padilla's military detention, but before the Supreme Court could review the Fourth Circuit's decision, the government changed course and transferred Padilla back into the criminal justice system in Miami, where he had been indicted on criminal charges.[103] Padilla was ultimately convicted of three counts relating to conspiracies to provide material support to terrorists and sentenced to seventeen years and four months in prison.[104]

Where Padilla was initially held as a material witness, then as an "enemy combatant," and finally tried and convicted in federal court, the path of Ali Saleh Kahlah al-Marri took the opposite path. Al-Marri, a citizen of Qatar, initially was indicted in New York and later Illinois on charges relating to credit card fraud.[105] On June 23, 2003, al-Marri was designated an "enemy combatant" and subsequently transferred to the Consolidated Naval Brig in Charleston, South Carolina. His counsel filed a habeas petition on his behalf.[106] The district court dismissed the petition, but a panel of the Fourth Circuit reversed, holding that al-Marri's military detention was unlawful.[107] The government's petition for rehearing en banc was granted,[108] and at the time of this writing, en banc consideration is still pending.

IV.
The Data on Cases Prosecuted in Federal Court

This White Paper is intended to be grounded, as much as possible, in the real-world experiences of how the criminal justice system has actually dealt with the prosecution of individuals involved in international terrorism. To do this most thoroughly, the effort requires building a data set of relevant terrorism cases. Unfortunately, there is no ready, comprehensive list of terrorism prosecutions; indeed, there can be differing views about what cases really are terrorism cases. The Justice Department's Executive Office for United States Attorneys ("EOUSA"), for example, has reported bringing 3,094 anti-terrorism cases against 3,925 defendants during fiscal years 2002 through 2006, and concluding 2,609 cases against 3,098 defendants during the same time frame.[109] The Administrative Office of the United States Courts ("AOUSC"), however, reports a total of ninety-nine terrorism cases filed against 153 defendants during the same period.[110] And in an op-ed piece published in the *Wall Street Journal* in the summer of 2007, Attorney General Michael B. Mukasey, prior to his appointment, estimated that criminal prosecutions of terrorists "have yielded about three dozen convictions" since the 1993 World Trade Center bombing.[111] Even within the Department of Justice, reported terrorism cases vary: in contrast to the thousands of anti-terrorism cases tallied by the EOUSA, the Department of Justice's Counterterrorism Section counted 527 defendants charged in international terrorism and terrorism-related cases between September 11, 2001 and November 15, 2007.[112] Given these varying pictures of the number of terrorism cases, we need to define, as best we can, what we mean by a "terrorism case."

The difference between the EOUSA's 3,094 terrorism cases and the AOUSC's ninety-nine cases can likely be explained by differences in classification and data collection.[113] While the EOUSA does not disclose which particular cases it classifies as terrorism or terrorism-related, it does provide a description of the categories of cases it includes in its numbers. The EOUSA total includes international terrorism, domestic terrorism, terrorism financing, terrorism-related hoaxes, and "anti-terrorism" prosecutions—i.e., any case where the underlying purpose of the prosecution is anti-terrorism-related, or intended to disrupt potential or actual terrorist threats, even though the offense charged is not facially a terrorism charge (e.g., immigration violations, document fraud, or drug trafficking).[114] Moreover, the EOUSA classifies as "anti-terrorism" any prosecution that arises out of a terrorism-related law enforcement effort, including any case referred by a Joint Terrorism Task Force, even if there is no apparent link between the particular defendant and any terrorist organization or terrorist activity.[115] The AOUSC, on the other hand, classifies cases according to the "major offense" charged. In a telephone call with the AOUSC's Statistics Division, the AOUSC reported that it does not publicly disclose its criteria for classifying major offenses. But even without knowing the specific criteria used, it seems likely that only cases involving substantive terrorism charges are included in the AOUSC statistics and that many cases the EOUSA might classify as "terrorism related" would be classified by the AOUSC according to a non-terrorism major offense.

Although we agree that a wide variety of criminal statutes may be—and should be—invoked against terrorists and their accomplices, the EOUSA's classification is, for purposes of this White Paper, overbroad in some important respects. For purposes of this White Paper, we focus on Islamist extremist terrorist organizations like al Qaeda and individuals and organizations that are ideologically or organizationally linked to such groups. This approach is consistent with the intelligence community's view of the primary terrorist threat to the United States as well as the conventional perception of what is often termed the "War on Terror."[116] Domestic terrorism prosecutions that are not linked to international Islamist extremist organizations like al Qaeda—such as domestic militias, single-issue organizations that resort to violence, and the like—are not generally thought to present the novel legal and practical issues raised by international Islamist extremist terrorism cases, and generally seem less likely to implicate military or intelligence responses.[117] Similarly, terrorism-related hoaxes, for the very reason that they involve hoaxes rather than actual cases of terrorism, are outside the scope of this White Paper.

We have not included all international terrorism cases in this White Paper. We do not include prosecutions related to foreign organizations that employ terrorist tactics to further local criminal or political goals. For example, we do not include separatist groups like the Liberation Tigers of Tamil Eelam or secular insurgents like the Mujahideen e-Khalq.[118] Similarly, although violent guerilla groups like the Colombian Autodefensas Unidas de Colombia (United Self-Defense Forces of Colombia, or "AUC") and Fuerzas Armadas Revolucionarias de Colombia (Revolutionary Armed Forces of Colombia, or "FARC") are extremely dangerous and have at times targeted Americans abroad for kidnapping, hostage-taking, and murder, these groups are not linked to any broader, international Islamist extremist movement and, again, do not implicate the legal, intelligence, and security concerns that are thought to make al Qaeda and similar groups a special threat to our national security.[119]

Accordingly, and as set forth above, our analysis is limited to prosecutions related to terrorism associated—organizationally, financially, or ideologically—with Islamist extremist terrorist groups like al Qaeda.[120] Such prosecutions may seek criminal sanctions for acts of terrorism, for attempts or conspiracies to commit acts of terrorism, or for providing aid and support to those engaged in terrorism. We have also attempted to identify and include prosecutions intended to disrupt and deter terrorism through other means, such as through charges of immigration violations, document fraud, false statements, or financial crimes. We include these cases if the indictment or information charges that the criminal activity was connected to terrorist organizations or terrorist activities or if there are other assertions or evidence in the case that concretely demonstrate the government's belief that there is such a connection in the particular case—for example, evidence introduced at a detention or sentencing hearing. While the government may bring non-terrorism charges to disrupt and deter terrorism without stating its belief that the defendant is connected to terrorism, we have found no reliable way to identify and locate such cases if the connection is not explicitly alleged in the case. Finally, we have limited our analysis to criminal prosecutions; we have not sought to analyze military courts martial, trials by military commissions, immigration proceedings (other than criminal prosecutions for immigration violations), or other non-criminal proceedings.

The process of identifying and gathering terrorism cases is inevitably an imperfect one. There is no practical, reliable method for identifying all terrorism cases brought since 9/11, much less a method for identifying all terrorism cases ever brought in the United States. One place to start might be with the thousands of cases that the DOJ itself considers terrorism prosecutions, but the DOJ does not identify which cases it has categorized as terrorism-related and has resisted Freedom of Information Act attempts to obtain those docket numbers.[121] Similarly, the Statistics Division at the AOUSC, as noted above, does not disclose the cases underlying the tables in the Judicial Business of the United States.

Accordingly, we have sought to identify terrorism cases through other methods that are necessarily somewhat ad hoc. First, we screened cases that have been publicly identified as terrorism-related by the DOJ as well as high-profile prosecutions that have garnered significant media attention. Second, we consulted lists of terrorism prosecutions compiled by other organizations, such as FindLaw,[122] the *Washington Post,*[123] and the NYU Center on Law and Security in its Terrorist Trial Report Card.[124] Third, we sought to identify cases charging the primary terrorism offenses in chapters 113B and 115 of Title 18 of the United States Code by Keyciting those statutes and by running searches of docket databases through Westlaw.[125] For purposes of measuring outcomes of terrorism-related cases brought under the DOJ's post-9/11 law enforcement priorities and strategies, we have focused on cases filed after September 11, 2001, though we also included some significant international terrorism prosecutions filed in the 1990s for discussion and reference. Through this search, we have identified 107[126] terrorism prosecutions in the years since 2001 that form the basis of our quantitative analysis. We also have considered a number of terrorism prosecutions from the late 1980s and 1990s in connection with our analysis of the legal and practical challenges involved in international terrorism prosecutions.

We believe our search methodology has yielded a data set that can be used to make observations and draw conclusions about the court system's ability to cope with international terrorism prosecutions. Our data set, however, almost certainly does not contain the full universe of terrorism cases, nor is it necessarily perfectly representative of that universe. Indeed, our data set may be the product of certain selection biases. For example, it may be skewed toward cases with characteristics that draw media attention and thus underrepresent lower-profile cases; or it may be biased toward cases brought in certain jurisdictions with more readily accessible or searchable filings. To some extent, these limitations may circumscribe our ability to draw conclusions about the entire population of cases. Even with these limitations, however, we believe the data set is sufficiently robust to identify certain recurring factual and legal circumstances, to analyze the judiciary's response to those circumstances, and to draw conclusions based on that analysis. Further, our interviews and examination of the views of other experts have helped us confirm that we have identified and focused on the salient issues in international terrorism prosecutions.

Terrorism Prosecutions Filed and Defendants Charged, 9/12/2001 – 12/31/2007

As discussed above, this Paper's analysis of the practical and legal issues presented in terrorism prosecutions is based on a substantial body of both pre- and post-9/11 cases. While we have sought to identify all of the post-9/11 terrorism cases meeting the criteria discussed above, we did not undertake a similarly comprehensive attempt to canvass all pre-9/11 cases. Accordingly, while many pre-9/11 cases play a significant role in our analysis throughout this Paper, for purposes of the quantitative analysis presented below we have restricted the data set to those cases filed between September 11, 2001 and December 31, 2007.

As shown in Figure 1, we have identified 107 cases filed since September 11, 2001 that meet the criteria discussed above. 256 defendants were charged in those cases, including one individual who in 2008 was added to a case that was originally filed in 2007. These cases include prosecutions of high-profile defendants such as Richard Reid, Zacarias Moussaoui, and Jose Padilla; material support prosecutions against defendants such as the cleric Mohammed Ali al-Moayad, the Holy Land Foundation for Relief and Development, and Benevolence International Foundation; prosecutions of alleged domestic terror cells like the Fort Dix plotters and the so-called Virginia Jihad Network; and a broad assortment of others cases alleging some link to Islamist extremist terrorism.

Figure 1: Total Number of Terrorism Cases and Defendants

	Cases	Defendants
Total	107	257

For purposes of tabulating these numbers, an individual who was separately charged in more than one case was counted as a defendant in each case. So, for example, Nuradin Abdi has been charged in separate cases in the Southern District of Ohio and in the Eastern District of Virginia, and we counted Abdi as a separate defendant in each case. Further, there may be circumstances where a single "case" may involve multiple jurisdictions. If a prosecution is dismissed in one jurisdiction so that charges may be filed in a separate jurisdiction, we generally have treated that circumstance as a single case in the second jurisdiction, with data from the prior prosecution noted as relevant procedural background. Also, if a case is transferred for sentencing pursuant to Federal Rule of Criminal Procedure 20, we have treated this as a single case in the originating court.

Figure 2 shows the cases in our data set broken down by the year of filing, and by the number of defendants first charged by year of the charging instrument.

Figure 2: Number of Terrorism Cases and Defendants by Year

	Cases	Defendants
2001	22	36
2002	22	58
2003	17	50
2004	14	36
2005	12	21
2006	10	19
2007	10	36

As these figures indicate, a large number of cases were filed and a large number of defendants were charged immediately after the 9/11 attacks. Overall, these figures show a generally declining trend in both numbers of cases filed and number of new defendants charged in each succeeding year since 2001, although there was a notable jump in newly charged defendants in 2007. The data in Figure 2 is shown graphically in Figures 5 and 6 (facing page).

Terrorism Prosecutions Filed by Jurisdiction

Figures 3 and 4 summarize the geographical distribution of cases in our data set. The leading jurisdictions, both by number of cases and number of defendants, are the Eastern District of Virginia, the Southern District of New York, and the Eastern District of New York. This data is shown graphically on page 27 in Figures 9, 10, and 11.

Figure 3: Top Jurisdictions by Cases Filed

		Cases	Defendants
1	E.D. Va.	22	34
2	S.D.N.Y.	13	26
3	E.D.N.Y.	9	19
4	D.N.J.	6	13
5	N.D. Ill.	4	8
6	D. Mass.	4	7
7	E.D. Mich.	3	19
7	S.D. Fla.	3	14
7	D. Ariz.	3	4
7	D. Conn.	3	4
7	S.D. Ohio	3	3
7	S.D. Tex.	3	3
23 jurisd.		2 or fewer	103 total
Total:		107	257

Figure 4: Top Jurisdictions by Defendants Charged

		Defendants	Cases
1	E.D.Va.	34	22
2	S.D.N.Y.	26	13
3	E.D.N.Y.	19	9
3	E.D. Mich.	19	3
5	N.D. Tex.	16	2
6	S.D. Fla.	14	3
7	D.N.J.	13	6
8	M.D. Fla.	11	2
8	D.D.C.	11	1
25 Jurisd.		8 or fewer	46 total
Total:		257	107

Pre-Trial Detention

Of the 257 defendants in our data set, 46 have yet to be brought into custody because they are fugitives, presently are subject to extradition proceedings or cannot be extradited, are deceased, or for some other reason. Another 6 defendants are legal entities rather than individuals, and bail information was not available for two individuals. Thus 203 individual defendants have been arrested and have had a bail determination made by the court.

Of these 203, 139 defendants were ordered detained without bail and 70 defendants were released on conditions. Six defendants are counted in each category, because either they were initially detained but later were granted release on conditions, or initially were granted release on conditions and later had bail revoked. Indeed, one of the defendants initially was ordered detained, later was granted release on conditions, and then had bail revoked. Figure 13 on page 29 presents graphically the data showing pre-trial detention compared with release on conditions.

These numbers do not reflect whether or not the defendants granted release on conditions actually were released, i.e., whether they were able to post the required bond or meet other conditions; they reflect only the fact that the court ordered that the defendant would be released if he met the conditions set forth in the order.

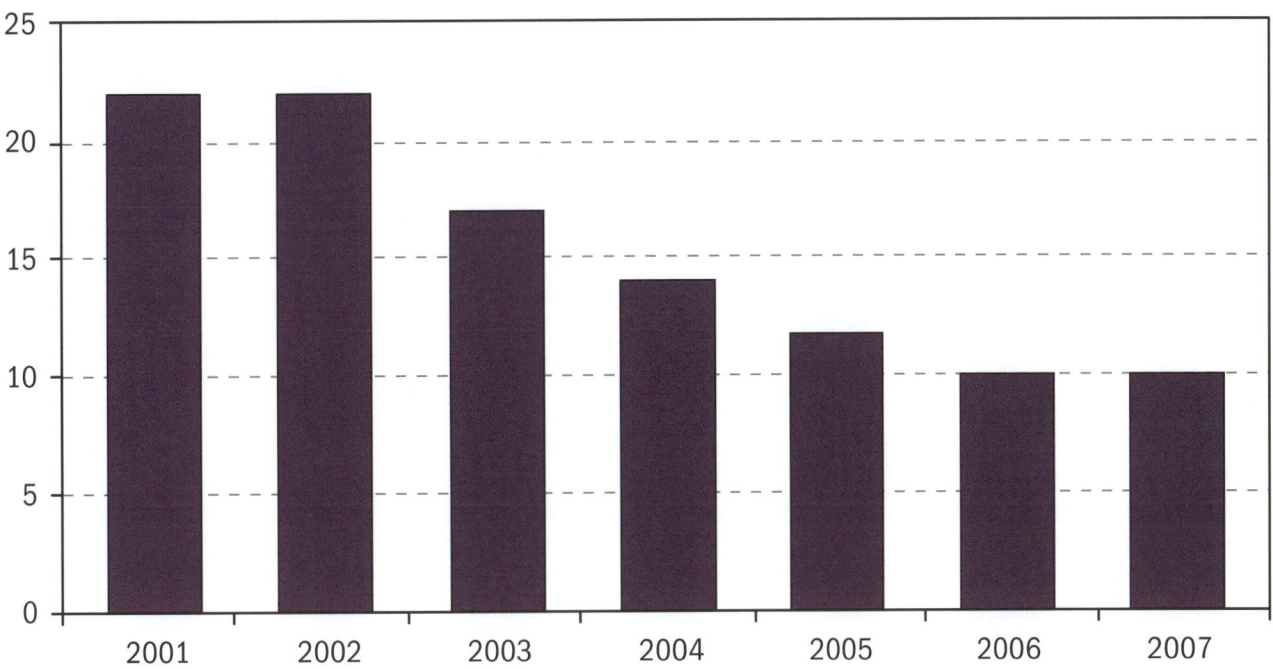

Figure 5: Number of Terrorism Cases Filed,
9/12/2001 – 12/31/2007

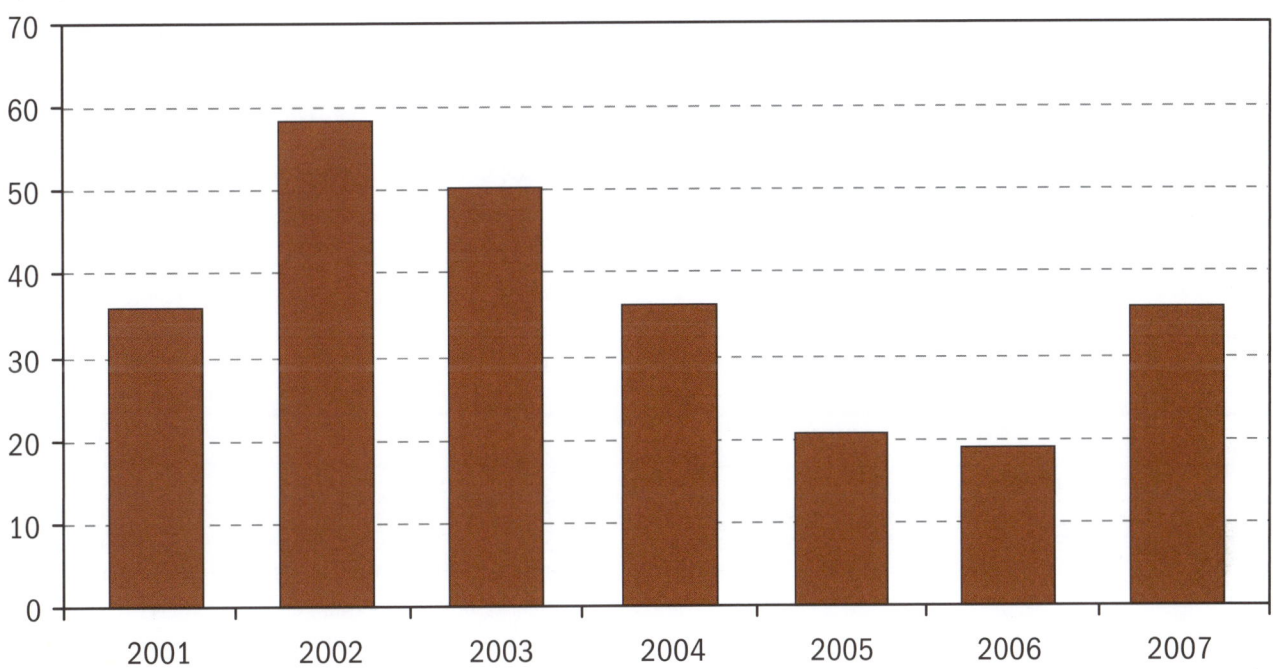

Figure 6: Number of Defendants Charged in Terrorism Cases Filed,
9/12/2001 – 12/31/2007

Outcomes in Terrorism Prosecutions

Of the 257 defendants included in our post-9/11 data set, 97 still have charges pending against them. This leaves 160 defendants who have had charges against them resolved, either by conviction, acquittal or dismissal of charges.

Of the 160 defendants who have had charges resolved, 145 were convicted of at least one count, either by a verdict of guilty after trial or by a guilty plea. We believe that these 145 cases should be viewed largely if not entirely as successful prosecutions for the government, which generally views a felony conviction on any single count as a success.

Fifteen defendants have been acquitted of all charges or have had all charges against them dismissed.[127] In some instances, however, the acquittal or dismissal did not ultimately represent a victory for the defendant. For example, in the *al-Marri* case, the government moved to dismiss all charges when it designated al-Marri as an "enemy combatant" and transferred him into military custody. Thus, although the criminal case against al-Marri was terminated with no conviction, he remained in custody and, under the Fourth Circuit's most recent decision, the government is free to file new criminal charges against him. Further, as demonstrated by cases such as *Arnaout* and *Benkahla*, even when the defendant can be said to have "won" by obtaining acquittal or dismissal of all charges that were originally filed, the government may bring new charges, and ultimately may win a conviction and lengthy sentence, by commencing an entirely separate prosecution.

Figure 7 shows the conviction data for the 160 defendants whose cases have been resolved. The same data is shown graphically in Figures 14 and 15 on page 29.

Figure 7: Outcomes in Terrorism Cases, 9/12/2001 – 12/31/2007

Defendants	257	
Charges still pending	97	
Charges resolved	160	
Convicted of any charge	145	90.625%
- Convicted at trial	45	28.125%
- Guilty plea	100	62.50%
Acquitted of all charges or all charges dismissed	15	9.375%

Figure 8 summarizes the sentencing data for defendants who have been convicted of at least one offense and, at the time of writing, had been sentenced. Of the 124 defendants convicted and sentenced, 111 were sentenced to some term of imprisonment. The other 13 defendants received no prison time; most of these were sentenced either to probation or to time served.

Figure 8: Sentencing Data from Terrorism Prosecutions, 9/12/2001 – 12/31/2007

Total defendants sentenced:	124
Defendants sentenced to imprisonment (excluding probation or time served):	111
Defendants receiving no prison term (i.e., probation or time served):	13
Defendants sentenced to a term of life imprisonment:	5
Average term of imprisonment (excluding life sentences):	100.71 months (8.39 years)
Median term of imprisonment:	55.5 months (4.63 years)
Median term of imprisonment, excluding defendants receiving no time:	60 months (5 years)

The five defendants sentenced to life imprisonment are Zacarias Moussaoui, Masoud Khan, Ali al-Timimi, Richard Reid, and Mohammed Jabarah. In addition, several defendants have received lengthy prison terms likely to amount to a life sentence, including Mohammed Ali al-Moayad, 75 years; Hemant Lakhani, 67 years; and Seifullah Chapman, 65 years.

Offenses Charged in Terrorism Prosecutions

Figure 12 shows the statutes most commonly charged against defendants in cases within our data set. The statutes are ranked by the number of separate defendants charged with any count alleging a violation of that statute. Because defendants often are charged with more than one offense, a single defendant may be counted multiple times in this chart, once for each statute that he is alleged to have violated. The most commonly charged statute in our data set is the federal aiding-and-abetting statute, 18 U.S.C. § 2, with 175 of the 270 defendants charged with at least one count alleging aiding and abetting. However, because aiding and abetting charges in our data set always are accompanied by substantive offenses, and because there are limited useful

In Pursuit of Justice 27

Figure 9: Number of Terrorism Cases Filed by Jurisdiction, 9/12/2001 – 12/31/2007

- ED Va (22)
- SDNY (13)
- EDNY (9)
- DNJ (6)
- ND Ill (4)
- D Mass (4)
- 29 Other Jurisdictions (49)

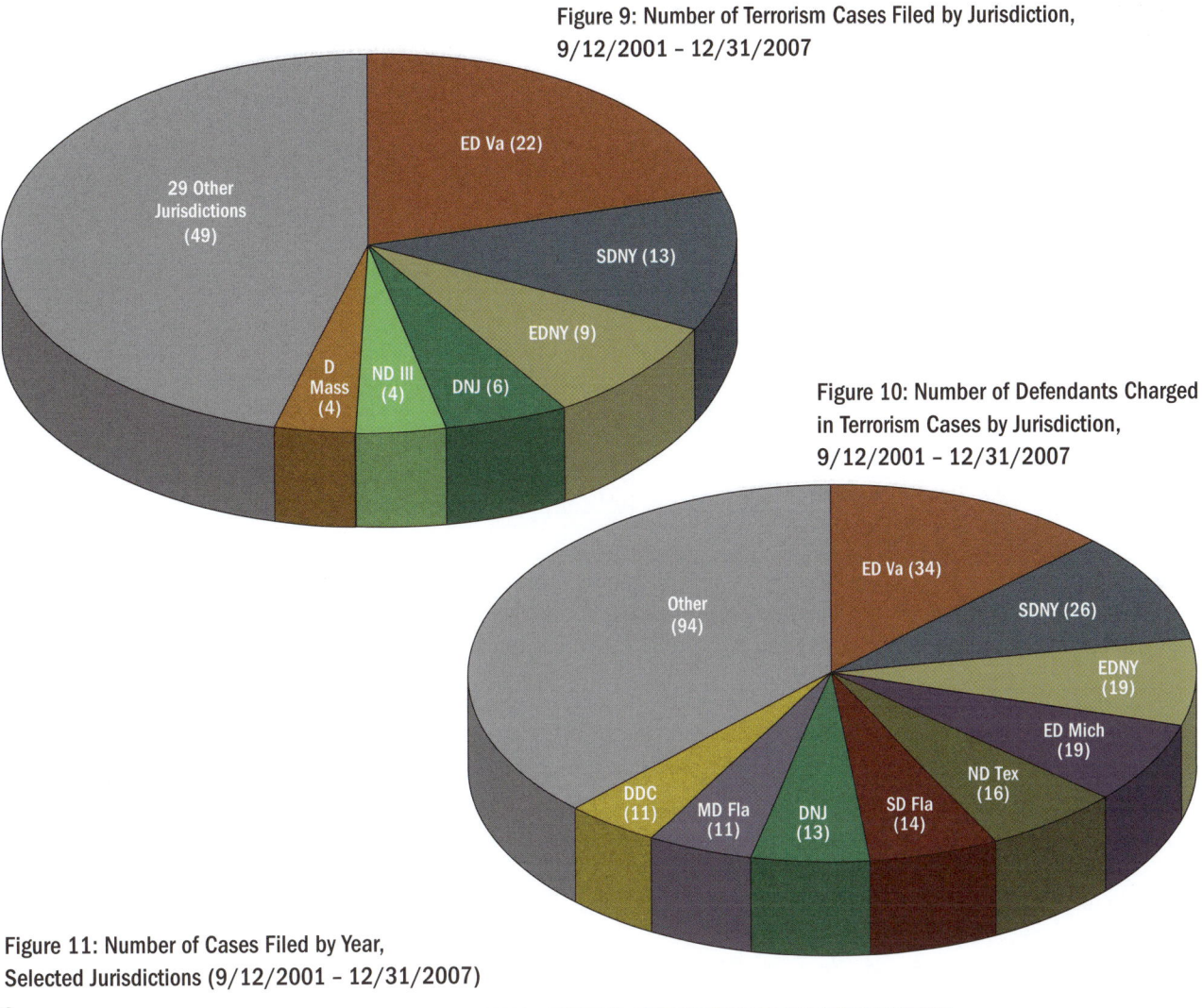

Figure 10: Number of Defendants Charged in Terrorism Cases by Jurisdiction, 9/12/2001 – 12/31/2007

- ED Va (34)
- SDNY (26)
- EDNY (19)
- ED Mich (19)
- ND Tex (16)
- SD Fla (14)
- DNJ (13)
- MD Fla (11)
- DDC (11)
- Other (94)

Figure 11: Number of Cases Filed by Year, Selected Jurisdictions (9/12/2001 – 12/31/2007)

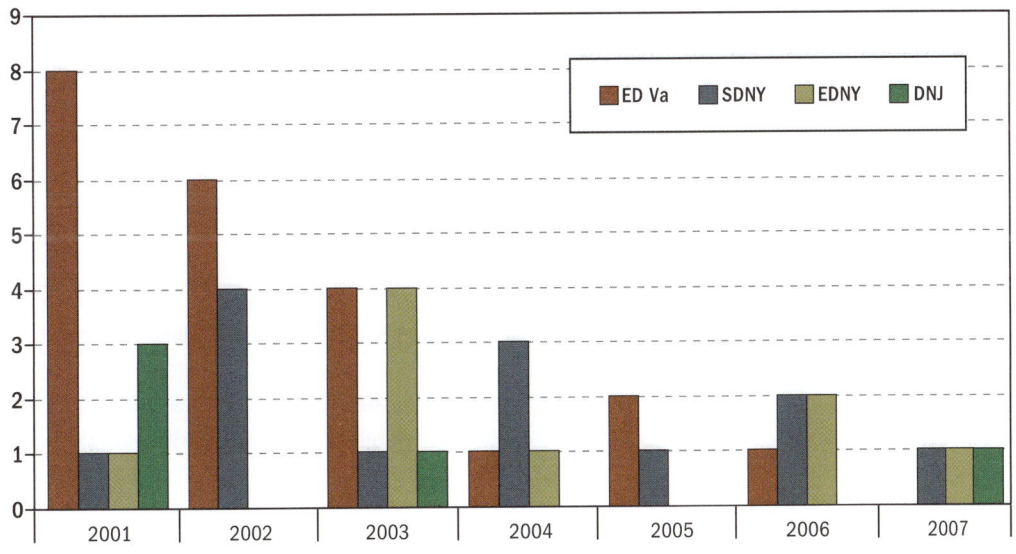

Figure 12: Table of Offenses Charged and Outcomes

	Offense		Defts	Defts with charge resolved	Defts convicted of the specific charge	Defts where the charge was dismissed as part of a plea	Defts convicted of any offense
1	18 U.S.C. § 2339B	Material support	82	52	26	13	46
2	18 U.S.C. § 2339A	Material support	58	32	19	6	27
3	50 U.S.C. §§ 1701-1706	IEEPA	52	31	23	3	26
4	18 U.S.C. § 1956	Money laundering	48	21	10	8	20
5	18 U.S.C. § 1001	False statements	39	32	23	2	28
6	18 U.S.C. § 924	Weapons charge	38	25	17	4	21
7	18 U.S.C. § 956	Conspiracy to commit murder	29	11	5	4	9
8	18 U.S.C. § 1962	RICO	25	18	12	2	16
9	18 U.S.C. § 2384	Explosives charges	21	14	6	5	11
10	18 U.S.C. § 1028	Document fraud	16	16	10	3	13

inferences to draw from the frequency of aiding-and-abetting charges, we have omitted this statute from the table.

The next most commonly charged offense is the federal conspiracy statute, 18 U.S.C. § 371. Like § 2 charges, § 371 charges in our data set are accompanied in each instance by a substantive offense that is the object of the conspiracy.

By far the most commonly charged substantive offenses in our data set are the material support statutes, 18 U.S.C. §§ 2339A and 2339B, followed by violations of the International Emergency Economic Powers Act by providing funds, services or support to a Specially Designated Global Terrorist under Executive Order 13224 (50 U.S.C. §§ 1701 - 1706). After these material support offenses, the next most commonly charged statute is money laundering (18 U.S.C. § 1956). Next are false statements (18 U.S.C. § 1001), weapons charges (18 U.S.C. § 924), and conspiracy to commit murder (18 U.S.C. § 956). Rounding out the list are RICO charges (18 U.S.C. § 1962), explosives charges (18 U.S.C. § 2384), and document fraud (18 U.S.C. § 1028).

The table also shows conviction data for these statutes, but a word of explanation is in order about this data. To begin with, we excluded defendants who still have charges against them pending. We then calculated the number of defendants who were convicted (either after trial or by guilty plea) of any count alleging a violation of the statute. But we also have noted the number of instances where all counts charging a violation of the statute were dropped as part of a plea to another charge. This is an important consideration because the dismissal of charges as part of a plea usually provides little useful insight into the strength of the government's evidence in support of the dismissed charge. Finally, we have included the instances where the defendant was ultimately convicted of some offense. Consistent with our approach to measuring outcomes in terrorism prosecutions, we believe the most important yardstick is whether the prosecution secured a conviction on any charge against the defendant. The precise statute of conviction is often (though not always) of lesser significance.

We have not sought to correlate sentences imposed against defendants with particular statutes the defendants have been charged with or convicted of, because the nature of sentencing is to focus on the overall criminal conduct involved in the case, rather than on particular statutory charges. Except for the application of statutory maximums and minimums, sentencing focuses on the defendant's individual characteristics; the entirety of the defendant's conduct in the course of preparing for, committing, and seeking to avoid detection for the offense; the reasonably foreseeable conduct of others involved in jointly undertaken criminal activity; the harm caused to the victims; and other characteristics of the offense as a whole. *See generally* U.S.S.G. § 1B1.3 (relevant conduct); §§ 3D1.1 - 3D1.5 (grouping counts for sentencing purposes); § 5G1.2 (sentencing on multiple counts).

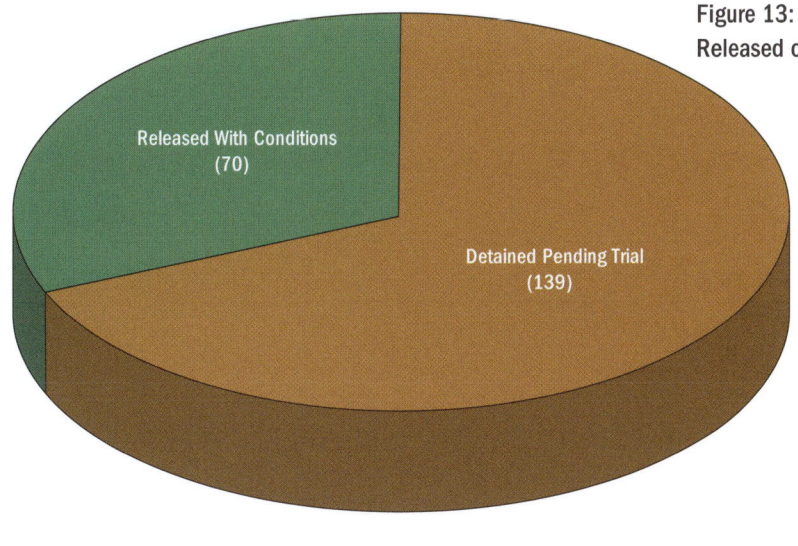

Figure 13: Number of Defendants Detained vs. Released on Conditions

- Released With Conditions (70)
- Detained Pending Trial (139)

Figure 14: Conviction Rates in Terrorism Cases, 9/12/2001 – 12/31/2007

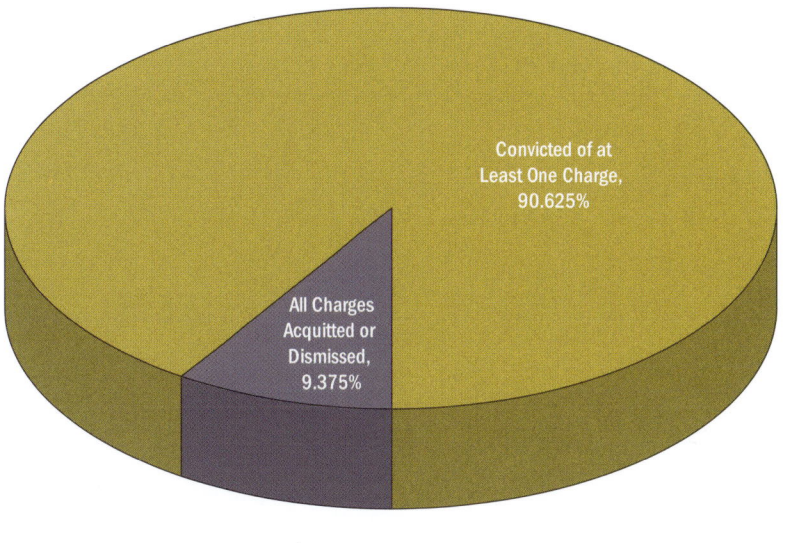

- Convicted of at Least One Charge, 90.625%
- All Charges Acquitted or Dismissed, 9.375%

Figure 15: Conviction Rates in Terrorism Cases, Guilty Plea vs. Trial, 9/12/2001 – 12/31/2007

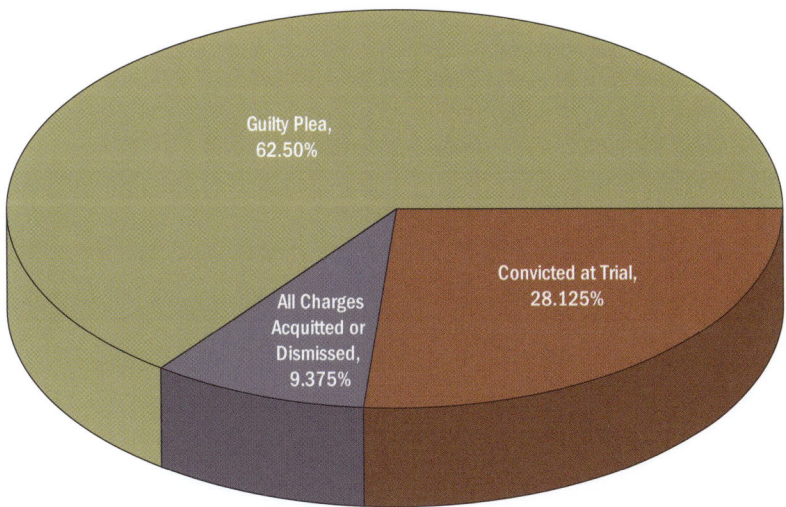

- Guilty Plea, 62.50%
- Convicted at Trial, 28.125%
- All Charges Acquitted or Dismissed, 9.375%

V.
Existing Criminal Statutes Cover a Broad Spectrum of the Crimes Committed by International Terrorists

The capability of the federal criminal justice system to effectively handle international terrorism cases depends heavily on the availability of statutes that can be used to prosecute the full breadth of terrorist conduct. Under U.S. criminal law, international terrorism is defined as "violent acts or acts dangerous to human life that are a violation of the criminal laws of the United States ... or that would be a criminal violation if committed within the jurisdiction of the United States" and which seek to influence, intimidate, coerce, or affect the conduct of a government or a people and occur in whole or in part outside the United States. 18 U.S.C. § 2331(1).[128] Given the central importance of combating international terrorism, it is no surprise that over time, and especially since 1996, Congress has cast its legislative net over a wide range of terrorist conduct. The federal criminal laws aimed at terrorism span conduct that may be merely preparatory to violent incidents, for example the material support statutes, to violent acts themselves after they have already occurred. Therefore, while some may debate who should be criminally prosecuted for terrorism, the decision not to prosecute a suspected terrorist is rarely, if ever, based on the unavailability of a statute under which to do so.

Understandably, since 9/11, the criminal justice system has emphasized a model of law enforcement that seeks to arm prosecutors with the tools to criminally charge individuals before they engage in violent acts. This early prevention model of enforcement has raised concerns about whether the government is targeting terrorist conduct, or whether in its zeal to protect the populace the government has strayed into prosecuting conduct for which there is insufficient specific criminal intent, or even whether the government is unconstitutionally prosecuting speech and association. While many criticisms may be levied at the justice system, there can be little doubt that the array of statutes to deal with terrorists has been broadened, especially over the last two decades, and has evolved to achieve both preventive and more traditional punitive goals; it also appears that the courts and Congress—perhaps slowly at times—have acted to draw better defined constitutional lines around these statutes.

This section of the White Paper discusses a number of the more significant and potentially useful terrorism statutes. We examine how and how widely these statutes have been used. We also examine where problems have occurred in prosecutions under these statutes. We further discuss what gaps may exist in the statutory scheme. Our primary focus in this section is on the substance of the statutes and not on the procedural or evidentiary problems that can arise in terrorism trials, which we discuss later in this report. A survey of all the statutes related to terrorism or the even broader group of other statutes used in terrorism prosecutions is beyond the scope of this White Paper, and we recognize that there are numerous other significant statutes which could merit discussion.[129] Nevertheless, the selection of statutes we have examined serves a dual purpose: it embraces most of the major current terrorism prosecutions that have taken place since 1993, and it provides some historical context to our country's adjustments to its criminal laws when faced with threats to its national security.

A. Material Support of Terrorist Organizations

Since 9/11, the so-called "material support" statutes, the most important of which are codified at Title 18, United States Code, §§ 2339A and 2339B, have proven to be among the most popular tools for prosecution of terrorist suspects in this country. According to our data, almost half of the terrorism cases that we have surveyed have included charges for offenses under either § 2339A or § 2339B. Section 2339A was originally enacted in 1994 as a response to the bombing of the World Trade Center in 1993. *See* Robert M. Chesney, *The Sleeper Scenario: Terrorism-Support Laws and the Demands of Prevention*, 42 Harv. J. on Legis. 1, 12 (2005). Two years later, § 2339A was amended and § 2339B was enacted as part of the Antiterrorism and Effective Death Penalty Act of 1996 ("AEDPA"), Pub. L. No. 104-132, §§ 303, 323, 110 Stat. 1214, 1250-53, 1255 (1996), in response to several tragic events that underscored the serious threat posed by terrorist activity, including the bombing of the Alfred P. Murrah Federal Building in Oklahoma City on April 19, 1995, which killed 168 people. *See* H.R. Rep. No. 104-383, pt. 1, at 37-38 (1995) (noting that the legislation was prompted by the Oklahoma City bombing, the bombing of Pan Am flight 103 over Lockerbie, Scotland, the kidnapping and murder of Colonel William Higgins by Hezbollah, the bombing of the World Trade Center, and the investigation, arrest, and conviction of CIA spy Aldrich Ames); *see also* Chesney, *The Sleeper Scenario*, at 1; Thomas C. Martin, *The Comprehensive Terrorism Prevention Act of 1995*, 20 Seton Hall Legis. J. 201, 210-19 (1996) (providing legislative history).

The purpose of the two statutes is to "prevent persons within the United States, or subject to the jurisdiction of the United States, from providing material support or resources to foreign organizations that engage in terrorist activities." *See* H.R. Rep. No. 104-383 at 58. Section 2339A stems the flow of material support only from those persons who intend this support to further a terrorist act; this statute has been used less frequently than § 2339B, which imposes an absolute ban on providing material support to organizations that are formally designated as foreign terrorist organizations by the Secretary of State.[130] Congress subsequently enacted two other material support statutes, §§ 2339C and 2339D, which address more specific aspects of terrorist financing and training camps and have begun to be invoked by prosecutors.[131]

1. Providing Material Support in Furtherance of a Terrorist Act (18 U.S.C. § 2339A)

Section 2339A makes it a crime to "provide[] material support or resources or conceal[] or disguise[] the nature, location, source, or ownership of material support or resources, knowing or intending that they are to be used in preparation for, or in carrying out" a number of specified offenses, including murder, kidnapping, and the violation of various terrorism statutes. 18 U.S.C. § 2339A(a). Section 2339A does not require that such support be given to a designated foreign terrorist organization because Congress intended it to cover the provision of material support to even non-designated terrorist organizations, so long as such support was provided in furtherance of the specified crimes. *See* H.R. Rep. No. 104-383 at 82. In this sense, § 2339A can be likened to a form of terrorism aiding and abetting statute. Prior to 9/11, § 2339A was rarely used; but in the years since the 9/11 attacks, over twenty defendants have been charged with at least fifty offenses under § 2339A. *See* Chesney, *The Sleeper Scenario*, at 18-20 (discussing the spike in § 2339A prosecutions after 9/11 through 2005 as compared to pre-9/11).

Prior to 1996, § 2339A did not define "material support." Since 1996, however, Congress has amended § 2339A by defining "material support" to include, among other things, the provision of property or services, money, lodging, training, false identification, weapons, communications equipment, transportation, "expert advice or assistance," and personnel. 18 U.S.C. § 2339A(b), *as amended by*, Pub. L. 108-458, § 6603(b), (g), Pub. L. 107-56, § 805(a)(2), and Pub. L. 104-132, § 323.[132] The term "personnel" has been broadly defined to include the providing of "a foreign terrorist organization with 1 or more individuals (who may be or include himself) to work under that terrorist organization's direction or control or to organize, manage, supervise, or otherwise direct the operation of that organization." 18 U.S.C. § 2339B(h). Most strikingly, the statutory definition explicitly states that a defendant can be prosecuted for providing himself as personnel. *See id.*; *accord United States v. Abdi*, 498 F. Supp. 2d 1048, 1054, 1058 (S.D. Ohio 2007) (affirming indictment on charges of, inter alia, conspiring to provide material support to terrorists in violation of § 2339A based on the fact that the defendant planned to attend a terrorist training camp and that he misrepresented the true purpose of his trip to immigration authorities on his application for a travel permit).

It also appears that courts follow the lead of the statutory definition in broadly construing what it means to provide others as personnel. Specifically, in *United States v. Sattar*, Lynne Stewart, the longtime attorney for Sheikh Omar Abdel Rahman, was found guilty of providing material support to a foreign terrorist organization in the form of "personnel" by relaying messages from Abdel Rahman, who was imprisoned in Minnesota, to the Islamic Group, the Egyptian terrorist organization he had helped lead, as well as to a Reuters reporter in Cairo. *See* 395 F. Supp. 2d 79, 100 (S.D.N.Y. 2005). The messages encouraged Abdel Rahman's followers to abandon an existing cease-fire between the Islamic Group and Egypt. *See id.* at 87-88. In upholding Stewart's conviction, the court found that the term "personnel" is not limited to the physical transfer of personnel, but includes "making personnel available—which is in accord with the ordinary and natural use of the term 'provide,' and is consistent with its placement in the statute and the purpose of proscribing the provision of resources used for a prohibited purpose." *Id.* at 99 (internal quotations omitted). Thus, the court reasoned that Stewart "provided" Sheikh Abdel Rahman as "personnel" to the Islamic Group by relaying his messages. *See id.*[133]

Section 2339A lists two items that do not constitute material support: the provision of medicine and religious materials. The "medicine" exception, however, has been construed narrowly. First, Congress noted that the medicine exception should be limited to medicine itself, and not include medical supplies. *See* H.R. Rep. No. 104-518, pt. 3, at 114 (1996) (Conf. Rep.). Moreover, in the only case so far construing this provision, the court refused to dismiss an indictment brought against a doctor for conspiring, attempting to provide, and providing medical services to a designated terrorist organization, holding that the term "medicine" does not include medical services. *See United States v. Shah*, 474 F. Supp. 2d 492, 498-500 (S.D.N.Y. 2007).[134] The doctor, who never actually succeeded in providing medical services to al Qaeda, was convicted for conspiring to and attempting to provide material support and sentenced to twenty-five years' imprisonment. *See* Judgment as to Rafiq Sabir, *United States v. Shah*, No. 05-cr-00673 (S.D.N.Y. Nov. 30, 2007) (Dkt. No. 176); *see also* Govt's Mem. in Opp'n to Rafiq Sabir's First Mot. to Set Aside Verdict at 21-23, *Shah* (S.D.N.Y. Sept. 11, 2007) (Dkt. No. 163) (discussing facts established at trial regarding Sabir's involvement in a conspiracy and his attempt to provide material support).

To violate § 2339A, a defendant must know or intend that his material support will be used in preparation for, or in carrying out, a terrorist activity. Because of this mens rea requirement, § 2339A has been upheld against challenges that it is unconstitutionally vague and overbroad in violation of the First and Fifth Amendments. *See United States v. Awan*, 459 F. Supp. 2d 167, 177-81 (E.D.N.Y. 2006); *see also Abdi*, 498 F. Supp. 2d at 1058-59.

Section 2339A has become a prominent prosecutorial tool for anticipatory prosecutions in which the defendants are arrested to preempt a terrorist strike. *See* Robert M. Chesney, *Beyond Conspiracy? Anticipatory Prosecution and the Challenge of Unaffiliated Terrorism*, 80 S. Cal. L. Rev. 425, 425 (2007) (quoting former Attorney General Alberto Gonzales saying, "Prevention is the goal of all goals when it comes to terrorism because we simply cannot and will not wait for these particular crimes to occur before taking action"). The benefits of such an approach are obvious, given the potentially catastrophic impact of a major terrorist attack. The approach, however, has drawn criticism from civil rights groups and others concerned that the government is prosecuting dissenting thought, rather than criminal acts. *See id.* at 426.[135]

To bring a case under § 2339A, the government need not prove that any predicate offense actually occurred. *See id.* at 479. In some respects, § 2339A is broader than conspiracy liability in that it does not even require proof of an actual agreement. Further, since § 2339A has no requirement to prove a "significant step" toward the commission of a crime, unlike an attempt charge, prosecutors can use the statute to bring charges well in advance of—and before any steps have been taken in furtherance of—a specific terrorism plot.

The case of *United States v. Lakhani* provides an example of how § 2339A has been used where other anticipatory statutes, such as conspiracy and attempt, were not available. In *Lakhani*, the government alleged that the defendant attempted to sell a surface-to-air missile to an undercover agent, believing that the agent planned to use it to shoot down airplanes. *See* Criminal Complaint, *United States v. Lakhani*, No. 03-cr-00880 (D.N.J. Aug. 11, 2003) (Dkt. No. 1); *see also United States v. Lakhani*, 480 F.3d 171, 174-77 (3d Cir. 2007). The defendant could not be charged with conspiracy because he negotiated with a government informant, *see Lakhani*, 480 F.3d at 174, and there was consequently no unlawful agreement. *See, e.g., United States v. Arbane*, 446 F.3d 1223, 1228 (11th Cir. 2006) ("It is axiomatic that you cannot have a conspiracy without an agreement between two or more culpable conspirators. If there are only two members of a conspiracy, neither may be a government agent or informant") (citation omitted). Further, since the defendant knew few details of how the missiles were purportedly to be used, it would have been hard to prove attempt of any underlying terrorism offense. *See*

Chesney, *Beyond Conspiracy?*, at 483; *see also Lakhani*, 480 F.3d at 174-77. Instead, he was charged with attempt to provide material support and other criminal violations. He was convicted and sentenced to forty-seven years in prison. *See Lakhani*, 480 F.3d at 174.

In another case, *United States v. Hayat*, the defendant was convicted of offenses, including a violation of § 2339A, for having traveled to Pakistan and provided "personnel in the form of his person" to receive "jihadist training, including training in physical fitness, firearms, and means to wage violent jihad," which he then intended to put to use in the United States. *See* Second Superseding Indictment, *United States v. Hayat*, No. 05-cr-00240 (E.D. Cal. Jan. 26, 2006) (Dkt. No. 162) (describing allegations against Hayat); *United States v. Hayat*, No. 05-cr-00240, 2006 WL 1686491, at *1 (E.D. Cal. June 19, 2006) (noting jury's conviction of Hayat on all counts of the indictment). Hayat was indicted upon his return to the United States, before he could "wage jihad in the United States." Second Superseding Indictment, *Hayat* (E.D. Cal. Jan. 26, 2006) (Dkt. No. 162). From the government's perspective this was a successful preemptive prosecution. The case was somewhat controversial, however, and demonstrated the long reach of § 2339A. Some of the evidence against the defendant related to his noxious views and opinions. The government alleged, for example, that Hayat had told an FBI informant that he was pleased about the murder of *Wall Street Journal* reporter Daniel Pearl and that he had read books about violent jihad. Other evidence, including the purpose of Hayat's trip to Pakistan, was disputed, and there was no allegation that Hayat had taken a step toward carrying out an act of terrorism while in the United States.[136]

2. Providing Material Support to Designated Terrorist Organizations (18 U.S.C. § 2339B)

Congress enacted § 2339B to fill a perceived gap in the terrorism laws that allowed terrorist organizations to receive funds or other material support from donors who intended their contributions to be used to support humanitarian causes. *See* H.R. Rep. No. 104-383 at 43-44; *see also Abdi*, 498 F. Supp. 2d at 1058 ("As § 2339A was limited to individuals (such as donors) who intended to further the commission of specific federal offenses, § 2339B encompassed donors who, though contributing to [foreign terrorist organizations], acted without the intent to further federal crimes"). Congress was concerned that financial resources and other forms of material support are fungible, and that any support given to a terrorist group frees up resources which may be used in furtherance of its terrorist activities. *See Abdi*, 498 F. Supp 2d at 1058 ("Congress made a specific finding that 'foreign organizations that engaged in terrorist activity are so tainted by their criminal conduct that any contribution to such an organization facilitates that conduct'") (quoting historical and statutory notes to 18 U.S.C. § 2339B); *Humanitarian Law Project v. Gonzales*, 380 F. Supp. 2d 1134, 1146 (C.D. Cal. 2005) (stating that Congress was concerned about terrorist organizations raising funds "under the cloak of a humanitarian or charitable exercise").

Although restrictions on fundraising are an important purpose of the law, § 2339B is by no means limited to financial contributions to terrorist organizations. To the contrary, § 2339B incorporates the same definition of "material support" as § 2339A and prohibits a broad range of assistance to designated terrorist organizations, including the provision of weapons, communications equipment, expert assistance, and personnel. *See* 18 U.S.C. § 2339B(g)(4).

Section 2339B prohibits donations of material support to an organization that is a designated "foreign terrorist organization." *Id.* § 2339B(a)(1). The designation process is governed by other provisions of federal law, which give the Secretary of State power to designate as a foreign terrorist organization any organization that is foreign and engages in terrorist activity or has the capability and intent to engage in it, where the terrorist activity threatens either the security of U.S. nationals or national security. *See* 8 U.S.C. § 1189(a)(1). The Secretary of State must publish notice of the designation in the Federal Register, and it becomes binding once published. *See id.* § 1189(a)(2). The designated organization then has thirty days to appeal the designation to the D.C. Circuit, and the appeal must be based solely on the administrative record unless the government wants to submit additional classified evidence ex parte. *See id.* § 1189(c). The reviewing court may only set aside the designation on limited grounds such as that it is arbitrary, capricious, or an abuse of discretion or in conflict with the Constitution or a statute. *See id.* § 1189(c)(3). Some organizations have challenged their designations but with little success. *See, e.g., People's Mojahedin Org. of Iran v. Dept. of State*, 327 F.3d 1238, 1241-45 (D.C. Cir. 2003) (affirming designation of foreign terrorist organization status upon organization that committed violent acts against Iranian government buildings and officials).

Once an organization is designated as a "foreign terrorist organization" under these procedures, a criminal defendant may not "raise any question concerning the validity of the issuance of such designation as a defense or objection at any trial or hearing." 8 U.S.C. § 1189(a)(8). Several defendants prosecuted under § 2339B have challenged the designation process, claiming that the inability to contest an element of a criminal offense infringes on their due process rights, but courts have rejected these arguments on several grounds, including: (1) lack of the defendants' standing to assert the rights of the organizations; (2) the ability of the organizations (and their members) to challenge the designations in civil proceedings; and (3) deference to Congress on national security matters. *See United States v. al-Arian*, 308 F. Supp. 2d 1322, 1343-47 (M.D. Fla. 2004); *see also United States v. Assi*, 414 F. Supp. 2d 707, 725-26 (E.D. Mich. 2006). Courts have also noted that defendants' challenges to the validity of the designations would be irrelevant at their criminal trials, because "Congress has provided that the *fact* of an organization's designation as [a foreign terrorist organization] is an element of § 2339B, but the *validity* of the designation is not." *United States v. Hammoud*, 381 F.3d 316, 331 (4th Cir. 2004) (emphasis in original); *accord Assi*, 414 F. Supp. 2d at 725-26.

Section 2339B has generated some controversy because of its limited criminal intent component.[137] As originally enacted, § 2339B contained no explicit mens rea requirement. The statute was then challenged by "legal and social service organizations and two individuals who [sought] to provide 'material support' to the non-violent humanitarian and political activities of Kurdish and Tamil organizations the Secretary designated as 'foreign terrorist organizations.'" *Humanitarian Law Project v. U.S. Dep't of Justice*, 352 F.3d 382, 385 (9th Cir. 2003). The plaintiffs argued that "§ 2339B [ran] afoul of the Fifth Amendment's right to due process of law because the statute [did] not require proof that a person charged with violating the statute had a guilty intent when he or she provided 'material support' to a designated organization." *Id.* at 394. In response, "to avoid the serious due process concerns raised by § 2339B," the Ninth Circuit construed § 2339B "to require the government to prove that a person acted with knowledge of an organization's designation as a 'foreign terrorist organization' or knowledge of the unlawful activities that caused the organization to be so designated." *Id*. at 393-94.

Another court went even further, construing § 2339B's implicit mens rea component to require "knowledge, in addition to the previous two requirements, that the recipient could or would utilize the support to further the illegal activities of the entity." *United States v. al-Arian*, 329 F. Supp. 2d 1294, 1298 (M.D. Fla. 2004). In 2004, Congress resolved the issue by adding the explicit mens rea requirement that exists in the statute today: "To violate this [provision], a person must have knowledge that the organization is a designated terrorist organization ... , that the organization has engaged or engages in terrorist activity ... , or that the organization has engaged or engages in terrorism." 18 U.S.C. § 2339B(a)(1). Thus, Congress required only knowledge of the terrorist designation or activity, rather than knowledge or intent that the support be provided in furtherance of criminal activity. *See Humanitarian Law Project v. Gonzales*, 380 F. Supp. 2d at 1147 ("This Court must assume that Congress, with full awareness of these decisions, incorporated the [Ninth Circuit's] holding into the statute and rejected the *Al-Arian* ruling requiring specific intent").

Subsequent courts have upheld the statute even though it does not require proof that the defendant knew that his contribution would be used specifically to advance terrorism. *See, e.g., Hammoud*, 381 F. 3d at 328-29; *Abdi*, 498 F. Supp. 2d at 1057-58; *Assi*, 414 F. Supp. 2d at 719-20; *Humanitarian Law Project v. Gonzales*, 380 F. Supp. 2d at 1142-48. In upholding the statute, those courts have noted that "§ 2339B does not prohibit mere association; it prohibits the *conduct* of providing material support to a designated [foreign terrorist organization]." *Hammoud*, 381 F.3d at 329 (emphasis in original); *accord Assi*, 414 F. Supp. 2d at 721 (§ 2339B "criminalizes the affirmative *conduct of providing material support or resources* to an organization designated as [a foreign terrorist organization]") (some emphasis omitted); *see also Humanitarian Law Project v. Gonzales*, 380 F. Supp. 2d at 1143-44 (§ 2339B "does not criminalize mere membership, association, or expressions of sympathy with foreign terrorist organizations," but rather "permits membership and affiliation with foreign terrorist organizations" and only "prohibits the conduct of providing material support or resources to an organization that one knows is a designated foreign terrorist organization or is engaged in terrorist activities").[138]

Though rarely used prior to 9/11, § 2339B has been charged frequently since that date.[139] It has increasingly been used to prosecute an organization's "foot soldiers and sympathizers" in a way that expands typical accomplice liability, since there is no requirement that the offender intended the support to facilitate any particular crime. *See* Tom Stacey, *The "Material*

Support" Offense: The Use of Strict Liability in the War Against Terror, 14 Kan. J.L. & Pub. Pol'y 461, 463 (2005). Another useful aspect of § 2339B is its extraterritorial reach: the statute explicitly confers jurisdiction over any offender who is a U.S. national or resident, who sets foot in the United States after committing the offense, or whose offense occurred at least in part anywhere in the United States or affected interstate commerce. See 18 U.S.C. § 2339B(d). The data from our research illustrates that § 2339B has served as a potent tool for the government in its campaign of "preemptive" prosecution, including cases where the defendants allegedly attended or planned to attend terrorist training camps.

For example, in one high-profile case, United States v. Goba, the government prosecuted six individuals from Lackawanna, New York, after learning that they had traveled to Afghanistan to train with al Qaeda and intercepting suspicious communications that raised concerns of a possible terrorist attack. See Indictment, United States v. Goba, No. 02-cr-00214 (W.D.N.Y. Oct, 21, 2002) (Dkt. No. 42); Larry Margasak, U.S. Still Investigating What 5 Were Plotting—Bush Praises Raids in Buffalo and Pakistan, Star-Ledger (Newark, NJ), Sept. 15, 2002, at 1. The government reportedly did not have enough information to prosecute the individuals, known as the "Lackawanna Six," for any other substantive terrorism offense. See John J. Goldman, Last of "Lackawanna Six" Terror Defendants Sentenced, L.A. Times, Dec. 18, 2003, at A38. Nonetheless, § 2339B allowed the government to prosecute the six individuals, leading to guilty pleas for conspiracy and attempt to provide material support and sentences of seven to ten years for each defendant. See Judgment as to Mukhtar al-Bakri, Goba (W.D.N.Y. Dec. 15, 2003) (Dkt. No. 220); Judgment as to Yasein Taher, Goba (W.D.N.Y. Dec. 15, 2003) (Dkt. No. 221); Judgment as to Yahya Goba, Goba (W.D.N.Y. Dec. 22, 2003) (Dkt. No. 224); Judgment as to Sahim Alwan, Goba (W.D.N.Y. Dec. 24, 2003) (Dkt. No. 226); Judgment as to Faysal Galab, Goba (W.D.N.Y. Dec. 30, 2003) (Dkt. No. 229); Amended Judgment as to Shafal Mosed, Goba (W.D.N.Y. Jan. 21, 2004) (Dkt. No. 235); Last Terror Cell Member Sentenced to Nine Years, Milwaukee J. Sentinel, Dec. 18, 2003, at 26A. Other material support cases under § 2339B have also led to convictions and severe sentences. See, e.g., United States v. Faris, 388 F.3d 452, 454-55 (4th Cir. 2004) (affirming guilty plea and twenty-year sentence for defendant who attended al Qaeda training camp in which he discussed possibility of severing cables of the Brooklyn Bridge); Amended Judgment & Indictment, United States v. Chandia, No. 05-cr-00401 (E.D. Va. Sept. 19, 2006) (Dkt. No. 226) (defendant sentenced to fifteen years in prison for conspiring and attempting to provide material support to the jihadi group Lashkar-e-Taiba).

Complementing its preemptive purpose, § 2339B also helps the government to cut off channels of support, financial or otherwise, to suspected terrorist groups. In United States v. Paracha, for instance, the government prosecuted a Pakistani citizen living in the United States for trying to obtain immigration documents for a known al Qaeda member and safeguarding al Qaeda assets through investment in a putatively legitimate business front. See United States v. Paracha, No. 03-cr-01197, 2006 WL 12768, at *2 (S.D.N.Y. Jan. 3, 2006). Paracha was convicted at trial for violations of three different statutes, including § 2339B, and was sentenced to thirty years in prison. See id. at *1. In the al-Arian case, the lead defendant, a professor at the University of South Florida, pled guilty following a mistrial to one count of violating § 2339B, which was based on the predicate acts of "operat[ing] and direct[ing] fundraising and other organizational activities" for the Palestinian Islamic Jihad-Shiqaqi Faction, "a foreign organization that uses violence, principally suicide bombings, and threats of violence to pressure Israel to cede territory to the Palestinian people." Al-Arian, 308 F. Supp. 2d at 1327; see Plea Agreement at 1, United States v. al-Arian, No. 03-cr-00077 (M.D. Fla. Apr. 14, 2006) (Dkt. No. 1563); Declaration of Mistrial, al-Arian (M.D. Fla. Dec. 7, 2005) (Dkt. No. 1464); see also Spencer S. Hsu, Former Fla. Professor to Be Deported, Wash. Post, Apr. 18, 2006, at A03.[140] The presiding judge exceeded the prosecutors' recommendation and sentenced al-Arian to fifty-seven months' imprisonment. See Judgment, al-Arian (M.D. Fla. May 1, 2006) (Dkt. No. 1574); Meg Laughlin, Judge Sentences Al-Arian to Limit, St. Petersburg Times, May 2, 2006, at 1A.[141]

In another significant case, Judge Sterling Johnson in the Eastern District of New York sentenced Yemeni cleric Mohammed Ali al-Moayad to seventy-five years in prison for attempting to raise money for terrorist organizations in violation of § 2339B. See Judgment, United States v. al-Moayad, No. 03-cr-01322 (E.D.N.Y. Aug. 1, 2005) (Dkt. No. 197); see also Jonathan Wald & Chris Kokenes, Cleric Sentenced in Terror Conspiracy, CNN.com, Aug. 2, 2005.[142] After a lengthy FBI investigation, al-Moayad was arrested in Germany during a meeting with a confidential informant, who had posed as a representative of a fictional donor who purportedly sought to make a $2 million contribution to terrorist groups. The investigation revealed that al-Moayad was in fact a conduit for forwarding large sums to terrorists. During the investigation, the informant recorded many incriminating statements of al-Moayad. See Affidavit in Support of Arrest Warrant, *al-Moayad* (E.D.N.Y Jan. 5, 2003) (Dkt. No. 1); Superseding Indictment, *al-Moayad* (E.D.N.Y Dec. 13, 2004) (Dkt. No. 94); *see also* Wald & Kokenes, *Cleric Sentenced in Terror Conspiracy*. Judge Johnson also sentenced al-Moayad's accomplice, Mohammed Mohsen Zayed, to forty-five years' imprisonment on material support charges. *See* Judgment, *al-Moayad* (E.D.N.Y. Sep. 14, 2005) (Dkt. No. 205).

This is not to say that the availability of § 2339B guarantees success for the government in its material support prosecutions. Indeed, the government has stumbled in some of these cases, including a few that have garnered significant attention. For example, in the fall of 2007, an eight-week trial involving officials of the Holy Land Foundation ended with a hung jury on most counts and one defendant being acquitted on all but one count. *See* Judgment of Acquittal & Order, *United States v. Holy Land Foundation for Relief & Dev.*, No. 04-cr-00240 (N.D. Tex. Oct. 22, 2007) (Dkt. No. 873); Peter Whoriskey, *Mistrial Declared in Muslim Charity Case*, Wash. Post, Oct. 23, 2007, at A03.[143] This was viewed as a significant failure for the government against a charitable organization that for years had been considered by the government to be closely linked to Hamas. *See* Whoriskey, *Mistrial Declared in Muslim Charity Case*. The government has also failed to secure convictions in other material support trials. *See, e.g.*, Verdict, *United States v. al-Hussayen*, No. 03-cr-00048 (D. Idaho June 10, 2004) (Dkt. No. 761) (Saudi student accused of providing material support to terrorist group under §§ 2339A and 2339B found not guilty by jury); *see also* Maureen O'Hagan, *A Terrorism Case That Went Awry*, Seattle Times, Nov. 22, 2004, at A1;[144] *cf.* Second Superseding Indictment, *United States v. Marzook*, No. 03-cr-00978, 2004 WL 5361379 (N.D. Ill. Aug. 19, 2004) (Dkt. No. 59) (defendant Abdelhaleem Ashqar accused of providing money and personnel to Hamas found not guilty of § 2339B violation by jury but convicted of obstruction of justice; Ashqar was subsequently sentenced to 135 months' imprisonment). Lapses such as *Holy Land Foundation* and *al-Hussayen* may reflect weaknesses in the government's trial strategy in these particular cases or that the evidence was simply insufficient to warrant a conviction. *See* O'Hagan, *A Terrorism Case that Went Awry* (member of jury that acquitted al-Hussayen explains that prosecutors had no hard evidence that al-Hussayen was involved in terrorism).

Prosecutors and defense lawyers who are familiar with material support cases agree that under some circumstances these cases may be challenging to prove. As an initial matter, the cases may lack a strong emotional impact for the jury because they may appear victimless and do not involve completed acts of terrorism. Thus, without direct evidence of the defendant's knowledge that his fundraising is intended to benefit a designated terrorist organization, such as an audiotape, it can be difficult for prosecutors to present a compelling case, especially if the prosecution relies solely on confusing financial records of contributions to an organization that in part is dedicated to bona fide humanitarian relief efforts. By the time these financial records are declassified and available they may be quite dated, which can raise questions in jurors' minds regarding the significance of the evidence. The prosecution may face additional obstacles if the jury perceives that the government is incorporating a controversial foreign-policy agenda (for example, taking sides in the Israeli-Palestinian conflict) as part of a material support prosecution. In *Holy Land Foundation*, for example, the latter issue may have been highlighted by the prominent testimony in the government's case of an agent from an Israeli intelligence service. *See* Jason Trahan, *Holy Land Trial Turns to Israeli Agent*, Dallas Morning News, Aug. 10, 2007, at 6B.[145]

Some prosecutors have expressed the concern that charitable organizations which serve as terrorist fronts have become adept at providing ready defenses to the government's theories of prosecution, for example by casting some of the support they get as necessary for the organization to provide for the "self-defense" of the ultimate beneficiaries. Thus, even if weapons are provided by the organization, a material support defendant could argue that he understood that the weapons were not for terrorism but for "self-defense." Congress may wish to consider further legislation to clarify this issue.

Moreover, in cases brought under § 2339B, the difficulties are often exacerbated because the organizations use fronts or offshoots with other names. However, proof problems and evidentiary challenges are by no means limited to material support cases; to the contrary, they are a feature of many complex federal prosecutions in all subject areas, including white-collar and organized crime. As experience has shown, convictions generally occur if the government follows a disciplined approach in gathering evidence, formulating charges, and presenting a tight and focused case to the jury, resisting the temptation to "over-try" the case.

At the same time, some commentators remain concerned that the material support statute sweeps too broadly. Despite the fact that courts have upheld the mens rea requirement in § 2339B, the statute continues to draw criticism because it lacks a requirement that a defendant have any specific criminal intent to support a terrorist act. *See* Stacey, *The "Material Support" Offense*, at 461; *see also Oversight of the USA PATRIOT ACT: Hearing Before the S. Comm. on the Judiciary*, 109th Cong. 389-405 (2005) (statement of David Cole, Professor of Law, Geo. Univ. Law Center) (arguing that the 2004 amendments have made the statute more vague and that the lack of a specific criminal intent makes the statute unconstitutional); David Henrik Pendle, Comment, *Charity of the Heart and Sword: The Material Support Offense and Personal Guilt*, 30 Seattle U. L. Rev. 777, 793-802 (2007) (suggesting that the lack of a requirement of personal guilt constitutes a violation of the Due Process Clause); Stephen Townley, *The Hydraulics of Fighting Terrorism*, 29 Hamline L. Rev. 65, 112-13 (2006) (concluding that several aspects of the statute, including the designation process, are unconstitutional). In order to ensure that the statute is used properly and does not become a vehicle for suppressing legitimate freedom of speech or association, it is critical for the government to conduct its material support investigations and evaluate the evidence in a disciplined and objective manner, bringing charges only where it is convinced that the proof is sufficient to secure a conviction beyond a reasonable doubt.

3. Providing or Collecting Funds to Be Used in an Act of Terrorism (18 U.S.C. § 2339C)

Section 2339C was enacted in 2002 as part of the Suppression of the Financing of Terrorism Convention Implementation Act of 2002. *See* H.R. Rep. No. 107-307, pt. 2, at 4 (2001). The statute makes it a crime to provide or collect funds "with the intention that such funds be used, or with the knowledge that such funds are to be used, in full or in part, in order to carry out" an act of terrorism. 18 U.S.C. § 2339C(a)(1). Section 2339C also prohibits a defendant from knowingly concealing or disguising the nature, location, source, ownership, or control of any material support or resources, or intending that the support or resources are to be provided, or were provided, in violation of § 2339B or in violation of the first part of § 2339C. *See id.* § 2339C(c). The statute defines "provide" to include the "giving, donating and transmitting" of funds and defines "collects" to include "raising and receiving" funds. *Id.* § 2339C(e). There is no requirement that the funds provided actually be used to carry out the predicate act of terrorism. The statute in its design parallels the traditional criminal laws against money laundering but applies them in the terrorism context. *See id.* §§ 1956, 1957. The government has used § 2339C in prosecuting an individual who allegedly "transferred and concealed the transfer of approximately $152,000 in funds that he believed were being sent to Pakistan and Afghanistan to be used to support a terrorist training camp in Afghanistan by, among other things, funding the purchase of equipment such as night-vision goggles." Superseding Indictment at ¶ 1, *United States v. Alishtari*, No. 07-cr-00115 (S.D.N.Y. Mar. 26, 2007) (Dkt. No. 8).[146]

4. Receiving Military Training from a Designated Foreign Terrorist Organization (18 U.S.C. § 2339D)

Section 2339D, which prohibits the receipt of military-type training from an organization that has been designated a foreign terrorist organization by the Secretary of State, was passed as part of the Intelligence Reform and Terrorism Prevention Act in 2004. *See* Pub. L. No. 108-458, § 6602, 118 Stat. 3638, 3761-62 (2004). It was intended to fill a perceived gap in § 2339B with regard to terrorist training camps. *See A Review of the Material Support to Terrorism Prohibition Improvements Act: Hearing Before the Subcomm. on Terrorism, Technology and Homeland Security of the S. Comm. on the Judiciary*, 109th Cong. 51 (2005) (joint statement of Daniel Meron, Principal Deputy Assistant Att'y Gen. Civil Div. & Barry Sabin, Chief, Counterterrorism Section Criminal Div.). Section 2339D's scope is limited to persons who knew the organization from which they received training was a designated foreign terrorist organization or knew of the organization's illegal aims. *See* 18 U.S.C. § 2339D(a). We are aware of at least one prosecution for a violation of § 2339D. *See generally* Criminal Complaint, *United States v. Maldonado*, No. 07-cr-00125 (S.D. Tex. Feb. 13, 2007) (Dkt. No. 1) (defendant charged with, inter alia, training in Mogadishu, Somalia, to fight against Ethiopian forces allied with the United States, and if necessary, U.S. forces themselves).[147]

B. Other Terrorism Statutes Under Chapter 113B of the Federal Criminal Code

In addition to the material support statutes, Chapter 113B of the Federal Criminal Code, entitled "Terrorism," contains many specific statutes that Congress has adopted for use against persons involved in terrorism. Some of these statutes are highly specialized and have been used sparingly or not at all; others are more broadly applicable and have been invoked with success by prosecutors and law enforcement. What follows is a brief survey of the different terrorism crimes in Chapter 113B.

1. Homicide or Serious Assault Against U.S. Nationals Outside the United States with Intent to Conduct Terrorism (18 U.S.C. § 2332)

Title 18 section 2332 of the United States Code, the first substantive statute in the "Terrorism" chapter, imposes broad criminal liability on anyone who unlawfully kills, conspires to kill, or attempts to kill a U.S. national, defined as a U.S. citizen or anyone who owes permanent allegiance to the United States, outside the United States. *See* 18 U.S.C. §§ 2332(a), 2331(3). The statute establishes escalating penalties depending on whether the homicide is classified as involuntary manslaughter, voluntary manslaughter, or murder. *See id.* § 2332(a).[148] It also criminalizes extraterritorial acts of physical violence against a U.S. national with the intent to cause or result of causing "serious bodily injury." *Id.* § 2332(c).[149]

At first blush, these statutes could be read as a global ban on homicides or serious assaults against U.S. citizens. In enacting § 2332, however, Congress made clear that the statute was not intended to have such a universal scope and was, instead, only intended to be used in terrorism cases. *See* H.R. Rep. No. 99-783, at 87 (1986) (Conf. Rep.), *as reprinted in* 1986 U.S.C.C.A.N. 1926, 1960 (noting that "[s]imple barroom brawls or normal street crime, ... are not intended to be covered by this provision"). Accordingly, the statute may be invoked only if the Attorney General or his highest ranking subordinate with responsibility for criminal prosecutions certifies that, in his judgment, the homicide or assault was "intended to coerce, intimidate, or retaliate against a government or a civilian population." 18 U.S.C. § 2332(d).[150] Importantly, however, the government is *not* required to prove the purpose of the killing in order to win a conviction, and the validity of the certification is not subject to judicial review or consideration by the jury. *See* H.R. Rep. No. 99-783.

Section 2332 was enacted as part of the Omnibus Diplomatic Security and Antiterrorism Act of 1986. *See* Pub. L. No. 99-399, § 1202(a), 100 Stat. 853, 896 (1986). Previously, U.S. criminal laws had reached only extraterritorial homicides or assaults against high-ranking officials, diplomats, and law enforcement agents. During Congressional debates, Senator Specter stated that § 2232 was "urgently needed to fill [a] critical gap in our antiterrorism arsenal." 132 Cong. Rec. 1718 (1986) (statement of Sen. Arlen Specter); *see also* 132 Cong. Rec. at 2355-56 (same); 132 Cong. Rec. 15356 (1986) (statement of Sen. Patrick Leahy) (indicating that the bill would close a "serious gap in our arsenal against terrorists").

Section 2332 represents an important tool in U.S. efforts to pursue and prosecute terrorist crimes. Although the certification requirement is a hurdle for prosecutors to clear before bringing such charges, prosecutors do not face the evidentiary challenges of proving that the purpose of the offense was to retaliate against or intimidate a government. Instead, the elements of this statute closely resemble longstanding homicide and assault statutes that are familiar, bread-and-butter material for prosecutors.

Section 2332 was charged in two of the most significant terrorism prosecutions in recent years—the Embassy Bombings case and the Shoe Bomber case. *See United States v. Bin Laden*, 93 F. Supp. 2d 484 (S.D.N.Y. 2000); Indictment, *United States v. Reid*, No. 02-cr-10013 (D. Mass. Jan. 16, 2002) (Dkt. No. 5). In the Embassy Bombings case, defendant Mohamed al-'Owhali sought dismissal of the charge of conspiracy to murder U.S. nationals on the ground that because the conspiracy was alleged to have occurred both inside and outside the United States, it could not constitute a violation of 18 U.S.C. § 2332(b). *See Bin Laden*, 93 F. Supp. 2d at 486. The court denied al-'Owhali's motion, finding no basis to dismiss the count "because, in addition to alleging a plain violation of a criminal statute, the count also alleges conduct that is, arguably, not prohibited by the statute." *Id.*; *see also id.* ("It is our view that so long as a count alleges acts committed outside the United States in furtherance of a conspiracy to kill United States nationals, it alleges a violation of 2332(b)."). The four defendants who proceeded to trial were convicted of more than 200 counts, including the § 2332 charges, and were sentenced to life in prison in October 2001. *See* Judgment as to Wadih el-Hage, *United States v. el-Hage*, No. 98-cr-01023 (S.D.N.Y. Oct. 22, 2001) (Dkt. No. 637); Judgment as to Khalfan Khamis Mohamed, *el-Hage* (S.D.N.Y.

Oct. 22, 2001) (Dkt. No. 638); Judgment as to Mohamed Rashed Daoud al-'Owhali, *el-Hage* (S.D.N.Y. Oct. 23, 2001) (Dkt. No. 640); Judgment as to Mohamed Sadeek Odeh, *el-Hage* (S.D.N.Y. Oct. 24, 2001) (Dkt. No. 641). In the Shoe Bomber case, Richard Reid eventually pled guilty to numerous charges, including attempted homicide of U.S. nationals under § 2332(b)(1), and was sentenced to life in prison plus 110 years on January 30, 2003. *See* Judgment, *Reid* (D. Mass. Jan. 31, 2003) (Dkt. No. 188).

2. Use of Weapons of Mass Destruction (18 U.S.C. § 2332a)

Section 2332a establishes criminal penalties for anyone who, "without lawful authority, uses, threatens, or attempts or conspires to use, a weapon of mass destruction" where any of the following jurisdictional predicates are satisfied:

- the intended victim is a U.S. national who is outside the United States;
- the weapon is to be used against any person or property inside the United States, provided that the offense affects interstate or foreign commerce;
- the weapon is to be used against property owned, leased, or used by the U.S. government anywhere in the world;
- the weapon is to be used against property located inside the United States that is owned, leased, or used by a foreign government; or
- the perpetrator of the crime is a U.S. national acting anywhere in the world.

18 U.S.C. §§ 2332a(a), 2332a(b). Violations of § 2332a carry a possible life sentence, and in cases "where death results" provide for imposition of the death penalty. *See id.* Congress enacted § 2332a in 1994, shortly after the first World Trade Center bombing, as part of the Violent Crime Control and Law Enforcement Act, *see* Pub. L. No. 103-322, § 60023(a), 108 Stat. 1796, 1980-81 (1994), and subsequently amended the statute in 1996, *see* Pub. L. No. 104-132, §§ 511(c), 725, 110 Stat. 1214, 1284, 1300-01 (1996).[151] The enactment of § 2332a was spurred by concern that "the use and threatened use of weapons of mass destruction ... gravely harm the national security and foreign relations interests of the United States, seriously affect interstate and foreign commerce, and disturb the domestic tranquility of the United States." H.R. Rep. No. 102-405, at 46 (1991) (Conf. Rep.).

In cases brought outside the terrorism context, courts have provided important interpretations of § 2332a that clarify the elements of the offense and the nature of evidence the government must offer to prove a violation of the statute. For example, in *United States v. Wise*, members of an organization seeking to remove federal government operations from the State of Texas had sent letters to federal law enforcement agencies threatening to infect federal employees with toxic viruses. *See* 221 F.3d 140, 143-47 (5th Cir. 2000). In a post-conviction appeal, the defendants challenged the government's failure to allege or prove that they had acted "without lawful authority." *See id.* at 147-48. The Fifth Circuit rejected this argument, holding that "without lawful authority" is not an essential element of the offense, but rather constitutes an affirmative defense that a defendant must prove. *See id.* at 150.[152]

Perhaps the most widely known cases involving charges of § 2332a are the prosecutions of Timothy McVeigh and Terry Nichols for the 1995 bombing of the Murrah Building in Oklahoma City. McVeigh raised several legal challenges following his conviction at trial, including a challenge to the intent element of his § 2332a convictions. Specifically, McVeigh argued that the trial court's jury instructions were in error because § 2332a requires proof of specific intent to kill. *See United States v. McVeigh*, 153 F.3d 1166, 1193-94 (10th Cir. 1998). The Tenth Circuit held that the phrase "if death results" in section 2332a is a sentencing factor and not an element of the offense. *See id.* at 1194. The court acknowledged that the statute contains no specificity as to the requisite level of intent, but instead of construing § 2332a as a strict liability crime, the *McVeigh* court concluded that the statute incorporates a "knowingly" standard. *See id.* at 1194. In other words, the government must prove that a defendant "(1) knowingly used, or attempted or conspired to use, a weapon of mass destruction and (2) knowingly did so against 'any property that is owned, leased, or used by the United States or by any department or agency of the United States.'" *Id.* at 1194; *accord United States v. Nichols*, 169 F.3d 1255, 1260-61 (10th Cir. 1999).

The government successfully invoked § 2332a in the Embassy Bombings case. During pre-trial proceedings, the defendants argued that they could not be prosecuted under this statute because they were not American citizens. The district court rejected the argument, reasoning that because § 2332a(a) explicitly provides for jurisdiction over attacks on U.S. property and nationals occurring outside the United States, foreign nationals could be charged under the statute. *See United States v. Bin Laden*, 92 F. Supp. 2d 189, 218 (S.D.N.Y. 2000); *accord United States v. Yousef*, 927 F. Supp. 673, 680-83 (S.D.N.Y. 1996).

In *Bin Laden*, defendant Mohamed Sadeek Odeh also challenged the constitutionality of § 2332a on the ground that Congress exceeded its legislative authority in the statute's extraterritorial application. *See Bin Laden*, 92 F. Supp. 2d at 220. Odeh asserted that the only potential constitutional grant of authority that could support the enactment of § 2332a is Article I, Section 8, Clause 10 of the Constitution, which grants Congress the authority "to define and punish Piracies and Felonies committed on the high Seas, and Offenses against the Law of Nations." *Id.* He argued that conduct proscribed by § 2332a was not widely considered to be an offense against the law of nations. *See id.* In rejecting this argument, Judge Sand noted that, even if some members of the international community would not consider these terrorist bombings to violate international law, Clause 10 not only provides Congress with the authority to punish offenses against international law, but also permits Congress to "define" such offenses. *See id.* at 220. Further, and more importantly, the court reasoned that Clause 10 is not the only basis for Congress' enactment of § 2332a. *See id.* at 221. Rather, based upon the concept of essential sovereignty, Congress is bestowed with the authority to protect the nation from destruction. *See id.* (citations omitted). In penalizing attacks on United States property, § 2332a was clearly designed to protect a vital U.S. interest.

3. Acts of Terrorism Within the United States that Transcend National Boundaries (18 U.S.C. § 2332b)

Section 2332b establishes serious criminal penalties for anyone who, "involving conduct transcending national boundaries ... kills, kidnaps, maims, commits an assault resulting in serious bodily injury, or assaults with a dangerous weapon any person within the United States" or who "creates a substantial risk of serious bodily injury to any other person" by destroying any property within the United States or by attempting or conspiring to destroy property within the United States. 18 U.S.C. § 2332b(a)(1). Enacted as part of the AEDPA, Pub. L. No. 104-132, § 702, 110 Stat. 1214, 1291 (1996), this statute only reaches conduct that occurs in a manner "transcending national boundaries," which is defined as "conduct occurring outside the United States in addition to the conduct occurring in the United States." *Id.* § 2332b(g)(1). Legislative history confirms that the statute is aimed at terrorist acts that take place within the United States but which "are in some fashion or degree instigated, commanded, or facilitated from outside the United States." 141 Cong. Rec. 11958 (1995) (Statement of Sen. Thomas Daschle); *see also* H.R. Rep. No. 104-383, at 83 (1995) (noting that "only those terrorist crimes that are truly trans-national in scope will be prosecuted under this section").[153]

Section 2332b(b) delineates the bases upon which the federal courts may exercise jurisdiction over such transnational terrorist activities. Specifically, jurisdiction exists where the conduct involves the use of the mail or any instrument of interstate or foreign commerce; the offense obstructs, delays, or affects interstate or foreign commerce; the victim is the United States, a member of the uniformed services, or any other federal employee; the property affected is, in whole or in part, owned or leased by the United States; or the offense is committed in the territorial sea, special maritime, or territorial jurisdiction of the United States. *See* 18 U.S.C. § 2332b(b). Although the government is required to prove that at least one of the jurisdictional grounds exists beyond a reasonable doubt, it is not required to prove that a defendant had any knowledge of the jurisdictional basis. *See id.* § 2332b(d); H.R. Rep. No. 104-383 at 83. Significantly, § 2332b also provides extraterritorial federal jurisdiction over any act of terrorism transcending national boundaries. *See* 18 U.S.C. § 2332b(e)(1).

Section 2332b was used to prosecute Zacarias Moussaoui, who pled guilty to engaging in extensive criminal conduct leading up to 9/11—both in the United States and abroad— including attending an al Qaeda-led training camp in Afghanistan in 1998, contacting U.S. flight schools by email from Malaysia, enrolling in a flight school in Oklahoma, inquiring about beginning a crop-dusting business, possessing flight manuals for commercial aircraft, placing multiple calls from public telephones to Germany (the location of an alleged al Qaeda terrorist cell), receiving a wire transfer of approximately $14,000 from Germany, and buying and possessing knives and fighting paraphernalia including shin guards and fighting gloves. *See* Superseding Indictment, *United States v. Moussaoui*, No. 01-cr-00455 (E.D. Va. June 19, 2002) (Dkt. No. 199). Moussaoui pled guilty before trial and was sentenced to life imprisonment that, under § 2332b(c)(2), must run consecutively to any other sentence imposed. *See* Minute Entry, Plea, *Moussaoui* (E.D. Va. Apr. 22, 2005); Judgment, *Moussaoui* (E.D. Va. May 4, 2006) (Dkt. No. 1854). He was also sentenced to four other life terms, to be served concurrently, under the remaining counts. *See* Judgment, *Moussaoui* (E.D. Va. May 4, 2006) (Dkt. No. 1854).

The government also charged a violation of § 2332b in the prosecution of Ahmed Ressam for attempting to bomb Los Angeles International Airport on the eve of the Millennium new year. *See* Second Superseding Indictment, *United States v. Ressam*, No. 99-cr-00666 (W.D. Wa. Feb. 14, 2001) (Dkt. No. 178). During the course of the case, Ressam began to cooperate extensively with the government, acting as a key source of information about al Qaeda. *See United States v. Ressam*, 474 F.3d 597, 599-601 (9th Cir. 2007); Transcript of Sentencing Proceedings at 4-11, 23, 25-26, 30-31, *Ressam* (W.D.Wash. July 27, 2005) (Dkt. No. 384); *see also* Nat'l Comm'n on Terrorist Attacks Upon the United States, *The 9/11 Commission Report*, at 275-76 (2004) (hereinafter *"The 9/11 Commission Report"*); Hal Bernton & Sara Jean Green, *Ressam Judge Decries U.S. Tactics*, Seattle Times, July 28, 2005, at A1.[154] Ressam, however, suddenly stopped cooperating in 2003, eventually forcing the government to drop charges in another case against a defendant, about whom Ressam had been expected to testify. *See* Transcript of Sentencing Proceedings at 25-26, *Ressam* (W.D. Wash. July 27, 2005) (Dkt. No. 384). At Ressam's sentencing, the government urged the court to impose a term of imprisonment of thirty-five years because Ressam's cooperation ceased prematurely. *See id.* at 30-31. The court, however, imposed a term of twenty-two years. *See id.* at 31.[155]

Another former cooperator, Mohammed Mansour Jabarah, was also charged with a violation of § 2332b. *See* Information at 1-3, *United States v. Jabarah*, No. 02-cr-01560 (S.D.N.Y. July 30, 2002) (Dkt. No. 1). Jabarah pled guilty to a number of charges, including conspiracy to kill U.S. nationals in violation of § 2332b, for his role in planning and conducting surveillance for bombings of U.S. embassies in the Philippines and Singapore—bombings that fortunately never occurred. *See* Sentencing Memorandum (Redacted) by U.S.A. at 4-11, *Jabarah* (S.D.N.Y. May 7, 2007) (Dkt. No. 7); *see also* Minute Entry, *Jabarah* (S.D.N.Y. July 30, 2002). After the 9/11 attacks, Jabarah was arrested in Oman, where he was working on establishing an al Qaeda "safehouse" after having fled Southeast Asia. *See* Sentencing Memorandum (Redacted) by U.S.A. at 9, *Jabarah* (S.D.N.Y. May 7, 2007) (Dkt. No. 7). He was subsequently deported to Canada, where he had been living prior to becoming involved with al Qaeda. *See id.* After Jabarah's arrival in Canada, Canadian officials began discussions with prosecutors from the U.S. Attorney's Office for the Southern District of New York, which led to a cooperation agreement between Jabarah and that office. *See id.* at 9-11. Jabarah was then brought to the Southern District of New York and charged with five counts, including conspiracy to violate § 2332b. *See id.* After his guilty plea, Jabarah provided substantial information to the government for several months, but his cooperation ended when the FBI discovered steak knives, nylon rope, and writings detailing violence and plans for revenge hidden in his room in FBI-secured housing. *See id.* at 11-17. Jabarah was then transferred to a high-security prison and ceased cooperating. *See id.* Judge Barbara Jones unsealed his case in January 2008 and sentenced Jabarah to life in prison for his role in planning bombings of U.S. embassies in the Philippines and Singapore. *See* Judgment, *Jabarah* (S.D.N.Y. Jan. 18, 2008) (Dkt. No. 15); *see also* Alan Feuer, *Canadian Gets Life in Qaeda Bomb Plot*, N.Y. Times, Jan. 19, 2008, at A8.[156]

In addition to its substantive provisions, § 2332b also contains a number of interesting procedural provisions that are intended to strengthen federal law enforcement. *See* 18 U.S.C. § 2332b(g)(5). For example, the statute defines a number of specified criminal acts as "Federal crime[s] of terrorism" and then provides that, with respect to each of these offenses, there is no statute of limitation if the commission of an offense listed in § 2332b(g)(5)(B) results in or creates a foreseeable risk of death of serious bodily injury—a risk that will not be difficult to prove in most terrorism cases. *See* 18 U.S.C. § 3286(b). Even if no such risk exists, the statute of limitations for crimes of terrorism is extended to eight years (as opposed to the customary five-year limitations period that generally applies to federal crimes). *See id.*; 18 U.S.C. § 3286(a). Separate provisions of federal criminal law provide that courts can issue "nationwide" arrest and search warrants for "federal crimes of terrorism," *see* Fed. R. Crim. P. 41(b)(3), and create a rebuttable presumption of pre-trial detention at bail hearings for defendants charged with any of these specified crimes. *See* 18 U.S.C. § 3142.[157]

4. Financial Transactions with Countries Supporting International Terrorism (18 U.S.C. § 2332d)

In the wake of the 1995 Oklahoma City bombing, Congress adopted 18 U.S.C. § 2332d, which broadly prohibits any financial transactions with the government of a country "designated ... as a country supporting international terrorism." 18 U.S.C. § 2332d(a).[158] There are five countries currently on this list: Cuba, Iran, North Korea, Sudan, and Syria. See U.S. Dep't of State, *State Sponsors of Terrorism* (Feb. 2008).[159] The statute forbids a broad range of financial transactions with the governments of these nations, including transactions involving the movement of funds by wire or other means, transactions involving one or more monetary instruments, or the transfer of title to any real property, vehicle, vessel, or aircraft. See 18 U.S.C. § 2332d(b)(1) (incorporating definition of "financial transaction" from 18 U.S.C. § 1956(c)(4)).[160] We are not aware of any international terrorism cases in which this statute has been invoked to date.

Although § 2332d broadly applies to nearly every conceivable type of financial transaction with designated governments, it applies only to "United States persons" (i.e., any U.S. citizen or permanent resident alien, any person in the United States, and any company incorporated in the United States). See 18 U.S.C. § 2332d(b)(2). The statute does not apply to foreign corporations, even if they are present in the United States. See *United States v. Chalmers*, 474 F. Supp. 2d 555, 565 (S.D.N.Y. 2007).[161] Further, it does not apply to foreign persons unless they are present in the United States. See 18 U.S.C. § 2332d(b). To be convicted of violating § 2332d, a defendant must know or have reasonable cause to know that a country is designated as one supporting international terrorism. See 18 U.S.C. § 2332d(a).[162]

5. Bombings of Places of Public Use (18 U.S.C. § 2332f)

In the wake of the July 1996 bombing of the Khobar Towers apartment building in Saudi Arabia, the United States sought an international treaty requiring mandatory prosecution or extradition for persons charged with bombing public or government facilities. The result was the International Convention for the Suppression of Terrorist Bombings, which the United States signed on January 12, 1998, and which went into international force on May 23, 2001. See H.R. Rep. No. 107-307, pt. 3, at 7 (2001). In 2002, Congress implemented the treaty by adopting 18 U.S.C. § 2332f as part of our domestic criminal law. See Terrorist Bombings Convention Implementation Act of 2002, Pub. L. No. 107-197, § 102(a), 116 Stat. 721, 721-23 (2002).

This statute makes it a crime to "unlawfully deliver[], place[], discharge[], or detonate[] an explosive or other lethal device in, into, or against a place of public use, a state or government facility, a public transportation system, or an infrastructure facility with the intent to cause death or serious injury, or with the intent to cause extensive destruction of such place, facility, or system, where such destruction results or is likely to result in major economic loss." 18 U.S.C. § 2332f(a). The statute also covers conspiracies and attempts. See 18 U.S.C. § 2332f(a)(2). Congress established broad-ranging jurisdiction for § 2332f. Thus, the statute applies to bombings where the attack occurs in the United States; the victim is a U.S. national; the perpetrator is found in the United States; the target is a facility belonging to the United States; the offense is calculated to force the United States to act or abstain from acting; or the offense is committed on an airplane or boat registered in the United States. See 18 U.S.C. § 2332f(b).[163]

Section 2332f applies not only to bombings that cause death and injury; it also applies broadly to bombings that cause economic loss.[164] The government successfully invoked § 2332f in *United States v. Siraj*. See 468 F. Supp. 2d 408, 413-14 (E.D.N.Y. 2007). The defendant was charged with four counts of conspiracy related to a plot to bomb the New York City subway station at 34th Street in Manhattan. See *id.* at 413. In the fourth count of the indictment, he was charged with violating § 2332f by "conspiring to deliver, place, discharge, or detonate an explosive device in a public transportation system with the intent to cause extensive destruction of such system, likely to result in major economic loss, in violation of 18 U.S.C. §§ 2332f(a)(2) and (a)(1)(B)." *Id.* at 413-14.[165] The jury convicted the defendant after hearing testimony from a cooperating witness, James Elshafay, who had pled guilty to a similar charge. See *id.* at 416; Press Release, U.S. Dep't of Justice, Shahawar Martin Siraj Sentenced to Thirty Years of Imprisonment for Conspiring to Place Explosives at the 34th Street Subway Station in New York (Jan. 8, 2007)[166] (noting that Elshafay pled guilty to conspiracy to damage or destroy a subway station by means of an explosive). The jury also heard hours of secretly recorded conversations between the defendant and a confidential informant in which the defendant discussed his hatred for America and his desire to bomb bridges and subway stations. See Siraj, 468 F. Supp. 2d at 415-16. Siraj was sentenced to thirty years' imprisonment and a life term of supervised release. See Judgment, United States v. Siraj, No. 05-cr-00104 (E.D.N.Y. Jan. 18, 2007) (Dkt. No. 182).[167]

6. Missile Systems Designed to Destroy Aircraft and Radiological Dispersal Devices (18 U.S.C. §§ 2332g and 2332h)

In the Intelligence Reform and Terrorism Prevention Act of 2004, Congress broadly criminalized the production, use, transfer, receipt, possession, importation, or exportation of two different types of highly dangerous weapons: (a) missile systems designed to destroy aircraft and (b) devices capable of releasing radiation or radioactivity at levels dangerous to human life. See Pub. L. No. 108-458, §§ 6903, 6905, 118 Stat. 3638, 3770-73 (2004) (codified at 18 U.S.C. §§ 2332g and 2332h). In enacting these statutes, Congress made clear that it viewed both types of weapons as distinctly threatening. Indeed, upon conviction under § 2332g or § 2332h, the court must impose a mandatory minimum sentence of at least twenty-five years' imprisonment. See 18 U.S.C. §§ 2332g(c)(1), 2332h(c)(1).

Lightweight, surface-to-air missile systems designed to take down aircraft are called "MANPADS" (a somewhat awkward acronym for the equally awkward name "Man-Portable Air Defense Systems"). They can fire explosive or incendiary rockets or missiles equipped with guidance systems and are designed to target low-flying aircraft, typically around the time of landing or departure. See 150 Cong. Rec. 11998-99 (2004) (statement of Sen. John Cornyn). Citing a 2000 State Department report and research conducted by the Congressional Research Service, Senator Cornyn stated that MANPADS were one of the leading causes of loss of life in commercial aviation worldwide—bringing down over thirty aircraft—and that there have been at least thirty-six known missile attacks on commercial planes in the last twenty-five years. See id. The statute also covers devices known colloquially as "dirty bombs." During Congressional debate, Senator Kyl noted that previously, no statute prohibited the mere possession of these devices. See 150 Cong. Rec. S11997 (2004) (statement of Sen. Jon Kyl).

Sections 2332g and 2332h establish broad extraterritorial jurisdiction over any person who commits an act involving these weapons that affects interstate or foreign commerce, who commits an act against a U.S. national while the national is outside the United States, or who commits an act against any property owned, used, or leased by the United States. See 18 U.S.C. §§ 2332g(b), 2332h(b). Jurisdiction also extends to any offender that aids and abets any person over whom jurisdiction exists. See 18 U.S.C. §§ 2332g(b)(5), 2332h(b)(5). Senator Kyl recognized the potential significance of aiding-and-abetting liability under these statues, noting that the statute would "deter middlemen and facilitators who are essential to the transfer of these weapons." 150 Cong. Rec. at S11997.

Perhaps because the statutes are still relatively new—and because, one hopes, missile systems and radiological devices are not easily accessible—the government has used §§ 2332g and 2332h infrequently. See U.S. Dep't of Justice, Counterterrorism Section, Counterterrorism White Paper Update 17 (2007); see also U.S. Dep't of Justice, Counterterrorism Section, Counterterrorism White Paper 24 (2006).[168] However, in 2006, the government secured a guilty plea from Chao Tung Wu for conspiracy to import missile systems designed to destroy aircraft in violation of § 2332g. See Minutes of Entry of Guilty Plea, United States v. Wu, No. 05-cr-00806 (C.D. Cal. Apr. 19, 2006) (Dkt. No. 97). According to Wu's plea agreement, he and Yi Qing Chen, a co-defendant, told an undercover FBI agent that he could procure 200 shoulder-fired missiles from China "with the assistance of a corrupt customs broker." U.S. Dep't of Justice, 2006 Counterterrorism White Paper, at 24. They were arrested before the deal was completed, and the missiles were never delivered. See id. As of the writing of this White Paper, Wu had not been sentenced. See generally Docket Sheet, Wu (C.D. Cal. Aug. 17, 2005). According to the docket, the government and Wu have agreed to multiple continuances of the sentencing hearing, and Wu, who has an undisclosed medical condition, is subject to home confinement pending sentencing. See, e.g., Sealed Document - Stipulation to Continuance of Sentencing Hearing, Wu (C.D. Cal. Sept. 19, 2007) (Dkt. No. 133); see Bond & Conditions of Release, Wu (C.D. Cal. June 18, 2007) (Dkt. No. 128). Chen has also pled guilty, but the entry of his guilty plea is sealed, and it is, therefore, unclear whether he pled guilty to the violation of § 2332g for which he was originally charged. See Sealed Document - Entry of Guilty Plea, Wu (C.D. Cal. Oct. 1, 2007) (Dkt. No. 141). Chen's sentencing hearing has not been scheduled yet. See generally Docket Sheet, Wu (C.D. Cal. Aug. 17, 2005).[169]

7. Harboring or Concealing Terrorists (18 U.S.C. § 2339)

In the immediate aftermath of 9/11, Congress passed a statute making it a crime to harbor or conceal any person whom a person knows, or has reasonable grounds to believe, is about to commit or has committed a terrorist act. *See* 18 U.S.C. § 2339. The statute provides for a maximum penalty of ten years' imprisonment. *See* 18 U.S.C. § 2339(a). During Congressional debate over this provision, Senator Leahy discussed the importance of the mens rea requirement, "[I]t is not enough that the defendant had 'reasonable grounds to *suspect*' that the person he was harboring had committed, or was about to commit, such a crime; the government must prove that the defendant knew or had 'reasonable grounds to *believe*' that this was so." 147 Cong. Rec. 20677 (2001) (statement of Sen. Patrick Leahy) (emphasis added).[170] Although there have not yet been any prosecutions brought under § 2339 and courts have not yet teased out the difference between a "reasonable belief" and a "reasonable suspicion" in the context of harboring or concealing a terrorist, Senator Leahy's comments suggest that conviction under the statute requires proof of heightened knowledge by the defendant.[171]

C. Treason (18 U.S.C. § 2381)

Treason is the oldest crime available for terrorism prosecutions and "the only crime defined by the Constitution." *Stephan v. United States*, 133 F.2d 87, 90 (6th Cir. 1943). Article III of the Constitution states that treason "shall consist only in Levying War against [the United States], or in adhering to their Enemies, giving them Aid and Comfort." U.S. Const. art. III, § 3. The Constitution also imposes an evidentiary burden, requiring for any treason conviction "the Testimony of two Witnesses to the same overt Act, or on Confession in open Court." *Id.* The treason statute essentially uses the Constitutional definition, with the following differences: (1) the statute applies only to defendants "owing allegiance to the United States" and (2) the statute specifies that the act of treason can take place "within the United States or elsewhere." 18 U.S.C. § 2381.

Since 9/11, there has been only one treason indictment in an international terrorism case—against Adam Gadahn, also known as "Azzam the American" or "Azzam al Amriki." *See* First Superseding Indictment, *United States v. Gadahn*, No. 05-cr-00254 (C.D. Cal. Oct. 11, 2006) (Dkt. No. 10). Gadahn grew up in rural California and then joined al Qaeda as a teenager after being proselytized at a mosque in Orange County, California. He has appeared in numerous inflammatory videos advocating al Qaeda's ideology and goals and harshly criticizing the United States.[172] *See id.* The indictment in *Gadahn* accuses the defendant of committing treason by propagandizing for al Qaeda. *See id.* As of the preparation of this White Paper, Gadahn was a fugitive from justice. However, as set forth below, the legal theory of treason set forth in the indictment against him appears to be viable.

Somewhat surprisingly, apart from Gadahn, the government has not brought any treason charges against suspected international terrorists in recent years.[173] Commentators from both the left and the right have expressed disappointment in the dearth of treason prosecutions. *See, e.g.*, Henry Mark Holzer, *Why Not Call It Treason?: From Korea to Afghanistan*, 29 S.U. L. Rev. 181, 220-21 (2002) (arguing that Lindh should be prosecuted for treason); Carlton F.W. Larson, *The Forgotten Constitutional Law of Treason and the Enemy Combatant Problem*, 154 U. Pa. L. Rev. 863, 923-25 (2006) (treason prosecutions should supplant enemy combatant detentions); Benjamin A. Lewis, Note, *An Old Means to a Different End: The War on Terror, American Citizens ... And the Treason Clause*, 34 Hofstra L. Rev. 1215, 1251-61 (2006) (Hamdi and Padilla should have been prosecuted for treason instead of being detained as enemy combatants); *see also Hamdi v. Rumsfeld*, 542 U.S. 507, 554-61 (2004) (Scalia and Stevens, JJ., dissenting) (suggesting that Hamdi could be tried for treason rather than being held as an enemy combatant).

The reluctance to prosecute for treason, however, is not a recent phenomenon. The gravity of treason "is emphasized by the fact that it is the only crime defined by the Constitution." *Stephan*, 133 F.2d at 90. In *Cramer v. United States*, a case arising from a naturalized U.S. citizen's alleged assistance to Nazi saboteurs during World War II, the Supreme Court noted that it had never before "had occasion to review a [treason] conviction," because even on the occasions in which defendants were convicted of treason "Presidents again and again have intervened to mitigate judicial severity or to pardon entirely." 325 U.S. 1, 24, 26 (1945). As the Court noted, "We have managed to do without treason prosecutions to a degree that probably would be impossible except while a people was singularly confident of external security and internal stability." *Id.* at 26.[174] This wariness of treason is well-evidenced by the scarcity of treason prosecutions through World War II, and "the absence of significant appellate decisions in the entire sixty-year period since the World War II cases." George P. Fletcher, *Law, Loyalty and Treason: How Can the Law Regulate Loyalty Without Imperiling It?*, 82 N.C. L. Rev. 1611, 1626 (2004).

On a more practical level, treason prosecutions face potential evidentiary problems. As mentioned before, treason is unique among all crimes in that it carries a constitutional requirement that any treasonous overt act be verified by two witnesses. Moreover, it might be difficult for the government to provide evidence of intent in certain situations. (The intent requirement is discussed in more detail below.) Consequently, while some consider John Walker Lindh the textbook case of a traitor, *see id.* at 1611, another commentator has observed the difficulties in finding two witnesses to any overt act committed by Lindh. *See* Melysa H. Sperber, Note, *John Walker Lindh and Yaser Esam Hamdi: Closing the Loophole in International Humanitarian Law for American Nationals Captured Abroad While Fighting With Enemy Forces*, 40 Am. Crim. L. Rev. 159, 192 (2003). Also, the prosecution might have found it difficult to produce evidence that Lindh intended to fight the United States in particular, rather than the Northern Alliance. *See id.*; Suzanne Kelly Babb, Note, *Fear and Loathing in America: Application of Treason Law in Times of National Crisis and the Case of John Walker Lindh*, 54 Hastings L.J. 1721, 1735-36 (2003).[175]

Further, the treason statute applies only to those individuals "owing allegiance to the United States." 18 U.S.C. § 2381. U.S. citizens clearly fit this definition, even if they are dual citizens, whether their treasonous acts occur in the United States or abroad. *See Kawakita v. United States*, 343 U.S. 717, 725-33 (1952) (dual Japanese-American citizen committed treason against United States while in Japan); *Gillars v. United States*, 182 F.2d 962, 981 (D.C. Cir. 1950); *Stephan*, 133 F.2d at 91; *United States v. Fricke*, 259 F. 673, 675 (S.D.N.Y. 1919). Resident aliens also appear to "owe allegiance" for purposes of the treason statute, although the issue has not been considered by courts since the 19th century. *See Carlisle v. United States*, 83 U.S. (16 Wall.) 147, 154-55 (1872) ("The alien, whilst domiciled in the country, owes a local and temporary allegiance, which continues during the period of his residence"); *accord Radich v. Hutchins*, 95 U.S. 210, 211-12 (1877); *United States v. Wong Kim Ark*, 169 U.S. 649, 693-94 (1898); *see also Charge to Grand Jury—Treason*, 30 F. Cas. 1039, 1040 (D. Mass. 1861) (No. 18,273) (hereinafter "*Mass. Grand Jury Charge*").[176] However,

persons who are not U.S. citizens or resident aliens very likely fall outside the scope of the treason statute.

Notwithstanding these historical limitations, and subject to the proviso that treason charges may only be brought against U.S. citizens and perhaps against resident aliens, treason remains a viable theory of prosecution. There are two independent theories of liability under the treason statute: (1) levying war against the United States and (2) adhering to the enemies of the United States, giving them aid and comfort. A brief discussion of each of these theories based principally on treason prosecutions from the early days of the nation's history as well as cases from the Civil War and World War II eras follows.

1. Levying War Against the United States

To "levy war," an individual must actually assemble a body of persons to wage war; merely conspiring to do it or enlisting individuals without physically gathering them is not sufficient. *See Ex Parte Bollman*, 8 U.S. (4 Cranch) 75, 127 (1807); *United States v. Burr*, 25 F. Cas. 2, 13 (Marshall, Chief Justice, C.C.D. Va. 1807) (No. 14692A); *Mass. Grand Jury Charge*, 30 F. Cas. at 1039.[177] Once the body has been assembled, "some actual force or violence must be used in pursuance" of executing the plan to levy war before a treason conviction can be sustained. *Bollman*, 8 U.S. at 128; *accord Burr*, 25 F. Cas. at 13. The "force," however, need only be a show of force: "if [the defendants] are armed and march in a military form, for the express purpose of overawing or intimidating the public ... that will, of itself, amount to a levy of war, although no actual blow has been struck, or engagement has taken place." *Charge to Grand Jury—Treason*, 30 F. Cas. 1046, 1047 (Story, Circuit Justice, C.C.D.R.I. 1842) (No. 18,275) (hereinafter "*R.I. Grand Jury Charge*"); *see also United States v. Greiner*, 26 F. Cas. 36, 39 (E.D. Pa. 1861) (No. 15,262) (same). Accordingly, the attempt to levy war does not have to be successfully executed to constitute treason. *See United States v. Greathouse*, 26 F. Cas. 18, 24 (Field, Circuit Justice, C.C.N.D. Cal. 1863) (No. 15,254).

Furthermore, once the body has been assembled, "all those who perform any part" in the plan to levy war, "however minute, or however remote from the scene of action, and who are actually leagued in the general conspiracy, are to be considered as traitors," even if they have not personally taken up arms. *Bollman*, 8 U.S. at 126; *accord Greathouse*, 26 F. Cas. at 22; *Charge to Grand Jury—Treason*, 30 F. Cas. 1036,

1037 (C.C.S.D. Ohio 1861) (No. 18,272) (hereinafter "*Ohio Grand Jury Charge*"); *see also Mass. Grand Jury Charge*, 30 F. Cas. at 1040 (sending arms, provisions, money, or intelligence may constitute treason).

The "levying war" prong of the treason statute has an intent requirement as well: namely "to overthrow the government, or to coerce its conduct." *Greathouse*, 26 F. Cas. at 22. A defendant has the requisite intent not just by planning to overthrow the government, but also to "prevent the execution of any one or more general and public laws of the government, or to resist the exercise of any legitimate authority of the government in its sovereign capacity." *R.I. Grand Jury Charge*, 30 F. Cas. at 1047; *see also Mass. Grand Jury Charge*, 30 F. Cas. at 1039 (treasonous to "prevent by force the execution of any public law of the United States, ... for it is entirely to overthrow the government as to one of its laws"); *United States v. Mitchell*, 26 F. Cas. 1277, 1281 (Patterson, Circuit Justice, C.C.D. Pa. 1795) (No. 15,788) (same); *United States v. Vigol*, 28 F. Cas. 376, 376 (Patterson, Circuit Justice, C.C.D. Pa. 1795) (No. 16,621) (same). The resistance to law, however, has to be intended to continue beyond a single incident: "the sudden outbreak of a mob, or the assembling of men in order, by force, to defeat the execution of the law, in a particular instance, and then to disperse, without the intention to continue together, or to re-assemble for the purpose of defeating the law generally, in all cases, is not levying war." *Mass. Grand Jury Charge*, 30 F. Cas. at 1039. Furthermore, the resistance to law has to have a "public" motive of resistance to the government, rather than a private motive. *See United States v. Hoxie*, 26 F. Cas. 397, 398 (Livingston, Circuit Justice, C.C.D. Vt. 1808) (No. 15,407); *accord United States v. Hanway*, 26 F. Cas. 105, 127-28 (Grier, Circuit Justice, C.C.E.D. Pa. 1851) (No. 15,299).

2. Adhering to Enemies, Giving Them Aid and Comfort

Since the Civil War, most treason prosecutions have focused on defendants who were charged with adhering to the enemies of the United States and giving them aid and comfort. The paradigmatic "enemy," of course, is a foreign sovereign state at war with the United States. *See, e.g., Stephan*, 133 F.2d at 90; *Fricke*, 259 F. at 675-76. The term "enemies" has also been limited to "the subjects of a foreign power in a state of open hostility with us." *Greathouse*, 26 F. Cas. at 22; *see also Hoxie*, 26 F. Cas. at 398 (adhering prong not applicable because, at time of act, the United States had "no public enemy"). It is unclear whether a foreign *stateless* actor, such as al Qaeda, would qualify as an "enemy" under this definition; the *Greathouse* court's use of the term "foreign power" arguably means a conflict against a foreign state. Various commentators, however, have argued for more expansive definitions of "enemies" that would include, at least in some circumstances, stateless actors. *See* Tom W. Bell, *Treason, Technology, and Freedom of Expression*, 37 Ariz. St. L. J. 999, 1016-1019 (2005) (arguing that if "enemies" meant only states at war with the United States, § 3 of Article III of the Constitution or § 2381 of title 18 of the U.S. Code could have been written accordingly); Larson, *The Forgotten Constitutional Law of Treason and the Enemy Combatant Problem*, at 923-25 (al Qaeda is an "enemy" based on post-9/11 legislation authorizing the President to use force against the perpetrators of the 9/11 attacks).

The text of the Congressional resolution authorizing the President to use military force after the 9/11 attacks (the "AUMF") strongly supports a broad construction of "enemies" to include al Qaeda. Under the AUMF, "the President is authorized to use all necessary and appropriate force against those nations, *organizations*, or persons he determines planned, authorized, committed, or aided the terrorist attacks that occurred on September 11, 2001, or harbored such organizations or persons, in order to prevent any future acts of international terrorism against the United States by such nations, organizations, or persons." Authorization for Use of Military Force, Pub. L. No. 107-40, § 2(a), 115 Stat. 224, 224 (2001) (emphasis added). The fact that this language refers to organizations in addition to nations strongly suggests that al Qaeda would be deemed an "enemy" under the treason statute.[178] This issue will likely be tested in the *Gadahn* case if he is apprehended and brought to justice.

The prohibited action of this prong of the treason statute is the "act of aid and comfort," while the phrase "adherence to the enemy" describes the intent required for conviction. *Cramer*, 325 U.S. at 29. A "finding that the accused actually gave aid and comfort to the enemy" satisfies the Constitution's requirement of an overt act proving treason. *Id.* at 34; *accord Haupt v. United States*, 330 U.S. 631, 634 (1947). If an individual owing allegiance to the United States "commits an act which weakens, or tends to weaken, the power of the United States to resist or to attack the enemies of the United States, that is in law giving aid and comfort to the enemies of the United States." *Fricke*, 259 F. at 676. Giving valuable information to the enemy is a paradigmatic example of such aid and comfort. See *United States v. Werner*, 247 F. 708, 711 (E.D. Pa. 1918). During World War II, the defendant in *Kawakita* was found guilty of giving aid and comfort to Japan when he committed acts of cruelty against American POWs at a Japanese work camp. See 343 U.S. at 963-65. Many of the other treason convictions based on "aid and comfort" were against American citizens propagandizing while in the employ of enemy powers during World War II. See *Chandler v. United States*, 171 F.2d 921, 937-41 (1st Cir. 1949); accord *Gillars*, 182 F.2d at 970-71; *Best v. United States*, 184 F.2d 131, 137-38 (1st Cir. 1950); *Burgman v. United States*, 188 F.2d 637, 639 (D.C. Cir. 1951). Importantly, the aid and comfort does not have to provide any actual benefit to the enemy; for instance, a propagandist working for Germany during World War II aided and comforted the Nazis simply by making recordings of propaganda aimed at Americans, even though the Nazis were never in a position to use those recordings. See *Chandler*, 171 F.2d at 941.

Given how many actions could conceivably aid a U.S. enemy, the intent requirement of "adherence to the enemy" is an important limiting factor on the applicability of the treason offense. The *Cramer* court recognized this fact when it stated that "a citizen may take actions, which do aid and comfort the enemy—making a speech critical of the government or opposing its measures, profiteering, striking in defense plants or essential work, and the hundred other things which impair our cohesion and diminish our strength—but if there is no adherence to the enemy in this, if there is no intent to betray, there is no treason." 325 U.S. at 29. The adherence element is essentially a specific intent to betray the United States. *Id.*; accord *Kawakita*, 343 U.S. at 742. Accordingly, if a defendant helps an enemy soldier out of some motive other than a desire to support the enemy or undermine the United States, he does not have the requisite intent for treason. See *Haupt*, 330 U.S. at 642 (father of German saboteur would not be guilty of treason if he had helped son purely out of parental concern rather than desire to help Germany); *Fricke*, 259 F. at 682 (defendant would not be guilty of treason if he had given money to German agent as a personal favor, rather than in the recipient's status as a German agent).[179] On the other hand, the intent to betray the United States by helping a recognized enemy is not mitigated by a sincere belief that helping the enemy will promote America's long-term interests, or by expressions of sympathy for U.S. soldiers. See *Chandler*, 171 F.2d at 942-44 (American citizen propagandizing for Nazis was guilty of treason despite belief that Nazi victory would be good for United States in long term); *D'Aquino v. United States*, 192 F.2d 338, 353 (9th Cir. 1951) (acts of kindness toward American POWs did not undermine finding that defendant bore treasonous intent). In the *Gadahn* case, it should not be difficult for the government to persuade a jury that the defendant "adhered" to al Qaeda based on his repeated, open, and notorious statements of support for al Qaeda.[180]

D. Seditious Conspiracy (18 U.S.C. § 2384)

The seditious conspiracy statute was enacted in 1861, during the Civil War. *Ohio Grand Jury Charge*, 30 F. Cas. at 1038. It reads:

> If two or more persons in any State or Territory, or in any place subject to the jurisdiction of the United States, conspire to overthrow, put down, or to destroy by force the Government of the United States, or to levy war against them, or to oppose by force the authority thereof, or by force to prevent, hinder, or delay the execution of any law of the United States, or by force to seize, take, or possess any property of the United States contrary to the authority thereof, they shall be fined under this title or imprisoned not more than twenty years, or both.

18 U.S.C. § 2384.[181] Interestingly, the seditious conspiracy statute has been characterized as an early effort "to help the government cope with and fend off urban terrorism." *United States v. Rodriguez*, 803 F.2d 318, 320 (7th Cir. 1986); accord *United States v. Rahman*, 854 F. Supp. 254, 259 (S.D.N.Y. 1994). In the middle of the 20th century, the government successfully brought seditious conspiracy cases against members of the Puerto Rican separatist movement; in the 1970s and 1980s, it was less successful in bringing such charges against alleged Marxist and white supremacist adherents. See Bradley T. Winter, *Invidious Prosecution: The History of Seditious Conspiracy—Foreshadowing the Recent Convictions of Sheikh Omar Abdel-Rahman and His Immigrant Followers*, 10 Geo. Immigr. L.J. 185, 188, 193-96, 202-04 (1996).[182]

The seditious conspiracy statute is an important weapon for prosecutors to use in prosecuting preparatory terrorist conduct, rather than merely punishing terrorist acts after the fact. The elements of seditious conspiracy are: (1) a conspiracy between two or more persons to (2) engage in any of the conduct described in § 2384. See *United States v. Khan*, 461 F.3d

477, 487 (4th Cir. 2006); *United States v. Rahman*, 189 F.3d 88, 123 (2d Cir. 1999).[183] Unlike treason, conviction for seditious conspiracy requires neither furtherance of the conspiracy's goal nor any overt act in pursuit of that goal. *See Rahman*, 854 F. Supp. at 259; *Anderson v. United States*, 273 F. 20, 23 (8th Cir. 1921). Moreover, the intent requirement for seditious conspiracy should not be confused with motive: if the defendant has intent to levy war against the government, the fact that levying war is not an end in itself but motivated by some further goal does not preclude conviction. *See Bryant v. United States*, 257 F. 378, 386 (5th Cir. 1919). The intent requirement, however, contains both a subjective and objective test; i.e., the intended object of the conspiracy must be both subjectively seditious (the defendant believed that the object was equivalent to the conduct described in § 2384) *and* objectively seditious (the object could objectively fit within the conduct described in § 2384). *See Rahman*, 854 F. Supp. at 258-61 (planned assassination of Egyptian president could be object of seditious conspiracy because assassination of foreign head of state on American soil could disrupt U.S. government's ability to conduct foreign relations; in contrast, planned assassination of Israeli citizen could not be object of seditious conspiracy even if defendants considered Israeli citizen to be in league with the United States because there was no indication that, objectively, the assassination "could further an end that [§ 2384] prohibits agreeing to further, wholly apart from what the defendants thought or believed").

Several defendants have challenged the seditious conspiracy statute on constitutional grounds, arguing that it circumvents the evidentiary requirements of the treason statute, *see, e.g., Rahman*, 189 F.3d at 112; *Rodriguez*, 803 F.2d at 320, but those arguments have been rejected on multiple grounds.[184] The Second Circuit has also rejected free speech challenges to the statute, explaining that the Supreme Court has allowed certain prohibitions on unlawful advocacy in precedents construing the Smith Act, and that the seditious conspiracy statute prohibits conduct "much further removed from the realm of constitutionally protected speech" because it prohibits the "conspir[acy] to *use* force, not just to *advocate* the use of force." *Rahman*, 189 F.3d at 115 (emphasis in original); *see also United States v. Lebron*, 222 F.2d 531, 536 (2d Cir. 1955) (seditious conspiracy statute did not violate free speech rights because it comported with Smith Act precedents). The Second Circuit was not swayed by Sheikh Omar Abdel Rahman's argument that, because he was an Islamic cleric, his speech should receive extra protection as religious speech. *See Rahman*, 189 F.3d at 116-18 (citing *Employment Div. v. Smith*, 494 U.S. 872, 879 (1990)).

The government achieved a significant victory in the 1990s by invoking the seditious conspiracy statute against Abdel Rahman and his co-defendants for conspiring to bomb New York tunnels and landmarks and for planning to assassinate Egyptian President Hosni Mubarak. *See Rahman*, 189 F.3d at 103. At the time, the Rahman case was "considered to be the most important international terrorism prosecution ever conducted in the United States." Joseph Grinstein, Note, *Jihad and the Constitution: The First Amendment Implications of Combating Religiously Motivated Terrorism*, 105 Yale L.J. 1347, 1349 (1996). Some commentators were surprised when the government chose to prosecute the defendants for seditious conspiracy as opposed to a more frequently prosecuted crime such as RICO; these commentators expressed concern that a seditious conspiracy prosecution could allow jurors' political beliefs to cloud their judgment, or that juries would balk at the proposition that the defendants actually intended to overthrow our government. *See* Tamar Lewin, *Conspiracy Case Against Sheikh Is Risky, Experts Say*, N.Y. Times, Aug. 28, 1993, §1, at 21.[185] The skeptics were proven wrong, however, when the defendants in *Rahman* were convicted for conspiring to conduct a bombing campaign in the United States and to assassinate the President of Egypt on U.S. soil, and these convictions were affirmed by the Second Circuit. *See* 189 F.3d at 123-24. After the trial, one observer noted that the political nature of the seditious conspiracy charge may have worked to the government's advantage by helping the prosecutors "cast their case in political terms, linking the defendants to Middle East terrorism." Richard Pérez-Peña, *The Terror Conspiracy: The Charges; A Gamble Pays Off as the Prosecution Uses an Obscure 19th-Century Law*, N.Y. Times, Oct. 2, 1995, at B5.[186]

In the years since 9/11, the government has continued to put the seditious conspiracy statute to use in cases targeting international terrorism. *See* Sealed Indictment, *United States v. Batiste*, No. 06-cr-20373 (S.D. Fla. June 22, 2006) (Dkt. No. 3) (seven defendants charged with plotting to blow up the Sears Tower in Chicago and federal buildings in Miami); Indictment, *United States v. James*, No. 05-cr-00214 (C.D. Cal. Aug. 31, 2005); Press Release, U.S. Dep't of Justice, *Four Men Indicted on Terrorism Charges Related to Conspiracy to Attack Military Facilities, Other Targets* (Aug. 31, 2005)[187] (four defendants in *James* indictment plotted to attack U.S. military facilities, Israeli government facilities and synagogues in the Los Angeles area); *United States v. Khan*, 309 F. Supp. 2d 789, 796 (E.D. Va. 2004) (conspiracy to travel to Pakistan to train to fight against American forces in Afghanistan); Plea Agreement, *United States v. Battle*, No. 02-cr-00399 (D. Or. Oct. 16, 2003) (Dkt. No. 351);[188] Press Release, U.S. Dep't of Justice, *Jeffrey Battle and Patrice Lumumba Ford Plead Guilty to Seditious Conspiracy in "Portland Cell" Case* (Oct. 16, 2003)[189] (seven defendants agreed to fly to Afghanistan to fight American forces). The prosecutions in *Khan* and *Ford* have led to convictions which have been upheld on appeal. *See United States v. Khan*, 461 F.3d 477, 487 (4th Cir. 2006); *United States v. Ford*, 216 F. App'x 652 (9th Cir. 2007). Three of the Los Angeles defendants have pled guilty to seditious conspiracy. *See* Plea Agreements as to Levar Washington and Kevin James, *James* (C.D. Cal. Dec. 14, 2007) (Dkt. Nos. 258, 259); Minutes of Change of Plea Hearing as to Gregory Patterson, *James* (C.D. Cal. Dec. 17, 2007) (Dkt. No. 263); *California: Guilty Pleas in Attack Plot*, N.Y. Times, Dec. 15, 2007, at A19.[190] As of the writing of this paper, there was no trial date scheduled for the other defendant in *James*. *See* Order to Continue Trial Date, *James* (C.D. Cal. Apr. 18, 2008) (Dkt. No. 298). In the first *Batiste* trial, one of the seven defendants was acquitted, and the judge declared a mistrial for the remaining six defendants. *See* Judgment of Acquittal, *Batiste* (S.D. Fla. Dec. 13, 2007) (Dkt. No. 707); Order Declaring Mistrial & Scheduling Trial Date, *Batiste* (S.D. Fla. Dec. 13, 2007) (Dkt. No. 710); Kirk Semple, *U.S. Falters in Terror Case Against 7 in Miami*, N.Y. Times, Dec. 14, 2007.[191] The second trial also resulted in a deadlocked jury and a mistrial. *See* Carmen Gentile, *Six Suspects Will Be Tried a Third Time in Sears Plot*, N.Y. Times., Apr. 24, 2008, at A18.[192]

One commentator, in reviewing the government's success in *Rahman*, has written at length of the virtues of the seditious conspiracy statute as an alternative to a treason prosecution, the latter of which he views negatively. *See* Babb, *Fear and Loathing in America*, at 1740-41 ("The end result of seeking the seditious conspiracy charge over one for treason is that courts are spared the inevitable drama of a treason trial, defendants are spared the highly prejudicial label of 'traitor,' prosecutors are spared the burden of meeting the stringent standards of treason, and those who have harmed or conspired to do harm to the national security are nonetheless made answerable"). The seditious conspiracy statute is not a panacea, however. First, because it is a conspiracy statute, it cannot be used against lone terrorists. Second, "[u]nlike treason, seditious conspiracy does not extend beyond United States jurisdictional boundaries." *Rodriguez*, 803 F.2d at 320. This jurisdictional limitation is softened somewhat by the rule that when any "act in furtherance of a conspiracy [takes place] in one district, that district has jurisdiction over all the conspirators, although some were never physically present there." *United States v. Valle*, 16 F.R.D. 519, 522 (S.D.N.Y. 1955); *accord United States v. Berry*, No. 84-cr-00529, 1985 WL 1587, at *8 (N.D. Ill. May 10, 1985). Thus, if one member of a seditious conspiracy committed any act within the U.S. jurisdiction, all conspirators would be prosecutable. However, a seditious conspiracy prosecution could not be brought against conspirators who have not yet taken any action within the U.S. jurisdiction, blunting to some extent the preemptive capabilities of this statute.

E. Recruitment of and Enlistment for Hostile Force (18 U.S.C. §§ 2389-90)

Mere enlistment into a force hostile to the United States or recruitment of such enlistees does not rise to the level of treasonous conduct. Accordingly, shortly after the beginning of the Civil War, Congress passed separate legislation criminalizing both recruitment and enlistment. *See Ohio Grand Jury Charge*, 30 F. Cas. at 1037 ("it seems to have been the view of the congress by which it was enacted, that recruiting or enlisting soldiers or sailors for the service of the enemy, or opening a recruiting station for that purpose, or the act of being enlisted, were not treasonable within the law of 1790, and that further legislation was therefore needed to warrant their punishment"). In its modern form, the recruitment statute establishes criminal penalties for: (1) recruitment of "soldiers or sailors within the United States, or in any place subject to the jurisdiction thereof, to engage in armed hostility against the same;" or (2) the opening "within the United States, or in any place subject to the jurisdiction thereof, a recruiting station for the enlistment of such soldiers or sailors." 18 U.S.C. § 2389. The enlistment statute, in turn, levies criminal punishment for any enlistment or engagement "within the United States or in any place subject to the jurisdiction thereof, with intent to serve in armed hostility against the United States." 18 U.S.C. § 2390.

The latter statute has been used by the government in a modern terrorism prosecution as the predicate statute of a conspiracy prosecution. In *Khan*, the government successfully argued that the defendant conspired to violate § 2390 when he agreed with others at a meeting in the United States to travel to Pakistan to train for fighting against the United States in Afghanistan. *See* 309 F. Supp. 2d at 819. The conviction was affirmed by the Fourth Circuit. *See Khan*, 461 F.3d at 487. Both the trial and appellate courts agreed on the elements of a § 2390 violation: enlistment or engagement within the United States or any place subject to the jurisdiction thereof, with intent to serve in armed hostility against the United States. *See Khan*, 309 F. Supp. 2d at 819; *Khan*, 461 F.3d at 487.

As the *Khan* opinions observe, both the recruitment and enlistment statutes confine their applicability to recruitment and enlistment within the United States even though the statutes were presumably intended to supplement the treason statute, which applies extraterritorially. Accordingly, in their present form, the recruitment and enlistment statutes could not be used against individuals who recruit and enlist on foreign soil for forces that intend armed hostility toward the United States. It is worth noting, however, that in *Khan*, only the recruitment or enlistment took place in the United States; the intended armed hostilities were to take place abroad, in Afghanistan. *See Khan*, 309 F. Supp. 2d at 819; *Khan*, 461 F.3d at 487.

F. Use of Alternative Statutes to Prosecute Defendants Believed to Be Complicit in Terrorism

After the attacks of 9/11, the Department of Justice announced that its foremost priority would be the prevention of terrorist acts. Attorney General John Ashcroft told the Senate Judiciary Committee that the attacks had changed the Department's approach: "From that moment, at the command of the President of the United States, I began to mobilize the resources of the Department of Justice toward one single, overarching and overriding objective: to save innocent lives from further acts of terrorism." *Dep't of Justice Oversight: Preserving Our Freedoms While Defending Against Terrorism: Hearing Before the S. Comm. on the Judiciary*, 107th Cong. 310 (2001) (statement of John Ashcroft, Att'y Gen. of the United States); *see also* Chesney, *The Sleeper Scenario*, at 26-34 (discussing the Department of Justice's emphasis on prevention post 9/11). The Attorney General put it simply to Congress: "We must prevent first, prosecute second." *Homeland Defense: Hearing Before the S. Comm. on the Judiciary*, 107th Cong. 9 (2001) (statement of John Ashcroft, Att'y Gen. of the United States).

Some terrorism statutes can be used preventively. For example, the material support statutes may be invoked to prosecute terrorists before they have committed a violent act. *See, e.g.*, Chesney, *The Sleeper Scenario*, at 39-44 (discussing the use of § 2339B, the material support statute, to arrest preventively the defendants in the Lackawanna Six case). However, as discussed above, these statutes have limitations because the defendant must be linked to a planned terrorist act or a designated terrorist group. Such evidence is not always available at the time prosecutors want to arrest a suspect whom they view as dangerous. Furthermore, if the government brings a case under the material support statutes, it will "tip its hand" and reveal publicly that it believes that the defendant is connected to terrorism. This may compromise sensitive information about the existence or scope of an ongoing terrorist investigation. Thus, in order to be able to arrest suspects at an early stage and not risk disclosure of sensitive information, prosecutors have adopted a familiar strategy of federal criminal prosecutions in other areas—the arrest of the suspect on an alternative, readily provable charge that does not, on its face, require any allegation that the defendant is linked to terrorism.[193]

The Department of Justice has an explicit strategy of employing alternative statutes for terrorism suspects:

> [T]he Department's counterterrorism efforts have broadened since September 11 to include pursuit of offenses terrorists often commit, such as identity theft and immigration violations. These statutes include 18 U.S.C. § 1546 (fraudulently obtaining travel documents), 18 U.S.C. § 1425 (immigration violations), and 18 U.S.C. § 1001 (making misrepresentations to federal investigators). Prosecution of terrorism-related targets on these types of charges is often an effective method—and sometimes the only available method—of deterring and disrupting potential terrorist planning and support activities without compromising national security information.

U.S. Dep't of Justice, *2006 Counterterrorism White Paper*, at 29. This strategy has proved effective because individuals who enter the United States to commit terrorist acts are likely to violate other laws, including statutes regarding immigration, financial, or credit-card fraud, or the laws related to procuring false documents or making false statements to federal officials. In just the past year, in fact, the government has charged individuals it suspects of having connections to terrorists with crimes such as document fraud, *see* U.S. Dep't of Justice, *2007 Counterterrorism White Paper Update*, at 20 (describing jury's guilty verdict against Mohamad Kamal Elzahabi, who was charged with lying to federal agents "about helping a man, later convicted in Jordan as a terrorist, to obtain a Massachusetts driver's license in 1997"), and marriage fraud, *see id.* (describing guilty plea of Ali Fouad Ayache, "a Hizballah associate and supporter who obtained his green card by entering into a fraudulent marriage with a United States citizen in 2002, lying to federal officers about it, and then attempting to persuade his 'wife' to lie to authorities").

Since many suspects who are arrested under these alternative statutes will be detained, the alternative prosecution strategy often achieves the objective of incapacitating dangerous individuals. Indeed, in some respects, the strategy serves almost as a surrogate for preventive detention—except for the crucial fact that it has the virtue and transparency of basing an individual's detention on actual charged criminal conduct. Former Assistant Attorney General Viet Dinh recognized the analogy, observing that "[w]e do not engage in preventive detention. In this respect, our detention differs significantly from that of other countries ... What we do here is perhaps best described as preventative prosecution." *See* Chesney, *The Sleeper Scenario,* at 31 (citation omitted) (calling the law enforcement strategy "preventive charging").

There can be little doubt that the ability to pursue alternative prosecutions can be, and in some cases has been, directly relevant to significant terrorism cases. As the 9/11 Commission noted in its report, as many as fifteen of the nineteen 9/11 hijackers were vulnerable to criminal charges based on their fraudulent travel documents. *See 9/11 Commission Report*, at 384, 384 n.32, n.33 (stating that two hijackers presented passports that were fraudulently altered in a manner associated with al Qaeda, that eleven other hijackers may have had passports altered in the same way, and that at least two other hijackers made false statements in their travel documents).[194] The 9/11 Commission Report underlined the difficulty terrorists can encounter in gaining entry to the United States:

> For terrorists, travel documents are as important as weapons. Terrorists must travel clandestinely to meet, train, plan, case targets, and gain access to attack. To them, international travel presents great danger, because they must surface to pass through regulated channels, present themselves to border security officials, or attempt to circumvent inspection points.

> In their travels, terrorists use evasive methods, such as altered and counterfeit passports and visas, specific travel methods and routes, liaisons with corrupt government officials, human smuggling networks, supportive travel agencies, and immigration and identity fraud.

Id. at 384. The attempt to slip through the bureaucratic net of immigration laws exposes terrorists to potential alternative prosecutions for each violation and lie along the way.

In pursuing the "preventive prosecution" strategy, the government is not limited to bringing criminal charges; in many cases it can commence civil immigration proceedings by arresting illegal aliens and detaining them pending removal. Although a detailed assessment of the government's immigration enforcement strategy is beyond the scope of this White Paper, the case of Zacarias Moussaoui illustrates how immigration enforcement can complement criminal charges as a means to arrest and detain dangerous individuals. Moussaoui, who at one time was believed to be the "20th hijacker," was a French national who entered the United States on February 23, 2001, under a visa waiver program. *See* Dep't of Justice, *2006 Counterterrorism White Paper*, at 25. He took flight training in Oklahoma and then went to Minnesota, where his focus on learning to fly large jets without obtaining a pilot's license first aroused suspicion in his flight instructor. *See 9/11 Commission Report*, at 247. On August 16, 2001, after the instructor reported him to the authorities, Moussaoui was arrested and detained by the Immigration and Naturalization Service (INS) for overstaying his visa. *Id.* at 273.

Although in many ways a tantalizing missed opportunity, the arrest of Moussaoui reflects many of the potential benefits of an arrest of a suspected terrorist on an alternative charge. First, Moussaoui's arrest resulted in the detention of a dangerous individual who was believed to be a terrorist—and who was later proven to be one.[195] Indeed, Moussaoui's arrest on immigration charges ultimately led to his guilty plea on serious terrorism charges and his imprisonment for life. *See* Judgment, *United States v. Moussaoui*, No. 01-cr-00455 (E.D. Va. May 4, 2006) (Dkt. No. 1854). Second, if news of Moussaoui's arrest had reached senior figures in al Qaeda, there is some reason to think they might have cancelled the 9/11 attacks. As reported in the 9/11 Commission Report, according to one cooperating witness, "had Bin Ladin and KSM [Khaled Sheikh Mohammed] learned prior to 9/11 that Moussaoui had been detained, they might have canceled the operation." *9/11 Commission Report*, at 247. Thus, even though an alternative prosecution may risk compromising an investigation, it may—even unknowingly—also help disrupt or forestall an attack. Third, if the government had managed to connect Moussaoui to al Qaeda in August 2001—as it did by September 13—questions would likely have been raised about an al Qaeda plot to hijack and pilot airliners, and the plot might have been foiled. See id. at 273, 275-76.[196]

It is a challenge to identify all the cases in which individuals who are connected to terrorism have been successfully arrested and prosecuted on alternative charges, but there are a number of examples. For instance, Soliman Biheiri was convicted in two separate trials of immigration violations and false statements. See Judgment, United States v. Biheiri, No. 03-cr-00365 (E.D. Va. Jan. 12, 2004) (Dkt. No. 47); Judgment, United States v. Biheiri, No. 04-cr-00201 (Jan. 14, 2005) (Dkt. No. 89). Although the charges did not facially reflect a connection to terrorism, a declaration in support of the defendant's pre-trial detention by a senior special agent from the Bureau of Immigration and Customs Enforcement ("ICE") stated that Biheiri through his company "may have transferred funds to or for terrorists" and that his company engaged in financial transactions with people who subsequent to or prior to those transactions were designated as terrorists. See Declaration in Support of Pre-Trial Detention of Special Agent David Kane ("Kane Decl.") at ¶ 19, Biheiri (E.D. Va. Sept. 4, 2003) (Dkt. No. 10). According to Agent Kane's declaration, Biheiri was the president and sole director of a New Jersey-based investment firm that received investments from organizations providing financing and other support to terrorist organizations, including Hamas, and may have transferred funds overseas used to finance the bombings of U.S. embassies in Africa. See id. ¶¶ 7, 11, 13-17, 26; see also Dep't of Justice, 2006 Counterterrorism White Paper, at 29-30. Biheiri also had the contact information for four individuals who were either Specially Designated Terrorists or Specially Designated Global Terrorists in his computer contact list. See Kane Decl. at ¶¶ 24-25. One of those contacts was Sami al-Arian, see id. ¶ 25, who pled guilty several years later in federal court in Florida to a charge of conspiracy to provide material support to Palestinian Islamic Jihad. See Judgment, United States v. al-Arian, No. 03-cr-00077 (M.D. Fla. May 1, 2006) (Dkt. No. 1574). Biheiri was eventually sentenced to a period of imprisonment to be followed by deportation.[197]

In United States v. Damrah, Fawaz Mohammed Damrah was convicted of unlawfully obtaining citizenship by making false statements in his citizenship application about his involvement with the Palestinian Islamic Jihad ("PIJ") and the Islamic Committee for Palestine ("ICP"). See 412 F.3d 618, 620 (6th Cir. 2005). The PIJ, a designated terrorist organization, opposes the existence of Israel and is committed to eliminating it. The ICP raised funds for the PIJ. See id. As the evidence showed, Damrah had spoken at videotaped fundraising events for the ICP and had noted that the organization's name had been chosen "for security reasons." Id. at 621. After a jury trial, Damrah was convicted and sentenced to two months' imprisonment, four months' home confinement, and three years of supervised release. See id. at 620. In addition, his citizenship was revoked. See id. at 622.

Other alternative prosecutions have not centered on immigration charges. For example, Mohammad Radwan Obeid was arrested after a librarian saw him viewing websites related to al Qaeda and the construction of explosive devices and reported him to the FBI. See Dep't of Justice, 2006 Counterterrorism White Paper, at 30. A search warrant executed on his computer turned up evidence that he had been communicating with others about terrorist activity. See id. When Obeid was questioned about that activity, he lied and was prosecuted under 18 U.S.C. § 1001(a)(2) for making false statements. See id.; Sealed Indictment, United States v. Obeid, No. 05-cr-00149 (S.D. Ohio Oct. 25, 2005) (Dkt. No. 5). Obeid pled guilty to one count of making a false statement and received a twelve-month sentence. See Amended Judgment, Obeid (S.D. Ohio July 10, 2006) (Dkt. No. 46).

Like Obeid, the defendant in United States v. Maflahi was charged and convicted of making a false statement under 18 U.S.C. § 1001(a)(2). See Indictment, Maflahi, No. 03-cr-00412 (E.D.N.Y. Apr. 9, 2003) (Dkt. No. 2). In the Maflahi case, the defendant told FBI agents that he was not involved in fund-raising done by a Yemeni sheikh, Abdullah Satar, during Satar's 1999 visit to the United States. See William Glaberson, Man Guilty of Lying to the F.B.I. in Sheik Case, N.Y. Times, Feb. 19, 2004, at 1.[198] Testimony from an FBI anti-terrorism agent contradicted these statements and showed that Maflahi frequently drove the sheikh around during the visit and took calls on his cell phone that were intended for the sheikh. See id. Maflahi was found guilty and sentenced to five years' imprisonment, followed by three years supervised release. See Judgment, Maflahi (E.D.N.Y. July 9, 2004) (Dkt. No. 50).

There are other notable examples of cases where the government has used alternative statutes to arrest and prosecute individuals with connections to terrorism. See, e.g.,

Indictment, *United States v. Abdulah*, No. 01-cr-00977 (D. Ariz. Oct. 25, 2001) (Dkt. No. 1) (charging defendant with making false statements under 18 U.S.C. § 1001(a)(2) and social security fraud under 42 U.S.C. §§ 408(a)(7)(A), (B)); Indictment, *United States v. al-Marri*, No. 03-cr-10044 (C.D. Ill. May 22, 2003) (Dkt. No. 5) (charging defendant with using false identification to open bank accounts under 18 U.S.C. § 1028(a)(7), making false statements to influence FDIC-insured accounts under 18 U.S.C. § 1014, making false statements to the FBI under 18 U.S.C. §§ 1001(a)(1), (2), and possession of more than fifteen unauthorized credit cards under 18 U.S.C. § 1029(a)(3)); Complaint, *United States v. Alrababah*, No. 01-cr-01284 (E.D. Va. Nov. 16, 2001) (Dkt. No. 1) (charging defendant with unlawful production of identification documents and aiding and abetting under 18 U.S.C. §§ 1028(a)(1), 1028(b)(1)(A)(ii), 1028(c)(3)(A) and conspiracy to commit identification document fraud under 18 U.S.C. § 1028(f)); Indictment, *United States v. Budiman*, No. 02-cr-00074 (E.D. Va. Feb. 21, 2002) (Dkt. No. 22) (same); Indictment, *United States v. Galicia*, No. 01-cr-00411 (E.D. Va. Oct. 25, 2001) (Dkt. No. 11) (same). In some alternative prosecutions, such as *United States v. Qureshi*, the government has convinced the defendant to cooperate and provide information about other terrorists. *See* Dep't of Justice, *2006 Counterterrorism White Paper*, at 30 (discussing Qureshi's proffer about al Qaeda member Wadih el-Hage and an organization that may have assisted in financing the embassy bombings in Kenya and Tanzania); Plea Agreement, *United States v. Qureshi*, No. 04-cr-60057 (W.D. La. Feb. 11, 2005) (Dkt. No. 31). In one of our interviews, a former prosecutor explained that by using alternative prosecutions the government had successfully disabled a Hezbollah cell in the United States. *See* Telephone Interview with Kenneth M. Karas, U.S. District Judge for the S.D.N.Y. & former Assistant U.S. Att'y in the S.D.N.Y. (Dec. 10, 2007).

Although frequently the sentences for such alternative prosecutions are less severe than the sentences for terrorism offenses, according to prosecutors these defendants once deported are often not able to re-integrate themselves into their former terrorist organizations. The reason is that the relatively short period of incarceration is viewed with suspicion by the members of the organization who believe that it is because the released defendant is cooperating. *See* Telephone Interview with Kenneth M. Karas (Dec. 10, 2007).

While some have criticized these sorts of prosecutions as "pretextual," *see, e.g.*, Daniel C. Richman & William J. Stuntz, *Al Capone's Revenge: An Essay on the Political Economy of Pretextual Prosecution*, 105 Colum. L. Rev. 583 (2005), these critics often fail to acknowledge that alternative prosecutions have been used effectively in law enforcement for many years. Indeed, we believe that it is a misnomer to label such prosecutions as "pretextual." To the extent that individuals are arrested on non-terrorism charges and law enforcement continues to pursue leads to see if terrorism charges can be developed, the government is not engaging in a pretext; it is conducting a legitimate and longstanding method of investigation and enforcement. A similar strategy was famously used by the New York City Police Department in the 1990s as it enforced minor crimes like turnstile jumping, not as a substitute for prosecuting felonies but as a way of targeting those who might have warrants or be linked to major felonies. *Id.* at 605-06. Additionally, many of the crimes called "pretextual" are in fact crimes that are characteristic of terrorists who, as explained above, must dodge numerous laws to enter and remain in this country undetected or finance their activities. Certain of these crimes (such as document and financial frauds) may in fact be terrorism "precursor" crimes; that is, crimes that precede an attack and are undertaken to support financially and otherwise the terrorist's presence in the United States. *See* Siobhan O'Neil, Congressional Research Service, *CRS Report for Congress—Terrorist Precursor Crimes: Issues and Options for Congress* 1 (2007).[199] Finally, even when the government proceeds under an alternative statute, the defendant must still be convicted beyond a reasonable doubt. The fact that the defendant may not in another era have been targeted or treated as severely is a function of the reality that the criminal justice system must be responsive to the dangers of the time. In our view, the ability to use alternative prosecutions is an important and legitimate part of the flexibility and responsiveness of the criminal justice system in combating terrorism.

G. Use of Generally Applicable Statutes Aimed at Violence or Conspiracy

In addition to employing terrorism-specific statutes or "alternative" statutes to incapacitate would-be terrorists and hamper the commission of terrorist acts, prosecutors regularly charge suspected terrorists with other generally applicable criminal statutes. For example, the government has initiated, and often successfully concluded, prosecutions of suspected terrorists for crimes as diverse as fraud, money laundering, racketeering, aircraft piracy, arms dealing, destruction of property, and murder. *See, e.g.*, Judgment, *United States v. Abu Ali*, No. 05-cr-00053 (E.D. Va. Apr. 17, 2006) (Dkt. No. 397) (reflecting convictions for, inter alia, conspiracy to commit aircraft piracy and conspiracy to destroy an aircraft, and resulting thirty-year prison sentence); *United States v. Bin Laden*, 397 F. Supp. 2d 465, 473 (S.D.N.Y. 2005) (noting that defendant el-Hage had been convicted of conspiracy to kill U.S. nationals and destroy U.S. property); Judgment, *United States v. Arnaout*, No. 02-cr-00892 (N.D. Ill. Aug. 18, 2003) (Dkt. No. 213) (reflecting guilty plea to count of racketeering and resulting 136-month prison sentence); Sealed Indictment, *Batiste* (S.D. Fla. June 22, 2006) (Dkt. No. 3) (charging defendants with conspiring to bomb the Sears Tower in Chicago and federal buildings in Miami); Sealed Indictment, *United States v. al-Mughassil*, No. 01-cr-00228 (E.D. Va. June 21, 2001) (Dkt. No. 1) (charging defendants with bombing of Khobar Towers, a housing complex used by U.S. employees and military personnel in Saudi Arabia, and ensuing murders and attempted murders); Indictment, *United States v. Assi*, No. 98-cr-80695 (E.D. Mich. Aug. 4, 1998) (Dkt. No. 12) (reflecting charges for, inter alia, unauthorized arms dealing).

Many of the above prosecutions included conspiracy charges. The government can bring these charges under specific conspiracy provisions contained in statutes outlining substantive offenses, *see, e.g.*, 18 U.S.C. § 32 (criminalizing conspiracy to commit air piracy as well as the actual commission of air piracy); 18 U.S.C. § 2339B (criminalizing conspiracy to provide material support as well as the actual provision of material support), or, if not available, under the general conspiracy statute, which makes it a crime to conspire to "commit any offense against the United States." 18 U.S.C. § 371. The elements of a conspiracy prosecution under § 371 are straightforward: (1) an agreement to pursue an unlawful objective, (2) the defendant's knowledge of that unlawful objective and intentional participation in the agreement, and (3) an overt act by one or more members to the agreement in furtherance of the conspiracy. *See United States v. Mann*, 493 F.3d 484, 492 (5th Cir. 2007); *United States v. Munoz-Franco*, 487 F.3d 25, 45 (1st Cir. 2007); *United States v. Blackwell*, 459 F.3d 739, 760 (6th Cir. 2006); *United States v. Soy*, 454 F.3d 766, 768 (7th Cir. 2006).[200]

Judge Learned Hand famously described the conspiracy statute as the "darling of the modern prosecutor's nursery." *Harrison v. United States*, 7 F.2d 259, 263 (2d Cir. 1925); *see also United States v. Townsend*, 924 F.2d 1385, 1416 (7th Cir. 1991) (quoting *Harrison* and then observing that the conspiracy charge's "attraction has not diminished with the passage of years"); *United States v. Reynolds*, 919 F.2d 435, 439 (7th Cir. 1990) (describing conspiracy charge as "inevitable because prosecutors seem to have conspiracy on their word processors as Count I; rare is the case omitting such a charge"); Jonathan Mahler, *The Bush Administration vs. Salim Hamdan*, N.Y. Times (Magazine), Jan. 8, 2006, at 44, 51[201] (explaining that "the conspiracy charge is a logical one for prosecuting members of organizations like Al Qaeda" because it "is especially popular among prosecutors going after organized-crime rings; it gives them leverage to lean on foot soldiers to testify against their superiors").

The pervasiveness of conspiracy charges in federal criminal cases is rooted in several prosecution-friendly traits of the statute. For example, because the gravamen of a conspiracy crime is the agreement itself, an individual does not have to proceed as far along a path of criminal conduct to be prosecuted for conspiracy as one does to be prosecuted for attempt. *See* Benjamin E. Rosenberg, *Several Problems in Criminal Conspiracy Laws and Some Proposals for Reform*, 43 No. 4 Crim. L. Bull. 427, 431-35 (2007). Indeed, one commentator claims that "the sole defensible rationale for the conspiracy doctrine is the belief that the prevention of the sort of group danger inherent in a conspiracy can be accomplished only through a mechanism that deters criminal group efforts before they begin." Marie E. Siesseger, Note, *Conspiracy Theory: The Use of the Conspiracy Doctrine in Times of National Crisis*, 46 Wm. & Mary L. Rev. 1177, 1190 (2004).

Perhaps the most striking substantive advantage a conspiracy prosecution confers upon the government is the ability to impose so-called "Pinkerton liability" under which any "defendant guilty of participating in a conspiracy may also be found guilty of any criminal acts committed by any co-conspirator in furtherance of the conspiracy, even if the defendant had no role in the commission of the criminal acts." Rosenberg, *Several Problems in Criminal Conspiracy Laws*, at 438; *see also* Philip Shenon, *The DeLay Inquiry: The Texas Republican; DeLay Goes on Radio and TV to Proclaim Innocence*, N.Y. Times, Sept. 30, 2005, at A26[202] ("Criminal law specialists noted that conspiracy charges were often sought by prosecutors because they did not require proof that a defendant participated directly in the crimes that resulted from the conspiracy"). Procedurally, meanwhile, a conspiracy charge allows prosecutors to "admit[] evidence that does not reflect directly on the crimes charged but is merely background of the conspiracy," Rosenberg, *Several Problems in Criminal Conspiracy Laws*, at 446 (internal quotations omitted), and to admit statements that "wouldn't be allowed in a non-conspiracy case because they would be considered hearsay." V. Dion Hayes, *Jurors Embrace "Darling" of Prosecutors*, Chi. Trib., Dec. 24, 1997, at 1; *see also* Harriet Chiang, *Charge Against Top Cops Tough to Prove*, S.F. Chron., Mar. 6, 2003, at A1[203] ("Proving a conspiracy allows prosecutors to bring in a potential gold mine of evidence, statements that may seem extraneous but are relevant to the crime").[204] The potent advantages of conspiracy prosecutions under § 371 are somewhat counterbalanced by the relatively low maximum statutory penalty of five years, which in serious cases would clearly cap the punishment at an inappropriately low level.

Prosecutors have effectively used conspiracy charges under § 371 in various terrorism prosecutions. *See, e.g., Khan*, 309 F. Supp. 2d at 818 (conspiracy to violate 18 U.S.C. §§ 924, 960, 2390); *Rahman*, 189 F.3d at 124 (conspiracy to violate 18 U.S.C. § 844(i)); *United States v. Yousef*, 327 F.3d 56, 81-85 (2d Cir. 2003) (describing conviction of Ramzi Yousef on count of conspiring to destroy an aircraft under 18 U.S.C. § 32(a) in the Manila bombing case); Indictment, *United States v. Abuali*, No. 01-cr-00686 (D.N.J. Oct. 25, 2001) (Dkt. No. 12) (conspiracy to defraud the United States); Indictment, *United States v. Dumeisi*, No. 03-cr-00664 (N.D. Ill. July 16, 2003) (Dkt. No. 5) (same); Superseding Information, *United States v. Shnewer*, No. 07-cr-00459 (D.N.J. Oct. 31, 2007) (Dkt. No. 85) (same); Indictment, *United States v. Rashed*, No. 87-cr-00308 (D.D.C. July 14, 1987) (Dkt. No. 12) (conspiracy to use explosives); Press Release, U.S. Dep't of Justice, Jose Padilla and Co-Defendants Convicted of Conspiracy to Murder Individuals Overseas, Providing Material Support to Terrorists (Aug. 16, 2007).[205]

H. Biological Weapons (18 U.S.C. §§ 175-78)

In 1990, Congress enacted the first statute aimed at prosecuting "modern" terrorism: the Biological Weapons Anti-Terrorism Act of 1989, Pub. L. No. 101-298, 104 Stat. 201 (1990) (codified as amended at 18 U.S.C. §§ 175, 176, 177, 178) (hereinafter "BWATA"). As the name of the statute implies, Congress passed BWATA to "implement the Biological Weapons Convention, an international agreement unanimously ratified by the United States Senate in 1974 and signed by more than 100 other nations" and to "protect the United States against the threat of biological terrorism." *Id.* § 2(a). Congress was concerned by domestic biological terrorist threats as well as the possibility that potentially hostile nations could obtain biological weapons. *See* S. Rep. No. 101-210, at 5-6 (1989), *reprinted in* 1990 U.S.C.C.A.N. 186, 190-91 (hereinafter "BWATA S. Rep.").

Although BWATA has not yet been used in terrorism prosecutions, it offers a comprehensive set of statutory provisions and could be an effective tool in an appropriate case. BWATA is codified in chapter 10 of title 18 of the United States Code, and carries several prohibitions. First, BWATA makes it a crime to "develop[], produce[], stockpile[], transfer[], acquire[], retain[] or possess[] any biological agent, toxin, or delivery system for use as a weapon, or knowingly assist[] a foreign state or any organization to do so, or attempt[], threaten[], or conspire[] to do the same." 18 U.S.C. § 175(a). The terms "biological agent," "toxin," and "delivery system" are broadly defined. *See* 18 U.S.C. § 178.[206] BWATA's legislative history broadly notes that "for use as a weapon" was intended to be broadly defined by what it is not. BWATA S. Rep. at 10. This definition in the negative has since been amended so that "for use as a weapon" means for any purpose *other than* "prophylactic, protective, bona fide research, or other peaceful purposes." 18 U.S.C. § 175(c). The statute specifically establishes "extraterritorial Federal jurisdiction over an offense under this section committed by or against a national of the United States." 18 U.S.C. § 175(a).

Some commentators expressed concern in the early part of this decade that prosecutions under § 175(a) could be difficult because the statute requires proof of intent to use a biological agent, toxin, or delivery system as a weapon. *See* Heather A. Dagen, Comment, *Bioterrorism: Perfectly Legal*, 49 Cath. U. L. Rev. 535, 539 (2000) ("[M]erely possessing dangerous pathogens is not a crime unless a prosecutor can prove that the possessor intended to use a pathogen as a weapon."); Timothy K. Gilman, *Search, Sentence, and (Don't) Sell: Combating the Threat of Biological Weapons Through Inspections, Criminalization, and Restrictions on Equipment*, 12 J. Transnat'l L. & Pol'y 217, 243 (2003) ("[T]he laws are ineffective at criminalizing behavior that takes place before the use of bioweapons in an attack.") (internal citations omitted); James W. Parrett, Jr., Note, *A Proactive Solution to the Inherent Dangers of Biotechnology: Using the Invention Secrecy Act to Restrict Disclosure of Threatening Biotechnology Patents*, 26 Wm. & Mary Envtl. L. & Pol'y Rev. 145, 155-56 (2001) ("[T]he effect of these laws is diluted by the fact that individuals must have the intent to use the biological agents").

Perhaps in response to such concerns, Congress inserted a new subsection (b) to § 175 as part of the Uniting and Strengthening America by Providing Appropriate Tools Required to Intercept and Obstruct Terrorism Act of 2001. *See* Pub. L. No. 107-56, § 817(1)(c), 115 Stat. 272, 385 (2001) (the "USA PATRIOT Act") (codified at 18 U.S.C. § 175(b)). Section 175(b) goes beyond § 175(a) by criminalizing knowing possession of "any biological agent, toxin, or delivery system of a type or in a quantity that, under the circumstances, is not reasonably justified by a prophylactic, protective, bona fide research, or other peaceful purpose." 18 U.S.C. § 175(b). This amendment to BWATA appears to address concerns about the potential difficulty of proving a defendant's intent to use biological agents as a weapon. *See* Keith Jamie Lewis, *The War on Terrorism Affects the Academy: Principal Post-September 11, 2001 Federal Anti-Terrorism Statutes, Regulations and Policies That Apply to Colleges and Universities*, 30 J.C. & U.L. 239, 244 (2004) ("This additional offense makes the mere knowing possession of agents or toxins a crime under certain circumstances, even if it is not known that the agents or toxins or their delivery systems are for use as a weapon.") (internal quotations omitted); Robert Eisig Bienstock, *Anti-Bioterrorism Research Post-9/11 Legislation: The USA PATRIOT Act and Beyond*, 30 J.C. & U.L. 465, 468 (2004) ("[I]nstead of having to prove use as a weapon, the prosecutor need only prove that the facts do not demonstrate one of the valued uses.").[207]

Congress has since added two other prohibitions to BWATA. First, Congress has prohibited the knowing possession and transfer of biological agents and toxins to unregistered persons and the knowing possession or shipment of certain agents to restricted persons, a designation including certain criminal defendants, convicted felons, fugitives, illegal aliens, and members of terrorist organizations. *See* USA PATRIOT Act § 817(2), 115 Stat. at 386 (codified at 18 U.S.C. § 175b); Public Health Security and Bioterrorism Preparedness and Response Act of 2002, Pub. L. No. 107-188 § 231, 116 Stat. 594, 660-62 (2002) (amending 18 U.S.C. § 175b);

Intelligence Reform and Terrorism Prevention Act of 2004, Pub. L. No. 108-458 § 6802(c), 118 Stat. 3638, 3767 (2004) ("IRTPA") (same).

Second, Congress has criminalized the production, engineering, synthesis, acquisition, transfer, receipt, possession, importation, exportation or use of "variola virus," the virus causing human smallpox. *See* IRTPA § 6906, 118 Stat. at 3773 (adding 18 U.S.C. § 175c). As with § 175, the more general statute governing biological agents and toxins, the variola virus statute applies extraterritorially. *See* 18 U.S.C. § 175c(b). Congress singled out the variola virus for special treatment because smallpox "is believed to pose the greatest potential threat for adverse public health impact and has a moderate to high potential for large-scale dissemination." IRTPA § 6902(a)(3), 118 Stat. at 3769. Moreover, Congress found that the variola virus has no legitimate purpose, *id.* § 6902(a)(5), 118 Stat. at 3769; and did not extend § 175's "peaceful purpose" affirmative defense to § 175c. Producing, engineering, synthesizing, acquiring, transferring, receiving, possessing, importing, or using of the variola virus for *any* purpose is criminal, unless authorized by the Secretary of Health and Human Services. *See* 18 U.S.C. § 175c(c)(2).[208]

I. Criminal Incitement Offenses: The Smith Act (18 U.S.C. § 2385) and Criminal Solicitation (18 U.S.C. § 373)

One recurring feature of terrorism cases is a figure of authority who incites followers to commit acts of violence. Often it is fiery orators and ideologues—sometimes Muslim clerics—who urge violence and terrorism by their followers against the United States. They may incite violent acts in person, through the media, or by issuing religious edicts such as fatwas. *See, e.g.*, Lawrence Wright, *The Looming Tower, Al-Qaeda and the Road to 9/11* ("*The Looming Tower*") 66 (2006) ("The theology of jihad requires a fatwa—a religious ruling—in order to consecrate actions that otherwise would be considered criminal."). In religious schools, such as some madrassas, scores of individuals may be incited—indeed, commanded—to direct violence against the United States and its citizens. The immediacy of the Internet and videotaped messages circulated across the globe have also been used effectively by terrorist leaders to exhort their followers, from afar, to commit violent acts against the United States and its citizens.[209]

It follows that terrorism cases in the United States frequently feature at their epicenter some form of speech that triggered the terrorist acts. For example, the indictment of Sheikh Omar Abdel Rahman portrayed him as an inciter of terrorist violence: he was alleged to have provided, through his words, religious authority and justification for terrorist acts. The indictment charged that Abdel Rahman was the "'emir' or leader of the Jihad Organization in the United States." Superseding Indictment at ¶ 4, *United States v. Rahman*, No. 93-cr-00181 (S.D.N.Y. Oct. 19, 1994) (Dkt. No. 361). It further charged that as the "emir," Abdel Rahman "provided necessary counsel regarding whether particular jihad actions, including acts of terrorism, were permissible under his radical interpretation of Islamic law" and that he urged direct terrorist acts by "solicit[ing] [members of the Jihad Organization] to commit violent jihad actions." *Id.* Similarly, Osama bin Laden has issued purported fatwas—Islamic decrees directing Muslims to certain actions—ordering direct violence. *See, e.g.*, Superseding Indictment at ¶¶ 3, 12(j), 12(o), 12(ww)-(zz), *United States v. Bin Laden*, No. 98-cr-01023 (S.D.N.Y. Mar. 12, 2001) (Dkt. No. 550) (describing Bin Laden's declaration of war against the United States and fatwas directing attacks against U.S. forces in the Arabian Peninsula and ordering the murder of any American, military or civilian); Indictment at ¶¶ 3, 5-10, *Moussaoui* (E.D. Va. Dec. 11, 2001) (Dkt. No. 1) (same). Courts and others have noted that fatwas or other inciting speech can be catalysts for terrorism by directing it and providing religious justification for it. *See, e.g., Rux v. Republic of Sudan*, 495 F. Supp. 2d 541, 551-52 (E.D. Va. 2007) (An al Qaeda fatwa "provided religious support for attacks directed at the U.S. Navy."); *The Homeland Security Implications of Radicalization: Hearing Before the Subcommittee on Intelligence, Information Sharing, and Terrorism Risk Assessment, House Committee on Homeland Security*, 109th Cong. 104, 45-60 (2006) (statement of Steven Emerson, Executive Director, the Investigative Project on Terrorism) (citing examples of terrorism cases in which defendants were motivated by speech to participate in terrorist acts) (hereinafter, "Emerson Statement").

1. The Smith Act

One potentially useful tool against such advocacy is the Smith Act, which was adopted in 1940 to protect the country from "violence, revolution and terrorism," *see Dennis v. United States*, 341 U.S. 494, 501 (1951) (Vinson, C.J., plurality); *accord United States v. Blumberg*, 136 F. Supp. 269, 270 (E.D. Pa. 1955) (quoting *Dennis*, 341 U.S. at 501), by prohibiting unlawful advocacy and membership in groups that engage in unlawful advocacy. *See* 18 U.S.C. § 2385. The statute criminalizes the advocacy, abetting, advising, or teaching of the "the duty, necessity, desirability, or propriety of overthrowing or destroying" any government in the United States (federal, state, or municipal) "by force or violence," whether through literature or other means. 18 U.S.C. § 2385. Although the statute has a checkered history as a tool for overreaching against purported Communists, the Supreme Court has "narrow[ed] the statutory language to avoid a construction which would violate the First Amendment." *United States v. Silverman*, 248 F.2d 671, 676 (2d Cir. 1957). The current state of First Amendment law is set forth in *Brandenburg v. Ohio*, which held that advocacy of the use of force cannot be proscribed unless it is "directed to inciting or producing imminent lawless action and is likely to incite or produce such action." 395 U.S. 444, 447 (1969).[210]

The membership clause of the Smith Act has been construed to require the prosecution to prove two elements: (1) the existence of a group that engages in unlawful advocacy; and (2) the defendant's active membership, with "knowledge of the [group's] illegal advocacy and a specific intent to bring about" the object of that advocacy "as speedily as circumstances would permit." *Scales v. United States*, 367 U.S. 203, 220-21 (1961); *accord Hellman v. United States*, 298 F.2d 810, 811-12 (9th Cir. 1961) (citing *Scales*, 367 U.S. at 220-21).[211] In *Scales*, the Court considered the "active membership" requirement crucial in deflecting concerns that the Smith Act violated the Fifth Amendment's prohibition against proving guilt by association. *See* 367 U.S. at 224-28. "[G]uilt is personal, and when the imposition of punishment on a status or on conduct can only be justified by reference to the relationship of that status or conduct to other concededly criminal activity ... , that relationship must be sufficiently substantial to satisfy the concept of personal guilt in order to withstand attack under the Due Process Clause of the Fifth Amendment." *Id.* at 224-25. The "active" membership requirement ensures that the statute reaches only those "having also a guilty knowledge and intent, and ... therefore prevents a conviction on what otherwise might be regarded as merely an expression of sympathy with the alleged criminal enterprise, unaccompanied by any significant action in its support or any commitment to undertake such action." *Id.* at 228. The specific intent requirement, on the other hand, is critical to avoid violation of the First

Amendment's rights of free association because "an active member with knowledge of both the legal and illegal aims [of his group] might personally intend to effectuate only the [group's] legal objectives." *Hellman*, 298 F.2d at 812; *see also Scales*, 367 U.S. at 228-29.

The Smith Act could conceivably be used to prosecute inciters of terrorism. Inflamed hortatory speech that leads to violence remains a consistent theme in terrorism cases and has not been limited to high-profile individuals such as Abdel Rahman and Bin Laden. *See, e.g.*, Superseding Indictment at ¶ 7, *United States v. Hassoun*, No. 04-cr-60001 (S.D. Fla. Nov. 17, 2005) (Dkt. No. 141) (alleging that the defendant published "a newsletter that promoted violent jihad as a religious obligation"); Indictment at 4, 6, *United States v. al-Timimi*, No. 04-cr-00385 (E.D. Va. Sept. 23, 2004) (Dkt. No. 1) (alleging that al-Timimi, a primary lecturer at an Islamic Center in Falls Church, Virginia, directed others that they had a duty to engage in "violent jihad" against American troops); *see generally* Emerson Statement (citing numerous cases in which there was evidence of inciting oral and written speech).

If a terrorist by dint of his authority or his religious standing commands others to "kill Americans and destroy their buildings and their government because it is evil," which is qualitatively similar to messages that have been reported in cases and the press, this is speech that is not worthy of protection under American law. Prosecutors may conclude that there is deterrent value in quelling the voices of influential figures who sanction murder, and that many terrorists will not take action without such sanction. They also may conclude that the *Brandenburg* test requiring an imminent threat is more easily met in an era when communications can be instantaneously disseminated around the world and where the weapons to be used may be nuclear or biological. On the other hand, the use of the Smith Act or a similar statute could raise First Amendment concerns. Prosecutions might end up focusing on Muslim clerics, which could be perceived as a selective attack on Islam and specifically its religious leaders. The use of the statute in this fashion would likely increase the policing of statements in mosques, pamphlets, and on the Internet. Such policing could overreach and ultimately debilitate the robust exchange of ideas on which our country prides itself, and could inhibit people from associating with controversial organizations. Some modern terrorism prosecutions, especially those based on the material support statutes, have implicated similar issues of balancing First and Fifth Amendment rights against the desire to prosecute individuals for their support of dangerous groups. Although courts have generally upheld material support convictions, speech-based prosecutions would go further and could be more controversial.

2. Criminal Solicitation

Alternatively, an inciter of violence could be prosecuted under the criminal solicitation statute, 18 U.S.C. § 373, which prohibits a person with "intent that another person engage in conduct constituting a crime described in Title 18" from "command[ing], induc[ing] or otherwise endeavor[ing] to persuade the other person to commit the felony." *Rahman*, 189 F.3d at 125 (internal quotations omitted). The acts constituting solicitation do not warrant First Amendment protection, even if they are religious in nature. *Id.* at 116-17.

Unlike the Smith Act, § 373 has already been successfully used by the government to prosecute individuals guilty of inciting terrorist violence, both inside and outside the Islamist extremist context. *See, e.g., Rahman*, 189 F.3d at 125-26 (affirming conviction of Sheikh Abdel Rahman for soliciting the bombing of U.S. military bases and the assassination of Egyptian President Hosni Mubarak); *United States v. Sattar*, 272 F. Supp. 2d 348, 374 (S.D.N.Y. 2003) (refusing to dismiss solicitation charge against individual who helped Abdel Rahman draft and disseminate a fatwa that "called on brother scholars everywhere in the Muslim world to do their part and issue a unanimous fatwah that urges the Muslim nation to fight the Jews and to kill them wherever they are") (internal quotations omitted); *Sattar*, 395 F. Supp. 2d at 82 (noting conviction on that solicitation charge); Superseding Indictment, *al-Timimi* (E.D. Va. Feb. 3, 2005) (Dkt. No. 47) (reflecting charging and conviction of defendant for solicitation of treason through his persuading defendants in *Khan* to fight against the United States in Afghanistan); *see also United States v. Hale*, 448 F.3d 971, 982-85 (7th Cir. 2006) (affirming conviction of white supremacist for soliciting the murder of a federal judge who entered judgment against his organization in a civil suit); *United States v. Polk*, 118 F.3d 286, 292-93 (5th Cir. 1997) (affirming conviction of individual for soliciting the destruction of federal buildings and the murder of the occupants of those buildings). Criminal solicitation also reaches inciting speech that the Smith Act does not, as one can be guilty under § 373 of inciting *any* felony under the federal criminal code, not merely overthrow of the government. *See, e.g., Rahman*, 189 F.3d at 125-26.

Nonetheless, for two reasons, the presence of § 373 could complement, rather than displace, the utility of the Smith Act. First, § 373 arguably contemplates the defendant's solicitation of particular individuals to engage in criminal acts, rather than the more open calls to overthrow the government that are prohibited by the Smith Act. *But see Sattar*, 272 F. Supp. 2d at 374 (unclear whether defendant was disseminating instruction to kill to specific individuals or to Muslim world at large). Secondly, the Smith Act carries a maximum sentence of twenty years' imprisonment, while criminal solicitation carries a maximum sentence equal to half the maximum sentence allowable for the predicate offense, or twenty years if the predicate offense carries a penalty of death or life imprisonment. *Compare* 18 U.S.C. § 2385 *with* 18 U.S.C. § 373. Thus, the Smith Act imposes a stiffer sentence than that which would accompany a charge of solicitation of any predicate crime with a sentence of less than forty years.

3. Considerations of Extraterritorial Application

Unlike the treason statute, the Smith Act and § 373 have no allegiance requirement. Further, unlike seditious conspiracy, the Smith Act and § 373 do not have the requirement of proving a conspiracy. These laws against incitement therefore can be used to target an individual who impels others to bloody deeds but keeps himself clear of the criminal group. Nor do the Smith Act or § 373 require the proof of non-speech conduct or linkage to a terrorist act or designated terrorist organization that the material support statutes require. However, unlike the treason statute and § 2339B, the Smith Act and § 373 do not include clauses applying them extraterritorially. Accordingly, it remains unclear under what circumstances they can be used to prosecute an individual who from abroad incites violence against the United States. *See, e.g., Ofori-Tenkorang v. Am. Int'l Group, Inc.*, 460 F.3d 296, 301 (2d Cir. 2006) ("Absent clear evidence of congressional intent to apply a statute beyond our borders, the statute will apply only to the territorial United States") (internal quotations and alteration omitted). Congress, however, has the power to remedy this gap in either or both of the incitement statutes. *See, e.g., In re French*, 440 F.3d 145, 151 (4th Cir. 2005) ("Although the presumption against extraterritoriality is important ... it nevertheless must give way when Congress exercises its undeniable authority to enforce its laws beyond the territorial boundaries of the United States") (internal quotations omitted).[212]

From a prosecutorial perspective, legislating extraterritorial application of the Smith Act and/or § 373 might be desirable. It would give the criminal justice system jurisdiction over individuals who incited imminent violence against the United States but who remained outside its borders. On the other hand, it would mean that, for example, a mullah from Pakistan, who preached violence against the United States in a mosque in Lahore, could travel to London or somewhere where the United States might cause his arrest. This hypothetical mullah could be arrested on a warrant for what he said in Pakistan and then extradited to the United States to be prosecuted for statements for which the Pakistani government did not see fit to arrest him.[213] Such a scenario could create foreign policy issues, and could even provoke the arrest of Americans abroad under foreign laws based on speech that is lawful in the United States. These considerations would be important in evaluating whether to apply either incitement statute extraterritorially.

VI.
Courts Have Consistently Exercised Jurisdiction Over Defendants Brought Before Them, Even if the Defendant Was Subjected to Forcible Treatment Outside the Scope of Normal Arrest or Extradition Proceedings

At the outset of a criminal case, the government must secure the defendant's presence in court to face the charges. Where the defendant is located within the United States, this is usually accomplished through an arrest by state or federal law enforcement officers or, on occasion, when the defendant voluntarily surrenders to the authorities. In either case, the defendant is promptly brought before a federal magistrate judge for his initial appearance and the criminal case begins.

When the defendant resides outside the United States, the government generally secures his presence in the United States through extradition proceedings. Under these proceedings, which are carried out pursuant to bilateral treaties between the United States and foreign countries, the U.S. government transmits a formal request, through diplomatic channels, to the authorities in the country where the defendant is believed to be present. The foreign government then handles the extradition request, which may include a separate request for the defendant's provisional arrest if he is not already in custody, according to procedures that are dictated by the treaty and by its own domestic laws and customs. If the foreign government grants extradition, it typically arranges for U.S. law enforcement agents to pick up the defendant at a specified time and place for transportation to the United States and presentment before a magistrate judge.

The standard procedures of arrest and extradition are well-established and non-controversial. Many defendants facing criminal charges in terrorism cases have been apprehended and brought before federal courts through these traditional means. These cases present no unusual or difficult issues.

In other international terrorism cases, however, defendants have been brought into the criminal justice system by unconventional means, including transfer by U.S. military authorities—sometimes after lengthy periods of detention and interrogation—or informal rendition by foreign officials outside the extradition process. In either scenario, the circumstances surrounding the defendant's apprehension may be murky, and the defendant may allege that he was subjected to forcible treatment or prolonged detention. Nonetheless, these procedures do not generally preclude a federal court from asserting jurisdiction over the defendant once he appears before a magistrate judge and the criminal case begins.

Under the *Ker-Frisbie* doctrine, named for a pair of Supreme Court cases decided respectively in 1886 and 1952, the constitutional requirements of due process are satisfied by affording the defendant all of the protections of the criminal justice system once the criminal case begins, and there is ordinarily no basis for a court's refusal to assert jurisdiction over the defendant based on irregularities that may have occurred during the process of bringing the defendant to court. In *Ker v. Illinois*, a messenger from the United States traveled to Peru, armed with formal extradition papers, to secure the extradition of an individual who had been indicted for larceny and embezzlement in Illinois state court. See 119 U.S. 436, 438 (1886). Upon arrival in Peru, however, the messenger did not serve the extradition papers or even make contact with the

Peruvian government, but instead forcibly abducted the defendant and held him as a prisoner on a lengthy ocean voyage to Hawaii and then California, from which the defendant was transported, still in custody, to Illinois. *See id.* at 438-39. On appeal, the Supreme Court rejected the defendant's claim that the charges against him should have been dismissed on account of these events, holding that "for mere irregularities in the manner in which [the defendant] may be brought into custody of the law, we do not think he is entitled to say that he should not be tried at all for the crime with which he is charged in a regular indictment." *Id.* at 440.

In *Frisbie v. Collins*, the Supreme Court reaffirmed this principle. *See* 342 U.S. 519 (1952). *Frisbie* was a habeas corpus action brought by a prisoner in Michigan who alleged that, while he was living in Chicago, Michigan police officers forcibly seized and blackjacked him before taking him to Michigan to face murder charges that were pending against him. *See id.* at 520. The prisoner alleged that his subsequent trial and conviction violated the Due Process Clause of the Fourteenth Amendment and the Federal Kidnapping Act, but the Court rejected the prisoner's claim. *See id.* at 521-23. The Court noted that it had "never departed from the rule announced in *Ker v. Illinois* ... that the power of a court to try a person for crime is not impaired by the fact that he had been brought within the court's jurisdiction by reason of a 'forcible abduction.'" *Id.* at 522 (quoting *Ker*, 119 U.S. at 444)). As the *Frisbie* Court reasoned, this rule of law:

> rest[s] on the sound basis that due process of law is satisfied when one present in court is convicted of crime after having been fairly apprized of the charges against him and after a fair trial in accordance with constitutional procedural safeguards. There is nothing in the Constitution that requires a court to permit a guilty person rightfully convicted to escape justice because he was brought to trial against his will.

Id.

Since *Frisbie*, courts have identified two narrow circumstances in which a defendant's irregular abduction might cause a federal court to lose jurisdiction over a criminal case: (a) if the abduction violates an explicit provision of a relevant extradition treaty or (b) if the abduction is accompanied by torture or other extreme conduct that "shocks the conscience" of the court. *See, e.g., United States v. Best, 304 F.3d 308, 312 (3d Cir. 2002); United States v. Anderson, 472 F.3d 662, 666 (9th Cir. 2006).* However, to our knowledge no defendant has successfully challenged a court's jurisdiction based on irregularities in the process by which he was captured or brought to court.

In *United States v. Alvarez-Machain*, the Supreme Court rejected a defendant's claim that his capture violated the extradition treaty between the United States and Mexico. *See* 504 U.S. 655 (1992). The defendant in *Alvarez-Machain* was a Mexican physician who was accused of participating in the kidnapping and murder of a Drug Enforcement Administration ("DEA") agent in Mexico. *See id.* at 657. When the Mexican authorities did not cooperate with the DEA's efforts to have the defendant handed over to the United States, a private party (who was paid by the DEA) forcibly kidnapped the defendant from his office in Guadalajara, Mexico, and then flew him against his will to Texas, where he was handed over to DEA agents. *See id.* at 657 n.2. Noting that the Mexican government had submitted letters protesting the abduction of the defendant, lower courts found that the abduction had violated the extradition treaty between the United States and Mexico and dismissed the indictment. *See id.* at 658-59. The Supreme Court, however, reinstated the indictment on grounds that the extradition treaty did not expressly prohibit forcible abductions. *See id.* at 663-66 (noting that "the current version of the Treaty, signed in 1978, does not attempt to establish a rule that would in any way curtail the effect of *Ker*"). The Court also rejected the argument that the treaty contained an implied term, rooted in customary international law, that prohibited each party from kidnapping the other party's citizens as a means of securing their presence in court. *See id.* at 667-69.

In the wake of *Alvarez-Machain*, lower courts have repeatedly rejected arguments that forcible abductions violate extradition treaties, noting that such arguments can prevail only if there is a violation of explicit language in the treaty. For example, in *Kasi v. Angelone*, defendant Mir Aimal Kasi sought habeas corpus relief after being convicted, in Virginia state court, of fatally shooting two CIA employees and wounding three others with an AK-47 in January 1993 as the employees drove to work in Northern Virginia. *See* 300 F.3d 487, 490-91 (4th Cir. 2002). After the murders, Kasi fled to Pakistan and remained a fugitive for the next four and a half years, residing mainly in Afghanistan. *See id.* at 491. In 1997, FBI agents abducted him from a hotel room in Pakistan and then transported him, hooded and shackled, by vehicle and air to a secret location where he was held "in a jail-like facility." *Id.* Two days later, Kasi was transported by U.S. military aircraft to Northern

Virginia to face the murder charges in Virginia state court. *See id.* On habeas review, the Fourth Circuit rejected Kasi's claim that his abduction was improper, reasoning that the U.S.-Pakistan extradition treaty did not expressly prohibit forcible abduction outside normal extradition process. *See id.* at 493-500.[214]

The second possible exception to the *Ker-Frisbie* doctrine—for abductions involving torture or other extreme conduct that shocks the conscience—has an uncertain legal footing and has never been applied to require a court to dismiss charges against a defendant. The leading case is *United States v. Toscanino*, in which the defendant alleged that he was forcibly seized near his home in Montevideo, Uruguay; driven, bound and blindfolded, to the Brazilian border; tortured and interrogated for seventeen days in Brazil by individuals including a U.S. federal law enforcement agent; and then drugged and transported to the United States to face federal narcotics charges. *See* 500 F.2d 267, 269-70 (2d Cir. 1974). The *Toscanino* defendant raised allegations of torture while in Brazil, including denial of adequate sleep and food; forced standing and walking for hours at a time; pinching of his fingers with metal pliers; and electric shocks applied to his earlobes, toes, and genitals. *See id.* at 270. The Second Circuit concluded that these facts, if proven, would raise a serious due process issue that would entitle the defendant to relief, potentially including dismissal of the charges. *See id.* at 275-76, 276 n.6. The court remanded for a possible evidentiary hearing. *See id.* at 281. On remand, however, the defendant failed to come forward with an affidavit or any other evidence to support the allegation that U.S. agents participated in his alleged mistreatment in South America, and the district court denied his motion to dismiss the indictment. *See United States v. Toscanino*, 398 F. Supp. 916, 917 (E.D.N.Y. 1975).

As years have gone by, some courts have expressed doubt as to the soundness of *Toscanino*, in part because of subsequent Supreme Court decisions that tend to undermine much of the Second Circuit's reasoning. *See United States v. Matta-Ballasteros*, 71 F.3d 754, 763 n.3 (9th Cir. 1995) (noting that the Second Circuit's prediction about the likely course of future Supreme Court decisions in this area "was not prescient"); *Best*, 304 F.3d at 312 ("Subsequent decisions of the Supreme Court indicate that there is reason to doubt the soundness of the *Toscanino* exception, even as limited to its flagrant facts").[215] Other courts have continued to hold out the possibility that an indictment could be dismissed based on outrageous conduct that shocks the conscience, *see, e.g., Anderson*, 472 F.3d at 666 (noting that "the Ker/Frisbie doctrine does not apply … [if] the United States government engaged in 'misconduct of the most shocking and outrageous kind'" to obtain the defendant's presence in court) (quoting *Matta-Ballesteros*, 71 F.3d at 764). But this doctrine has not been tested, and its contours are uncertain at best. One reason why the validity of *Toscanino* has never been clearly settled is that no case has arisen in which there has been credible evidence that U.S. government officials participated in torturing an individual before he was transferred to the civilian court system. If such a case were presented, the viability of *Toscanino* would be squarely tested.

In the Philippine Airline Bombing case, defendant Ramzi Yousef sought to invoke *Toscanino* by alleging that he was abducted from his relatives' home in Pakistan and then tortured for several months in a desert jail cell before being turned over to U.S. law enforcement agents in Islamabad on February 8, 1995. *See United States v. Yousef*, 927 F. Supp. 673, 677 (S.D.N.Y. 1996). However, Judge Kevin Thomas Duffy rejected Yousef's allegations as "incredible," citing evidence that Yousef had traveled in Thailand during the period that he claimed to have undergone torture in the Pakistani desert. *Id.* at 676-77. Judge Duffy also noted that Yousef did not provide any credible evidence that U.S. agents participated in the alleged torture and, more generally, that *Toscanino* had been "interpreted … narrowly" and that no court had ever granted relief under that case. *Id.*

In the *Padilla* case, where the defendant was held in military custody in South Carolina for some three-and-a-half years before being turned over to law enforcement authorities in Miami to face criminal charges, the district court rejected the defendant's claim that the conditions of his military detention and interrogation in the Naval Brig constituted outrageous conduct sufficient to warrant dismissal of the indictment.[216] *See generally United States v. Padilla*, No. 04-cr-60001, 2007 WL 1079090 (S.D. Fla. Apr. 9, 2007). The court noted that *Toscanino* had been questioned by the Eleventh Circuit and, more generally, that little clear guidance exists on the dismissal of an indictment based on outrageous government conduct. *See id.* at *2-3, *5 n.11. As the district court noted in *Padilla*, this "doctrine has never been effectively applied in any context" and has almost always been discussed in the quite different context of entrapment-type scenarios where the government was intimately involved in the events leading to the defendant's alleged violation of the law. *Id.* at *2-3 (discussing cases such as *United States v. Russell*, 411 U.S. 423 (1973), and *Hampton v. United States*, 425 U.S. 484 (1976), both of which involved undercover narcotics investigations in which the police provided defendants with the means to sell or manufacture the controlled substance).[217] The court, however, did take into account Padilla's conditions of confinement in the Naval Brig when sentencing Padilla, ordering seventeen years and four months in prison instead of the life sentence the government sought. *See* Judgment, *Padilla* (S.D. Fla. Jan. 22, 2008) (Dkt. No. 1333); Kirk Semple, *Padilla Gets 17 Years in Conspiracy Case*, N.Y. Times, Jan. 23, 2008, at A14.[218]

VII.
In the Overwhelming Majority of Cases, Existing Law Provides an Adequate Basis to Detain or Appropriately Monitor Terrorism Suspects

What should happen when the government identifies a person who is suspected of participating in international terrorism? Often, the short answer is that the suspect should be detained or monitored closely by the government. In cases where criminal charges have already been filed, or can be filed in short order, the criminal justice system is well-equipped to detain or appropriately monitor terrorism suspects. The government also has ample authority to detain aliens suspected of complicity in terrorism who are subject to removal under the federal immigration laws. Further, under the law of war, the military may capture and detain enemy combatants "to prevent captured individuals from returning to the field of battle and taking up arms once again." *Hamdi v. Rumsfeld*, 542 U.S. 507, 518 (2004); *see also id.* ("detention of individuals" who fought against the United States in Afghanistan as part of the Taliban is a "fundamental and accepted ... incident to war" and may extend "for the duration of the particular conflict in which they were captured"); W. Winthrop, *Military Law and Precedents* 788 (rev. 2d ed. 1920) ("A prisoner of war is no convict; his imprisonment is a simple war measure"); *In re Terito*, 156 F.2d 142, 145 (9th Cir. 1946) ("The object of capture is to prevent the captured individual from serving the enemy").[219]

Over the years, acting under these provisions of civilian and military law, the government has been able to lawfully detain a large number of individuals suspected of terrorism. However, under longstanding principles of American law, preventive detention is not generally permitted within our civilian justice system. As a result, in some cases where the government has been unable or unwilling to proceed with criminal charges or immigration proceedings following an arrest by civilian law enforcement agents, it has faced difficulty in its efforts to detain an individual without charges. In some of these situations, the government has invoked controversial tactics such as aggressive theories of military detention. The result, in a handful of exceptional cases such as those of Jose Padilla and Ali Saleh Kahla al-Marri, both of which are discussed in detail below, has been protracted litigation.

Reasonable persons might differ as to whether, in extraordinary circumstances, it is necessary for the government to wield authority to hold an individual in preventive detention. While other countries permit it on a limited basis,[220] our history reflects a longstanding aversion to the practice, save shameful episodes such as the mass detention of Japanese-Americans during World War II. Some have suggested that this traditional reluctance to hold individuals in preventive or investigative detention can no longer be maintained given the contemporary risk to our national security. *See, e.g.*, Jack L. Goldsmith & Neal Katyal, *The Terrorists' Court*, N.Y. Times, July 11, 2007, at A19;[221] Jack L. Goldsmith & Eric A. Posner, *A Better Way on Detainees*, Wash. Post, Aug. 4, 2006, at A17.[222] However, we do not believe that the need for a brand-new scheme of administrative detention has been established. In the overwhelming majority of terrorism cases that have arisen to date, the government has been able to lawfully detain individuals based on criminal or immigration charges or based on non-controversial applications of the law of war. In other words, cases such as *Padilla* and *al-Marri* are rare exceptions, they are not the rule, and we believe that it is a mistake to draw generalized conclusions about the efficacy of the criminal justice system from these isolated and in some ways anomalous cases. Further, a brand-new administrative detention scheme would reflect a significant shift in our country's traditional approach to this very important subject, could be susceptible to abuse, and would raise serious constitutional issues. In this White Paper, we do not respond to specific proposals for a new administrative detention scheme, but we do believe that the foregoing considerations are important.

A. Detention of Persons Charged with a Federal Crime

After a defendant is charged with a federal crime, a federal magistrate judge must promptly convene a hearing, at which the defendant is entitled to be represented by counsel, to determine whether the defendant should be detained or released on bail. *See* Fed. R. Crim. P. 5. The magistrate judge's bail decision is governed by the Bail Reform Act, 18 U.S.C. § 3142, which generally applies to alleged terrorists in the same way that it applies to criminal suspects. *See* 18 U.S.C. § 3242(f)(1).

The Bail Reform Act requires the release of the defendant on the "least restrictive" condition or conditions that the "judicial officer determines will reasonably assure the appearance of the person as required and the safety of any other person and the community." 18 U.S.C. § 3142(c)(1)(B). Generally speaking, pre-trial detention of a defendant is only appropriate "upon a judicial finding that 'no condition or combination of conditions will reasonably assure the appearance of the person as required and the safety of any other person and the community.'" *United States v. Goba*, 240 F. Supp. 2d 242, 246 (W.D.N.Y. 2003) (quoting 18 U.S.C. § 3142(e)). However, the Bail Reform Act also includes a legislatively mandated presumption that a defendant charged with federal terrorism offenses should be detained. Specifically, § 3142(e) provides that a rebuttable presumption exists that no condition or combination of conditions will reasonably assure the safety of any other person and the community where the defendant is facing federal terrorism charges or has been convicted of or released from prison within five years on similar charges. This presumption shifts the burden onto the terrorism suspect to demonstrate that he will not pose a risk to the community or danger of flight. In litigating a detention hearing, the government is permitted to introduce hearsay and other evidence that would not be admissible at trial under the Federal Rules of Evidence. *See* 18 U.S.C. § 3142(f). Thus, the government may proffer information without being required to produce a witness with firsthand knowledge or, in some circumstances, without disclosing the source or means by which the information was gathered. *See id.*

In practice, courts have applied these standards and, depending on the individual defendant, have either ordered detention without bail or fashioned an appropriate bail package. *See, e.g.*, Order of Detention, *United States v. al-Moayad*, No. 03-cr-01322 (E.D.N.Y. Nov. 17, 2003) (Dkt. No. 6); Order, *United States v. Warsame*, No. 04-cr-00029 (D. Minn. Feb. 9, 2004) (Dkt. No. 11) (ordering that Warsame be detained pending trial); Order, *Warsame* (D. Minn. Feb. 16, 2007) (Dkt. No. 93) (denying Warsame's motion for release from custody); Order Setting Conditions of Release, *United States v. al-Timimi*, No. 04-cr-00385 (E.D. Va. Sept. 24, 2004) (Dkt. No. 2) (ordering al-Timimi's release upon posting $75,000 secured bond and satisfaction of additional conditions); Order Setting Conditions of Release, *United States v. Idris*, No. 02-cr-00306 (E.D. Va. Mar. 22, 2002) (Dkt. No. 5) (ordering Idris released on a personal recognizance bond with conditions).

The prosecution of Wadih el-Hage, charged in the Embassy Bombings case, highlights the government's ability to ensure that terrorism defendants are not only detained pre-trial, but detained for a lengthy period if necessary. El-Hage was initially arrested on September 16, 1998, five weeks after the bombings, and charged with eight counts of perjury and three counts of false statements in connection with a grand jury investigation of terrorism. *See United States v. el-Hage*, 213 F.3d 74, 77 (2d Cir. 2000). Despite the non-violent charges and despite the fact that el-Hage was an American citizen who had lived with his family in Texas for the better part of twenty-two years, el-Hage was detained as a flight risk. *See id.* This decision by the magistrate judge was based in part on el-Hage's extensive foreign ties and foreign travel and the underlying contention that el-Hage had significant al Qaeda ties. *See id.* Upon his detention, the government imposed special security measures on el-Hage, which resulted in his solitary confinement for the first fifteen months of detention and a limitation on his ability to contact anyone other than family members. *See id.* at 78. After superseding charges including conspiracy counts were brought against el-Hage, a trial date was set such that his pre-trial detention period was expected to be between thirty and thirty-three months. *See id.*

at 76. El-Hage challenged the length and nature of his pre-trial detention as a violation of his due process rights. *See id.*

On appeal, the Second Circuit upheld el-Hage's pre-trial detention period. *See id.* at 81. In measuring the constitutionality of el-Hage's detention, the court weighed four factors: (1) its length, (2) the extent of the prosecution's responsibility for delay of the trial, (3) the gravity of the charges, and (4) the strength of the evidence upon which detention was based, i.e. the evidence of risk of flight and dangerousness. *See id.* at 79 (citing *United States v. el-Gabrowny*, 35 F.3d 63, 65 (2d Cir. 1994)). Although the court recognized the length of el-Hage's pre-trial detention, it placed a significant emphasis on the gravity of the charges against el-Hage and his risk of flight. *See id.* at 80. In doing so, the court cited the potential danger of el-Hage's ability to share non-classified pre-trial discovery materials as a basis for his detention. *See id.*

The factors upon which the Second Circuit focused in upholding el-Hage's detention are likely to be present in other terrorism prosecutions, and therefore it is no surprise that most of these defendants are subject to pre-trial detention. The co-conspirators of foreign terrorist entities necessarily have ties abroad and a record of foreign travel that heighten their risk of flight. The seriousness of terrorism charges is self-evident. And many terrorism cases also present the same risks of pre-trial discovery as in *el-Hage*.

B. Detention of Aliens Subject to Removal

Complementing its authority to seek detention for individuals who have been charged with a crime, the government also may arrest, and in many circumstances detain, aliens accused of being unlawfully present in the United States. If determined to be unlawfully present in the United States, aliens are subject to the immigration removal process, which affords the government the opportunity to detain some terrorist suspects in those instances where it otherwise may be unable or unwilling to bring criminal charges.

Under 8 U.S.C. § 1226(a), "[o]n a warrant issued by the Attorney General, an alien may be arrested and detained pending a decision on whether the alien is to be removed from the United States." 8 U.S.C. § 1226(a).[223] Detention is mandatory in certain situations—for example, where the alien was previously convicted of an aggravated felony or is reasonably believed likely to be engaged in terrorist activity.

See 8 U.S.C. §§ 1226(c)(1), 1226a(a)(3). Otherwise, the statute vests the Attorney General with broad discretion to determine whether the alien should be detained in immigration custody or released on bond or parole pending removal proceedings. *See* 8 U.S.C. § 1226(a). Under the statute, the Attorney General's "discretionary judgment" regarding detention under the immigration statute "shall not be subject to judicial review" and "[n]o court may set aside any action or decision by the Attorney General under [§ 1226] regarding the detention or release of any alien." 8 U.S.C. § 1226(e).

The Supreme Court has held that mandatory detention under 8 U.S.C. § 1226(c) does not violate a defendant's due process rights. *See Demore v. Kim*, 538 U.S. 510, 513 (2003) (holding that "Congress, justifiably concerned that deportable criminal aliens who are not detained continue to engage in crime and fail to appear for their removal hearings in large numbers, may require that persons ... be detained for the brief period necessary for their removal proceedings."). At the end of the proceedings in immigration court, when a final order of removal has been entered, the government generally has ninety days to secure the alien's removal, but this period may be extended in some cases. *See* 8 U.S.C. §§ 1231(a)(1), 1231(a)(6). In *Zadvydas v. Davis*, the Supreme Court held that an alien's detention during the post-removal period cannot be indefinite and must be limited to a period reasonably necessary to bring about that alien's removal from the United States. *See* 533 U.S. 678, 682 (2001). The Supreme Court recognized six months as a presumptively reasonable amount of time to remove an alien. *See id.* at 701. After the six-month period, if an alien provides good reason to believe that there is no significant likelihood of removal in the reasonably foreseeable future, the government must provide evidence sufficient to rebut that showing. *See id.*[224]

In the wake of the 9/11 attacks, the government aggressively used its immigration enforcement authority to arrest and detain hundreds of aliens. Within months of the 9/11 attacks, law enforcement authorities had detained, at least for questioning, more than 1,000 individuals nationwide. *See Center for Nat'l Security Studies v. Dep't of Justice*, 331 F.3d 918, 921 (D.C. Cir. 2003) ("In the course of the post-September 11 investigation, the government interviewed over one thousand individuals about whom concern had arisen"); *Elmaghraby. v. Ashcroft*, No. 04-cv-01809, 2005 WL 2375202, at *2 (E.D.N.Y. Sept. 27, 2005) (noting that in the months following 9/11, the FBI arrested and detained "thousands of Arab

Muslim men ... as part of its investigation into the attacks"); Teresa A. Miller, *Blurring the Boundaries Between Immigration and Crime Control After September 11th*, 25 B.C. Third World L.J. 81, 90 (2005). Eleven months after the attacks, 762 non-citizens were reportedly in INS custody, detained on immigration violations. *See* U.S. Dep't of Justice, Office of the Inspector General, *The September 11 Detainees: A Review of the Treatment of Aliens Held On Immigration Charges In Connection With The Investigation of the September 11 Attacks* ("*OIG September 11 Detainees Report*") (June 2003);[225] U.S. Dep't of Justice, Office of the Inspector General, *Supplemental Report on September 11 Detainees' Allegations of Abuse at the Metropolitan Detention Center in Brooklyn, New York* (Dec. 2003);[226] *see also Center for Nat'l Security Studies*, 331 F.3d at 921 ("Over 700 individuals were detained on INS charges"). One high-ranking Department of Justice official told the Inspector General that the strategy was "we have to hold these people until we find out what is going on," and that it was understood that the Department of Justice was detaining individuals on immigration charges that had not been enforced in the past. U.S. Dep't of Justice, *OIG September 11 Detainees Report*, at 13.[227]

The sweep was instructive because it demonstrated that non-citizens are vulnerable to detention and/or prosecution based on immigration charges. *See id.* at 5 ("It is important to note that nearly all of the 762 aliens we examined violated immigration laws, either by overstaying their visas, by entering the country illegally, or some other immigration violation.") At the same time, however, it prompted accusations of racial profiling and overbroad enforcement, which can have negative consequences for law enforcement. *See, e.g.*, Martha Minow, *The Constitution as Black Box During National Emergencies: Comment on Bruce Ackerman's "Before the Next Attack: Preserving Civil Liberties in an Age of Terrorism"*, 75 Fordham L. Rev. 593, 603 (2006) (criticizing Department of Homeland Security for "the round-up of Muslims, resulting in widespread mistreatment of detainees and not one charge related to terrorism"). If sweeps are based—or perceived to be based—on nationality or ethnicity, they may foster ethnic or racial prejudice and, on a pragmatic level, could chill the cooperation that law enforcement may otherwise receive from law-abiding members of minority communities.

In addition, some immigration detainees brought legal challenges to the sweep, raising serious allegations of abuse and other violations of the rights of those detained. In general, courts have upheld the government's authority to detain individuals but have allowed claims based on mistreatment while in custody to proceed. In one case, eight alien detainees contended "that the government used their status as illegal aliens as a cover, as an excuse to hold them in jail while it pursued its real interest—determining whether they were terrorists, or could help catch terrorists." *Turkmen v. Ashcroft*, No. 02-cv-02307, 2006 WL 1662663, at *1 (E.D.N.Y. June 14, 2006). In dismissing this claim, the court accepted that the government held the detainees in jail not because it needed the time to remove them on immigration charges, but because the government wanted the detainees available if it was determined that they could be charged with criminal offenses. *See id.* The court supported the prosecution strategy of pursuing immigration charges with an eye toward a more serious criminal prosecution, stating that: "[T]he government may use its authority to detain illegal aliens pending deportation even if its real interest is building criminal cases against them." *Id.* The court, however, did not dismiss the detainees' claims of physically and psychologically abusive treatment at the prison facilities where they were detained, and that portion of the case is still pending. *See, e.g., id.* at *1, *4-*21.[228]

In addition to providing an independent basis for the government to detain individuals suspected of terrorism, the immigration laws can provide a backstop for the government in criminal cases where the bail statute would otherwise require a defendant's release. The case of the *United States v. al-Shannaq* is instructive. *See* 02-cr-00319 (D. Md. July 2, 2002). In 2002, Rasmi Subhi Salah al-Shannaq, a Jordanian resident who was the roommate of two of the 9/11 hijackers, Hani Hanjour and Nawaf al-Hazmi, was arrested for illegally purchasing a visa. *See Hijackers' Roommate Confesses To Fake Visa*, Daily Press (Newport News, Va.), Nov. 24, 2002, at A7; *Sept. 11 Hijackers' Roommate Enters Plea*, S. Fla. Sun-Sentinel, Nov. 24, 2002, at 9A. Al-Shannaq was indicted by a federal grand jury on a visa fraud charge. *See* Indictment, *al-Shannaq* (D. Md. July 2, 2002) (Dkt. No. 1); William Douglas, *Illegal Visas Probed: Feds Seek Links Between Fraudulent Operation, 9/11 Hijackers*, Newsday (Long Island, NY), July 11, 2002, at A07. Al-Shannaq pled not guilty, and U.S. Magistrate Judge Susan Gauvey of the District of Maryland released him under twenty-four-hour electronic monitoring into his family's custody in Baltimore after they raised $434,000 to secure his bail. *See* Minute Entry, *al-Shannaq* (D. Md. July 11, 2002); Appearance Bonds & Agreements to Forfeit Property, *al-*

Shannaq (D. Md. July 10, 2002) (Dkt. Nos. 9-21); Douglas, *Illegal Visas Probed*; Warren P. Strobel & Cassio Furtado, *3 in Visa Plot Have Hijack Links*, Miami Herald, July 11, 2002, at 3A. The magistrate judge ruled that the government could not continue to detain al-Shannaq on the fraudulent visa count because prosecutors had not produced evidence linking him to terrorism and because the court did not consider him to be a flight risk. *See* Douglas, *Illegal Visas Probed*. However, the government then turned al-Shannaq over to the INS and advised the court that al-Shannaq was not going to be released on bail and was instead facing an immigration detainer based on an immigration-related charge that he had overstayed his visa. Strobel & Furtado, *3 in Visa Plot Have Hijack Links*. About four months later, al-Shannaq entered into a plea agreement, was returned to the criminal justice system, pled guilty to fraudulently obtaining a visa, and was sentenced to time served. *See* Judgment, *al-Shannaq* (D. Md. Nov. 22, 2002) (Dkt. No. 29); *Hijackers' Roommate Confesses To Fake Visa*. Al-Shannaq was then remanded into the custody of immigration authorities and was subsequently deported to Jordan. *See Hijackers' Roommate Confesses To Fake Visa*.

C. The Material Witness Statute

In situations where the government is unable or unwilling to file criminal charges and a person is not subject to detention under immigration laws, the government has only limited authority under the criminal law to hold the person in custody. In recent years, the government has invoked the material witness statute in terrorism cases, but that statute imposes numerous procedural safeguards and may properly be used only for a limited period of time.

The material witness statute states that if a person's testimony is shown to be "material in a criminal proceeding, and if it is shown that it may become impracticable to secure the presence of the person by subpoena," then a court may issue an arrest warrant for the individual, who thereafter must appear before a magistrate judge for a bail hearing. 18 U.S.C. § 3144. The statute provides, however, that detention is inappropriate where the testimony can be secured by deposition and "further detention is not necessary to prevent the failure of justice." *Id*. Moreover, Federal Rule of Criminal Procedure 46(h)(2) requires judicial oversight of the government's use of the statute to detain material witnesses:

> An attorney for the government must report biweekly to the court, listing each material witness held in custody for more than 10 days pending indictment, arraignment, or trial. For each material witness listed in the report, an attorney for the government must state why the witness should not be released with or without a deposition being taken under Rule 15(a).

Fed. R. Crim. P. 46(h)(2). In light of this text, it is clear that the material witness statute offers only limited authority for detaining individuals without charge.

After the 9/11 terrorist attacks, Attorney General Ashcroft "announc[ed] a policy of 'aggressive detention' of material witnesses." *See* Serrin Turner & Stephen J. Schulhofer, Brennan Ctr. for Justice at N.Y.U. Sch. of L., *The Secrecy Problem in Terrorism Trials* 38 (2005).[229] Although the precise number of individuals detained as material witnesses is unclear due to grand jury secrecy rules, the American Civil Liberties Union ("ACLU") has documented more than seventy cases based on interviews with witnesses, their family members, lawyers, and government officials. *See* Anjana Malhotra, International Civil Liberties Report, *Overlooking Innocence: Refashioning the Material Witness Law to Indefinitely Detain Muslims Without Charges* 1-2 (Dec. 10, 2004)[230]; *see also* Human Rights Watch & ACLU, *Witness to Abuse: Human Rights Abuses Under Material Witness Law Post September 11* ("*Witness to Abuse*") (June 2005).[231] According to a joint Human Rights Watch and ACLU report, of the seventy post-9/11 material witness cases, over one-third of those arrested were incarcerated under material witness warrants for at least two months, some for more than six months, and at least one individual spent over a year in prison.[232] *See* Human Rights Watch & ACLU, *Witness to Abuse*, at 3. The government was accused in some cases of misusing the material witness statute to detain terrorism suspects—rather than material witnesses—while it developed evidence to bring charges or identified another means of detaining the suspect. The *Washington Post* has reported that twenty of the forty-four persons detained on material witness warrants in 2002 were never brought before a grand jury. *See* Steve Farinau & Margot Williams, *Material Witness Law Has Many in Limbo: Nearly Half Held in War on Terror Haven't Testified*, Wash. Post, Nov. 24, 2002, at A01.[233] On the other hand, individuals who were involved in the Justice Department's review process of the material witness warrants have asserted strongly that there was painstaking review of the basis for each material witness warrant issued, even before there was judicial review. Law enforcement officials have also noted that all individuals were provided with counsel, many were released, and others were detained only on consent of counsel or after criminal charges were filed.

The spate of material witness warrants used after the 9/11 attacks demonstrates the urgency felt by law enforcement to investigate what had happened and potentially disrupt future incidents. Indeed, officials involved in the investigation were feverishly trying to determine whether there would be a second wave of attacks. *See, e.g.*, Nat'l Comm'n on Terrorist Attacks Upon the U.S., *The 9/11 Commission Report* 326 (2004) (hereafter "*9/11 Commission Report*").

However, the use of the material witness statute after 9/11 does raise legal questions. Many of the individuals who were arrested on material witness warrants after 9/11 were likely viewed as potential suspects in addition to being material witnesses. Indeed, in most complex criminal investigations, it often is not clear whether an individual is primarily a witness or primarily a suspect; often, they are potentially both. In many cases, as may well have been the fact after the 9/11 attacks, the government may suspect an individual but also want that individual's testimony if he is willing to give it. In such a scenario, is it proper for the government to seek an individual's arrest and detention as a material witness?

Although the law on this point is not settled, we believe that the courts would uphold the use of the material witness statute in such a "mixed motive" case so long as the government has a concurrent, real, and good-faith intention to seek the individual's testimony as a material witness. Such an approach would be faithful to the purpose of the material witness statute without requiring courts to embark, in all cases, on open-ended, and probably futile, dissections of prosecutors' subjective motivations in an effort to divine the "dominant" reason for seeking a particular individual's arrest, even assuming the doubtful proposition that the dominant motive can be the determining factor in deciding the appropriateness of the material witness warrant. Of course, if a court were confronted with evidence that the government was abusing the material witness statute by seeking arrest warrants with no intention of calling the individuals as witnesses, then judicial action would be warranted.

The case of Osama Awadallah makes clear both the legitimate uses and the limitations of the material witness statute. Awadallah was a student in San Diego and an acquaintance of two of the 9/11 hijackers. *See United States v. Awadallah*, 349 F.3d 42, 45-48 (2d Cir. 2003). His phone number was found in the vehicle that one of the hijackers had abandoned at Dulles Airport in Virginia. *See id.* Ten days after the 9/11 attacks, the government arrested him in San Diego, as a material witness in a Southern District of New York grand jury investigation regarding the 9/11 attacks. *See id.* Awadallah appeared before a magistrate judge in San Diego, who ordered him detained pending his removal to New York. *See id.* at 47. Upon his arrival in New York on October 2, 2001, Awadallah appeared before then-Chief Judge Michael B. Mukasey, who ordered his continued detention. *See id.* In mid-October 2001, Awadallah appeared twice before the grand jury and testified about his knowledge of the 9/11 hijackers. *See id.* at 48. He was subsequently indicted for perjury based on his allegedly false denials of knowing one of the hijackers and also based on his denials that certain handwriting was his own. *See id.* A jury eventually acquitted Awadallah of these charges.[234] *See* Judgment of Acquittal, *United States v. Awadallah*, No. 01-cr-01026 (S.D.N.Y. Nov. 20, 2006) (Dkt. No. 116).

During pre-trial proceedings, the Second Circuit upheld the validity of the indictment against Awadallah. *See Awadallah*, 349 F.3d at 45. In doing so, the court affirmed that the material witness statute may be employed to arrest and detain potential grand jury witnesses but made clear it may only be used for this purpose: "The district court noted (and we agree) that it would be improper for the government to use § 3144 for other ends, such as the detention of persons suspected of criminal activity for which probable cause has not yet been established." *Id.* at 59. Although this language does not explicitly address the "mixed motive" scenario addressed above, it does not prohibit the arrest of material witnesses who are also viewed as potential suspects.

Perhaps the most controversial use of the material witness statute occurred in the case of Oregon lawyer Brandon Mayfield, but the problems in that case appear to have been caused by defective fingerprint analysis and investigative failures rather than misuse of the material witness statute per se. In connection with the investigation of the March 11, 2004, bombing of a train in Madrid, Spain, the Spanish National Police recovered a plastic bag near the bombing site that had a fingerprint, which the FBI determined matched a known fingerprint of Mayfield. *See* Steven T. Was & Christopher J. Schatz, *A Multitude of Errors: The Brandon Mayfield Case*, Nat'l Ass'n of Criminal Defense Lawyers Champion Magazine, Sept.-Oct. 2004, at 6.[235] While a question developed among the investigative teams as to the validity of the fingerprint match, the government obtained a material witness warrant for Mayfield's arrest on May 5, 2004. *See id.* The following day, Mayfield was arrested and detained after a bail hearing, and the government executed search warrants at his home and office. *See id.* Mayfield remained incarcerated until May 18, 2004, when, reportedly after receiving further confirmation from the Spanish authorities that the latent fingerprint did not match Mayfield, the government moved for his release from custody. *See id.* A few days later, the government moved to dismiss the material witness proceeding. *See id.*

Mayfield subsequently filed a civil action against the government for his arrest and for the government's execution of search warrants, which the government settled by agreeing to pay a total of $2 million to Mayfield and his immediate family members. *See Mayfield v. United States*, 504 F. Supp. 2d 1023, 1026 (D. Or. 2007) (acknowledging that court signed stipulated settlement agreement on November 29, 2006); Dan Eggen, *U.S. Settles Suit Filed by Ore. Lawyer*, Wash. Post, Nov. 30, 2006, at A03[236]. In connection with the settlement, the government issued a statement apologizing to Mayfield and his family "for the suffering caused by the FBI's misidentification of Mr. Mayfield, including his arrest as a material witness in connection with the 2004 Madrid train bombings and execution of search warrants and other court orders in the Mayfield family home and in Mr. Mayfield's law office." *Apology Note*, Wash. Post, Nov. 29, 2006.[237]

D. Evaluating the Detention of Terrorism Suspects Under Existing Law

As the foregoing discussion makes clear, the civilian justice system offers several different avenues, under existing law, for the government to secure the detention of an individual whom it believes is complicit in terrorism. If the government files criminal charges, it can seek detention under the bail statute. If the suspect is an alien not lawfully present in the United States, the government has broad latitude to arrest and detain him pending removal proceedings. The government may also seek an individual's arrest on a material witness warrant, but this approach is viable only for a limited time period and carries with it important procedural safeguards.

Of these three methods, the first is often the most direct and effective. However, the government may face a quandary in determining whether to bring criminal charges against a terrorism suspect. In some cases, the government may face the problem of insufficient admissible evidence to support a criminal charge—even though it may firmly believe, perhaps based on reliable but inadmissible intelligence information, that an individual presents a real danger. In other cases, an arrest may be feasible but could impair the government's ability to successfully prosecute the defendant by interrupting the investigation and thus cutting off the government's ability to develop additional evidence. In some such cases, a public arrest may damage ongoing investigations of larger terrorism networks by revealing the government's scrutiny and tipping off co-conspirators.

For years, prosecutors have faced these sorts of challenges in serious criminal matters such as organized crime and gang prosecutions. The problem of insufficient evidence is generally, though not always, surmountable for a creative and energetic federal prosecutor. Given the breadth of the Federal Criminal Code, and the fact that most dangerous criminals break a multitude of laws, prosecutors often are able to develop evidence to support *some* criminal charge—sometimes with more serious or additional charges to follow later. In our experience, it is infrequent that an imminently dangerous individual is known to law enforcement and will be able to avoid all criminal charges on grounds of insufficient evidence.

Further, the Department of Justice and other law enforcement agencies are periodically faced with the need to protect ongoing investigations in narcotics trafficking, organized crime, and violent gang investigations. Law enforcement sometimes learns about imminent criminal activity—for example, a wiretap or an informant might suggest that a murder or a violent attack is being planned, or that a large-scale shipment of illegal narcotics will soon arrive, flooding the streets of a U.S. city— and it must weigh the benefits of immediate arrest with the impact on the larger investigations, often in the face of potential danger to the community that could result from a failure to act. Although these situations are challenging, prosecutors and agents historically have used creative methods to arrest suspects and thwart potential harm while preserving ongoing investigations. Among other methods, prosecutors may bring limited or unrelated charges against suspects, employ heightened surveillance (including, for example, traffic stops of vehicles to seize weapons or drugs), or draft charging instruments to limit the disclosure of the larger investigation. Even short of an arrest, a traffic stop or other overt contact by law enforcement is often successful in disrupting an ongoing conspiracy, causing the conspirators to spend their energy wondering how law enforcement found out about them and altering their plans in an effort to avoid arrest.

It might reasonably be argued that terrorism cases are "different" because of the overriding need to protect national security interests and the potential for truly disastrous consequences if a terrorist attack occurs or if sensitive national-security information is improperly disclosed. In the abstract, it is difficult to evaluate the number of terrorism cases in which traditional solutions such as an arrest on lesser charges or heightened surveillance will not serve to protect ongoing investigations. It is our observation, based on public information about cases that have been brought, that the government has successfully arrested and incapacitated many terrorism defendants—including violent and dangerous individuals—without obvious damage to ongoing investigations. This record of success inspires some confidence in law enforcement's ability to handle these situations in the terrorism context, but that conclusion cannot be tested based solely on public-record information.

However, in two very unusual cases, *Padilla* and *al-Marri*, the government has shunned the existing legal bases for detention and has sought to invoke novel and potentially far-reaching theories of military detention. In the next section of this Paper, we discuss those cases.

1. The *Padilla* Case

Jose Padilla, an American citizen and former Chicago gang member, was initially detained on a material witness warrant, later designated as an "enemy combatant" and detained in a Naval Brig in South Carolina, and finally, more than three years after his initial detention, charged in a federal indictment. In 2007, Padilla was convicted of serious terrorism charges in federal court in Miami. *See Padilla v. Bush*, 233 F. Supp. 2d 564, 569 (S.D.N.Y. 2002) ("*Padilla I*"); Jury Verdict, *United States v. Padilla*, No. 04-cr-60001 (S.D. Fla. Aug. 16, 2007) (Dkt. No. 1193). As the following summary illustrates, the road from Padilla's initial capture to the courtroom in Miami was circuitous in the extreme.

In 2002, the government obtained a material witness warrant for Padilla, whom it suspected of being involved in the alleged Dirty Bomb plot to stage a radioactive terrorist attack within the United States. *See Padilla I*, at 568. The warrant was issued by Chief Judge Mukasey of the federal court in Manhattan. *See id.* Padilla was arrested in Chicago on May 8, 2002, and was transported to New York, where he was detained. *See id.* at 568-69. On or about May 22, 2002, Padilla, through counsel, challenged the propriety of his detention under the material witness warrant and moved to vacate the warrant. *See id.* at 571. On or about June 9, 2002, just two days before Judge Mukasey was scheduled to preside over a court conference on Padilla's motion to vacate the material witness warrant, President Bush issued an order designating Padilla an "enemy combatant" pursuant to the Authorization for the Use of Military Force ("AUMF") passed by Congress a week after the 9/11 attacks. *See id.* Padilla was removed from federal custody, transferred into military custody, and detained by the Department of Defense at the Naval Brig in Charleston, South Carolina. *See id.* at 572. Judge Mukasey, upon motion of the government, vacated the material witness warrant. *See id.* At this point, Padilla had been effectively plucked out of the criminal justice system.

Padilla filed a motion for a writ of habeas corpus, challenging, among other things, his designation and detention as an "enemy combatant" as being unlawful and seeking access to counsel. *See id.* at 569. In *Padilla I*, Judge Mukasey ruled that Padilla's designation as an "enemy combatant" was a lawful exercise of the President's military powers as the Commander in Chief under the AUMF. *See id.* at 610. Judge Mukasey did, however, rule that Padilla was entitled to counsel during the period of his detention. *Id.* Judge Mukasey's decision was appealed to the Second Circuit by both the government (primarily on the holding that Padilla was entitled to counsel) and by the defendant (primarily on the holding that President Bush's authorization of Padilla's designation and detention as an "enemy combatant" was lawful). *See Padilla v. Rumsfeld*, 352 F.3d 695, 699 (2d Cir. 2003) ("*Padilla II*").

The Second Circuit, although affirming certain portions of Judge Mukasey's decision, reversed other portions and held that President Bush did not have the authority to designate and detain Padilla as an "enemy combatant." *See id.* The Second Circuit ordered that the lower court issue a writ of habeas corpus releasing Padilla from military custody within thirty days, but stayed its order to permit the government to appeal its decision to the Supreme Court. *See id.*

The Supreme Court heard the government's appeal and, on June 28, 2004, issued a ruling that would precipitate an entirely new round of legal wrangling. Rather than address the substance of the Second Circuit's ruling, the Supreme Court dismissed Padilla's petition for a writ of habeas corpus on jurisdictional grounds, holding that it should have been filed in federal court in South Carolina, the site of his detention, rather than in New York. See *Rumsfeld v. Padilla*, 542 U.S. 426, 451 (2004) ("*Padilla III*"). Accordingly, Padilla remained detained by the Department of Defense in the U.S. Naval Consolidated Brig in Charleston.

After the Supreme Court's ruling, Padilla refiled his petition for a writ of habeas corpus in South Carolina federal court. In the litigation that ensued, the District Court in South Carolina ruled, unlike Judge Mukasey, that Congress did not authorize the indefinite detention of Padilla and that President Bush exceeded his authority in compelling the detention of Padilla as an "enemy combatant." See *Padilla v. Hanft*, 389 F. Supp. 2d 678 (D.S.C. 2005) ("*Padilla IV*"). On appeal, however, the Fourth Circuit reversed the South Carolina court, finding that President Bush did in fact have the authority to detain Padilla under the AUMF. See *Padilla v. Hanft*, 423 F.3d 386, 396 (4th Cir. 2005) ("*Padilla V*"). Padilla immediately pressed his legal fight to the Supreme Court, and filed a petition for certiorari to seek review of the legality of his detention.

It is here where Padilla's saga took yet another twist. The government sought and received an extension of its time to oppose Padilla's petition for certiorari to the Supreme Court. Just days prior to the due date of the government's brief to the Supreme Court, however, the government indicted Padilla on charges unrelated to the Dirty Bomb plot and moved to have the Fourth Circuit withdraw its opinion as moot and authorize the transfer of Padilla from military custody to federal civilian custody. See *Padilla v. Hanft*, 432 F.3d 582, 583-84 (4th Cir. 2005) ("*Padilla VI*"). The Fourth Circuit, displeased with the government's tactics, denied the request for the transfer and criticized the government for "at least an appearance that the government may be attempting to avoid consideration of our decision by the Supreme Court." *Id.* Subsequently, however, the Supreme Court overruled the Fourth Circuit and granted the government's request to transfer Padilla into federal civilian custody. See *Hanft v. Padilla*, 546 U.S. 1084 (2006).

Padilla was ultimately tried in federal court in Miami and was convicted of serious terrorism charges by a jury on August 16, 2007. *See* Jury Verdict, *Padilla* (S.D. Fla. Aug. 16, 2007) (Dkt. No. 1193). On January 22, 2008, he was sentenced to just over seventeen years' imprisonment—much less than the life sentence that the government sought.[238] See Judgment, *Padilla* (S.D. Fla. Jan. 22, 2008) (Dkt. No. 1333); Kirk Semple, *Padilla Gets 17 Years in Conspiracy Case*, N.Y. Times, Jan. 23, 2008, at A14.[239] In sentencing Padilla, Judge Marcia Cooke took into consideration, among other things, the "harsh" conditions he was subjected to in the Naval Brig and gave Padilla credit for the three and a half years he was confined there. See Semple, *Padilla Gets 17 Years in Conspiracy Case*, at A14.

2. The *al-Marri* Case

The *al-Marri* case presents a different sequence of events. The case traces its origins to September 10, 2001—the day before 9/11—when Ali Saleh Kahlah al-Marri, a citizen of Qatar, lawfully entered the United States with his wife and children to pursue a master's degree at Bradley University in Peoria, Illinois. See *al-Marri v. Wright*, 487 F.3d 160, 164 (4th Cir. 2007) (rehearing en banc pending). On December 12, 2001, FBI agents arrested al-Marri at his home in Illinois on a material witness warrant issued in the Southern District of New York. Al-Marri was transported to New York and, in February 2002, was indicted on counterfeit credit-card charges. See *id.* About a year later, in January 2003, the government filed a superseding indictment charging al-Marri with false statements to the FBI and false statements to a bank. See *id.* In May 2003, a court in New York dismissed the charges for lack of venue, at which point the government transferred al-Marri to Peoria and indicted him in the Central District of Illinois on the same charges. See *id.* The Illinois court set a trial date in late July 2003 and scheduled a hearing in late June on al-Marri's pre-trial motions, including a motion to suppress statements allegedly obtained by torture. See *id.*

On June 23, 2003, before the hearing, the government moved to dismiss the indictment, transferred al-Marri into military custody, and brought him to the Naval Brig in South Carolina, where he was detained. See *id.* at 164-65. At that point, as with Padilla, al-Marri had been removed from the justice system. The government asserted that it had authority to detain al-Marri indefinitely without charge as an "enemy combatant." See *id.* at 165. For the first sixteen months of his confinement, al-Marri had no access to his family or his attorneys. See *id.* In a subsequent civil lawsuit, he claimed that he was subjected to mistreatment during his military confinement. See *id.*

Al-Marri filed a petition for habeas corpus in a federal court in Illinois, but the petition was dismissed for lack of venue and the Seventh Circuit affirmed the dismissal. See *id.* at 165. Al-Marri then refiled his petition in South Carolina. See *id.* In response, the government submitted a declaration from the director of an intelligence task force who asserted that al-Marri was closely associated with al Qaeda, met with Osama bin Laden in the summer of 2001, and entered the United States "to serve as a 'sleeper agent' to facilitate terrorist activities and explore disrupting this country's financial system through computer hacking." *Id.* Al-Marri denied the government's allegations but did not offer any specific rebuttal; as a result, the South Carolina court dismissed the habeas corpus action. *See id.* at 166.

On appeal, after a lengthy analysis of the law of war and relevant statutes, a panel of the Fourth Circuit ruled that the government lacked legal authority to detain al-Marri under the law of war but that the government was free to prosecute al-Marri in the criminal justice system, initiate deportation proceedings against him, detain him as a material witness in connection with a grand jury investigation, or detain him for a limited time under the USA PATRIOT Act's detention provisions. *See id.* at 160, 164, 195. At the time this White Paper was prepared, the Fourth Circuit had granted rehearing and heard oral argument en banc but the en banc court had not yet rendered a decision. The case may ultimately end up before the Supreme Court.

3. Assessing *Padilla* and *al-Marri*

What lessons can be drawn from the *Padilla* and *al-Marri* sagas? For one thing, the many rounds of legal wrangling and contradictory lower-court decisions tell us that the legal basis for the government's prolonged military detention of Padilla and al-Marri was uncertain at best. At some point, perhaps in connection with the *al-Marri* case, which in the spring of 2008 was still working its way through the lower courts, the Supreme Court may clarify whether it is permissible to hold an individual in military detention when that individual is not an enemy alien and was arrested by civilian law enforcement far away from the battlefield at a time when he was not engaged in traditional warfare against the United States. Until then, there is likely to be disagreement on this fundamental question.

But is the prolonged military detention of Padilla and al-Marri justifiable? Some might contend that the lengthy military detention was necessary in order to permit the government to extract intelligence from the two individuals. At an early stage of the litigation, the government made this sort of argument to Judge Mukasey in an effort to prevent Padilla from consulting with counsel. *See Padilla v. Rumsfeld*, 243 F. Supp. 2d 42, 49-50 (S.D.N.Y. 2003) (declaration from Director of Defense Intelligence Agency arguing that lengthy detention of individual without counsel was necessary to "create an atmosphere of dependency and trust between the subject and the interrogator").[240] But the argument ultimately begs the question as to whether there was any lawful basis to detain Padilla and al-Marri. The government may frequently wish to obtain intelligence from individuals, but under our Constitution and laws it does not generally have license to arrest and detain them without filing criminal charges or invoking other legal authority. Furthermore, from the public record it is unclear what if any intelligence was actually gathered from Padilla and al-Marri, and different people would likely disagree as to whether gathering intelligence from Padilla, for example, was "worth it" when measured against the cost of holding an American citizen, without charge, for many years inside the United States following his arrest by the FBI at O'Hare Airport. This sort of balancing may well present a constitutional issue to be resolved by the Supreme Court in the context of *al-Marri* or some other case.

The *Padilla* and *al-Marri* cases might also be viewed as demonstrating that the effort to keep a terrorist suspect beyond the reach of the justice system can consume even more time and resources than are consumed by dealing with him through normal criminal channels. This point would be an interesting rebuttal to the argument that using the criminal justice system for terrorists is too big a drain on the nation's resources.

Another lesson might focus on the conventional ending to the *Padilla* case. After his indictment in 2005, Padilla was transferred back to civilian custody in Miami, presented before a magistrate judge, and detained under the Bail Reform Act; his case then proceeded with discovery, pre-trial motions, a trial before a jury, and, ultimately, a conviction and a prison sentence. In light of that very ordinary denouement to a prolonged and extraordinary saga, one might ask whether it was necessary for the government to go through years of contortions to justify Padilla's military detention—which in the end led to a reduced sentence for Padilla. There may be reasons why it was not possible for the government to bring criminal charges against Padilla sooner, but those reasons are not obvious to an outside observer.

Nevertheless, it may well be the case that the government faced a difficult choice in June 2002, when it initially moved Padilla into military custody. At that time, Padilla was contesting his material witness detention. The government apparently was convinced that Padilla was a highly dangerous al Qaeda adherent but may have lacked admissible evidence sufficient to justify charging him at that time. There are some circumstantial indications that this was the case. Padilla, a former gang member, had significant prior experience with the criminal justice system and likely knew enough not to be induced into making incriminating post-arrest statements. (Many less experienced detainees, including individuals charged in serious terrorism cases, have been more talkative upon arrest.) Further, because Padilla was a U.S. citizen, he was not subject to immigration detention. In addition, the charges that were ultimately filed against Padilla rested on complex evidence that may not have been available or usable in the spring of 2002.

To be sure, some aspects of the *Padilla* situation suggest overreaching and even gamesmanship by the government. But some have hypothesized a rare situation, possibly resembling *Padilla*, where the government has located a dangerous individual far away from the traditional battlefield without sufficient evidence to file criminal charges and where the individual is a U.S. citizen and thus is not subject to immigration detention. Some have suggested that in such a scenario, the government would face a dilemma, especially if the individual were believed capable of causing a massive attack. It appears that this sort of scenario—as seemingly unusual as it is—is what motivates some people to be concerned that the available means of detention in the criminal justice system are not sufficient. Others, however, would argue that adopting a long-term administrative detention scheme to address the scenario of the unchargeable but dangerous individual would undermine and corrupt the foundational principles and character of our system of justice.

The *al-Marri* case presents an entirely different factual scenario from *Padilla*. There, the government *was* able to bring substantial criminal charges against the defendant in a timely fashion, including charges of making false statements to the FBI and committing financial crimes such as false statements to a bank and possession of counterfeit credit cards. From the public record there is no reason to doubt the legitimacy of these charges or the strength of the evidence against the defendant. Courts in New York and Illinois had ordered his detention. Yet while the prosecution of al-Marri was ongoing, the government plucked him out of the justice system and transferred him to a Naval Brig. This course of events cannot be explained as a means to secure al-Marri's detention; the only explanation that seems to make sense is that the government wanted to interrogate him. As noted above, reasonable people may differ as to the costs and benefits of such a maneuver, but at a minimum the transfer of al-Marri into military custody raises significant constitutional issues.

Ultimately, we believe that the most important lesson to be drawn from *Padilla* and *al-Marri* is that the Byzantine history of these cases is unusual. It is true, of course, that our analysis of this issue may be incomplete because it is limited to public record. Nevertheless, based on the unusual history of these cases, we believe that people should be extremely wary of using them to draw broad-ranging conclusions about the justice system as a whole. In our view, it makes more sense to focus on the fact that in the overwhelming majority of cases in which an individual is identified as a participant in international terrorism, the government possesses ample tools to detain that person through the criminal justice system, under the immigration laws, or through non-controversial application of the law of war. The proven usefulness of these existing tools suggests to us that a brand-new scheme of administrative detention has not been shown to be necessary.

Further, any administrative detention scheme aimed at solving the quandary the government may have faced with Padilla would have to be severe. Based on our conversations with many who have prosecuted terrorism cases, administratively detaining a defendant like Padilla for days, or even up to two weeks as may be allowed in some jurisdictions in Europe, would not provide sufficient time to develop a case with admissible evidence. Therefore, as a practical matter, critics of the justice system who advocate an administrative detention scheme, are advocating—whether overtly or implicitly—a long-term system of administrative detention. Such a system would very likely carry significant deleterious consequences, including actual and/or perceived debasement of our legal culture, and would raise serious constitutional problems.

VIII.
Using Statutes Such as FISA and CIPA, Courts Have Effectively Managed the Challenge of Dealing with Classified or Sensitive Evidence that Implicates National Security

In some terrorism cases, the government may seek to rely on evidence that is probative of the defendant's guilt but which implicates sensitive national security interests. Navigating these situations is challenging, but especially in recent years, courts have been able to make effective use of two key statutes: the Foreign Intelligence Surveillance Act ("FISA") and the Classified Information Procedures Act ("CIPA"). The two statutes are different in their focus and in the procedures that they mandate, but together they provide a framework for allowing the government and the defense to offer relevant evidence while safeguarding the secrecy that is often required to protect national security.

A. The Foreign Intelligence Surveillance Act

Originally enacted in 1978, FISA permits the government to lawfully conduct electronic surveillance (i.e., wiretapping), as well as physical searches, in the course of gathering foreign intelligence within the United States without satisfying the normal Fourth Amendment requirement of establishing probable cause to believe that the surveillance will yield evidence of a crime.[241] Congress originally adopted FISA because of three related concerns: (1) judicial confusion over the existence, nature, and scope of a foreign intelligence exception to the Fourth Amendment's warrant requirement that arose in the wake of the Supreme Court's 1972 decision in *United States v. U.S. Dist. Court*, 407 U.S. 297 (1972); (2) Congressional concern over perceived Executive Branch abuses of such an exception; and (3) the perceived need to provide the Executive Branch with an appropriate means to investigate and counter foreign intelligence threats.[242] FISA accommodates these concerns by establishing a detailed process for the government to collect foreign intelligence information "without violating the rights of citizens of the United States." *United States v. Hammoud*, 381 F.3d 316, 332 (4th Cir. 2004), *vacated on other grounds*, 543 U.S. 1097 (2005), *reinstated in pertinent part*, 405 F.3d 1034 (4th Cir. 2005). Although originally limited to electronic surveillance, FISA's coverage has now been expanded to include physical searches as well.[243]

From its inception, FISA provided a framework for evidence to be used in criminal cases, but in the 1990s an internal "wall" developed within the Department of Justice that made it difficult to use FISA evidence in court. In the wake of 9/11, Congress amended the Act to make it easier for the government to use FISA evidence in criminal trials, and since then FISA evidence has played an important role in a number of international terrorism cases, including the following:[244]

- *United States v. al-Arian*: In a prosecution alleging material support of a terrorist organization called Palestinian Islamic Jihad ("PIJ"), among the evidence to be used at trial was some 21,000 hours of telephone recordings in Arabic that were obtained under FISA. See *United States v. al Arian*, 267 F. Supp. 2d 1258, 1260 (M.D. Fla. 2003). In December 2005, after a decade-long investigation and a six-month trial, the jury found lead defendant Sami Amin al-Arian, a university professor, not guilty on eight of seventeen charges. See Jury Verdict, *United States v. al-Arian*, No. 03-cr-00077 (M.D. Fla. Dec. 7, 2005) (Dkt. No.

1463). However, al-Arian subsequently pled guilty to a single charge of conspiracy to provide support to the PIJ and was sentenced to serve fifty-seven months in prison. Judgment, *al-Arian* (M.D. Fla. May 1, 2006) (Dkt. No. 1574).

- *United States v. Arnaout*: Searches of Enaam Arnaout's home and the Illinois office of Benevolence International Foundation were conducted pursuant to FISA, leading to the recovery of key records and documents used in the successful criminal prosecution of Arnaout, who pled guilty to racketeering conspiracy. The government recorded conversations in Arnaout's house involving a Saudi who was believed to be a top al Qaeda financier. *See* Complaint, *Arnaout*, No. 02-cr-00414 (N.D. Ill. Apr. 29, 2002) (Dkt. No. 1); Gov't's Resp. to Def.'s Mot. to Dismiss Indictment, *Arnaout* (N.D. Ill. Aug. 2, 2002) (Dkt. No. 53); John Ashcroft, U.S. Att'y Gen., Transcript of Att'y Gen. John Ashcroft Regarding Guilty Plea by Enaam Arnaout Media Availability Following Speech to Council on Foreign Relations (Feb. 10, 2003);[245] Glenn R. Simpson & Jess Bravin, *New Power Boosts Terror Fight: Prosecutors Capitalize on Increased Access to Wiretap Evidence*, Wall St. J., Jan. 21, 2003, at A4.[246]

- *United States v. Galab*: Faysal Galab, a member of the "Lackawanna Six," agreed to plead guilty on January 10, 2003, and cooperate with investigators. FISA evidence was reportedly described to him during plea negotiations, leading his defense lawyer to comment, "I've got to believe there was tons of surveillance of these guys when they got back to this country." *See* Simpson & Bravin, *New Powers Fuel Legal Assault On Suspected Terror Supporters.*

- *United States v. Hassoun*: FISA evidence in this case included 275 transcripts of secretly recorded conversations and more than 300 summaries of those intercepts. In granting a protective order, Magistrate Judge Ann E. Vitunac decided that the "FISA intercepts, or any copies thereof, are now and will forever remain the property of the U.S. government." Protective Order, *United States v. Hassoun*, No. 04-cr-60001 (S.D. Fla. Jan. 8, 2004) (Dkt. No. 34). Hassoun's lawyer, Fred Haddad, said he did not object to the government's control over the FISA wiretap information because "I've now got boxes of this stuff, 10,000 to 12,000 pages, and I'm only through some of it... I don't have to file 6,000 motions to get all this stuff to defend my client. They're being very above-board with me." Dan Christensen, *Widening Terror Probe*, Miami Daily Bus. Rev., June 25, 2004, at 1.[247]

- *United States v. Holy Land Foundation*: In the prosecution of a charitable organization and its leaders for providing material support to Hamas, the government produced fifty boxes of FISA materials over a ten-month period. *See* Gov't's Classified Combined Mem. in Opp'n to Def.'s Joint Mot. to Suppress FISA Evidence, *United States v. Holy Land Foundation*, No. 04-cr-00240 (N.D. Tex. Nov. 2, 2006) (Dkt. No. 445). The *Holy Land Foundation* trial extended over eight weeks and resulted in a hung jury on most counts with one defendant being acquitted on all but one count. *See* Peter Whoriskey, *Mistrial Declared in Muslim Charity Case*, Wash. Post, Oct. 23, 2007, at A03.[248]

- *United States v. Paul*: In the spring of 2007, the government charged Christopher Paul, a resident of Columbus, Ohio, with conspiracy to provide material support to terrorists based on approximately fifteen years of conduct including meetings with al Qaeda figures in Pakistan and Afghanistan, receiving training with weapons and grenades, possession of equipment to make false documents, and possession of manuals on how to make explosives at his father's residence in Columbus, Ohio. Less than two weeks after Paul's arrest, the government served notice of its intent to use evidence obtained from electronic surveillance and physical searches under FISA. *See* Notice of Intent to Use FISA Information, *United States v. Paul*, No. 07-cr-00087 (S.D. Ohio Apr. 23, 2007) (Dkt. No. 19).

- *United States v. Sattar*: In the prosecution of Lynne Stewart and her co-defendants, the government made extensive disclosures to the defense of materials obtained pursuant to FISA, including over 85,000 audio recordings, 63 audio tapes of phone calls, the FBI's written summaries of approximately 5,300 voice calls, approximately 150 draft transcripts of voice calls, approximately 10,000 pages of e-mails, and videotapes made of prison visits between Stewart and her client, Sheikh Abdel Rahman. *See United States v. Sattar*, No. 02-cr-00395, 2003 WL 22137012 (S.D.N.Y. Sept. 15, 2003).

What follows is a brief overview of FISA procedures, as well as a summary of the way the "wall" was erected in the 1990s and then dismantled after 9/11.

1. Overview of FISA Procedures

FISA's provisions for obtaining judicial authorization for a search or electronic surveillance differ from the procedures followed in a normal criminal investigation. In the usual criminal case, if a prosecutor wants to obtain a search warrant, he must persuade a neutral magistrate, based on sworn testimony from a law enforcement agent, that there is probable cause to believe that a search will yield evidence of a crime, after which the magistrate issues a search warrant with place, time, and subject matter limitations for its execution that is later given to the target of the search. For electronic surveillance in a criminal investigation, Title III of the Omnibus Crime Control and Safe Streets Act of 1968, 18 U.S.C. §§ 2510 et seq., establishes analogous procedures that law enforcement must stringently follow before commencing, and while conducting, a wiretap. Again, the focus is on demonstrating probable cause that the electronic surveillance will yield evidence of a crime. *See* 18 U.S.C. § 2518(3).

In contrast, FISA authorizes a special court, the Foreign Intelligence Surveillance Court ("FISC"), that meets ex parte and in secret to consider whether to authorize surveillance under FISA.[249] Although the statute contains special procedures to be used in emergencies and other unusual situations, in most instances, the FISA procedure begins with the government's filing of a sealed, ex parte application with the FISC.[250] This application must be approved by the Attorney General and must include detailed information, including the identity of the target of the surveillance, a description of the information sought, certifications that the information is believed to be foreign intelligence information and cannot reasonably be obtained by normal investigative techniques, and information about any prior applications for surveillance of the same targets.[251]

After review of the application, a judge of the FISC determines whether the application satisfies a number of specific requirements and whether there is probable cause to believe that:

- the target of the electronic surveillance or physical search is a foreign power or an agent of a foreign power, except that no U.S. person may be considered a foreign power or an agent of a foreign power solely upon the basis of activities protected by the First Amendment to the Constitution of the United States; and

- for electronic surveillance, each of the facilities or places at which the electronic surveillance is directed is being used, or is about to be used, by a foreign power or an agent of a foreign power; or

- for physical searches, the premises or property to be searched is owned, used, possessed by, or is in transit to or from an agent of a foreign power or a foreign power.[252]

FISA defines a "foreign power" to include "a group engaged in international terrorism or activities in preparation therefor." 50 U.S.C. § 1801(a)(4).

If the FISC judge finds that the government has established probable cause to support these findings and has satisfied the statute's other requirements, the judge must issue an ex parte order approving the surveillance or search. The order must describe the target of the search, the information sought, and the means of acquiring that information. *See* 50 U.S.C. §§ 1805(c)(1), 1824(c)(1). The order must also set forth the period of time during which the electronic surveillance or physical searches are approved, which is generally ninety days or until the objective of the electronic surveillance or physical search has been achieved. *See* 50 U.S.C. §§ 1805(e)(1), 1824(d)(1). The government may make applications to renew the order, but such applications must generally be made upon the same basis as the original application and require the same findings by the FISC. *See* 50 U.S.C. §§ 1805(e)(2), 1824(d)(2).

FISA authorizes the collection of "foreign intelligence information," which the statute defines to include information that relates to the "the ability of the United States to protect against (A) actual or potential attack or other grave hostile acts of a foreign power or an agent of a foreign power; (B) sabotage or international terrorism by a foreign power or an agent of a foreign power; or (C) clandestine intelligence activities by an intelligence service or network of a foreign power or by an agent of a foreign power" or, with respect to a foreign power or a foreign territory, information that relates to "(A) the national defense or the security of the United States; or (B) the conduct of the foreign affairs of the United States." 50 U.S.C. § 1801(e).

2. The Use of FISA Evidence in Criminal Cases— The Creation and Demise of the FISA "Wall"

Although focused on the collection of foreign intelligence information, from its inception FISA has explicitly allowed the use of such evidence in criminal prosecutions. *See* 50 U.S.C. §§ 1806(k), 1825(k). If the Attorney General approves the use of evidence collected pursuant to FISA in a criminal prosecution, and the government intends to use or disclose FISA evidence at the trial of anyone who was subject to surveillance or a search under FISA, the government must first notify the defendant and the court that the government intends to disclose or use the FISA evidence. *See* 50 U.S.C. §§ 1806(c), 1825(d). On receiving such notification, the defendant may move to suppress any evidence derived from FISA surveillance or searches on the grounds that: (1) the evidence was unlawfully acquired; or (2) the electronic surveillance or physical search was not conducted in conformity with the order of authorization or approval. *See* 50 U.S.C. §§ 1806(e), 1825(f). However, upon the filing of an affidavit by the Attorney General stating that disclosure of such material would harm national security, the district court must review the FISA warrant application and related materials in camera and ex parte to determine whether the surveillance or search "of the aggrieved person was lawfully authorized and conducted." 50 U.S.C. §§ 1806(f), 1825(g). The certifications contained in the applications—including that the information sought was believed to be foreign intelligence information and could not be obtained by normal investigative techniques—should be "presumed valid." *United States v. Duggan*, 743 F.2d 59, 77 n.6 (2d Cir. 1984); *United States v. Rosen*, 447 F. Supp. 2d 538, 545 (E.D. Va. 2006). During this process, the FISA application is never disclosed to the defendant, due to the possibility that such disclosure might compromise the ability of the United States to gather foreign intelligence effectively. *Rosen*, 447 F. Supp. 2d at 546. This stands in marked contrast to conventional wiretap applications under Title III, as well as affidavits supporting search warrants, which are routinely disclosed to the defense before trial to enable defendants to challenge the admissibility of the evidence obtained under a wiretap order or search warrant.

Despite these provisions explicitly envisioning the use of FISA evidence in criminal trials, in the years leading up to 9/11 the Department of Justice created an internal "wall" that, in practice, resulted in separation between prosecutors and agents involved in law enforcement and those engaged in intelligence-gathering. *See In re Sealed Case*, 310 F.3d 717, 723 (FISA Ct. Rev. 2002) ("it is quite puzzling that the Justice Department, at some point during the 1980s, began to read the statute as limiting the Department's ability to obtain FISA orders if it intended to prosecute the targeted agents"). The origins of the FISA wall can be traced back to language in the original version of FISA that required a senior Executive Branch official to certify, as part of every FISA application, that "the purpose of the surveillance is to obtain foreign intelligence information." *See* 50 U.S.C. § 1804(a)(7)(B) (2000) (prior to the 2001 and 2004 amendments). Before 9/11, surveillance that was not for "the purpose" of obtaining foreign intelligence was considered improper under FISA. *See, e.g., In re Sealed Case*, 310 F.3d at 725; *United States v. Koyomejian*, 970 F.2d 536, 540 (9th Cir. 1992). Conversely, federal courts that approved the use of FISA evidence in criminal cases relied on findings that "the primary purpose" of the surveillance was to gather foreign intelligence. *See United States v. Johnson*, 952 F. 2d 565, 572 (1st Cir. 1991); *United States v. Pelton*, 835 F.2d 1067, 1076 (4th Cir. 1987); *United States v. Sarkissian*, 841 F.2d 959, 964 (9th Cir. 1988).

In the mid-1990s, a Department of Justice working group sought an opinion from the Department of Justice's Office of Legal Counsel ("OLC") on whether the FISC could approve a search under FISA only when the collection of foreign intelligence was the "primary purpose" of the search, or whether it sufficed that such collection was among the purposes of the search. *See* Nat'l Comm'n on Terrorist Attacks upon the United States, *The 9/11 Commission Report* 79 (2004) (hereafter "*9/11 Commission Report*"). In February 1995, OLC concluded that "courts are more likely to adopt the 'primary purpose' test than any less stringent formulation." *Implementation of the USA Patriot Act: Section 218—Foreign Intelligence Information ("The Wall"): Hearing Before the Subcomm. on Crime, Terrorism, and Homeland Security of the H. Comm. on the Judiciary*, 109th Cong. Serial No. 109-16 at 17-34 (Apr. 28, 2005) (statement of David S. Kris, Senior Vice President, Time Warner Inc.) (hereafter "Kris Statement")[253]; *see also* William C. Banks, *The Death of FISA*, 91 Minn. L. Rev. 1209, 1236-37 (2007). OLC determined that "the greater the involvement of prosecutors in the planning and execution of FISA searches, the greater is the chance that the government could not assert in good faith that the 'primary purpose' was the collection of foreign intelligence." Kris Statement at 4. OLC recommended that "an appropriate internal process should be established that FISA certifications are consistent with the 'primary purpose' test." Banks, *The Death of FISA*, at 1237 (internal citations and quotations omitted).

OLC's reading of the statute, along with internal Justice Department procedural requirements imposed by the Office of Intelligence Policy and Review ("OIPR"), which in effect served as the central gatekeeper within the Department of Justice for all FISA applications, led to special procedures that, in practice, made it difficult for law enforcement agents and prosecutors to coordinate with government personnel who were conducting intelligence-gathering. *Id.* at 1234-35.[254] Indeed, in the 1990s the FBI developed a parallel system of "dirty" teams for gathering intelligence and "clean" teams for criminal law enforcement. *See id.* at 1239. The teams could investigate the same target at the same time, but they rarely talked with one another. *See id.*

Shortly after 9/11, Congress passed the USA PATRIOT Act, which modified the language in FISA and paved the way for this internal "wall" to be torn down. Initially, the Justice Department proposed an amendment that would have replaced FISA's certification requirement that "the purpose" of surveillance was to obtain foreign intelligence with "'a' purpose." *Id.* at 1243. According to the Justice Department, the change "would eliminate the current need continually to evaluate the relative weight of criminal and intelligence purposes, and would facilitate information sharing between law enforcement and foreign intelligence authorities." U.S. Dep't of Justice, Anti-Terrorism Act of 2001, Section-by-Section Analysis (2001)[255]; *see also* Banks, *The Death of FISA*, at 1243. During the course of the congressional debate, members and outside experts questioned the constitutionality of the change to "a" purpose, from "the" or "primary" purpose. Banks, *The Death of FISA*, at 1244. At a Senate Judiciary Committee hearing, Senator Feinstein urged Attorney General Ashcroft to consider "substantial or significant purpose" as an alternative formulation of the purpose requirement, rather than adopting "a purpose." *Id.* at 1245. The Attorney General agreed to support a slight change in the proposal, and the eventual USA PATRIOT Act amended FISA to provide that obtaining foreign intelligence must be "a significant purpose" of the surveillance. *Id.*; *see also In re Sealed Case*, 310 F.3d at 732-33 (reviewing legislative history of amendments to FISA as part of USA PATRIOT Act).[256]

The adoption of the "significant purpose" standard has resulted in a marked increase in FISA warrants. According to the Justice Department, in 2006 the DOJ submitted 2,181 FISA applications—more than twice as many as in 2001—and the FISC rejected only one of those applications. *See* Letter from Richard A. Hertling, Acting Assistant Att'y Gen., to Hon. Nancy Pelosi (April 27, 2007).[257] The "significant purpose" standard has survived Fourth Amendment challenge in both the Seventh Circuit and the United States Foreign Intelligence Surveillance Court of Review ("FISCR"). *See In re Grand Jury Proceedings of Special April 2002 Grand Jury*, 347 F.3d 197, 206 (7th Cir. 2003); *In re Sealed Case*, 310 F.3d at 717; *see also United States v. Ning Wen*, 477 F.3d 896, 898-99 (7th Cir. 2007) (upholding the use of FISA evidence in a domestic criminal case when the foreign intelligence investigation was complete). However, a recent opinion from a federal district court in Oregon in the *Mayfield* case rejects the FISCR opinion, finding that the "significant purpose" language impermissibly violates the Fourth Amendment. *See Mayfield v. United States*, 504 F. Supp. 2d 1023, 1042-43 (D. Or. 2007). The Oregon court rejected the new language because "for the first time in our Nation's history," the government would be permitted to "conduct surveillance to gather evidence for use in a criminal case without a traditional warrant, as long as it presents a non-reviewable assertion that it also has a significant interest in the targeted person for foreign intelligence purposes." *Id.* at 1036. It remains to be seen whether this holding will withstand appellate review.[258] *See id., appeal docketed*, No. 07-35865 (9th Cir. Oct. 19, 2007).

FISA continues to be a subject of debate in Congress, with some observers suggesting that the statute needs to modernized and reformed. On August 6, 2007, President Bush signed into law a temporary amendment to Section 105 of FISA, through the Protect America Act of 2007, Pub. L. No. 110-55, 121 Stat. 552 (2007). The new legislation contains three significant amendments to existing law.[259] The impact of this legislation remains to be seen. Irrespective of the new legislation, FISA evidence has made important contributions to terrorism cases, and the statute is a powerful tool for the government in prosecuting international terrorism cases in the post-9/11 era.

B. The Classified Information Procedures Act

When there is the potential that classified information will be disclosed in a criminal case, CIPA, Pub. L. No. 96-456, 94 Stat. 2025, 2025-31 (1980) (codified at 18 U.S.C. app. 3), establishes pre-trial, trial, and appellate procedures intended to protect national security information from improper or unnecessary disclosure—whether by the prosecution or the defendant—while at the same time balancing the defendant's fundamental right to a fair trial. As described by one author, CIPA gives "the defendant a sword in his battle to avoid a conviction and the government a shield to protect its national security interests." Timothy Shea, Note, *CIPA Under Siege: The Use and Abuse of Classified Information in Criminal Trials*, 27 Am. Crim. L. Rev. 657, 662 (1990).

CIPA was enacted by Congress in 1980 against the backdrop of difficulties encountered in the criminal prosecution of Cold War spies. CIPA is commonly understood to have been directed at the practice of "graymailing," in which a defendant, who had knowledge of or access to classified information, threatened to disclose this information as part of his defense. *See* S. Rep. No. 96-823, at 2-4 (1980), *reprinted in* 1980 U.S.C.C.A.N. 4294, 4295-97; H.R. Rep. No. 96-831, pt. 1, at 6-10 (1980); *see also United States v. Smith*, 780 F.2d 1102, 1105 (4th Cir. 1985) (recognizing that CIPA was enacted "in an effort to combat the growing problem of graymail"). This practice often left prosecutors facing an all-or-nothing dilemma—either disclose the classified information and pursue prosecution or dismiss the indictment. While Congress might have had certain types of cases in mind in enacting CIPA, the statute is not limited to any particular type of criminal proceeding.[260]

CIPA's procedures apply in three scenarios in which classified information could be disclosed as part of a criminal proceeding: (1) when the defendant requests classified information from the government for use at trial; (2) when the defendant already has classified information that he intends to use at trial; and (3) when the government needs to use classified information at trial. CIPA provides two primary safeguards against the disclosure of classified information in these situations. First, it allows the presiding judge to review any classified information to determine if the information is relevant. Second, if the court finds that the information is relevant, CIPA authorizes the substitution of the classified information with an unclassified alternative or, if necessary, the implementation of additional measures if the information cannot fairly be provided to the defendant in a substitute form. What follows is a discussion of CIPA's detailed provisions and an assessment of how CIPA has worked in terrorism cases.[261]

1. Overview of CIPA's Provisions

At the outset of a criminal case, CIPA provides a mechanism for either party to alert the court that the case involves classified information by moving for a pre-trial conference "to consider matters relating to classified information that may arise in connection with the prosecution." 18 U.S.C. app. 3 § 2. Following such a motion, the court "shall promptly hold a pretrial conference to establish the timing of requests for discovery, the provision of notice required by section 5 of [CIPA], and the initiation of the procedure established by section 6 of [CIPA]" to determine the use, relevance, or admissibility of classified information. *Id.*

With respect to discovery materials, CIPA authorizes the court to conduct an evaluation outside the presence of the defendant and defense counsel when discovery contains classified information. *See* 18 U.S.C. app. 3 § 4. Upon a finding that classified discovery materials are relevant, the court can order that the discovery be provided in a substitute form. *Id.*[262] Specifically, the court "may authorize the United States to delete specified items of classified information from documents to be made available to the defendant, to substitute a summary of the information for such classified documents, or to substitute a statement admitting relevant facts that the classified information would tend to prove." *Id.*

CIPA does not change the government's discovery obligations or alter the rules of evidence. *See United States v. Baptista-Rodriguez*, 17 F.3d 1354, 1363 (11th Cir. 1994) (stating that CIPA does not create new law governing the admissibility of evidence); *United States v. Wilson*, 732 F.2d 404, 412 (5th Cir. 1984) (same); *United States v. Pickard*, 236 F. Supp. 2d 1204, 1209 (D. Kan. 2002) (same); *United States v. Clegg*, 740 F.2d 16, 18 (9th Cir. 1984) (granting discovery because the classified materials submitted in camera "are relevant to the development of a possible defense"). In practice, however, this principle has been tested from time to time as courts have applied either a heightened standard of relevance or have balanced relevance with national security interests to decide whether information is discoverable. *See United States v. Yunis*, 867 F.2d 617, 623 (D.C. Cir. 1989) (stating that protection of government's classified information requires a higher threshold of materiality for disclosure); *United States v. Sarkissian*, 841 F.2d 959, 965 (9th Cir. 1988) (allowing balancing for both discovery and admissibility); *United States v. Pringle*, 751 F.2d 419, 427

(1st Cir. 1984) (stating that CIPA requires a balancing test for discovery).

The analysis in *Yunis* exemplifies how courts have evaluated classified information under CIPA in the terrorism context. There, the defendant, who was charged with air piracy, conspiracy, and hostage taking in connection with the June 11, 1985, hijacking of Royal Jordanian Airlines flight 402, sought discovery of classified transcripts of taped conversations between himself and a confidential informant. *See Yunis*, 867 F.2d at 618-19. The district court ordered the transcripts disclosed to the defendant, but the D.C. Circuit reversed. *See id.* at 620-21. In doing so, the D.C. Circuit held that the defendant must make a threshold showing that the requested material is relevant to his case. If the defendant makes this showing, the court must "determine if the assertion of privilege by the government is at least a colorable one," in which case the court will inquire into whether the information is "helpful to the defense of [the] accused." *Id.* (citing *Roviaro v. United States*, 353 U.S. 53, 60-61 (1957)).[263] The *Yunis* court applied this test after reviewing the classified information ex parte and in camera, and held that "[n]othing in the classified documents in fact goes to the innocence of the defendant *vel non*, impeaches any evidence of guilt, or makes more or less probable any fact at issue in establishing any defense to the charges." *Id.* at 624. The court also noted that because the defendant was present during each of the conversations contained in the transcripts, withholding the transcripts "does not impose upon him any burden of absolute memory, omniscience, or superhuman mental capacity." *Id.*

If the court determines that the classified information must be disclosed but cannot be provided to the defendant in a substitute form, CIPA gives the court discretion to enter a protective order "against the disclosure of any classified information disclosed by the government to any defendant in a criminal case." 18 U.S.C. app. 3 § 3. In terrorism cases, courts have required that the disclosure of classified information be limited to defense counsel who have passed a formal security clearance and have prohibited defense counsel from disclosing the information to the defendant. *See, e.g., United States v. Moussaoui*, No. 01-cr-00455, 2002 WL 1987964, at *1 (E.D. Va. Aug. 29, 2002); *United States v. Bin Laden*, No. 98-cr-01023, 2001 WL 66393, at *2 (S.D.N.Y. Jan. 25, 2001); *United States v. Bin Laden*, 58 F. Supp. 2d 113, 116-17 (S.D.N.Y. 1999).

In order to eliminate the possibility of a surprise disclosure of classified information at trial, CIPA requires that the defendant provide the court and the government with written notice if he "reasonably expects to disclose or to cause the disclosure of classified information in any manner in connection with any trial or pretrial proceeding involving the criminal prosecution of such defendant." 18 U.S.C. app. 3 § 5(a). The defendant must provide this notification "within the time specified by the court or, where no time is specified, within thirty days prior to trial." *Id.* Once notified, the government can request a hearing to determine the relevance or admissibility of the information. *See* 18 U.S.C. app. 3 § 6(a). If the government intends to use classified information, it can invoke the same procedures and request a hearing. *See id.*

The purpose of the hearing is "to make all determinations concerning the use, relevance, or admissibility of classified information that would otherwise be made during the trial proceedings." *Id.* Unlike discovery hearings, which can be held ex parte, CIPA mandates that the pre-trial hearing be held with both parties in camera. *See id.* Courts have found that a defendant can be prohibited from attending the hearing and his interests can be adequately represented solely by his counsel's presence. *See Bin Laden*, 2001 WL 66393, at *6-7. Prior to the hearing, the government must:

> provide the defendant with notice of the classified information that is at issue. Such notice shall identify the specific classified information at issue whenever that information previously has been made available to the defendant by the United States. When the United States has not previously made the information available to the defendant in connection with the case, the information may be described by generic category... rather than by identification of the specific information of concern to the United States.

18 U.S.C. app. 3 § 6(b)(1). At the hearing, the court hears from counsel and then rules on whether the classified information identified is admissible under the Federal Rule of Evidence. The court must state in writing the basis for its determination. *See id.* § 6(a).

Like the procedure outlined by CIPA for discovery, if the court determines that the classified information should be disclosed, CIPA provides for an alternative procedure that allows for the substitution at trial of the classified information with a summary or a statement admitting relevant facts that the classified information would tend to prove. *See id.* § 6(c)(1). In support of a motion for substitution, the government may submit an affidavit from the Attorney General (or authorized high-ranking Justice Department official) explaining why the information is classified and what harm to national security would result from disclosure. *See id.* § 6(c)(2).[264] The motion for substitution must be granted if the court finds "that the statement or summary will provide the defendant with substantially the same ability to make his defense as would disclosure of the specific classified information." *Id.* § 6(c)(1).

If, however, the court finds that a proposed substitution is inadequate and the government cannot offer another alternative, then the prosecution must make a choice: it can either disclose the information, or file an affidavit from the Attorney General with the court "objecting to disclosure of the classified information at issue," in which case the court must order that the information remain secret and impose an appropriate sanction on the government. *Id.* § 6(e). Depending on the level of unfairness to the defendant of the non-disclosure, there are a variety of sanctions available to the court, ranging from the most severe—dismissal of the indictment—to lesser sanctions, including "dismissing specified counts of the indictment or information; finding against the United States on any issue as to which the excluded classified information relates; or striking or precluding all or part of the testimony of a witness." *Id.* § 6(e)(2).

CIPA also includes procedures aimed at preventing the improper disclosure of classified information during trial. CIPA authorizes the court to "order admission into evidence of only part of a writing, recording, or photograph ... unless the whole ought in fairness be considered." *Id.* § 8(b). During trial, the government may "object to any question or line of inquiry that may require the witness to disclose classified information not previously found to be admissible," in which case the court must take suitable action to safeguard against the compromise of classified information. *Id.* § 8(c). For example, the court can require either party to provide a summary of the response or the nature of the information that either party seeks to elicit or about which a party expects to testify.

CIPA provides the government a right to an interlocutory appeal "from a decision or order of a district court in a criminal case authorizing the disclosure of classified information, imposing sanctions for nondisclosure of classified information, or refusing a protective order sought by the United States to prevent disclosure of classified information." *Id.* § 7. CIPA also requires that the Court of Appeals consider the appeal on an expedited basis. *See id.*

In addition to the foregoing substantive provisions, CIPA addresses the practical, everyday need to protect classified information that is in the possession of the courts during the course of a criminal proceeding. As required by CIPA, then-Chief Justice Burger issued procedural rules intended to safeguard against the disclosure of classified information. *See* Security Procedures Established Pursuant to Pub. L. 96-456, 94 Stat. 2025, By the Chief Justice of the United States for the Protection of Classified Information, at ¶¶ 1-15, *reprinted following* 18 U.S.C.A. app. 3, § 9. Those rules require:

- the appointment of a court security officer to supervise security measures in any criminal case or appeal therefrom involving classified information;
- the identification of secure quarters within the courthouse where proceedings involving classified information will take place;
- security clearances for court personnel with access to classified information;
- specific procedures for the storage, custody and transmittal of classified information within the court;
- the creation of operating procedures for handling classified information; and
- the establishment of procedures for disposal of classified information.

See id. ¶¶ 2-4, 7-11. In addition, the rules authorize the government to investigate "the trustworthiness of persons associated with the defense." *Id.* ¶ 5. The rules do not require background checks of jurors but instruct the trial judge to "consider a government request for a cautionary instruction ... regarding the release or disclosure of classified information." *Id.* ¶ 6.

2. The Use of CIPA Procedures in Terrorism Cases

Courts have broadly upheld CIPA's constitutionality in the context of criminal terrorism cases. *See, e.g., Bin Laden*, No. 98-cr-01023, 2001 WL 66393, at *9 (S.D.N.Y. Jan. 25, 2001); *United States. v. Abdi*, 498 F. Supp. 2d 1048, 1087

(S.D. Ohio 2007); *United States v. Holy Land Found. for Relief and Dev.*, No. 04-cr-00240, 2007 WL 628059, at *2 (N.D. Tex. Feb. 27, 2007).

Further, since the late 1980s, when the statute was first used in the terrorism context, courts have applied CIPA in a large number of terrorism cases. *See, e.g., Aref v. United States*, 452 F.3d 202, 204 (2d Cir. 2006) (discussing trial court's issuance of a protective order in criminal terrorism trial pursuant to CIPA); *United States v. Hammoud*, 381 F.3d 316, 338 (4th Cir. 2004) (finding that CIPA's sanctions provisions were never implicated because trial court found that classified information sought by defendant was not relevant); *United States v. Rezaq*, 134 F.3d 1121, 1142-43 (D.C. Cir. 1998) (affirming trial court's substitution of summaries for classified information under CIPA in criminal terrorism trial and finding that "district court did a commendable job of discharging its obligations under CIPA"); *United States v. Yunis*, 867 F.2d 617, 619-20 (D.C. Cir. 1989) (holding that district court abused its discretion by ordering discovery of classified information under CIPA in criminal terrorism trial); *United States v. Abdi*, 498 F. Supp. 2d 1048, 1087 (S.D. Ohio 2007) (applying CIPA in criminal terrorism trial and requiring defense counsel to undergo security clearance in order to view CIPA materials); *United States v. Hayat*, No. 05-cr-00240, 2007 WL 1454280 (E.D. Cal. May 17, 2007) (referencing sealed order filed in criminal terrorism trial addressing CIPA issues); *United States v. Hassoun*, No. 04-cr-60001, 2007 WL 1200951, at *6 (S.D. Fla. Apr. 15, 2007) (referencing sealed order filed in criminal terrorism trial addressing CIPA issues); *United States v. Holy Land Found. for Relief and Dev.*, No. 04-cr-00240, 2007 WL 959029, at *2 (N.D. Tex. Mar. 28, 2007) (applying CIPA in criminal terrorism trial and allowing ex parte submissions by government); *United States v. Warsame*, No. 04-cr-00029, 2007 WL 748281, at *3 (D. Minn. Mar. 8, 2007) (implementing CIPA procedures in criminal terrorism trial); *United States v. Salah*, 462 F. Supp. 2d 915, 925 (N.D. Ill. 2006) (authorizing substitutions in lieu of classified information in criminal terrorism trial pursuant to CIPA); *United States v. Abu Marzook*, 435 F. Supp. 2d 708, (N.D. Ill. 2006) (issuing partially redacted order consistent with CIPA and discussing application of CIPA procedures employed during suppression hearing in criminal terrorism trial); *United States v. Abu Marzook*, 412 F. Supp. 2d 913, 928 (N.D. Ill. 2006) (granting in part government's motion to employ certain special procedures pursuant to CIPA during suppression hearing in criminal terrorism trial); *United States v. Aref*, No. 04-cr-00402, 2006 WL 1877142, at *2 (N.D.N.Y. July 6, 2006) (ordering that documents identifying information submitted pursuant to CIPA in criminal terrorism trial be sealed); *United States v. Koubriti*, 307 F. Supp. 2d 891, 895 (E.D. Mich. 2004) (referencing sealed order filed in criminal terrorism trial addressing CIPA issues); *United States v. Ressam*, 221 F. Supp. 2d 1252, 1255 (W.D. Wash. 2002) (identifying docket items filed under seal in criminal terrorism trial pursuant to CIPA); *United States v. Rezaq*, 899 F. Supp. 697, 708 (D.D.C. 1995) (holding that §§ 5 and 6 of CIPA "provide more than adequate procedural protections against public disclosure of classified information" in denying prosecution's request for modification of protective order in criminal terrorism trial); *United States v. Bin Laden*, 58 F. Supp. 2d at 115-17, 124 (implementing security measures and entering protective order in criminal terrorism trial pursuant to CIPA); *United States v. Rahman*, 870 F. Supp. at 49-53 (applying CIPA procedures in criminal terrorism trial to determine whether, and if so, how, classified information should be disclosed). Even when CIPA does not technically apply, for example when the court attempts to determine the need for the deposition of a witness, courts have analogized to CIPA to resolve issues involving classified information.

Importantly, "CIPA is neither exhaustive nor explicitly exclusive with respect to the presentation of classified testimony or documents at trial." *United States v. Rosen*, No. 05-cr-00225, 2007 WL 3243919, at *7 (E.D. Va. Nov. 1, 2007). Thus, while CIPA has provided a flexible, practical mechanism for problems posed by classified evidence, Congress did not intend the statute to ossify the courts' ability to deal with these issues. Rather, Congress' express intent in enacting CIPA was that federal district judges, and thus the criminal justice system, "'must be relied on to fashion creative and fair solutions to these problems,' i.e., the problems raised by the use of classified information in trials." *Id.* (quoting S. Rep. 96-283, *reprinted in* 1980 U.S.C.C.A.N. 4294). Following this principle, courts have fashioned remedies for dealing with classified information that were not explicitly authorized by CIPA. For example, courts have permitted witnesses whose identity is secret to be referred to by a pseudonym, or to testify using a mask or some other method to shield the witness's identity. *See United States v. Moussaoui*, 382 F.3d 453, 456, 480 n.37 (4th Cir. 2004) (recognizing that, in order to protect national security, district court could allow the use of "alternate names for people or places" in creating substitutions for certain witnesses' proposed testimony); *United States v. Abu Marzook*, 435 F. Supp. 2d at 715 (allowing use of pseudonyms at a suppression hearing to protect the classified identities of secret agents of the Israel Security Agency); *see also* Neil A. Lewis, *Admitting He Fought in Taliban, American Agrees to 20-Year Term*, N.Y. Times, July 16, 2002, at A1[265] (reporting that the court in the John Walker Lindh trial was prepared to allow intelligence agents to testify at a hearing under assumed names and to be shielded in the courtroom so that the defendant and his counsel could confront the agents and the public would be able to hear but not see them). Thus, CIPA-like remedies continue to evolve to meet the needs of particular trials.

The Embassy Bombings case highlights many aspects of CIPA's application in terrorism cases. From the outset, Judge Sand recognized the government's heightened concerns because the investigation was "ongoing, which increases the possibility that unauthorized disclosures might place additional lives in danger." *Bin Laden*, 58 F. Supp. 2d at 121. Judge Sand entered a protective order that, among other things, required all defense counsel to undergo background checks and ordered that documents only be shown to counsel, and not to defendants. *See Bin Laden*, 2001 WL 66393, at *2. Judge Sand also conducted in camera reviews and ex parte hearings as necessary and made document-specific determinations regarding whether disclosure of classified information was required. *See Bin Laden*, 58 F. Supp. 2d at 115-17, 121-23; *Bin Laden*, 2001 WL 66393, at *4-7. In addition, because several witnesses—including law enforcement agents and former al Qaeda members who were cooperating with the government—possessed sensitive information, the court monitored the questioning to preempt the disclosure of classified information. *See* Ass'n of the Bar of the City of N.Y., Comm. on Fed. Courts, *The Indefinite Detention of "Enemy Combatants": Balancing Due Process and National Security in the Context of the War on Terror* 143 (Feb. 6. 2004).[266]

In certain terrorism cases where substitutions of evidence authorized by CIPA have been found insufficient to protect classified information, courts have employed an obscure and rarely used evidence presentation technique called the "silent witness rule." *See Rosen*, 2007 WL 3243919, at *5. As the *Rosen* court observed, the silent witness rule has not been explicitly approved or endorsed in a published opinion and at the time of the decision the government had only proposed using the rule in three reported non-terrorism cases. *See id.* at *6 n.11 (citing cases). The effect of the rule is akin to closing the courtroom. Evidence designated by the government is shown to the judge, the jury, counsel, and witnesses but the public is not permitted to see it. *See id.* at *5. Under this procedure:

> [A] witness referring to this evidence would not specifically identify or describe it, but would instead refer to it by reference to page and line numbers of a document or transcript, or more commonly by use of codes such as "Person 1," "Country A," etc. The jury, counsel, and the judge would have access to a key alerting them to the meaning of these code designations; the public, however, would not have access to this key. Any recordings containing the portions designated for SWR treatment would be played in open court, but would revert to static when the portions designated to be treated under the SWR are reached; thus the public would not hear these portions. At the same time, however, jurors, counsel, and the judge would listen on headphones to the unredacted recording.

Id. Because it effectively closes the courtroom, the silent witness rule must meet the stringent test required to override a defendant's right to a public trial, and the court must be satisfied that the procedure does not unfairly impede the defense. *See id.* at *8 (citing *Press-Enter. Co. v. Super. Court of Cal.*, 464 U.S. 501 (1984) and *Waller v. Georgia*, 467 U.S. 39 (1984)). The *Rosen* court applied a hybrid test under *Press-Enterprise* and CIPA that required the government to establish: (1) an overriding reason for closing the trial; (2) that the closure is only as broad as necessary to protect that interest; (3) that there is no reasonable alternative to closure; and (4) that the defendant is able to present substantially the same defense with the silent witness rule as he could with full public disclosure of the evidence. *See id.* at *10.

Although we are not aware of any reported decisions in terrorism cases, we understand that the silent witness rule was used in *United States v. Moussaoui* and *United States v. Abu Ali* to protect information for which CIPA procedures were deemed an insufficient safeguard. The rule is also available to a defendant whose counsel seeks to use evidence that remains classified and is not subject to substitution through the CIPA process. The rule therefore may be invoked more frequently in the future, which raises the possibility that greater portions of trials may be closed. Trial closure is an issue that warrants close scrutiny.[267]

3. Assessing CIPA's Effectiveness in Terrorism Cases

The proper handling of classified information is one of the most important and difficult challenges presented by international terrorism cases. In the blockbuster cases of the 1990s, the government was aware that it might need to "pull the plug" on the prosecutions if the court system was unable to fashion viable methods of handling classified evidence. *See* Interview with Mary Jo White, former U.S. Att'y for the S.D.N.Y. (Nov. 16, 2007). Over the years, however, courts have repeatedly demonstrated that they can use CIPA and analogize from CIPA to fashion solutions that protect the fair-trial rights of defendants while ensuring that classified information is not compromised.

Prior evaluations of CIPA have found that CIPA is "effective not only in espionage prosecutions but in terrorism prosecutions as well," *see* Serrin Turner & Stephen J. Schulhofer, Brennan Ctr. for Justice at N.Y.U. Sch. of L., *The Secrecy Problem in Terrorism Trials* 22 (2005),[268] and that there is "no indication that [CIPA], reasonably interpreted by federal judges, is inadequate to the task of protecting national security interests while affording defendants a fair trial." Ass'n of the Bar of the City of N.Y., *The Indefinite Detention of "Enemy Combatants,"* at 143. Patrick Fitzgerald, a prosecutor in the Embassy Bombings case, was quoted as saying, "When you see how much classified information was involved in that case, and when you see that there weren't any leaks, you get pretty darn confident that the federal courts are capable of handling these prosecutions. I don't think people realize how well our system can work in protecting classified information." Turner & Schulhofer, *The Secrecy Problem in Terrorism Trials*, at 25 (citing to a Consultation with Patrick Fitzgerald (Nov. 29, 2004)). Defense counsel in the Embassy Bombings trial also agreed that the case did not result in the disclosure of any sensitive intelligence information. *See id.* at 9 (citing to Consultations with Joshua Dratel (Sept. 9, 2004) and Sam Schmidt (Sept. 7, 2004), defense counsel for Wadih el-Hage). The experts whom we interviewed broadly agreed with these assessments, although some noted that CIPA becomes strained in cases that are dominated by classified evidence because relevance determinations and key evidentiary rulings must be made in camera and without a well-developed context rather than in open court as is the norm.[269]

As a result of CIPA's effectiveness, the government has been able to use information obtained from foreign law-enforcement and intelligence sources without compromising the integrity of those sources. For example, in the Embassy Bombings case, the government offered the testimony of L'Houssaine Kherchtou, a former al Qaeda member. *See* Turner & Schulhofer, *The Secrecy Problem in Terrorism Trials*, at 24. Prior to Kherchtou becoming a cooperating witness, he had been questioned by a foreign intelligence service for five days concerning his knowledge of al Qaeda. That questioning was taped, provided to the United States, and contained information relevant to the case, but the foreign intelligence service insisted that its involvement not be disclosed. "CIPA effectively resolved the issue: in discovery, a transcript of the debriefing was provided to defense counsel with references to the foreign intelligence service blacked out; at trial, defense counsel's questioning of Kherchtou on the witness stand was monitored to ensure that the foreign intelligence service was not identified." *Id.* It is our understanding that foreign intelligence agencies have become more willing to share information with the United States over time, as CIPA has proved to be effective in a number of cases. Even in cases where CIPA's procedures have not been involved, Courts have permitted the government to maintain the secrecy of sensitive law-enforcement information. For example, in *United States v. al-Moayad*, Judge Sterling Johnson granted motions in limine to preclude defense cross-examination of German law-enforcement witnesses on sensitive, technical aspects of electronic surveillance that had been employed in Germany. *See* Motion in Limine, *United States v. al-Moayad*, No. 03-cr-01322 (E.D.N.Y. Dec. 22, 2004) (Dkt. No. 100); Interview with Kelly Anne Moore, former Assistant U.S. Att'y in the E.D.N.Y. (Oct. 8, 2007).

As those who have worked with it can attest, however, CIPA is not particularly efficient. "Crafting substitutions that are both fair and effective can be a time-consuming, labor-intensive process, as can be the task of monitoring trial proceedings to ensure that classified information is not released through witness testimony." Turner & Schulhofer, *The Secrecy Problem in Terrorism Trials*, at 25. According to a former CIA general counsel, "CIPA is awkward and cumbersome, but it works." *Id.* (citing Consultation with Jeffrey Smith (Sept. 21, 2004)). Nevertheless, courts and counsel have repeatedly exhibited the patience and care that is necessary to use the CIPA procedures effectively.

Some critics have argued that CIPA violates a defendant's right "to secure effective assistance of counsel and to be able to confront the evidence against him." Ellen C. Yaroshefsky, *The Slow Erosion of the Adversary System: Article III Courts, FISA, CIPA and Ethical Dilemmas*, 5 Cardozo Pub. L. Pol'y & Ethics J. 203, 205 (2006); *see also* Sam A. Schmidt & Joshua L. Dratel, *Turning the Tables: Using the Government's Secrecy and Security Arsenal for the Benefit of the Client in Terrorism Prosecutions*, 48 N.Y.L. Sch. L. Rev. 69, 82 (2003/2004). CIPA's critics point to three basic shortcomings in support of their claims: (1) defense counsel is typically excluded from the court's initial review of classified material to determine whether information is discoverable and, because of their different roles, the court and the government do not share the defense's perspective as to what evidence might be material or relevant; (2) because counsel cannot discuss classified evidence with the defendant, it makes it difficult to prepare a defendant to testify, to conduct an adequate investigation, and to prepare a defense; and (3) defendants lose the right to confront the evidence against them, a right that is personal to the defendant and is not exercisable merely through counsel. *See* Yaroshefsky, *The Slow Erosion of the Adversary System*, at 213-19; Schmidt & Dratel, *Turning the Tables*, at 82-83.[270] As noted above, however, courts have repeatedly upheld CIPA's constitutionality. The criticism that defense counsel is excluded from the initial determination of whether classified material is discoverable is not readily distinguishable from the well-accepted (though, in some cases, problematic) practice in criminal cases that determinations of discovery material and *Brady* material are made by the government without defense or court participation. Further, these criticisms are addressed generally, at least to some extent, by the judicially-enforced requirement that CIPA substitutions be equally effective, from a defense perspective, as the underlying evidence.

Criticizing CIPA from the other end of the spectrum, proponents of a national security court or military tribunal for terrorism defendants claim that CIPA does not provide enough protection for sensitive information related to national security. *See, e.g.*, Andrew C. McCarthy & Alykhan Velshi, *We Need a National Security Court* (July 16, 2007) (unpublished manuscript, on file with the Foundation for Defense of Democracies).[271] It is true that, like any rule of law or procedure, CIPA is not foolproof and security breaches may sometimes occur. However, based on the public record, we are not aware of any important security breach in any terrorism case in which CIPA has been invoked. It has been reported that a breach occurred during trial of Sheikh Omar Abdel Rahman in Manhattan in the 1990s, when the government turned over to the defense a list of some 200 names of people, including Osama bin Laden, and entities who were alleged to be unindicted co-conspirators. *See 9/11 Commission Report*, at 427 n.8; McCarthy & Velshi, *We Need a National Security Court*, at fn.19; *see also* Michael B. Mukasey, Op-Ed., *Jose Padilla Makes Bad Law*, Wall St. J., Aug. 22, 2007, at A15.[272] The reports claim that the list eventually reached Bin Laden in Khartoum, alerting him to the fact that his connection to the case had been discovered. *See* McCarthy & Velshi, *We Need a National Security Court*, at fn.19.[273] However, in that case, it is our understanding that the government did not seek to invoke CIPA or other protections regarding the names on the list of unindicted co-conspirators. Had the government sought a court order restricting dissemination of the list, perhaps it would not have been disseminated to Bin Laden. In fact, in later terrorism cases, such as the Embassy Bombings case, protective orders have been employed to restrict the dissemination of sensitive materials. *See* Protective Order, *United States v. el-Hage*, No. 98-cr-001023 (S.D.N.Y. Dec. 17, 1998) (Dkt. No. 27).[274]

The other example most commonly cited for the proposition that terrorism trials have led to security breaches can be dismissed as factually inaccurate. It has been variously claimed that during the trial of Ramzi Yousef or during the Embassy Bombings trial the admission of phone records into evidence tipped Bin Laden off that the United States was monitoring his satellite phone and caused him to cease using it. *See, e.g.*, Mukasey, *Jose Padilla Makes Bad Law* (claiming the evidence was disclosed in the *Yousef* trial).[275] Both claims are plainly wrong. As an initial matter, the phone records related to Bin Laden's satellite phone were introduced into evidence in the Embassy Bombings case, not the *Yousef* trial. Indeed, the phone records were not obtained until after the *Yousef* trial. More importantly, the record makes clear that Bin Laden had stopped using the phone years before the records were offered in evidence at trial.

Documents regarding the satellite phone were seized in the September 23, 1998, search by New Scotland Yard of the London home of Khalid al-Fawwaz, an alleged al Qaeda associate who handled public relations.[276] Subsequently obtained records indicated that the phone was not used at all after October 9, 1998, and that the phone's use had dropped off dramatically after August 21, 1998, which was the day after the U.S. cruise missile attack on Bin Laden.[277] There are at least two reasons that neither the presentation of the phone records evidence in the Embassy Bombings trial, nor even the disclosure of those records to the defense in discovery, could possibly have caused Bin Laden to stop using the monitored phone: (1) the phone records seized from al-Fawwaz's home were not the subject of trial testimony until March 20, 2001, almost two-and-a-half years after the phone went dead,[278] and (2) discovery regarding the phone records was not turned over to the defense until well after the phone had gone dead.[279] Therefore, while there is no doubt that terrorism trials can pose risks for the disclosure of sensitive information and put strain on all the participants to take great care, the primary examples that are used to illustrate these risks are unfounded.

CIPA has provided flexibility to allow courts to address situations that were not originally envisioned. Indeed, the problem CIPA was intended to address—the disclosure of classified material already in the possession of the defendant—is different from the situation typically presented in terrorism trials, in which the classified information is known only to the government. Nevertheless, courts have dealt with this problem by entering protective orders to require security clearance of defense counsel and to prohibit defendants from access to the classified information. Certain situations, however, are beyond the express scope of CIPA's provisions.

For example, CIPA does not address the proper outcome when a defendant attempts to represent himself pro se, a situation that came to bear for a time in *Moussaoui*.[280] In *Mousssaoui*, the court denied the defendant's pro se request for access to classified discovery materials, finding that his interests could be protected by providing standby defense counsel with access to the classified materials. *See Moussaoui*, 2002 WL 1987964, at *1. Questions regarding Moussaoui's access to classified information and the use of standby counsel have been appealed to the Fourth Circuit, which will determine whether Judge Brinkema's reasoning was sound.

Although the Supreme Court has recognized a constitutional right to self-representation in criminal cases, *see Faretta v. California*, 422 U.S. 806 (1975), the courts have also recognized restrictions on that right. For example, even if a defendant invokes the right to self-representation, the court may appoint standby counsel to assist the defendant with courtroom procedures and mechanics. *See, e.g., McKaskle v. Wiggins*, 465 U.S. 168, 183 (1984) ("*Faretta* rights are also not infringed when standby counsel assists the *pro se* defendant in overcoming routine procedural or evidentiary obstacles to the completion of some specific task ... Nor are they infringed when counsel merely helps to ensure the defendant's compliance with basic rules of courtroom protocol and procedure."); *United States v. Irorere*, 228 F.3d 816, 828 n.2 (7th Cir. 2000) ("When a criminal defendant decides to proceed *pro se*, it is generally advisable for the district court to appoint 'shadow counsel' to be available to assist the defendant if needed."). Under these authorities, we anticipate that courts would recognize that a criminal defendant cannot plausibly claim an entitlement to see classified information by the simple expedient of firing his lawyer and that, in this area, standby counsel can be relied upon to protect the defendant's interests.

Moussaoui also highlighted that CIPA does not address the potential expansion of the scope of classified information that may be sought by a defendant who is facing the death penalty. In capital cases, the jury must consider statutory mitigating and aggravating factors in determining whether to impose a death sentence. *See* 18 U.S.C. § 3592 (enumerating factors). For example, one criterion is the relative participation of the individual involved in the criminal act. Facing the death penalty, Moussaoui requested classified information that extended beyond what was relevant to guilt or innocence and encompassed the criteria that are weighed by the jury. Specifically, he sought access to other detained suspects who he felt could corroborate his low rank and level of responsibility in al Qaeda and the charged criminal conduct, or could corroborate other mitigating factors. According to participants in the *Moussaoui* trial, this was a complicating factor in dealing with the classified information issues. *See* Matthew Barakat, *Moussaoui Judge: Terror Trials Work*, Assoc. Press, Feb. 2, 2008 ("U.S. District Judge Leonie Brinkema said in a speech ... that the zealous pursuit of a death sentence opened up numerous issues of exposing classified information that otherwise could have been avoided."). The challenges raised as a result of the death penalty charge were also reflected in Judge Brinkema's rulings regarding the trial testimony of three individuals, which the defense sought and the prosecution opposed because of the national security interest in gathering intelligence vital to saving American lives and winning an ongoing war. *See United States v. Moussaoui*, No. 01-cr-00455, 2003 WL 21263699, at *4 (E.D. Va. March 10, 2003) (addressing relevance of testimony of certain detained al Qaeda associates "support the defense argument that Moussaoui should not be sentenced to death" because information from that testimony "may be considered mitigating evidence of the defendant's minor role in the offense(s)"); *United States v. Moussaoui*, 282 F. Supp. 2d 480, 482 (E.D. Va. 2003) (noting that the court has previously found that "the United States may not maintain this capital prosecution while simultaneously refusing to produce witnesses who could, at minimum, help the defendant avoid a sentence of death").

Some observers have suggested that CIPA should be amended to address the statute's perceived limitations. For example, it has been suggested that basic amendments to CIPA, such as adding a provision mandating the application of CIPA to terrorism proceedings and adding a provision that expressly allows for the exclusion of a defendant from trial proceedings in limited circumstances, would be desirable. *See* James N. Boeving, *The Right to be Present Before Military Commissions and Federal Courts: Protecting National Security in the Age of Classified Information*, 30 Harv. J.L. & Pub. Pol'y 463, 552 (2007). In addition, the Department of Justice has identified two areas in need of improvement: (1) clarification of the appropriate application and scope of CIPA regarding access to witnesses and witness testimony as highlighted in *Moussaoui* and (2) a provision giving the government the ability to explain its reasons for invoking CIPA to the court under seal. *See* U.S. Dep't of Justice, Counterterrorism Section, *Counterterrorism White Paper* 49 (2006).[281]

As a solution to balancing a defendant's right of compulsory process to produce witnesses in his favor with the government's interest in preventing witness testimony from harming national security, Professor Stephen Schulhofer has suggested prohibiting the witness from testifying in court but allowing videotaped depositions to be played with a delay mechanism to allow the court to monitor classified information. *See* N.Y.U. Sch. of Law, The Ctr. on Law and Sec., *Prosecuting Terrorism: The Legal Challenge*, The N.Y.U. Rev. of Law and Sec., Issue No. 7, at 27 (April 2006). However, it is unclear whether such a solution would pass muster under the Confrontation Clause. *See United States v. Yates*, 438 F.3d 1307, 1312-18 (11th Cir. 2006) (where witnesses testified by means of two-way video hookup court held that in the absence of a showing that the video method was necessary to further an important public policy and that the reliability of the testimony was assured, Confrontation Clause was not overridden); *see also id.* at 1314-15 (citing Justice Scalia's statement objecting to amendment to Federal Rule of Criminal Procedure 26(b) allowing for testimony by two-way video conferencing). Some prosecutors who have handled terrorism cases have expressed the view that they are impeded by the limitations on the ability to get two-way video testimony and the concern that if they use such testimony it could lead to the overturning of a verdict.

IX.
Courts Have Effectively Applied the *Brady* Rule and the Government's Other Disclosure Obligations in Terrorism Cases

In the landmark case of *Brady v. Maryland*, the Supreme Court established the rule that "the suppression by the prosecution of evidence favorable to the accused upon request violates due process where the evidence is material either to guilt or to punishment, irrespective of the good faith or bad faith of the prosecution." 373 U.S. 83, 87 (1963). This rule upholds the notion that the government does not "win" a case simply when it secures a conviction, but rather that "the United States wins its point whenever justice is done its citizens in the courts." *Id.* In order to discharge its *Brady* obligations, the government must disclose exculpatory information to the defense early enough to permit the defense to effectively investigate and use the evidence at trial. *See United States v. Coppa*, 267 F.3d 132, 144 (2d Cir. 2001).

In *Giglio v. United States*, the Supreme Court held that *Brady* extends to evidence that may be used to impeach government witnesses as well as evidence that tends to directly bear on the defendant's guilt or innocence. *See* 405 U.S. 150, 154 (1972) ("when the 'reliability of a given witness may well be determinative of guilt or innocence,' non-disclosure of evidence affecting credibility falls within" the *Brady* doctrine) (quoting *Napue v. Illinois*, 360 U.S. 264, 269 (1959)). The government, however, is obligated to disclose impeachment evidence only relating to witnesses that are actually testifying, or whose statements as hearsay declarants are admissible under the Federal Rules of Evidence, and is only required to turn over such evidence in order to permit its effective use during cross-examination. *See* Fed. R. Evid. 806; *Coppa*, 267 F.3d at 144. The government's failure to properly discharge its *Brady* and *Giglio* obligations is a violation of the Due Process Clause of the Fourteenth Amendment.[282]

In 1985, the standard for what evidence constitutes *Brady* information was crystallized by the Supreme Court in *United States v. Bagley*. *See* 473 U.S. 667 (1985). In *Bagley*, the Court held that "[t]he evidence is material only if there is a reasonable probability that, had the evidence been disclosed to the defense, the result of the proceeding would have been different. A 'reasonable probability' is a probability sufficient to undermine confidence in the outcome." 473 U.S. at 682. Ten years later, the Supreme Court in *Kyles v. Whitley* further refined the *Brady* rule, holding that the government's disclosure obligation under *Brady* turns on the cumulative effect of the withheld evidence, not an item-by-item analysis. 514 U.S. 419, 436-37, 436 n.10 (1995). Recent Supreme Court cases affirm the vitality of the *Brady* rule.[283]

In addition to the duties imposed by *Brady*, the government must comply with discovery obligations created by Federal Rule of Criminal Procedure 16. Although pre-trial discovery in criminal cases is far more limited than in civil litigation, under Rule 16 the government must produce all written or recorded statements of the defendant as well as the substance of any oral statements of the defendant to government agents, plus other information including documents or objects that the government intends to use in its case in chief or that are "material to preparing the defense." Fed. R. Crim. P. 16(a).

Separately, before a government witness testifies, the government must turn over the witness' prior statements pursuant to the Jencks Act, 18 U.S.C. § 3500. While the statute does not literally require that such statements be disclosed to the defense until *after* the witness has testified on direct examination, in our experience most courts recognize that this is unfair to the defense and unworkable because it occasions delay as the defense needs time to review the disclosed material. As a result, most courts require disclosure of Jencks Act material in advance of the hearing or trial at which the witness will testify, or alternatively the court will order that disclosure occur at some reasonable point in advance of the government witness' direct examination.

The government's *Brady*, discovery, and Jencks Act obligations are fundamental, and violations can have dramatic consequences. A notorious example involves *United States v. Koubriti*, commonly known as the "Detroit Sleeper Cell" case. No. 01-cr-80778 (E.D. Mich. Sept. 18, 2001). In *Koubriti*, the defendants, alleged members of an al Qaeda sleeper cell, were indicted for material support of a terrorist organization. *See* First Superseding Indictment, *Koubriti* (E.D. Mich. Apr. 3, 2002) (Dkt. No. 121). The *Koubriti* case attracted national attention because the defendants were arrested within a week of the 9/11 attacks, and the case was billed as the government's first major terrorism trial in the wake of 9/11. *See* Gov't's Consol. Resp. Concurring in the Def.'s Mots. for a New Trial & Gov't's Mot. to Dismiss Count One Without Prejudice & Mem. of Law in Support Thereof ("Gov't's Consol. Resp.") at 6, *Koubriti* (E.D. Mich. Aug. 31, 2004) (Dkt. No. 562)[284]; Danny Hakim, *U.S. Asks for Dismissal of Terrorism Convictions*, N.Y. Times, Sept. 1, 2004, at A17;[285] David Johnston, *A Nation Challenged: The Investigation; 3 Held in Detroit After Aircraft Diagrams Are Found*, N.Y. Times, Sept. 20, 2001, at B2.[286] After a jury trial in 2003, two of the four defendants were convicted of terrorism charges based on evidence that they had "cased" various sites for a planned terrorist attack. *See* Verdict, *Koubriti* (E.D. Mich. June 3, 2003) (Dkt. No. 367); Gov't Consol. Resp. at 10-13, *Koubriti* (E.D. Mich. Aug. 31, 2004) (Dkt. No. 562). After the conviction, however, the defendants moved to dismiss the trial based on prosecutorial misconduct. *See* Mot. for Judgment of Acquittal, Koubriti (E.D. Mich. Oct. 15, 2003) (Dkt. No. 422); Mot. for Judgment Notwithstanding the Verdict or in the Alternative for New Trial, *Koubriti* (E.D. Mich. Oct. 15, 2003) (Dkt. No. 424); Am. Mot. for Judgment Notwithstanding the Verdict or in the Alternative for New Trial, *Koubriti* (E.D. Mich. Oct. 17, 2003) (Dkt. No. 425); *see also* Bennett L. Gershman, *How Juries Get it Wrong—Anatomy of the Detroit Terror Case*, 44 Washburn L.J. 327, 338-54 (2005) (discussing specifics of prosecutorial misconduct). In 2004, after a court-ordered internal review by the Justice Department, which resulted in the Department of Justice conceding error, the court dismissed the terrorism convictions and allowed a new trial on lesser document fraud charges. *United States v. Koubriti*, 336 F. Supp. 2d 676, 682 (E.D. Mich. 2004).

In its detailed court filing confessing error, the government acknowledged that its trial team had violated *Brady* by failing to tell the defendants that, among other things, a sketch alleged to show terrorist plotting against a U.S. airbase in Turkey instead was just a map of the Middle East and that a video alleged to reveal terrorist surveillance of U.S. attractions such as Disneyland and Las Vegas was merely a tourist videotape depicting young Tunisians visiting the United States. *See* Gov't's Consol. Resp. at 14-42, *Koubriti* (E.D. Mich. Aug. 31, 2004) (Dkt. No. 562). The government acknowledged that prosecutors also violated *Giglio* by failing to produce evidence calling into question the credibility of a government informant. *Id.* at 42-49. Due to the overwhelming amount of exculpatory evidence that had been suppressed, the Department of Justice asked that the terrorism charges be dropped, a development that the trial judge praised as being "not only the legally and ethically correct decision," but also "in the highest and best tradition of Department of Justice attorneys." *Koubriti*, 336 F. Supp. 2d at 679.

Thereafter, in a stunning development, the Department of Justice announced the indictment of Richard G. Convertino, the lead prosecutor in the case, and Harry R. Smith III, a security officer for the State Department who assisted in the prosecution, based on the *Brady* violations. *See* Indictment, *United States v. Convertino*, No. 06-cr-20173 (E.D. Mich. Mar. 29, 2006) (Dkt. No. 1); *see also* Paul Egan, *Terrorism Prosecutor Is Now a Defendant*, Detroit News, Oct. 8, 2007, at 1A;[287] Eric Lichtblau, *Ex-Prosecutor Accused of Concealing Evidence in Terror Case*, N.Y. Times, Mar. 29, 2006, at A18.[288] The two were indicted on charges of obstruction of justice and conspiracy to obstruct justice. *See* Indictment, *Convertino* (E.D. Mich. Mar. 29, 2006) (Dkt. No. 1). On October 31, 2007, after less than a day of deliberations, a jury acquitted Convertino and Smith of all charges. *See* Jury Verdict Form, *Convertino* (E.D. Mich. Oct. 31, 2007) (Dkt. No. 195); *see also* Philip Shenon, *Ex-Prosecutor Acquitted of Misconduct in 9/11 Case*, N.Y. Times, Nov. 1. 2007, at A18.[289] These tangled events illustrate the importance of the government's *Brady* obligations and the potentially grave consequences of violations for defendants who are wrongfully convicted and for those who are blamed for the miscues.

A. Balancing the Government's *Brady* Obligations Against the Need to Protect Sensitive National-Security Information

In applying the *Brady* rule and enforcing the government's disclosure obligations, courts must balance the defendant's due process rights to a fair trial and the government's interest in protecting national security. In some terrorism cases, achieving this balance has proved challenging for courts given the classified nature of some of the government's evidence and the fact that some key witnesses are either being detained by the government or are involved in ongoing counterterrorism efforts.

The high-profile case of *United States v. Moussaoui* dealt squarely with these challenges. In *Moussaoui*, defense counsel sought *Brady* material in the form of access to notorious terrorism figures who were in government custody and had made statements tending to exculpate Moussaoui. The government countered that providing Moussaoui with access to these individuals could interfere with ongoing interrogations and endanger national security. Finding that the witnesses' testimony was critical to Moussaoui's defense, the district court ordered the government to make the detainees available for questioning, suggesting a system whereby the witnesses could be deposed via closed-circuit feed from a remote location, with lag time to edit out sensitive information. *See United States v. Moussaoui*, 382 F.3d 453, 458 (4th Cir. 2004).[290]

On appeal, the Fourth Circuit took a different approach. The Fourth Circuit began by framing the questions presented by Moussaoui's *Brady* motion as ones of "grave significance" that "test the commitment of this nation to an independent judiciary, to the constitutional guarantee of a fair trial even to one accused of the most heinous of crimes, and to the protection of our citizens against additional terrorist attacks." *Id.* at 456. The Fourth Circuit then held that while Moussaoui was entitled to the witnesses' exculpatory information pursuant to *Brady*, carefully crafted summaries of interviews or interrogations of these witnesses would satisfy the government's *Brady* obligation and that depositions were unnecessary. *Id.* at 456-57.

In so holding, the Fourth Circuit discussed in detail the need to balance the defendant's rights with the government's need to protect national security. The court noted the government's argument that presenting the witnesses for depositions would create an unacceptable threat to national security for three reasons: (1) interruption of ongoing investigations and interrogations "could result in the loss of information that might prevent future terrorist attacks"; (2) "production of the witnesses would burden the Executive's ability to conduct foreign relations" because "if the Executive's assurances of confidentiality can be abrogated by the judiciary, the vital ability to obtain the cooperation of other governments will be devastated"; and (3) production of the witnesses might have a "bolstering effect ... on our enemies." *Id.* at 470-71. As a counterbalance, the court emphasized that Moussaoui's "Sixth Amendment right to compulsory process is not subject to question—it is integral to our adversarial criminal justice system." *Id.* at 471. Accordingly, after determining that the witnesses had material evidence that could benefit Moussaoui, the court held that Moussaoui was constitutionally entitled to the witnesses' testimony. *Id.* at 471-76.

The Fourth Circuit explained that determining whether to penalize the government for not complying with the defendant's "constitutionally guaranteed access to evidence" while taking into consideration the government's burdens in producing these witnesses was not unique and had been dealt with by the Supreme Court on "numerous occasions." *Id.* at 474 (quoting *Arizona v. Youngblood*, 488 U.S. 51, 55 (1988)). However, while the issue was perhaps not unique, the solution presented by the court was. The Fourth Circuit analogized the issue in *Moussaoui* to ones often faced under the Classified Information Procedures Act ("CIPA"). *Id.* at 471-72, 472 n.20, and 476-77.

As outlined above, CIPA enables the government to submit summaries of classified information in lieu of original evidence as a way to provide the defendant with relevant information while also protecting the most sensitive aspects of that information. *See id.* at 476-77. In *Moussaoui*, the Fourth Circuit utilized a CIPA-like solution whereby the government was required to produce summaries that were as unedited and true to the original statements of the witnesses as possible without compromising national security. Specifically, the Fourth Circuit proposed that summary evidence would be a sufficient substitution for deposition testimony so long as "the crafting of the substitutions [is] an interactive process among the parties and the district court" and the substitutions are crafted so that they "use the exact language ... to the greatest extent possible." *Id.* at 480. The court suggested that these parameters would be best accomplished by the defense first identifying the portions of the summaries it wanted to admit and then allowing the government to suggest additional portions in the interest of completeness. *Id.*[291] Based on the combined suggestions by the government and the defense, the district court should then create an appropriate set of substitutions. *Id.*

Commentators have noted that the solutions proposed by both the district court and the Fourth Circuit in *Moussaoui* show the ability of federal courts to come up with creative and effective solutions when dealing with the difficult balancing issues faced in terrorism trials.[292] Nevertheless, some have commented that the balance struck by the Fourth Circuit in *Moussaoui* was problematic, because in agreeing to admit summary evidence instead of producing the *Brady* witnesses for live questioning, Moussaoui's ability to exculpate himself was hampered. *See, e.g.*, Serrin Turner & Stephen J. Schulhofer, Brennan Ctr. for Justice at N.Y.U. Sch. of L., *The Secrecy Problem in Terrorism Trials* 44 (2005)[293] (while praising the flexibility and ingenuity of the *Moussaoui* courts, the authors nonetheless note that "the appeals court decision allowing written summaries to substitute for actual deposition testimony is certainly subject to criticism, and the compromise it endorsed should not necessarily be considered acceptable. It is something of a stretch to say that mere summaries will provide Moussaoui with 'substantially the same ability to make his defense' as would allowing him to call the detainees to testify, either at trial or in a deposition."); *see also* Megan A. Healy, *Compulsory Process and the War on Terror: A Proposed Framework*, 90 Minn. L. Rev. 1821, 1840 (2006) ("The Fourth Circuit's ruling exposed the difficulties inherent in prosecuting a terrorism defendant in the civilian criminal justice system. While the court effectuated Moussaoui's right to compulsory process in form, it gutted that right in substance. By employing a balancing test, the Fourth Circuit allowed asserted governmental interests to emasculate the defendant's right to compulsory process. Thus, the court failed to protect both Moussaoui's constitutional rights and the government's national security interest."). Others have raised the issue of whether CIPA's "substitute evidence" framework "violates the accused's constitutional right to a fair, public trial."[294]

It seems likely, however, that the summaries would have been helpful for the defense given the Fourth Circuit's admonitions that the summaries be as close to verbatim as possible and that the government could not offer inculpatory evidence as part of the summaries. Indeed, under CIPA, to which the district court and the Fourth Circuit looked for guidance in *Moussaoui*, summaries may be used in lieu of the underlying evidence *only* if they give the defendant "substantially the same ability to make his defense as would disclosure of the specified classified information." 18 U.S.C. app. 3 § 6(c)(1). It is true that the effect of a CIPA summary may fall short of favorable testimony from a live witness. On the other hand, live testimony may not be available in some cases, because accomplice witnesses often refuse to testify under oath to avoid incriminating themselves. Furthermore, even if an accomplice witness is willing to testify, experienced trial lawyers know that the effect of any particular witness' live testimony is difficult to predict and, in some cases, a witness' testimony can actually "boomerang" and wind up hurting the party who calls the witness if the witness is not perceived as credible or if damaging information is exposed on cross-examination. Therefore, from a defense perspective there may be clear advantages to CIPA-type summaries—that they can be admitted regardless of whether the witness would have asserted his Fifth Amendment rights and they cannot be undone on cross-examination by the government.

In the Embassy Bombings trial, defense counsel concluded that CIPA-type summaries were more useful than the underlying evidence would have been. In that trial, the defense sought to introduce cross-examination material regarding the "Black Hawk Down" episode in Somalia, but the government insisted that the information remain classified. *See* Sam A. Schmidt & Joshua L. Dratel, *Turning the Tables: Using the Government's Secrecy and Security Arsenal for the Benefit of the Client in Terrorism Prosecutions*, 48 N.Y.L. Sch. L. Rev. 69, 84 (2003-04). The defense agreed not to use that material in exchange for a stipulation "that was completely different than the projected cross-examination material, but which made [the defense's] point explicitly." *Id.* According to defense counsel, the "stipulation accomplished much more than the cross-examination would have. Even a perfectly executed cross-examination would not have established [what the defense sought to establish]." *Id.* at 85.

In *United States v. Paracha*, the Southern District of New York adopted a balancing approach that tracked the Fourth Circuit's decision in *Moussaoui* and that, in our view, underscores the practicality of the *Moussaoui* approach. In *Paracha*, defendant Uzair Paracha was accused of providing material support to al Qaeda by posing as another person, an alleged al Qaeda figure named Majid Khan, in order to make it easier for Khan to enter the United States. *See United States v. Paracha*, No. 03-cr-01197, 2006 WL 12768, at *1-*2, *11 (S.D.N.Y. Jan. 3, 2006). Specifically, the defendant was accused of obtaining immigration documents in Khan's name, using Khan's credit card in the United States, and conducting financial transactions with more than $200,000 in al Qaeda funds. *Id.* A jury ultimately found Paracha guilty of all charges against him. *Id.* at *1. Before trial, Paracha requested permission to depose four witnesses. *Id.* at *2-3. One of the witnesses, Paracha's father, Saifullah Paracha, was being held at Guantánamo as an "enemy combatant"; the other three, Majid Khan, Ammar al-Baluchi, and Khalid Sheikh Mohammad, were in government custody in undisclosed locations. *Id.* at *3, *5.

The government conceded that Paracha's father had made exculpatory statements during his testimony before a Combatant Status Review Tribunal at Guantánamo, and the parties agreed on procedures that would have permitted Paracha to depose his father at Guantánamo. *Id.* at *3. Just twelve days before the scheduled deposition, however, the defense informed the government that it had decided not to proceed with the deposition. *Id.* The reasons why are unclear from the public record. Thereafter, Paracha sought an order requiring the government to produce the father for live testimony at trial, but the court rejected this motion on grounds of national security. *Id.* at *3, *16-*18. Further, noting that Paracha had forfeited the opportunity to take his father's deposition before trial, the court held that the defense would not be permitted, at trial, to offer a CIPA-type summary of the father's statements. *Id.* at *18.

With respect to the other three witnesses, the court held that Mohammed's testimony was not material but that Khan and al-Baluchi possessed information that was material and favorable for the defense. *Id.* at *11-13, *16. The court found that it was not possible to arrange pre-trial depositions of Khan and al-Baluchi because of national security concerns, including the risk of disclosure of classified information, the disruption of intelligence-gathering, and the impairment of foreign policy efforts. *Id.* at *11-13. In accordance with *Moussaoui*, however, and with the consent of the defendant, the court concluded that the defendant's rights would be adequately protected through the admission of unclassified summaries of Khan and al-Baluchi's information, along with appropriate jury instructions to permit the jury to evaluate the circumstances under which the information in the summaries was obtained. *Id.* at *13-15. As the court noted, the summaries were favorable for the defense because the defendant could "present the witness's exculpatory statements without the introduction by the government of any inculpatory statements they might have made, and without subjecting the witnesses to cross-examination by the government." *Id.* at *13. Perhaps the best indication that this observation was correct is that the defendants consented to the use of the summaries.

B. Managing Problems Presented by Voluminous FISA Materials and Overclassification

It has been observed that defendants may be disadvantaged from a *Brady* perspective because of the government's practice of recording a large number of conversations under FISA but then following through with review, translation, and transcription for only a small number of the intercepted communications. Indeed, in the view of Joshua Dratel, a noted defense attorney who has participated in several high-profile terrorism cases, FISA effectively "reverses the obligation imposed upon the Government, pursuant to *Brady v. Maryland*, i.e., to provide the defense with exculpatory material within its custody and control. By not listening to the vast majority of FISA intercepts, the Government places the burden on defense counsel to find *Brady* material." Joshua L. Dratel, *Sword or Shield? The Government's Selective Use of its Declassification Authority for Tactical Advantage in Criminal Prosecutions*, 5 Cardozo Pub. L. Pol'y & Ethics J. 171, 178 (2006).

Any lawyer who has been involved in a large case with voluminous computer-stored evidence will be naturally sympathetic to this complaint. The profusion of electronic evidence does indeed present real problems for defense counsel and sometimes even the government in many modern-day criminal cases. However, such problems are by no means unique to international terrorism cases; to the contrary, in this era of electronic evidence, it has become all too common for defense counsel to be deluged with millions of pages of electronic documents.[295] In many large criminal cases, courts and counsel must deal with voluminous electronic evidence as thoroughly as possible by using techniques such as search terms and electronic databases. In the terrorism context, the problem would be reduced if intelligence agencies were able to more efficiently digest information such as FISA intercepts.[296] Ultimately, however, the challenge of managing vast arrays of evidence is simply a fact of life in modern-day litigation. In terrorism cases, courts have generally provided counsel with time to digest voluminous FISA evidence upon a showing that counsel is diligently attacking the problem. *See* Mem. Order & Op., *United States v. Holy Land Found. for Relief and Dev.*, No. 04-cr-00240 (N.D. Tex. Nov. 2, 2006) (Dkt. No. 443) (granting five-and-a-half-month continuance of trial date so defense could analyze voluminous amount of FISA materials, including English-language and foreign-language intercepts); *United States v. al-Arian*, 267 F. Supp. 2d 1258, 1260-64 (M.D. Fla. 2003) (granting eighteen-month continuance so defense could review 21,000 hours of recordings intercepted under FISA as well as 550 videotapes, thirty hard drives from seized computers, and hundreds of boxes of documentary evidence).

If voluminous FISA evidence is designated as "classified" by the government, defense counsel faces an even more difficult task in reviewing and analyzing the material for trial. Before reviewing classified FISA evidence, defense counsel must obtain a security clearance and then must locate and hire a qualified translator with a security clearance. Finding a translator is not always easy to do, especially where the government has filed its indictment far away from any major city. Further, defense counsel may not share the evidence with their client unless and until it is declassified—a limitation that may substantially impair defense counsel's ability to understand the evidence. *See* Dratel, *Sword or Shield?*, at 177-78 (citing several cases in which defense counsel struggled to deal with voluminous FISA intercepts that were designated as classified by the government); Mem. Op. & Order, *Holy Land Found. for Relief and Dev.* (N.D. Tex. July 5, 2007) (Dkt. No. 704) (denying defendants' motion to declassify certain FISA intercepts that the government intended to use at trial and noting that while defendants themselves were not permitted to review certain classified FISA intercepts, the intercepts had been provided to defense counsel, who had obtained appropriate security clearances). Finally, if voluminous FISA intercepts are treated as classified, it magnifies the burden on the parties and the court of going through CIPA procedures to balance the defendant's rights against the need to protect classified information.

Many lawyers whom we interviewed agree that, in general, there is a tendency for the government to be overly broad in designating evidence as classified. The declassification procedures are bureaucratic and time-consuming, but prosecutors have reported success in working through those procedures and declassifying significant evidence. Indeed, the traditional practice in the Southern District of New York has been to promptly declassify all FISA recordings of the defendants' own conversations that are produced to the defense in discovery. *See* Dratel, *Sword or Shield?*, at 179. In some other jurisdictions, the government has been accused of delay in declassifying FISA materials in order to gain a tactical advantage over the defense. *See generally id.* at 171. It is difficult to evaluate the merits of this accusation, but certainly courts should provide appropriate relief—whether through necessary adjournments or sanctions against the government if gamesmanship can be proven—in order to allow defense counsel to meaningfully assess the evidence.[297]

C. The Scope of the Prosecution's Obligation to Search for *Brady* Material

Under Supreme Court precedent, prosecutors have a duty to hand over *Brady* material that is in their own files as well as to "learn of any favorable evidence known to the others acting on the government's behalf in the case, including the police." *Kyles*, 514 U.S. at 437; *see also Pennsylvania v. Ritchie*, 480 U.S. 39 (1987). To meet this duty, the general rule is that the government must search its own files as well as the files held by other branches of government "closely aligned" with the prosecution. *United States v. Brooks*, 966 F.2d 1500, 1503 (D.C. Cir. 1992).

What constitutes "closely aligned" is a source of some debate among the courts. Many circuits follow what is known as the "prosecution team" model, which dictates that the government must search material held by its investigative and prosecutorial personnel. *See, e.g., United States v. Pelullo*,

399 F.3d 197, 217-18 (3d Cir. 2005); *United States v. Morris*, 80 F.3d 1151, 1169 (7th Cir. 1996); *United States v. Meros*, 866 F.2d 1304, 1309 (11th Cir. 1989); *United States v. Antone*, 603 F.2d 566, 569 (5th Cir. 1979). Under this approach, "the Government must produce only those documents to which it has access [and] the prosecutor is not required to conduct a separate investigation for the purpose of responding to a defendant's discovery requests." *United States v. Giffen*, 379 F. Supp. 2d 337, 343 (S.D.N.Y. 2004) (*citing United States v. Avellino*, 136 F.3d 249, 255 (2d Cir. 1998)).

Some courts take a slightly different approach. For example, the Ninth Circuit's approach dictates that "the scope of the government's obligation to produce documents under Rule 16 turns on the extent to which the prosecutor has knowledge of and access to the documents." *United States v. Santiago*, 46 F.3d 885, 894 (9th Cir. 1995) (*quoting United States v. Bryan*, 868 F.2d 1032, 1036 (9th Cir. 1989)) (rejecting government's argument that Rule 16 and *Brady* material need not be disclosed if located outside of the district in which the prosecution was pending); *see also United States v. Poindexter*, 727 F. Supp. 1470, 1473-76 (D.D.C. 1989). However, even under this approach, the Ninth Circuit has stated that boundaries exist, and that "a prosecutor need not comb the files of every federal agency which might have documents regarding the defendant in order to fulfill his or her obligations under [Rule 16]." *Bryan*, 868 F.2d at 1036; *see also United States v. Liquid Sugars, Inc.*, 158 F.R.D. 466, 474 (E.D. Cal. 1994) ("for obvious practical reasons, not every governmental agency can be considered as part of the 'government' for discovery purposes"). A broad definition of the government's duty to search was initially set forth by a district judge in *United States v. Safavian*, where the court held that the definition of "government" under Rule 16 "includes any and all agencies and departments of the Executive Branch of the government and their subdivisions, … and other law enforcement agencies." 233 F.R.D. 12, 14 (D.D.C. 2005). However, the *Safavian* court later tempered this position, explaining that "[w]hile, in this Court's view, the term 'government' encompasses all Executive Branch agencies and departments and the obligation to search files extends beyond agencies 'closely aligned' with the prosecution, it should be apparent that prosecutors are not required to search, or cause to be searched, the files of all Executive Branch agencies and departments in every criminal case." *United States v. Safavian*, 233 F.R.D. 205, 207 fn.1 (D.D.C. 2006).[298]

The government's burden to search may be expanded in cases where the U.S. government is working with foreign governments in a "joint investigation," although the parameters of a "joint investigation" are not always clear. The Second Circuit in *United States v. Paternina-Vergara* established that "in the course of a joint investigation undertaken by United States and foreign law enforcement officials, … United States officials [must engage] in a good-faith effort to obtain the statements of prosecution witnesses in the possession of the foreign government." 749 F.2d 993, 998 (2d Cir. 1984) (applying the doctrine in the context of the Jencks Act). The court emphasized that it would only go so far as to impose a "good faith" requirement, stating that "[t]he investigation of crime increasingly requires the cooperation of foreign and United States law enforcement officials, but there is no reason to think that Congress expected that such cooperation would constitute the foreign officials as agents of the United States …." *Id*. In *Paternina-Vergara*, the court held that where the prosecutor had made a good faith effort to secure documents held by Canadian authorities, the prosecutor had satisfied constitutional requirements even though Canadian authorities chose to withhold some of the documents requested by the defense, because "[w]hatever was withheld reflects the preference of the Canadian authorities, not the reluctance of the United States authorities." *Id*. Other courts have applied this reasoning in coming to similar conclusions. *See, e.g., United States v. Yousef*, 327 F.3d 56, 129-30 (2d Cir. 2003) (government's good faith effort to obtain documents held by the Philippines was sufficient despite the fact that those efforts turned out to be futile because the Philippine government withheld them as classified); *United States v. Webber*, 933 F.2d 1018 (Table), 1991 WL 88172, at *2 (9th Cir. May 17, 1991) (government satisfied its duty to attempt to obtain documents held by the Canadian government where the documents were withheld due to the "preference of Canadian authorities [and] not the reluctance of the United States authorities") (quoting *Paternina-Vergara*, 749 F.2d at 998); *United States v. Tseng*, No. 07-cr-00178, 2007 WL 3237520, at *3 (S.D. Cal. Oct. 30, 2007) (government satisfied its duty to attempt to obtain documents held by the Venezuelan government where it did not have "possession or control" of the documents and made a good faith effort to obtain them); *see also United States v.*

Karake, 281 F. Supp. 2d 302, 308 (D.D.C. 2003) (allowing discovery to proceed regarding whether the United States and Rwanda were acting jointly in order to allow defendants to determine whether statements made to Rwandan officials in Rwanda may be suppressed).

As the government investigates a complex international terrorism case, the investigation may encompass the efforts (coordinated or otherwise) of many different law enforcement and intelligence agencies both in the United States and abroad. One commentator has theorized that courts could potentially require the government to conduct broad-ranging *Brady* searches through the files of multiple government agencies, potentially resulting in the disclosure of sensitive information. *See* Mark D. Villaverde, *Structuring the Prosecutor's Duty to Search the Intelligence Community for Brady Material*, 88 Cornell. L. Rev. 1471, 1478 (2003) (arguing that overbroad *Brady* obligations make it "questionable whether the federal courts are the appropriate forum in which to try suspected international terrorists"). Lawyers whom we interviewed told us that, in practice, it is not always easy to conduct a thorough *Brady* search in a large-scale investigation in which agencies such as the CIA or the Defense Department may have worked closely with the prosecutors. Although these agencies have reportedly become more responsive to the needs of the justice system over time, their sometimes complicated recordkeeping systems and far-flung operations can present obstacles to an efficient *Brady* review.

The risks associated with *Brady* reviews in cases involving multiple agencies were recently highlighted in *Moussaoui*. On October, 25, 2007, well after Moussaoui's conviction and sentence had become final, the prosecutors notified the court and Moussaoui's defense counsel that they had learned of three recordings made during the CIA interrogations of certain detained al Qaeda associates that had been at issue during the criminal case. *See* Redacted Letter from U.S. Dep't of Justice dated Oct. 25, 2007, *United States v. Moussaoui*, No. 01-cr-00455 (E.D. Va. Nov. 9, 2007) (Dkt. No. 1898). None of these recordings had been previously provided to the defense or disclosed to the court. *See id.* While this disclosure is unlikely to jeopardize Moussaoui's conviction given that the recordings "neither mention Moussaoui nor discuss the September 11 plot," *id.* at 2-3, and that Moussaoui pled guilty, it serves as a reminder that the prosecution might not be in possession of, or even aware of the existence of, information that could qualify as *Brady* material.

In practice, courts have generally applied *Brady* in a sensible and realistic manner in international terrorism cases. For example, in *Padilla* the defendant demanded that the prosecution team search the materials possessed by foreign governments and law enforcement officials; U.S. local, state, and federal officials involved in the case and related cases; and no less than fifteen specified federal agencies, including the CIA, the NSA, and the Defense Department. *See* Mot. by Jose Padilla for Specific *Brady* Material, *Giglio* and *Kyles* Information at 3, *United States v. Padilla*, No. 04-cr-60001 (S.D. Fla. March 22, 2006) (Dkt. No. 254). The government objected, and the court followed established precedent by requiring the government to search the files of the prosecution team (i.e., "the prosecutor or anyone over whom he has authority") as well as the files of any other agencies that "have cooperated intimately from the outset of [the] investigation" and the files of any other agencies where the prosecutor gains "access to [evidence] in preparing his case for trial." *See* Order at 2, *Padilla* (S.D. Fla. May 19, 2006) (Dkt. No. 346) (quoting *Meros*, 866 F.2d at 1309; *Antone*, 603 F.2d at 569-70; and *United States v. Brazel*, 102 F.3d 1120, 1150 (11th Cir. 1997)).

In *United States v. Ressam* (the Millennium Bomber case), the defendant, who had lived for many years in Canada, was arrested in December 1999 as he attempted to enter the United States from Canada. He was bound for Los Angeles, where he planned to detonate a bomb at Los Angeles International Airport on the eve of the Millennium. During pre-trial proceedings, Ressam demanded that the government make a formal request to the government of Canada, under the Mutual Legal Assistance Treaty ("MLAT") between the United States and Canada, for *Brady* materials as well as prior statements of government witnesses under the Jencks Act. *See* Mem. of Law in Support of Def.'s Mot. to Compel Gov't to Make Request for *Brady* and *Jencks* Material through the Mutual Legal Assistance Treaty at 4, *United States v. Ressam*, No. 99-cr-00666 (W.D. Wash. Sept. 01, 2000) (Dkt. No. 119). In its response, the government represented that it had already made efforts to determine whether the Canadian authorities possessed *Brady* material. *See* Gov't's Resp. to Def.'s Mot. to Compel Gov't to Make Requests for *Brady* and *Jencks* Material, *Ressam* (W.D. Wash. Oct. 4, 2000) (Dkt. No. 132). The court denied the defendant's motion, explaining that the defendant could not compel the government to make a MLAT request and that, in any event, the Constitution "does not require the government to obtain Jenks, *Brady* and *Giglio* information from foreign governments ... ." Order at 4, *Ressam* (W.D. Wash. Nov. 7, 2000) (Dkt. No. 145).

X.
The *Miranda* Rule: Applying the Fifth Amendment Protections Against Coerced Confessions in a Practical Manner in Terrorism Cases

The famous warnings enunciated in *Miranda v. Arizona*—which begin with "You have the right to remain silent"—are deeply entrenched in the U.S. legal system. Courts have generally required U.S. law enforcement agents to administer the *Miranda* warnings when they question a suspect who is held in custody, even if the person is being held overseas by foreign authorities. Some have found anomalous the notion that U.S. law enforcement must issue *Miranda* warnings to suspected terrorists freshly captured on foreign soil.[299] To date, however, *Miranda* has arisen in contexts that resemble traditional police interrogation situations much more than the battlefield, and to our knowledge the *Miranda* rule has not prevented the government from obtaining convictions in any terrorism cases. Further, if *Miranda* issues are raised in a future case presenting a battlefield capture situation, there is good reason to believe that courts would interpret *Miranda* flexibly to recognize that warnings are not required in that context.

In *Miranda*, the Supreme Court held that custodial interrogation is intrinsically coercive and therefore "[u]nless adequate protective devices are employed to dispel the compulsion inherent in custodial surroundings, no statement obtained from the defendant can truly be the product of his free choice." 384 U.S. 436, 458 (1966). Accordingly, the Supreme Court enunciated the rule that "[p]rior to any questioning, the person must be warned that he has a right to remain silent, that any statement he does make may be used as evidence against him, and that he has a right to the presence of an attorney, either retained or appointed." *Id.* at 444. Further, while the defendant may choose to waive those rights, the waiver must be made "voluntarily, knowingly and intelligently." *Id.* Additionally, all questioning must cease if the suspect indicates that he would like to speak to an attorney or if the suspect indicates that he does not wish to be interrogated, regardless of any admissions already made. *Id.* at 444-45. As the Supreme Court noted in 2000, the *Miranda* rights have "become embedded in routine police practice to the point where the warnings have become part of our national culture." *Dickerson v. United States*, 530 U.S. 428, 443 (2000).

In cases where the defendant is arrested within the United States, the application of the *Miranda* rule is clear, although it is also subject to some well-recognized exceptions under Supreme Court precedent. But does Miranda apply to persons who are captured abroad? As the following discussion makes clear, the answer is different depending on whether the interrogation is conducted by foreign officials or U.S. law enforcement.

A. Application of the *Miranda* Rule in International Terrorism Cases Where the Defendant Is Subject to Custodial Interrogation Outside the United States

In the appeal of Ramzi Yousef's conviction following separate trials from the 1993 World Trade Center bombing and the Philippine-based Airline Bombing case, the Second Circuit held that *Miranda* does not apply to interrogations conducted overseas by foreign officials without participation by U.S.

personnel. Thus, statements elicited by foreign law enforcement are generally admissible in U.S. courts, regardless of whether any *Miranda*-type warnings were given, as long as the statements were voluntarily made. *See United States. v. Yousef*, 327 F.3d 56, 145 (2d Cir. 2003);[300] *see also United States. v. Abu Ali*, 395 F. Supp. 2d 338, 373-74 (E.D. Va. 2005) (holding that inculpatory statements made by an American citizen to Saudi Arabian officials without *Miranda* warnings were admissible because they were not the product of a "joint venture" relationship between U.S. and Saudi officials, nor were they produced by means that "shock the judicial conscience"); *United States v. Suchit*, 480 F. Supp. 2d 39, 54 (D.D.C. 2007) ("[b]ecause Suchit was not in custody at the time of either FBI interview, no *Miranda* warnings were required to render the statements admissible at the trial of this matter").

However, in the Embassy Bombings case, Judge Leonard B. Sand of the Southern District of New York held that *Miranda* does generally apply when U.S. agents question a detainee outside the United States. *See United States v. Bin Laden*, 132 F. Supp. 2d 168, 173-79 (S.D.N.Y. 2001). In that case, defendant Mohamed al-'Owhali, a citizen of Saudi Arabia, was apprehended and detained by Kenyan authorities in Kenya after the bombing of the U.S. embassy in Nairobi. *Id.* Over nine separate days, FBI agents and other U.S. law enforcement personnel (including a New York City Police Detective and an Assistant United States Attorney ("AUSA")) were permitted to question him while he remained in foreign custody in Kenya. *Id.* During the questioning, al-'Owhali made numerous inculpatory statements that he later moved to suppress on grounds that he was not given adequate *Miranda* warnings. *Id.*

The government responded by arguing that *Miranda* simply did not apply because the defendant was "a non-resident alien whose only connections to the United States are his alleged violations of U.S. law and his subsequent U.S. prosecution." *Id.* at 181. Describing the issue as one of first impression, Judge Sand disagreed with the government, holding that al-'Owahali, "insofar as he is the present subject of a domestic criminal proceeding, is indeed protected by the privilege against self-incrimination guaranteed by the Fifth Amendment." *Id.* As Judge Sand reasoned, "[w]hether or not Fifth Amendment rights reach out to protect individuals while they are situated outside the United States is beside the point" because the constitutional violation occurs "not at the moment law enforcement officials coerce statements through custodial interrogation, but when a defendant's involuntary statements are actually used against him at an American criminal proceeding." *Id.* Addressing the government's argument that these procedural requirements might impede intelligence-gathering, Judge Sand made clear that the *Miranda* doctrine did not preclude U.S. agents from questioning suspects without giving *Miranda* warnings. As Judge Sand noted, "*Miranda* only prevents an unwarned or involuntary statement from being used as evidence in a domestic criminal trial; it does not mean that such statements are never to be elicited in the first place." *Id.* at 189.

Judge Sand went on to hold "that courts may and should apply the familiar warning/waiver framework set forth in *Miranda* to determine whether the government, in its case-in-chief, may introduce against such a defendant evidence of his custodial statements—even if that defendant's interrogation by U.S. agents occurred wholly abroad and while he was in the physical custody of foreign authorities." *Id.*; *see also id.* at 185-86. Under Judge Sand's analysis, American agents questioning a non-citizen abroad must notify the suspect that he has a right to remain silent, in relation to the U.S. agent and regardless of whether the suspect has already spoken to local officials, and must also notify the suspect that any statements made may be used against him in an American court. *Id.* at 187-88. Where applicable, the agent should also notify the suspect that he has a right to the assistance of counsel, and that counsel may be present. The American agent is not required to tell the suspect that he has the right to counsel in nations where the individual does not otherwise have such a right. However, in such circumstances, the suspect should still be told that he may refuse to speak to the American agent without an attorney. Moreover, if there are "no obvious hurdles to the implementation of an accused's right to assistance and presence of counsel, due care should be taken not to foreclose an opportunity that in fact exists." *Id.* at 188-89.

On the facts of the case before him, Judge Sand criticized the printed "Advice of Rights" form used by the FBI agents before they questioned al-'Owhali. That form contained warnings resembling those prescribed in *Miranda* except with respect to the issue of counsel; the printed form stated only that al-'Owhali would have had the right to counsel if he were being interrogated in the United States. *Id.* at 173-74, 175. Judge

Sand held that the form erroneously suggested that counsel was not available under any circumstances outside the United States, see id. at 190-92, but found that subsequent clarifications by the AUSA cured the violation and that al-'Owhali knowingly waived his Miranda rights after the AUSA clarified them. Id. at 192-93.[301]

Since Judge Sand's ruling in 2001, several courts have applied the principle set forth in Bin Laden; i.e., that Miranda applies when U.S. agents conduct custodial interrogations overseas.[302] In United States v. Abu Ali, for example, the defendant, who was arrested and detained by the Saudi government on June 8, 2003, was initially questioned by Saudi law enforcement, but later the U.S. government provided questions for the defendant and observed additional interrogation of him by Saudi law enforcement through a two-way mirror. See 395 F. Supp. 2d at 343. No Miranda warnings were given. The court denied the defendant's motion to suppress, concluding that Miranda warnings were not required since U.S. law enforcement officials did not act in a "joint venture" with Saudi officials in the arrest, detention, or interrogation of the defendant and Saudi law enforcement officials act did not act as agents of the United States. Id. at 382. The court reasoned that the Saudi government controlled every aspect of questioning of the defendant and that although U.S. government officials were permitted to submit a list of questions for interrogations, they were not allowed to determine the content or form of the questions and the Saudi government did not permit them to directly interview the defendant. Id. The court stated that "[t]he only direct interrogation of the defendant conducted by U.S. officials was done by the FBI and Secret Services [later on] in September, 2003. And while Miranda warnings were not given during that interrogation, the government had indicated that it does not seek to use any statements obtained during that interrogation in its case-in-chief." Id.; see also United States v. Karake, 443 F. Supp. 2d 8, 49 (D.D.C. 2006) (where defendants made statements in the presence of American and Rwandan investigators overseas, government conceded that Miranda applied so long as American officials were participating in the interrogation).

B. The Implications of Judge Sand's Ruling in *Bin Laden*

Some have argued that it would be absurd to apply Miranda to battlefield situations where U.S. military personnel have captured an enemy fighter.[303] We fully agree that Miranda warnings are not—and need not be—administered in battlefield situations, but we do not believe that this argument has significant implications for criminal terrorism prosecutions.[304] As an initial matter, few defendants have been placed on trial for terrorism crimes following a battlefield capture. However, in the event that a person is put on trial in a U.S. federal court following capture in battle and that the government seeks to offer the defendant's statements following his capture, it is likely that the courts would recognize an exception to Miranda under the "public safety" exception first articulated in New York v. Quarles, 467 U.S. 649 (1984), or, more generally, based on the argument that civilian law-enforcement principles such as Miranda simply do not apply in battlefield conditions.

In Quarles, the police apprehended a rape suspect in an A&P supermarket after a woman had run up to the police on the street, reported that she had just been raped, and told the officers that the rapist had entered the supermarket and was armed. See 467 U.S. at 651-52. Inside the supermarket, the police surrounded the suspect and asked questions about the location of the gun, all without administering Miranda warnings. See id. The defendant made incriminating statements, and the lower courts ruled that those statements were inadmissible because of the failure to give Miranda warnings. See id. at 649-50. On appeal, however, the Supreme Court reasoned that although the defendant was in police custody at the time he made his statements, and thus Miranda applied, a "public safety" exception to the Miranda requirements was applicable in the context of this case. See id. at 650-52, 655-56. As Justice Rehnquist reasoned, "[i]n a kaleidoscopic situation such as the one confronting these officers, where spontaneity rather than adherence to a police manual is necessarily the order of the day," the defendant's statements should be admissible even if the officers were seeking to elicit incriminating statements. Id. at 656.

In United States v. Khalil, the Second Circuit applied Quarles to permit the government to introduce incriminating statements made prior to the administration of Miranda warnings. See 214 F.3d 111, 121-22 (2d Cir. 2000). An informant told police that two Islamic extremists were planning to detonate pipe bombs in a subway station or bus terminal to express anger over the treatment of Palestinians. *See id.* at 115. The police raided an apartment in Brooklyn that was believed to contain the pipe bombs. *See id.* Once inside the apartment, the police shot the two inhabitants when they attempted to fight back; the two men were taken to the hospital. *See id.* In the apartment, the police found a black bag with bombs inside, one of which had been switched on. *See id.* At the hospital, the police questioned one of the defendants about the bombs without giving *Miranda* warnings. *See id.* The defendant stated that he had made five bombs; that all contained gunpowder; and that each would explode when four switches were flipped. *See id.* When police asked the defendant if he had planned to kill himself in the explosion, he answered "Poof." *See id.* On appeal, the Second Circuit held that all of these statements were properly admitted under *Quarles*. *See id.* at 121.

Some commentators have suggested that the *Quarles* exception should be applied to permit questioning of persons captured in combat, involved in terrorist plots, or "to ferret out potential terrorist activity."[305] Although the scope of any *Quarles*-type exception would have to be carefully defined so that it is does not swallow the general *Miranda* rule, it may well be sensible to extend *Quarles* to battlefield capture situations. The case of John Walker Lindh illustrates how *Quarles* might be applied to such a scenario.

Lindh, the so-called "American Taliban," was captured around November 23, 2001, along with other Taliban fighters in Afghanistan by Northern Alliance Forces, and was later identified as a U.S. citizen after participating in a bloody prison uprising in the Mazar-e-Sharif fort where he was being held. *See* Gov't's Opp'n to Def.'s Mot. to Suppress at 3, *United States v. Lindh*, No. 02-cr-00037 (E.D. Va. July 1, 2002) (Dkt. No. 269). On December 1, 2001—eight days after he was captured—Lindh was taken into custody of U.S. Special Forces. *Id.*; *see also* Gov't's Resp. to the Def.'s Proffer of Facts at 9, *Lindh* (E.D. Va. July 1, 2002) (Dkt. No. 273).

According to a proffer of facts filed by Lindh's attorneys in federal court in Virginia, after a few hours of detention in U.S. custody, Lindh was loaded onto a truck and taken to a hospital to tend to the gunshot wound to his leg. *See* Proffer of Facts in Support of Def.'s Suppression Mots. at 11, *Lindh* (E.D. Va. June 14, 2002) (Dkt. No. 229).[306] Although Lindh received medical treatment, he later alleged that a decision was made to leave the bullet in his leg to protect the government's chain of custody. *See id.* at 13.[307]

Thereafter, U.S. Special Forces allegedly transported Lindh to a nearby Northern Alliance compound and interrogated him without providing *Miranda* warnings. *See id.* at 14. According to Lindh's allegations, on the morning of December 2, 2001, U.S. Special Forces soldiers bound Lindh's hands with rope, placed a hood over his head and drove him back to the Mazar-e-Sharif area where he was confined in a dark room. *See id.* at 14-15. Blindfolded and bound, Lindh stayed in this room for approximately five days. *See id.* at 15. On about the third day, he was interrogated for several hours and repeatedly interrogated thereafter. *See id.* He was not read his *Miranda* rights at any time in this period. *See id.* Nevertheless, Lindh later alleged that on more than one occasion, he asked to see a lawyer and a doctor. *See id.* at 15-16.

According to the proffer filed by Lindh's attorneys, on December 7, 2001, Lindh was blindfolded, placed in a truck, transferred to an airplane and flown to Camp Rhino about seventy miles south of Kandahar, Afghanistan, where he was stripped naked, taped to a stretcher with his chest, arms and ankles pinioned, and held in a metal container without insulation, heat, or light. *See id.* at 17-18. By December 9, an FBI agent arrived at Camp Rhino to interview Lindh. *See id.* at 20. Around that time, Lindh was advised of his *Miranda* rights but was told that no lawyers were available for him. *See id.* According to Lindh, he signed a *Miranda* waiver form because he feared he would have to return to the metal container with no insulation, heat or light. *See id.* After repeated interrogations at Camp Rhino, Lindh was transported to an amphibious assault ship with a flight deck, the USS *Peleliu*, about fifteen miles off the shore of Pakistan on December 14, 2002, underwent surgery to remove the bullet lodged in his leg, and was held for another seventeen days until December 31, 2001. *See* Mem. in Opp'n to Def.'s Mot. to Compel Production of Discovery at 7, *Lindh* (E.D. Va. Mar. 29, 2002) (Dkt. No. 57). On December 31, 2001, Lindh was taken to another amphibious assault ship, the USS *Bataan*, and held for another twenty-three days. *See id.* at 8. On January 22, Lindh was transported to the United States to be taken before a U.S. magistrate judge. *See id.* He was permitted to consult with counsel for the first time on January 24, 2002. Lindh's parents claimed that they retained counsel for Lindh on December 2, but that the government blocked delivery of this message to Lindh.

After Lindh's arraignment, his lawyers argued that any statements he made while in custody prior to December 9, 2001, were not admissible because he had not received *Miranda* warnings. *See* Mot. to Supress Statements for Violation of Fifth Amendment Rights (*Miranda* and *Edwards*) at 6-12, *Lindh* (E.D. Va. June 14, 2002) (Dkt. No. 224). Lindh's lawyers also argued that his statements made on December 9 and 10 to the FBI agent were inadmissible because the agent did not obtain a valid waiver of Lindh's rights due to the highly intimidating and coercive circumstances under which Lindh was held by the U.S. government. *See id.* at 12-18. The government opposed Lindh's suppression motion on two grounds. The government first argued that *Miranda* does not extend to information gathering related to intelligence and military operations and emphasized that *Miranda* requirements are directed toward criminal law enforcement investigations, not interrogations of enemy prisoners in the context of military operations. *See* Gov't Opp'n to Def.'s Mot. to Suppress Statements at 9, *Lindh* (E.D. Va. July 1, 2002) (Dkt. No. 271). The government also argued that Lindh's pre-*Miranda* statements were admissible under a battlefield exception based on an analogy to the *Quarles* public safety exception because "Interrogation of enemy combatants seized in battle may relate directly to the safety and protection of American troops, who are constantly exposed to the dangers of combat." *Id.* at 18-19.

Approximately one month after Lindh's lawyers filed their motions to suppress, and on the very day that the court was scheduled to conduct a hearing on his motions to suppress, Lindh pled guilty pursuant to a plea agreement. *See* Minute Entry (Change of Plea Hearing), *Lindh* (E.D. Va. July 15, 2002); M.K.B. Darmer, *Lessons from the Lindh Case: Public Safety and the Fifth Amendment*, 68 Brook. L. Rev. 241, 242 (2002). Although it is impossible to determine how the court would have ruled on Lindh's suppression motion involving *Miranda*, historically courts have applied *Miranda* in a common-sense manner, and there is every reason to expect such an approach if and when the issue is presented in a future case.

XI.
Courts Have Generally Applied the Federal Rules of Evidence in a Common-Sense, Practical Manner in Terrorism Cases

In congressional testimony in December 2001, former Secretary of Defense Donald Rumsfeld and former Deputy Secretary of Defense Paul Wolfowitz asserted that "[f]ederal rules of evidence often prevent the introduction of valid factual evidence for public policy reasons that have no application in a trial of a foreign terrorist." See Donald H. Rumsfeld & Paul Wolfowitz, U.S. Sec'y of Def., Prepared Statement: Senate Armed Services Committee "Military Commissions" (Dec. 12, 2001).[308] Others have expressed similar critiques. See Spencer J. Crona & Neal A. Richardson, *Justice for War Criminals of Invisible Armies: A New Legal and Military Approach to Terrorism*, 21 Okla. City U. L. Rev. 349, 382 (1996) ("The uncertainty of verdicts in the civilian criminal justice system is attributable to the various rules which result in the exclusion of relevant evidence"); *Id.* at 386 ("It would provoke laughter to suggest that soldiers in Desert Storm should have obtained search or arrest warrants before capturing Iraqi soldiers and their equipment"); *see also* Harvey Rishikof, *Is It Time for a Federal Terrorist Court? Terrorists and Prosecutions: Problems, Paradigms and Paradoxes*, 8 Suffolk J. Trial & App. Advoc. 1, 12-13 (2003) (with respect to terrorism cases, "the federal rules of evidence are too restrictive: hearsay, the exclusionary rule, rules for chain of custody and authentication, and others require the court to have a more 'latitudinarian' approach to create a broader record").[309]

However, these critics rarely offer specific examples of criminal terrorism prosecutions that have been affected, much less derailed, by the Federal Rules of Evidence; instead, their objections rest largely on unrealized theoretical concerns.[310] One law review article cites the Pan Am Flight 103 (Lockerbie) bombing case in arguing that it is unwieldy to develop admissible evidence of a wide-ranging terrorist attack, but that discussion, too, is largely theoretical, as the defendants were never tried in the United States following their conviction in Scotland.[311]

Those who complain of the allegedly "overly restrictive" evidentiary rules generally point to three broad issues as primary obstacles: (a) authentication and chain-of-custody requirements; (b) the difficulties of putting on witnesses from all over the world, some of whom may be serving active duty in the armed forces during a trial; and (c) the hearsay rule. *See generally* Crona & Richardson, *Justice for War Criminals of Invisible Armies*, at 382-86; Rishikof, *Is It Time for a Federal Terrorist Court?*, at 12-13; Tung Yin, *Ending the War on Terrorism One Terrorist at a Time: A Noncriminal Detention Model for Holding and Releasing Guantánamo Bay Detainees*, 29 Harv. J.L. & Pub. Pol'y 149, 177 (2005). However, these issues have traditionally been addressed in a common-sense manner, and our research indicates that to date they have not presented a significant obstacle to the government's terrorism prosecutions.

First, the Federal Rules of Evidence provide a relatively low burden for proving the authenticity of evidence, requiring only that "sufficient proof has been introduced so that a reasonable juror could find in favor of authenticity or identification." *United States v. Ruggiero*, 928 F.2d 1289, 1303 (2d Cir. 1991). The admission of evidence is a decision of the trial judge. *See* Fed. R. Evid. 104(a) (admissibility of evidence is a decision for the court); Fed. R. Evid. 104(b) (preliminary questions of admissibility where the relevance of evidence turns on a conditional fact are for the court). Once a judge decides that evidence is admissible, the weight given the evidence is a question for the trier of fact. Fed. R. Evid. 104(e).

Rules 901 and 902 of the Federal Rules of Evidence address the process of authenticating evidence. If a piece of evidence falls into any of the enumerated categories of self-authenticating documents in Rule 902, the evidence garners a rebuttable presumption of authenticity. If not, the trial judge is to make an admissibility decision under Rule 901. Rule 901(a) states that "the requirement of authentication or identification as a condition precedent to admissibility is satisfied by evidence sufficient to support a finding that the matter in question is what its proponent claims." Fed. R. Evid. 901(a). The prima facie showing required for admissibility is not even a preponderance of the evidence. "Rather, all that is required is substantial evidence from which the trier of fact might conclude that a document is authentic." *Zenith Radio Corp. v. Matsushita Elec. Indus. Co.*, 505 F. Supp. 1190, 1219 (E.D. Pa. 1980). Rule 901(b) illustrates ten potential ways of satisfying the 901(a) authentication requirement, many of which can be used to satisfy the requirement for the purposes of evidence collected in a terrorism case.

In practice, the authentication rules have not appeared to impose a barrier to the prosecution of terrorism cases. For example, in *United States v. al-Moayad*, the prosecution relied on a "Mujahidin Form" to demonstrate al-Moayad's predisposition to support terrorist activities and to rebut the impression created by the defense that there were no documents or other evidence establishing al-Moayad's involvement in supporting terrorism early on in the alleged conspiracy. *See* Brief for Appellee at 85, *United States v. al-Moayad*, No. 05-4186-cr (2d Cir. Mar. 14, 2007). The Mujahidin Form was the English translation of a form filled out in 1999 by a person who sought to attend an al Qaeda training camp in Afghanistan. *See* Brief for Appellant at 96, *al-Moayad* (2d Cir. June 1, 2006). It was part of a collection of documents and materials that were seized by American personnel from an al Qaeda training site, al Qaeda safehouses, and other locations near Kandahar, Afghanistan. *See id.* at 97; Brief for Appellee at 96, *al-Moayad* (2d Cir. Mar. 14, 2007). Al-Moayad was identified on the Form as the person who recommended the prospective trainee. *See* Brief for Appellant at 96, *al-Moayad* (2d Cir. June 1, 2006). Accordingly, the form was an important piece of evidence against al-Moayad.

In order to authenticate the document at trial, the prosecution offered the testimony of FBI Special Agent Jennifer Keenan and former Mujahidin trainee, and cooperating witness, Yahya Goba. *See* Brief for Appellee at 96, *al-Moayad* (2d Cir. Mar. 14, 2007). To establish a chain of custody, Agent Keenan testified that she was the FBI's Assistant Legal Attaché in Islamabad, Pakistan, that she received the form as part of shipments of items found and seized by in Afghanistan, that she and her staff inventoried and created a chain of custody for the items in the shipments received from Afghanistan, and that she forwarded them to the FBI in Washington, D.C., where they were secured until trial. *Id.* The prosecution also offered the testimony of Goba, who had trained at an al Qaeda camp in 2001 and who testified that he had filled out a form identical to the Mujahidin Form to gain admission to the camp. *Id.* at 97. Despite defense counsel's failure to object to the form on authentication grounds at trial, al-Moayad has challenged the authentication on appeal. As of early May 2008, the Second Circuit had not yet ruled on the appeal. *See generally* Docket, *al-Moayad* (2d Cir. Aug. 3, 2005).

Subsequently, in the *Padilla* case, a key piece of evidence against Jose Padilla was a similar al Qaeda training camp application bearing Padilla's fingerprints recovered from the camp in Afghanistan. At trial, this document became the subject of a chain-of-custody dispute, but the court ruled that the document was admissible. *See* Peter Whoriskey, *Defense Cites Ambiguities in Evidence Against Padilla*, Wash. Post, May 19, 2007, at A06.[312] In order to authenticate the training camp application in *Padilla*, the government relied on similar testimony as in the *al-Moayad* case and also took the additional step of producing a confidential witness, whose identity was protected, who testified that he came into possession of the application in Kandahar, Afghanistan, before it was shipped to Agent Keenan in Pakistan. *See* Gov't's Mot. in Limine Regarding Proposed Procedures for One Chain of Custody Witness, *Padilla* (S.D. Fla. Mar. 22, 2007) (Dkt. No. 928); *see also* Adam Liptak, *Padilla Case Offers New Model of Terrorism Trial*, N.Y. Times, Aug. 18, 2007, at A1[313] (calling the application "the strongest piece of evidence in Mr. Padilla's case").

Second, alleged problems with unavailable witnesses are not supported based on our review of the cases that have been brought. The government often requires its employees to suspend their normal activities and travel to a courthouse if their testimony is needed. For example, Brian Murphy, the FBI agent who conducted much of the investigative work leading up to the prosecution of al-Moayad in the Eastern District of New York, was also a member of the Marine reserves and, by the time of trial, was on active duty in Iraq as a Marine captain where he was stationed in the so-called "Triangle of Death." However, after coordination between the Defense and Justice Departments, Agent Murphy was ordered back to the United States to testify against al-Moayad and to assist in the successful prosecution of the case. See Interview with Kelly Anne Moore, former Assistant U.S. Att'y in the E.D.N.Y. (Oct. 8, 2007); John H. Richardson, *Brian Murphy v. The Bad Guys*, Esquire, Feb. 26, 2007.[314] Similarly, in the *Lindh* case, we understand that active-duty military personnel, including Special Forces officers, were at the courthouse ready, willing, and able to testify at John Walker Lindh's suppression hearing, but that their testimony was not necessary in light of Lindh's guilty plea shortly before the hearing was to commence. See Telephone Interview with David N. Kelley, former U.S. Att'y for the S.D.N.Y. (Nov. 26, 2007).

In *United States v. Ressam*, the court addressed another problem—witnesses who were not willing to travel to the United States to testify at trial but who were amenable to being deposed, with the understanding that their deposition testimony would be used at trial. See Order, No. 99-cr-00666 (W.D. Wash. June 23, 2000) (Dkt. No. 111). In *Ressam*, the court granted the government's motion, over the defendant's Confrontation Clause objection, to allow depositions of Canadian witnesses who were outside the court's subpoena power and who were unable or unwilling to testify at trial in the United States. The court was satisfied that constitutional requirements were met where: (1) the defense counsel had the ability to cross-examine witnesses at deposition, (2) the deposition was to be video-taped to allow jury to observe demeanor of witnesses, and (3) the defendant would virtually be present at the depositions through video conference equipment and a private telephone line between defendant and his counsel.

In situations of genuine unavailability, several circuits have allowed the admission of witness testimony by two-way videoconferencing. *See, e.g.*, *United States v Gigante*, 166 F.3d 75, 79-82 (2d. Cir. 1999) (allowing two-way videoconference trial testimony when the witness is unavailable because he was placed at undisclosed location under federal witness protection program); *see also United States v Weekley*, 130 F.3d 747, 752-54 (6th Cir. 1997); *United States v. Carrier*, 9 F.3d 867, 869-71 (10th Cir. 1993); *United States v. Quintero*, 21 F.3d 885, 892-93 (9th Cir. 1994). *But see United States v. Bordeaux*, 400 F.3d 548, 552-55 (8th Cir. 2005) (holding that two-way video conferencing does not satisfy the Confrontation Clause); *United States v. Yates*, 438 F.3d 1307, 1312-18 (11th Cir. 2006) (discussing Justice Scalia's statement objecting to amendment to Federal Rule of Criminal Procedure 26(b) allowing for testimony by two-way video conferencing and holding that where witnesses testified by means of two-way video hookup court Confrontation Clause was not overridden in the absence of a showing that the video method was necessary to further an important public policy and that the reliability of the testimony was assured).

In other cases, courts have permitted witnesses to testify under aliases or using other security measures to protect a witnesses' identity. *See generally* Order, *United States v. Holy Land Foundation*, 04-cr-00240 (N.D. Tex. May 4, 2007) (Dkt. No. 628) (official from the Shin Bet, Israel's domestic security agency, testified at trial under an alias); *see also* Greg Krikorian, *Holy Land Federal Witnesses Go Uncalled*, L.A. Times, Sept. 2, 2007, at A31.

Courts have also made accommodations for defense witnesses to give testimony even if they are in remote locations. In *al-Moayad*, the court authorized travel expenses for witnesses from Yemen to travel to Brooklyn to testify for the defense. *See, e.g.*, Order, *United States v. al-Moayad*, No. 03-cr-01322 (E.D.N.Y. Jan. 28, 2005) (Dkt. No. 135) (court ordered U.S. Marshal to prepay roundtrip transportation and other appearance expenses for four defense character witnesses from Yemen to testify at trial in New York). In *United States v. Paracha*, the court authorized a videotaped deposition of the defendant's father, who was being held at Guantánamo. *See* No. 03-cr-01197, 2006 WL 12768, at *1, *17-18 (S.D.N.Y. Jan. 3, 2006),

Third, the hearsay rules contain numerous exceptions that allow judges flexibility to admit out-of-court statements in a criminal case, whether involving terrorism or otherwise. A statement offered not to prove the truth of its contents, but only to show that it was made, is not excluded as hearsay. *See* Fed. R. Evid. 801. Likewise excluded from the hearsay rule are declarations against interest, *see* Fed. R. Evid. 804(b)(3), statements of a co-conspirator made during the course and in furtherance of the conspiracy, *see* Fed. R. Evid.

801(d)(2)(E), and admissions by a party-opponent, *see* Fed. R. Evid. 801(d)(2).

Out-of-court statements have been admitted under a hearsay exception—or treated as non-hearsay—in support of terrorism prosecutions. *See, e.g.*, *United States v. Abu Ali*, 395 F. Supp. 2d 338, 373 (E.D. Va. 2005) (inculpatory statements of defendant, charged with rendering or conspiring to render assistance or support to designated terrorist organization, made to Saudi Arabian interrogators while being detained, were voluntary and consequently admissible); *United States v. Salameh*, 152 F.3d 88, 112 (2d Cir. 1998) (upholding trial court's admission into evidence as non-hearsay terrorist materials seized from defendant "that discussed (1) the desirability of attacking enemies of Islam; and (2) how to produce and use explosives"; Second Circuit affirmed decision to admit evidence to prove existence of bombing conspiracy and to prove conspirator's intent and motives, which are non-hearsay purposes).

XII.
Terrorism Trials Have Not Presented Novel Speedy Trial Problems

The right to a speedy trial, embodied in the Sixth Amendment as well as the Speedy Trial Act of 1974, 18 U.S.C. § 3161 (2000), is a bedrock principle of our criminal justice system. The Speedy Trial Act generally requires that a defendant be indicted within thirty days after his arrest and that he brought to trial within seventy days of indictment. See 18 U.S.C. §§ 3161(b), 3161(c)(1). Yet in some terrorism cases, defendants have been held in custody for much longer than 100 days—sometimes two years or more—before their cases proceeded to trial.[315] Do these delays contravene the speedy trial guarantees established by the U.S. Constitution and the Speedy Trial Act?

The answer, to date, has been "no." As an initial matter, lengthy pre-trial delays are by no means unique to terrorism cases. To the contrary, courts have adopted pre-trial schedules extending for months or years following a defendant's arrest in criminal cases as diverse as narcotics-trafficking, armed robbery, and large-scale conspiracies.[316] Indeed, it is well-settled that courts are permitted to fashion lengthy pre-trial schedules according to the complexity and magnitude of a particular case. The Supreme Court has held that whether a defendant's constitutional guarantee of a speedy trial has been violated must be assessed in each case given a variety of factors including the reason for the delay and any prejudice to the defendant. See Barker v. Wingo, 407 U.S. 514, 530-33 (1972).[317] Further, the Speedy Trial Act explicitly provides that the seventy-day post-indictment period may be tolled for reasons such as pre-trial motions, plea discussions, the need to gather evidence abroad, and other legitimate purposes. See 18 U.S.C. § 3161(h). Further, the Speedy Trial Act recognizes that additional delays may be required in "unusual or complex" cases where it would be "unreasonable to expect adequate preparation for pretrial proceedings or for the trial itself within the time limits established by this section." 18 U.S.C. § 3161(h)(8)(B)(ii).

To date, an opinion in the United States v. al-Arian provides the most extensive analysis of the right to a speedy trial in the context of a terrorism prosecution. See 267 F. Supp. 2d 1258 (M.D. Fla. 2003). In al-Arian, the defendants, including Sami Amin al-Arian, a professor at the University of South Florida, were alleged members of the Palestinian Islamic Jihad-Shiqaqi Faction (the "PIJ"), an organization that allegedly used "violence, principally suicide bombings, and threats of violence to pressure Israel to cede territory to the Palestinian people." United States v. al-Arian, 308 F. Supp. 2d 1322, 1328 (M.D. Fla. 2004). The defendants allegedly operated and directed fundraising and other organizational activities in the United States for almost twenty years. See id. at 1328. Reflecting the duration of the alleged conspiracy, the indictment spanned more than nineteen years of activity and contained some fifty counts, including conspiracy to commit murder outside the United States and conspiracy to provide material support to terrorists. See al-Arian, 267 F. Supp. 2d at 1260. Three of the four defendants in the case waived their right to a speedy trial and moved for a continuance of at least eighteen months, arguing that "this case is a complex case with voluminous discovery, novel questions of fact and law, in a relatively new and complex area (terrorism), such that it is unreasonable to expect adequate preparation for trial and for pretrial proceedings within seventy days." Id. at 1263. Al-Arian agreed that it was a complex case, but objected to the continuance, arguing that it would violate his right to a speedy trial. See id.

The evidence in *al-Arian* was complex and voluminous, resulting in pre-trial delay. Perhaps most burdensome, among the evidence to be provided to the defense was some 21,000 hours of Arabic-language telephone recordings, obtained pursuant to FISA. Some of the recordings were classified and thus the defendants were required to hire interpreters who would be able to obtain the proper security clearances. *Id.* at 1260, 1264. Other evidence in the case included 550 videotapes, thirty computer hard drives, hundreds of boxes of documentary evidence, and numerous foreign documents written in Hebrew. *Id.* at 1260. The prosecution indicated it would seek protection under CIPA, further complicating matters. *Id.* at 1260 n.3. The court noted that both sides would likely seek to take depositions in foreign countries, and both sides acknowledged that the trial would likely last for six months to a year. *Id.* at 1260-61. Lastly, the parties estimated that it would take some eighteen months for both sides to review the telephone recordings and conduct other discovery in the case. *Id.* at 1261.

In rejecting al-Arian's claim that the continuance would violate his speedy trial rights, the court explained that the delays caused by the numerous pre-trial motions filed by the defendants (including nine by al-Arian himself) fell within the exception outlined in § 3161(h)(1)(F) of the Speedy Trial Act and were therefore appropriate. *Id.* at 1262-63. The court then determined that: (1) the case "is a complex, multi-defendant case in a relatively new area of law;" (2) the court would be "faced with novel questions of fact and law throughout" the case; and (3) "discovery in this case is voluminous." *Id.* at 1264. All of those factors led the court to grant the co-defendants' motions for a continuance on grounds that a delay would best serve the "ends of justice" and outweighed al-Arian's right to a speedy trial. *Id.* In so holding, the court noted that al-Arian failed to argue that the delay was "unreasonable" and failed to make a showing of any actual prejudice to his case given that discovery would likely consume the entire eighteen-month period. *Id.* at 1264 n.16.

Other courts have reached similar results. For example, in *Moussaoui*, Judge Brinkema issued an order granting the parties' joint motion to certify the case as "complex," agreeing with the parties that the case was highly complex "due to the international scope of the evidence, the potential for the death penalty, and the probability that information subject to [CIPA] is involved." *United States v. Moussaoui*, No. 01-cr-00455, 2001 WL 1887910, at *1 (E.D. Va. Dec. 27, 2001). Accordingly, Judge Brinkema ruled that "the seventy day time limit between arraignment and trial, which is normally required by the Speedy Trial Act, will not permit either the government or the defense sufficient time to prepare adequately for either pretrial motions or trial." *Id.*

As noted above, a separate provision of the Speedy Trial Act requires that criminal charges generally be filed within thirty days of the defendant's arrest. *See* 18 U.S.C. § 3161(b). In *United States v. Abu Ali*, the defendant argued that the government violated this provision by indicting him more than thirty days after his arrest. 395 F. Supp. 2d 338, 384-85 (E.D. Va. 2005). The determination of the defendant's claim turned on when the thirty-day clock began to run. The defendant was arrested in Saudi Arabia on June 8, 2003, but was not indicted in the United States for more than a year and a half thereafter. *Id.* at 343. However, as the court held, the defendant's arrest in Saudi Arabia was not effected as part of any joint venture with the U.S. government and was instead carried out by the Saudi Arabian government for its own purposes. *Id.* at 384-85. In the United States, charges were not filed against the defendant until February 3, 2005, and the defendant was not taken into custody by U.S. agents until February 21, 2005. On these facts, the court held that the indictment was filed within thirty days of the defendant's date of arrest, because his detention by Saudi Arabian officials in 2003 was not done "in connection with such charges" as required by the statute. *Id.*

Likewise, in *United States v. Rezaq*, Judge Lamberth denied the defendant's request for discovery regarding his speedy trial defense. 899 F. Supp. 697, 704-706 (D.D.C. 1995). In *Rezaq*, the defendant and two others were found guilty under Maltese law of hijacking a plane en route from Athens to Cairo in 1985. *Id.* at 701. Upon release by Maltese authorities in 1993, after Rezaq had served only seven of his twenty-five year sentence, Rezaq boarded a plane to Ethiopia via Ghana and Nigeria. *Id.* Upon landing in Ghana, Rezaq was detained there for four months before being transferred into U.S. custody. *Id.* In support of his motion seeking discovery relevant to his claim that his speedy trial rights had been violated, Rezaq argued that his thirty-day speedy trial clock began to run upon his detention in Ghana, because Ghana, Nigeria, and perhaps Malta, were acting as agents of the United States. *Id.* at 704. In Judge Lamberth's original decision, he granted Rezaq's discovery request, stating "[a]t bottom, the government's case against this Speedy Trial Act defense is a factual one: that Ghana detained Mr. Rezaq independent of the United States' influence." *United States v. Rezaq*, 156 F.R.D. 514, 522 (D.C.C. 1994). However, upon the government's motion for reconsideration, Judge Lamberth reversed this decision, holding that Rezaq's motion failed as a matter of law. *Rezaq*, 899 F. Supp. at 705. Specifically, Judge Lamberth held that, "[d]efendant's detention at the hands of foreign law enforcement officials cannot be said to have triggered the running of the statutory period under the Speedy Trial Act because the Speedy Trial Act can only be triggered by a *federal* arrest made in connection with *federal* charges, and at no time was defendant subjected to *federal* arrest pursuant to *federal* charges while detained in Ghana, Nigeria, and Malta." *Id.* (emphasis in original). Further, the court rejected Rezaq's agency theory, stating, "[f]ederal involvement does not magically transform an arrest conducted by a foreign sovereign into a *federal* arrest. Similarly, federal involvement or federal cooperation in foreign prosecutions and detentions does not constitute federal deputization of foreign government law enforcement officials." *Id.* at 706 (emphasis in original).

Similarly, as the *Padilla* case makes clear, speedy trial rights are not triggered when an individual is held in military custody. Jose Padilla was arrested in Chicago on May 8, 2002, but then was held in custody within the United States for more than three-and-a-half years without charge, first as a material witness in New York, and later as an alleged "enemy combatant" at a Naval Brig in South Carolina. It was not until November 17, 2005, that Padilla was indicted in federal court in Miami. *See* Def.'s Mot. to Dismiss Indictment at 1-2, *United States v. Padilla*, 04-cr-60001 (S.D. Fla. Oct. 4, 2006) (Dkt. No. 596); *see also* Gov't's Opp'n to Def.'s Mots. to Dismiss Indictment at 2-4, *Padilla* (S.D. Fla. Nov. 13, 2006) (Dkt. No. 658). After his arraignment in Florida, Padilla moved to dismiss the indictment based on speedy trial violations, but the court denied his motion, ruling that the speedy trial clock does not begin to run until the defendant is charged with a crime. *See* Order Denying Def. Padilla's Mot. to Dismiss Indictment, *Padilla* (S.D. Fla. Apr. 3, 2007) (Dkt. No. 951); *see also* Peter Whoriskey, *Judge Refuses to Dismiss Padilla's Charges*, Wash. Post, Mar. 24, 2007, at A09.[318]

XIII.
In Many Terrorism Cases, Federal Sentencing Laws Result in Severe Sentences and Sometimes Lead to Cooperation and Guilty Pleas

Under the federal sentencing laws, courts have in many cases meted out harsh sentences to individuals convicted of terrorism-related offenses. The severity of the sentences for terrorism crimes has served not only to incapacitate convicted terrorists but also, in some cases, to encourage cooperation from terrorist defendants who hope to garner sentencing leniency.

The starting point for an examination of sentencing procedures is the statutory maximum sentence that can be imposed on a particular offense. As discussed earlier, a wide range of statutes are used to prosecute individuals who the government believes have committed terrorism-related offenses, and the statutory maximums vary accordingly. For instance, the statutory maximum sentence for a conviction under the material support statutes is fifteen years imprisonment, or, if a death results, "any term of years or for life." See 18 U.S.C. §§ 2339A(a), 2339B(a)(1). The maximum penalty for extraterritorial homicide of a U.S. national in connection with terrorism ranges from death or life imprisonment (if the homicide is classified as murder) to a maximum sentence of ten years' imprisonment (if it is deemed voluntary manslaughter). See 18 U.S.C. § 2332(a). Persons convicted of participating in a bombing of a public place face a maximum sentence of any term of years or life imprisonment or, if death results, a capital sentence. See 18 U.S.C. § 2332f(c) (incorporating penalty provision of 18 U.S.C. § 2332a(a)). Seditious conspiracy carries a maximum sentence of twenty years' imprisonment, see 18 U.S.C. § 2384, while the general conspiracy statute authorizes a maximum prison term of five years. See 18 U.S.C. § 371.[319]

Though a particular offense may have an established maximum sentence, courts maintain a great deal of discretion in determining whether defendants convicted of multiple counts should serve the sentence associated with each count concurrently or consecutively. For example, following Ramzi Yousef's conviction in connection with the first World Trade Center bombing and other criminal acts, Judge Kevin Thomas Duffy of the Southern District of New York sentenced him to consecutive prison terms on several counts resulting in a term of imprisonment of life plus 240 years. See Judgment, *United States v. Yousef*, No. 93-cr-00180 (S.D.N.Y. Jan. 8, 1998) (Dkt. No. 655).

Within the outer boundaries of the statutory maximums, a court's sentencing discretion is informed by 18 U.S.C. § 3553. Section 3553(a) states that "the court shall impose a sentence sufficient, but not greater than necessary" to comply with the objectives of sentencing: i.e., the need for the sentence to reflect the seriousness of the offense, promote respect for the law, provide just punishment, afford deterrence, protect the public, and provide the defendant with needed education, training, or medical care. 18 U.S.C. § 3553(a). In determining the particular sentence to be imposed, a court must consider, in addition to the foregoing factors, (1) the nature and circumstances of the offense and the history and characteristics of the defendant; (2) the kinds of sentences available; (3) the kinds of sentence and the sentencing range established by the Guidelines; (4) policy statements issued by the Sentencing Commission; (5) the need to avoid unwarranted sentence disparities among defendants with similar records who have been found guilty of similar conduct; and (6) the need to provide restitution to victims of the offense. *See id.*

The third component of the federal sentencing regime is the Sentencing Guidelines, which operate within the statutory maximums described above and are informed by the factors of § 3553. The Guidelines were first promulgated by the United States Sentencing Commission in 1989 and are updated regularly. Under the landmark *Booker* decision, the Guidelines are now only advisory, rather than mandatory. *See United States v. Booker*, 543 U.S. 220, 258-65 (2005). Federal judges are required to consider the applicable Sentencing Guidelines Range along with other generalized sentencing factors described by § 3553 (e.g., the need for deterrence), but are no longer bound to impose a Guidelines sentence. At the same time, a sentence within the Guidelines range has been held to be presumptively reasonable on appeal and still carries persuasive force. *See Rita v. United States*, 127 S. Ct. 2456, 2472-73 (2007).

The Guidelines assign a value to each federal statutory crime—the "offense level"—and a value to each defendant's criminal history—the "criminal history." The defendant's offense level and criminal history taken together yield a specific sentencing range on the Guidelines' Sentencing Table, calculated in months. For example, a defendant convicted of violating 18 U.S.C. § 2339B, one of the material support statutes, is assigned a "base offense level" of twenty-six, which corresponds to a range of imprisonment between sixty-three and 150 months, depending on the individual's criminal history. Thus, a defendant lacking any prior convictions could be sentenced to a term of sixty-three to seventy-eight months, barring the application of certain offense-specific enhancements or reductions. However, when a defendant is found to have committed a specific crime in a certain manner or under certain specified conditions, enhancements or reductions to the offense level are included—called "specific offense characteristics"—thereby increasing or decreasing the total offense level.

In the terrorism context, the Sentencing Commission adopted a severe enhancement provision that is applicable to a host of terrorism cases, including material support prosecutions. Section 3A1.4 of the Guidelines states that:

> (a) If the offense is a felony that involved, or was intended to promote, a federal crime of terrorism, increase [the offense level] by 12 levels; but if the resulting offense level is less than level 32, increase to level 32.

> (b) In each such case, the defendant's criminal history category ... shall be Category VI.

U.S.S.G § 3A1.4. In increasing the offense level to a minimum offense level of thirty-two and elevating the defendant's criminal history category to Category VI—the highest criminal history category available—the Guidelines dictate that a defendant who qualifies for the terrorism enhancement will face a Guidelines range of no less than 210 to 262 months.

This sentencing enhancement provides the government with a potentially devastating weapon in prosecuting cases that involved a terrorism crime or were intended to promote one. In order to convince a federal judge to apply the terrorism enhancement, the government must only prove that the enhancement is appropriate by a preponderance of evidence. The government must meet this reduced burden in a separate sentencing hearing before only a federal judge, in which hearsay evidence and forms of proof inadmissible at trial are permitted. What results is an opportunity for the government to charge a suspected terror defendant with a lesser, non-terrorism specific crime that would typically carry lesser penalties, and subsequently seek the sentencing enhancement to ensure a lengthy sentence of incarceration.

In practice, the government has pursued such a strategy with mixed results. In *United States v. Benkahla*, the government indicted the defendant on federal charges of making false declarations to a grand jury, obstruction of justice, and making false statements to an FBI agent in connection with his visit to a jihad training camp, and the defendant was convicted at trial. *See* No. 06-cr-00009, 2007 WL 2254657, at *1-2 (E.D. Va. Aug. 3, 2007). The Guidelines range that corresponded with the offense level for the defendant's charged offense and his criminal history was thirty-three to forty-one months. However, the government sought application of the terrorism enhancement at a sentencing hearing. The district court found that the government had shown by a preponderance of the evidence that the defendant had been questioned in an "investigation of a federal crime of terrorism," and that, therefore, application of the terrorism enhancement under § 3A1.4 of the Guidelines was warranted. *Id.* at *5-7. Application of the terrorism enhancement resulted in an increased Guidelines range of 210 to 264 months, nearly seven times the range that his offenses of conviction and his criminal history would have otherwise carried. *See id.* at *2.

In exercising its discretion, however, the sentencing court in *Benkahla* held that a downward departure was warranted, as permitted by § 4A1.3 of the Guidelines, because Benkahla's criminal history category, as calculated pursuant to the terrorism enhancement, substantially overrepresented his criminal history or the likelihood that he would commit other crimes. *See id*. at *9.[320] The district court further noted that other defendants sentenced as a result of the investigation "all committed and were convicted of more dangerous and more violent offenses than Defendant, but none received a sentence as severe as his guidelines range suggests." *Id*. at *13. Consequently, the district court reduced his criminal history category from VI to I, which resulted in a Guidelines range of 121 to 151 months. *See id*. at *10. The court alternatively held that a sentence within the range of 210 to 264 months violated its mandate to impose a sentence "'sufficient, but not greater than necessary' to reflect the seriousness of the offense, promote respect for the law, provide just punishment, afford adequate deterrence, protect the public from further crimes, and provide adequate treatment to the defendant." *Id*. at *10-12 (citing 18 U.S.C. § 3553(a)). In so holding, the court noted that it had received more letters on behalf of Benkahla, a U.S. citizen born and raised in Virginia with a Master's degree from Johns Hopkins University, than "any other defendant in twenty-five years, all attesting to his honor, integrity, moral character, opposition to extremism, and devotion to civic duty." *Id*. at *11. After taking these factors into consideration, the court ultimately sentenced Benkahla to 121 months. *See id.* at *10.

Benkahla represents the first time that the enhancement was imposed for "obstructing an investigation of a federal crime of terrorism," rather than directly promoting a federal crime of terrorism, and marked only the third time the government has sought the enhancement for this type of offense. *Id*. at *2. While the district court's downward departure dampened the potential impact of the terrorism enhancement, the sentence imposed upon the defendant was still about three times the usual maximum for these offenses under the Guidelines.[321]

In contrast to the sentencing in *Benkahla*, another court in the Eastern District of Virginia previously declined to impose the terrorism enhancement in similar circumstances. *See United States v. Biheiri*, 356 F. Supp. 2d, 590, 591-92 (E.D. Va. 2005). In *Biheiri*, the government charged a defendant with making false statements. At the time of his indictment in 2003, substantial evidence existed that Biheiri had also financed terrorist acts in violation of federal law, but the five-year statute of limitations on that more serious offense had already expired. *See id*. at 591. Ultimately, the defendant was convicted of making false statements to federal agents about his business relationships with Islamist groups, including senior members of Hamas and the Palestinian Islamic Jihad. *See id.* at 591-92.

In sentencing Biheiri for the false statement conviction, the Court held that the terrorism enhancement could not be applied to a defendant who had merely *attempted* to obstruct an investigation of a federal crime of terrorism, but failed because the government already possessed information that indicated he was lying. *See id*. at 598. Without the terrorism enhancement, the Court noted that the Guidelines recommended a sentence of eight to fourteen months and, due to Biheiri's previous conviction for immigration fraud, sentenced Biheiri to thirteen months. *See id*. at 602-04.

A comparison of the *Benkahla* and *Biheiri* sentencings illustrates the potentially dramatic outcomes that result from application of the Guidelines' terrorism enhancement to relatively low-level offenses. In the *Benkahla* case, the government was able to secure a sentence of incarceration that was substantially higher than punishments normally commensurate with the crimes for which the defendant had been convicted.[322]

In all federal criminal cases, defendants who plead guilty prior to trial may be granted limited leniency under the Guidelines, and the harsh penalties meted out by federal courts following conviction on terrorism-related charges provide additional incentive for defendants to choose to plead guilty. Defendants who plead guilty in advance of trial are granted a two to three level reduction in their offense level guidelines in recognition of their acceptance of responsibility. *See* U.S.S.G. §3E1.1. In addition, the Guidelines provide an even greater incentive for defendants who agree to forego trial and cooperate with the government by providing information and intelligence to law enforcement. Under the Guidelines, the court may, on the motion of the government, depart from the Guidelines range for a defendant who has "provided substantial assistance in the investigation of another person who has committed an offense." U.S.S.G. §5K1.1.[323] Moreover, a cooperating defendant may also avoid mandatory minimum sentences imposed by statute. *See id.*; 18 U.S.C. § 3553(e). The prospect of lengthy sentences of incarceration often motivates defendants with valuable information about criminal conduct to cooperate with the government in hopes of leniency.

In practice, the government wields considerable control over the cooperation process. A defendant commences the cooperation process by meeting with the government in private—accompanied, of course, by his counsel. In this session, known as a "proffer," the defendant typically must confess first to his own criminal conduct and provide the government with information about the criminal conduct of others. The government typically takes the information provided by the defendant in these proffer sessions and attempts through its own investigation to verify the defendant's truthfulness and the utility of the information provided.

Usually after multiple proffers, if the government is satisfied with the defendant's truthfulness regarding his own criminal conduct and the conduct of others, the government enters into a written cooperation agreement with the defendant. The government requires the defendant to forego his right to trial and plead guilty to many or all of the crimes that he admitted during his proffer sessions.[324] The defendant is required as a part of this cooperation agreement to continue to cooperate with the government, truthfully respond to its inquiries and, if asked, testify truthfully in court against other defendants. In exchange, the government agrees to make a motion under Guidelines § 5K1.1 to inform the court of the defendant's cooperation at sentencing, a motion that permits the court under the Guidelines to reduce the defendant's sentence.[325] This letter is commonly known in criminal justice circles as a "5K1 Letter," after the Guidelines section upon which it is based.[326] Armed with the 5K1 letter, the judge has absolute discretion to grant the defendant a sentence reduction if the judge deems it appropriate after measuring the defendant's cooperation, irrespective of the Guidelines range normally applicable to the defendant's criminal culpability.

The cooperation process has proven historically to be one of the government's most powerful tools in gathering intelligence. In many instances, it is only through the narrative of a cooperating defendant—a true insider speaking with first-hand knowledge—that law enforcement can fully decode criminal conspiracies and effectively prosecute other wrongdoers. Indeed, the government recognizes that cultivating cooperation pleas is an effective intelligence gathering tool for all types of criminal investigations, including significant terrorist cases. In a webpage devoted to "Waging the War on Terror," the Department of Justice touts that it is "gathering information by leveraging criminal charges and long prison sentences." Website, U.S. Dep't of Justice, *Waging the War on Terror*.[327] According to the site, individuals pleading guilty in exchange for shorter sentences "have provided critical intelligence about al-Qaida and other terrorist groups, safehouses, training camps, recruitment, and tactics in the United States, and the operations of those terrorists who mean to do Americans harm." *Id.*

Although opinions differ, some experienced lawyers believe that defendants in terrorism cases are no less likely to cooperate than other defendants charged with serious offenses. One widely publicized example is Yahya Goba, one of six defendants indicted in the Lackawanna Six case. Goba pled guilty in March 2003 to providing material support to al Qaeda, in violation of 18 U.S.C. § 2339B, in connection with his attendance at an al Qaeda training camp in Afghanistan. *See* Plea Agreement, *United States v. Goba*, No. 02-00214 (W.D.N.Y. Mar. 25, 2003) (Dkt. No. 113); Change of Plea, *Goba* (W.D.N.Y. Mar. 25, 2003) (Dkt. No. 116); Press Release, U.S. Dep't of Justice, Defendant Yahya Goba Pleads Guilty to Providing Material Support to Al Qaeda (March 25, 2003).[328] As part of the plea agreement, Goba pled to conduct, and agreed to a Guidelines calculation, that would have resulted in a sentence under the Guidelines of 188 to 235 months. *See* Plea Agreement at 6-8, *Goba* (W.D.N.Y. Mar. 25, 2003) (Dkt. No. 113). After pleading guilty to a violation of 18 U.S.C. § 2339B, Goba was sentenced to 120 months in prison. *See id.* at 1-2; Judgment as to Yahya Goba, *Goba* (W.D.N.Y. Dec. 22, 2003) (Dkt. No. 224).[329]

Goba's plea agreement required his full cooperation with the government's investigation of the Lackawanna Six, as well as other terrorism investigations. *See id.* In 2005, Goba was a government witness at the trial of Mohammed Ali al-Moayad, where he testified about paperwork required of recruits prior to attending al Qaeda training camps, a point considered crucial by the prosecution in that case. *See* Brief for the Appellee at 97, *United States v. al-Moayad*, No. 05-4186-cr (2d Cir. Mar. 14, 2007); William Glaberson, *Judge in Case Against Sheik Allows Talk of Bin Laden*, N.Y. Times, Mar. 2, 2005, at B8.[330] Then, in May 2007, Goba testified at the trial of Jose Padilla on the same paperwork as he had in *al-Moayad*. *See* Decision and Order as to Yahya Goba, *Goba*

(W.D.N.Y. Dec. 14, 2007) (Dkt. No. 288); Peter Whoriskey, *Defense Cites Ambiguities in Evidence Against Padilla*, Wash. Post, May 19, 2007, at A06.[331] In addition, Goba testified in an Australian prosecution, *Crown v. Jack Thomas*; testified in *United States v. al-Hussayen*; and provided information for and was identified as a potential government witness in *United States v. Mohamed Albanna*, a matter that was ultimately resolved by plea agreement. *See* Decision and Order as to Yahya Goba at 4, *Goba* (W.D.N.Y. Dec. 14, 2007) (Dkt. No. 288). As a result of Goba's cooperation, which exceeded what was required of him under the plea agreement and subjected him to harsher prison conditions than he would have faced if he had not cooperated, the government moved for a twelve-month reduction in Goba's sentence under Federal Rule of Criminal Procedure 35(b)(2). *See* Gov't's Mot. for Reduction of Sentence, *Goba* (W.D.N.Y. Oct. 12, 2007) (Dkt. No. 285). The court granted the motion and reduced Goba's sentence to 108 months. *See* Decision and Order as to Yahya Goba at 4, *Goba* (W.D.N.Y. Dec. 14, 2007) (Dkt. No. 288); Amended Judgment, *Goba* (W.D.N.Y. Jan. 3, 2008) (Dkt. No. 289).

In another example, Earnest James Ujaama pled guilty to conspiring to provide goods and services to the Taliban in violation of the International Emergency Economic Powers Act (50 U.S.C. § 1705) in connection with his attendance at a jihad training camp in Afghanistan. *See* Plea Agreement (Redacted), *United States v. Ujaama*, No. 02-cr-00283 (W.D. Wash. Apr. 14, 2003) (Dkt. No.75); *see also* Press Release, U.S. Dep't of Justice, Earnest James Ujaama Pleads Guilty to Conspiracy to Supply Goods and Services to the Taliban, Agrees to Cooperate with Terrorism Investigations (Apr. 14, 2003).[332] Though that charge could have carried a maximum penalty of 120 months in prison, the court sentenced Ujaama to only twenty-four months in prison, along with three years supervised release. *See* Judgment, *Ujaama* (W.D. Wash. Feb. 13, 2004) (Dkt. No. 101). The sentence was what the government had recommended in its 5K1 submission in exchange for Ujaama's complete and truthful cooperation with the government. *See* Gov't's Sentencing Mem., *Ujaama* (W.D. Wash. Feb. 3, 2004) (Dkt. No. 94).[333] In acknowledging Ujaama's plea, then-Attorney General John Ashcroft stated, "[a]n important part of our war against terrorism is to obtain the cooperation of insiders who have direct knowledge of the activities of dangerous terrorists … . We expect his cooperation to lead to the arrest of additional terrorists and the disruption of future terrorist activity." Press Release, U.S. Dep't of Justice, Earnest James Ujaama Pleads Guilty to Conspiracy to Supply Goods and Services to the Taliban, Agrees to Cooperate with Terrorism Investigations.

Complications may arise when a defendant after initially cooperating with the government later withdraws his cooperation. In these situations, the court has been able to determine an appropriate sentence based on the specific circumstances of the case. For example, in *Jabarah*, Judge Barabara Jones called Jabarah's subsequent refusal to cooperate in violation of his cooperation agreement "extremely foolish." Alan Feuer, *Canadian Gets Life in Qaeda Bomb Plot*, N.Y. Times, Jan. 19, 2008, at A8.[334] His refusal to cooperate, in addition to the evidence found in Jabarah's room suggesting a plan to attack the FBI agents and prosecutors working on his case, led Judge Jones to sentence Jabarah to life imprisonment without any reduction based on his earlier period of cooperation. *See id.*; Judgment, *United States v. Jabarah*, No. 01-cr-01560 (S.D.N.Y. Jan. 18, 2008) (Dkt. No. 15).

The case of the Millennium Bomber, Ahmed Ressam, is another example. Ressam was convicted in 2001 for his role in a plot to detonate explosives at Los Angeles International Airport on the eve of the Millennium. Ressam cooperated with authorities for two years, but then refused to provide further information and assistance to authorities. *See* Sarah Kershaw, *Terrorist in '99 U.S. Case is Sentenced to 22 Years*, N.Y. Times, July 28, 2005, at A20.[335] Citing the detrimental effect of his refusal to further cooperate, including being forced to abandon certain terrorism-related indictments, prosecutors sought a prison term of thirty-five years at sentencing. *See* Tr. of Sentencing Proceedings at 30-31, *United States v. Ressam*, No. 99-cr-00666 (W.D.Wash. July 27, 2005). The sentencing judge, however, noted Ressam's significant assistance to counter-terrorism efforts within that two-year period, and sentenced him to a lower term of twenty-two years in prison. *See id.* at 31-32. This term was three years less than the initial sentence the government offered in exchange for a guilty plea, which Ressam had rejected before trial. *See id.* at 5.

Although the government and the court did not agree on the sentence imposed in the *Ressam*, they found common ground in stressing the ability of federal courts to handle terrorism cases.[336] After delivering the sentence, Judge John Coughenour stated that "our courts have not abandoned our commitment to the ideals that set our nation apart. We can deal with the threats to our national security without denying the accused fundamental constitutional protections." *Id.* at 33:6-9. He further emphasized that Ressam, a foreign person intent on killing Americans, "received an effective, vigorous defense, and the opportunity to have his guilt or innocence determined by a jury of 12 ordinary citizens," *id.* at 33:10-14, and that the entire proceeding took place "in the sunlight of a public trial. There were no secret proceedings, no indefinite detention, no denial of counsel." *Id.* at 33:15-17.[337] Meeting with reporters after the sentencing hearing, U.S. Attorney John McKay "said he agreed with the judge's assessment that the U.S. legal system could handle cases such as Ressam's." Hal Bernton & Sara Jean Green, *Ressam Judge Decries U.S. Tactics*, Seattle Times, July 28, 2005, at A1.[338] McKay added that the sentence "sent an important message to would-be terrorists around the world … and that is in the United States a fair trial will be given … and where it is found that terrorism was committed, a lengthy prison sentence will be imposed." *Id.*

XIV.
The Court System Generally Is Able to Assure the Safety and Security of Trial Participants and Others

By definition, international terrorists seek to carry out acts of violence. It is not surprising, therefore, that defendants in many terrorism prosecutions are dangerous and volatile, posing a real safety risk to those around them and to society at large. Experience has shown the risks of security breaches in terrorism cases. For example, consider two separate incidents during the Embassy Bombings case before Judge Leonard B. Sand in the Southern District of New York. First, on June 22, 1999, defendant Wadih el-Hage charged the bench during a pre-trial conference, coming within feet of Judge Sand before being tackled by a U.S. Marshal amid a chaotic breakdown of order in the courtroom. See Benjamin Weiser, *Terrorist Suspect Charges Toward Judge, but Is Tackled*, N.Y. Times, June 23, 1999, at B6.[339] A little over a year later, in November 2000, another defendant in the case, Mamdouh Mahmud Salim, stabbed Louis Pepe, a federal prison guard at the Metropolitan Correctional Center (MCC) in Manhattan, in the eye with a sharpened comb. See Benjamin Weiser, *Stabbing May End Debate on Restrictions for Terrorism Suspects*, N.Y. Times, Nov. 5, 2000, § 1, at 55;[340] see also Phil Hirschkorn, *Bin Laden Aide Sentenced to 32 Years in Prison for Jail Stabbing*, CNN.com, May 4, 2004.[341] The attack was brutal. Salim and a co-defendant first subdued Pepe by spraying hot sauce in his eyes and tying him up with pillow case strips; Salim then lodged the weapon three inches in Pepe's skull. See Press Release, Office of Sen. Charles E. Schumer, Schumer Secures Van, Ambulette, Home Upgrades for NYC Federal Prison Guard Paralyzed and Blinded by Bin Laden Aide (July 7, 2004).[342] Pepe survived the attack but suffered severe brain damage and partial paralysis, and lost his left eye. See id.

These incidents graphically illustrate a recurring issue in international terrorism cases: how to protect trial participants and others from violence at the hands of the defendants or their sympathizers. Security risks may extend broadly to prison guards, judges, jurors, court employees, witnesses, prosecutors, and defense counsel. In many cases, it is a real challenge to provide safety for these individuals; in some cases, extraordinary measures are necessary.

However, the problem of violent defendants is hardly unique to international terrorism cases. Based on our discussions with government experts on courtroom security, security threats associated with terrorism trials, while perhaps more serious than those associated with other types of trials, represent a difference in degree rather than a difference in kind. See Telephone Interview with courtroom security expert (Jan. 2008). Although completed acts of violence are infrequent, judges have occasionally been the victims of violent attacks stemming from a variety of civil and criminal cases. For instance, in 1989, Eleventh Circuit Judge Robert Vance was killed by a mail bomb sent by a man who had unsuccessfully endeavored to have a 1972 criminal conviction overturned. See *A Man is Convicted By an Alabama Jury Of Killing a Judge*, N.Y. Times, Nov. 6, 1996, at A19.[343] In February 2005, federal district judge Joan Humphrey Lefkow's mother and husband were murdered by a pro se civil litigant whose suit against doctors for disfiguring him during cancer treatment had been dismissed by Judge Lefkow. See Jodi Wilgoren, *In Suicide Note, Bitter Plaintiff Says He Killed Judge's Family*, N.Y. Times, Mar. 11, 2005, at A1.[344] Threats and violence targeted to judges, prosecutors, defense counsel, and others involved in the criminal and civil justice system are not uncommon. See Deborah Sontag, *In Courts, Threats Become Alarming Fact of Life*, N.Y. Times, Mar. 20, 2005, § 1, at 1.[345] Thus, for many years, the federal courts have been faced with dangerous defendants charged with all manner of brutal crimes, as well as disgruntled civil litigants, and the prison system and the courts, primarily through the U.S. Marshals Service, have developed a number of tools to minimize safety risks.[346] Although no safeguards are foolproof, and although the costs of maintaining security are real and should not be discounted, experience has shown that it is indeed possible to prosecute terrorism defendants without jeopardizing the safety or security of trial participants or others in the justice system. Based on experience working with, and our discussions with, law enforcement personnel involved in courtroom security, as long as the U.S. Marshals Service and other courthouse security personnel have access to adequate resources and are given adequate leeway to implement security measures, security threats associated with terrorism trials are capable of being managed. *See, e.g.*, Telephone Interview with courtroom security expert (Jan. 2008).

A. Courtroom and Juror Security

To prevent violent incidents directed at jurors or others in the courtroom, judges and the U.S. Marshals Service have employed a variety of measures. In the Embassy Bombings case, for example, a second metal detector was installed directly outside the courtroom entrance (this in addition to the normal metal detector at the entrance to the courthouse); marshals in plainclothes were present throughout the courtroom; and the defendants were forced to wear leg shackles during trial (the shackles were concealed from the jury by draperies hanging from the tables where the defendants sat). *See* Phil Hirschkorn, *Tight Security Blankets Embassy Bombings Trial*, CNN.com, Jan. 10, 2001.[347] Judge Sand threatened unruly defendants with the prospect of being removed from the courtroom and having to watch the proceedings from a cell via closed-circuit television if they sought to disrupt the proceedings. *See* Benjamin Weiser, *First Day of Jury Selection In U.S. Embassy Bombings*, N.Y. Times, Jan. 3, 2001, at B3.[348] During the sentencing in October 2001, only weeks after the 9/11 attacks on the nearby World Trade Center, security around the exterior of the courthouse was extreme: there were even soldiers in the nearby streets. *See* Alan Feuer, *Tight Security At Sentencing For Bombings*, N.Y. Times, Oct. 17, 2001, at B10;[349] Benjamin Weiser, *4 Are Sentenced to Life in Prison In 1998 U.S. Embassy Bombings*, N.Y. Times, Oct. 19, 2001, at A1.[350]

Heightened security measures such as those described above were adopted in several other terrorism-related cases, including those of Zacarias Moussaoui, Ramzi Yousef, and others. *See* Jerry Markon, *Trial Tests Courthouse's Neighbors: Moussaoui Case a Big Presence In a Dense Area of Alexandria*, Wash. Post, Mar. 2, 2006, at VA12;[351] Richard Bernstein, *4 Are Convicted In Bombing At the World Trade Center That Killed 6, Stunned U.S.*, N.Y. Times, Mar. 5, 1994, §1, at 1.[352] Such measures are not new to the civilian criminal court system, however, and have been used in varying forms for many years where the defendants or their associates pose a risk of violence in the courtroom. For example, the 1998 trial of Colombian drug lord Carlos Ledher at times involved security from marshals armed with automatic weapons. *See* John Nordheimer, *In a Quiet Setting, U.S. Concludes Its Biggest Drug Trafficking Case*, N.Y. Times, May 11, 1988, A23.[353] More recently, at the April 2005 sentencing of Matthew Hale, a white supremacist convicted of plotting to assassinate a federal judge, extra security measures included bomb-sniffing dogs and an additional metal detector outside the courtroom entrance, as well as four additional armed guards inside. *See* Jodi Wilgoren, *40-Year Term for Supremacist in Plot on Judge*, N.Y. Times, Apr. 7, 2005, at A16.[354] In high-threat cases, U.S. Marshals offices can draw on the expertise of other offices across the country with experience formulating security measures under similar circumstances and can draw, if approved, on money from a special assignments fund to obtain the necessary resources for extraordinary security measures. *See* Telephone Interview with courtroom security expert (Jan. 2008); U.S. Dep't of Justice, Office of the Inspector Gen., *The United States Marshals Service Judicial Security Process* 8 (Sept. 2007).[355]

Trial courts have ample discretion to impose extraordinary security measures when necessary, so long as they make efforts to minimize prejudice to the defendant. The Supreme Court has held that amplifying customary courtroom security does not violate a defendant's right to a fair trial, though courts' discretion to impose security restrictions is not limitless and requires a case-by-case assessment of whether such measures are justified. *See, e.g.*, *Holbrook v. Flynn*, 475 U.S. 560, 570-72 (1986) (presence of four additional armed, uniformed officers in the gallery did not violate defendant's right to a fair trial); *Illinois v. Allen*, 397 U.S. 337, 343-44 (1970) (physical restraints may be permissible last resort for violent or abusive defendants). Although heightened security measures might affect the jury's view of a defendant, the principle that judges retain broad authority to control their courtrooms and ensure security has been widely acknowledged. *See, e.g., United States v. Smith*, 426 F.3d 567, 571 (2d Cir. 2005) ("partial closing" of the courtroom need only be justified by a "substantial reason"); *Holladay v. Haley*, 209 F.3d 1243, 1255 (11th Cir. 2000) (trial court has "reasonable discretion" to balance state's interest in shackling and the defendant's right to appear "untainted by physical reminders of his status as an accused") (citation omitted); *United States v. McKissick*, 204 F.3d 1282, 1299 (10th Cir. 2000) (where defendant's fellow gang members may disrupt trial, requiring defendant to wear stun belt under clothing was within trial court's discretion); *United States v. Buford*, 106 F. App'x 400, 403-05 (6th Cir. 2004) (unpublished) (security escort for witness in the courtroom was not unconstitutionally prejudicial).

Given these general principles, it is unsurprising that heightened security measures at terrorism-related trials have been upheld on review. For example, following his conviction in the Embassy Bombings case, Wadih el-Hage sought a new trial based, in part, on jurors' alleged knowledge that he and the other defendants wore leg shackles during the trial. *See United States v. Bin Laden*, No. 98-cr-01023, 2005 WL 287404, at *2 (S.D.N.Y. Feb. 7, 2005). The district court rejected el-Hage's argument that this was irreparably prejudicial and noted Judge Sand's extensive efforts to conceal the restraints from the jury. *See id.* at *3-4. It held that, because the Second Circuit has not deemed sightings of shackles on defendants to be presumptively prejudicial, a defendant seeking relief is required to show specific prejudice from such sightings. *See id.* This el-Hage failed to do. *See id.*

The primary means of protecting jurors at potentially high-risk trials is to conceal their identities from the defendants and spectators by empaneling an "anonymous jury," where the names of the jurors are not known to the parties or the public, and in some cases, sequestering the jurors. The use of anonymous juries and other jury-related security procedures is well-established in organized crime trials and violent gang prosecutions and is by no means unique to terrorism cases. For example, anonymous juries were used in the 2007 murder trial of Kenneth McGriff, a notorious Queens drug kingpin; the 2006 trial of gang member Ronell Wilson for the murder of two undercover police officers; and the 2003 trial of mafia boss Peter Gotti. *See* William K.

Rashbaum, *Jury Votes Against Execution in Trial of Drug Dealer Convicted in 2 Killings*, N.Y. Times, Feb. 10, 2007, at B3;[356] William K. Rashbaum, *Trial Begins in Case of 2 Slain Detectives*, N.Y. Times, Nov. 27, 2006, at B3;[357] William Glaberson, *A Big-Name Defendant, and a Jury of Peers Without Names*, N.Y. Times, Jan. 6, 2003, at B4.[358] Similarly, in the 2005 trial of Yemeni cleric Mohammed Ali al-Moayad for funneling money to al Qaeda and Hamas, Judge Sterling Johnson of the Eastern District of New York empaneled an anonymous jury. *See* William Glaberson, *Defense for Sheik and Aide is Suspicious of Tape Gaps*, N.Y. Times, Jan. 5, 2005, at B3.[359] Judges Sand and Duffy also empaneled anonymous juries in the Embassy Bombings case and the first World Trade Center trial. *See* Weiser, *First Day of Jury Selection In U.S. Embassy Bombings*; Benjamin Weiser, *Bomb Trial Judge Tries To Put the Jury At Ease*, N.Y. Times, Aug. 10, 1997, § 1, at 31.[360]

Though an anonymous jury implicates a defendant's interest in participating in voir dire and in the presumption of innocence, it is nevertheless constitutional "when there is 'strong reason to believe the jury needs protection' and the district court 'takes reasonable precautions to minimize any prejudicial effects on the defendant and to ensure that his fundamental rights are protected.'" *United States v. Wong*, 40 F.3d 1347, 1376 (2d Cir. 1994) (quoting *United States v. Paccione*, 949 F.2d 1183, 1192 (2d Cir. 1991)). In deciding whether to empanel an anonymous jury or sequester a jury, a court may consider factors such as: (1) the seriousness of the charges; (2) the defendant's dangerousness; (3) previous attempts by the defendant or his associates to interfere with the judicial process; (4) the defendant's or his associates' ability to harm jurors; and (5) expected publicity at trial that may impair jurors' ability to be fair. *See United States v. Cacace*, 321 F. Supp. 2d 532, 534 (E.D.N.Y 2004) (citations omitted); *see also United States v. Wilson*, 493 F. Supp. 2d 397, 400-02 (E.D.N.Y. 2006) (same).

The more extreme measure of sequestration can protect jurors from tampering or physical harm, as well as from potentially prejudicial exposure to media coverage or other influences outside of admissible evidence. Sequestration may require the jury to remain separated from friends, family, and colleagues pending the conclusion of trial, as in the trials of mob bosses John Gotti and Vittorio Amuso. *See* Arnold H. Lubasch, *Man Said to Rule Mob Family With Terror*, N.Y. Times, May 19, 1992, at B3;[361] Arnold H. Lubasch, *Gotti*

Guilty of Murder and Racketeering, N.Y. Times, Apr. 3, 1992, at A1.[362] Partial sequestration may also be imposed to ensure jurors' safety, including such measures as requiring jurors to meet in a new place each day before being escorted to the courthouse by U.S. Marshals. *See, e.g.*, *Wilson*, 493 F. Supp. 2d at 400 (granting government's motion that the jury eat lunch and travel to the courthouse together under U.S. Marshals Service protection due to security concerns).

An important component of ensuring the safety of cooperating witnesses is the Witness Security Program, which provides for the immediate and long-term safety of government witnesses, and their immediate dependents, whose lives are threatened due to their testimony against terrorists, organized crime members, and other dangerous criminals. Since its inception in 1971, the Witness Security Program has protected, relocated, and given new identities to over 8,000 witnesses and 9,700 of their family members. *See* U.S. Marshals Service, *Witness Security Program Fact Sheet*, Dec. 3, 2007.[363] Relocated witnesses may also be provided with medical care, job training, housing, and employment. *See id.* According to the U.S. Marshals Service, the program has been highly successful: no participant following the program's security guidelines has ever been harmed, and a conviction rate of eighty-nine percent has been achieved in cases where protected witnesses testified. *See id.*

The U.S. Marshals Service also provides security directly to federal judges, U.S. Attorneys, and other court officers. In recent years, the Marshals Service has provided full-time protection for Southern District of New York Judge Kevin Thomas Duffy and former Judge, now Attorney General, Michael B. Mukasey, both of whom presided over high-profile terrorism trials involving the 1993 attack on the World Trade Center and the seditious conspiracy led by Sheikh Omar Abdel Rahman. *See* Sontag, *In Courts, Threats Become Alarming Fact of Life.* In 2006, members of the federal judicial system received 1,111 threats and inappropriate communications, almost double the number from only a few years ago. *See* U.S. Dep't of Justice, *The United States Marshals Service Judicial Security Process*, at 4. Of these threats, 684 were directed at federal judges, 162 were directed at prosecutors, and 265 were directed at other persons protected by the U.S. Marshals Service.[364] *See id.* at 5. To counter the threat, in 2006 the U.S. Marshals Service provided additional security resources for 135 "high-threat" trials and eleven terrorism trials, as well as protective details for forty-four federal judges. *See id.* at 2.

A recent report by the Department of Justice's Office of the Inspector General ("OIG") suggests weaknesses in the U.S. Marshals Service's centralized threat assessment process, conducted by the Office of Protective Intelligence ("OPI"). The OIG concluded that Deputy Marshals at the local district level place only limited value on OPI threat assessments because the assessments do not provide sufficient information about the threatener's behavior to be useful in local protective investigations and security responses. *See* U.S. Dep't of Justice, *The United States Marshals Service Judicial Security Process*, at 31. The OIG further concluded that the OPI is unable effectively to identify potential threats, *see id.* at 34, a possibly serious shortcoming in light of the fact that only approximately ten percent of violent acts or attempted violence against judicial participants are preceded by a threat. *See id.* at 36. The responsibility of assessing and appropriately responding to threats and potential threats thus appears to rest primarily with individual districts.[365]

B. Security Within the Bureau of Prisons

For every hour that a dangerous defendant spends sitting in a courtroom, he can expect to spend weeks or months locked up in pre-trial detention. And if a defendant ultimately is convicted of a serious terrorism offense, he is likely to face many years of imprisonment. Over the past decade, the Bureau of Prisons, upon the direction of the Attorney General, has developed a regime of Special Administrative Measures ("SAMs") to ensure security for highly dangerous defendants. SAMs are intended to prevent violence within the prison system and also to prevent inmates from sending communications to others outside of prison that may create a risk of violence or terrorism. *See* 28 C.F.R. § 501.3(a). SAMs are inmate-specific and may be imposed only upon findings of necessity by the Attorney General. *See id.* § 501.3(c). SAMs may be imposed for a maximum period of one year, but are renewable upon notification from the Attorney General, the head of a federal law enforcement agency, or the head of an intelligence agency that the measures continue to be justified by a risk of death or serious bodily injury. *See id.* They apply to pre-trial detainees and material witnesses as well as prisoners who have been convicted and sentenced. *See id.* § 500.1(c); *United States v. Ali*, 396 F.

Supp. 2d 703, 708 (E.D. Va. 2005); *United States v. Reid*, 214 F. Supp. 2d 84, 86-87 (D. Mass. 2002).

The regulations provide that SAMs "ordinarily" may include housing a prisoner in administrative segregation, sometimes known colloquially as "the hole" or "lockdown," as well as denying privileges such as "correspondence, visiting, interviews with representatives of the news media, and the use of the telephone." 28 C.F.R. § 501.3(a). In addition, if the Attorney General provides an express directive, SAMs may be imposed to permit the monitoring of otherwise privileged attorney-client communications, after giving notice both to the inmate and their counsel, when "reasonable suspicion exists to believe that a particular inmate may use communications with attorneys or their agents to further or facilitate acts of terrorism." *Id.* § 501.3(d). To our knowledge, however, these latter SAM provisions have been imposed infrequently, and no court has determined whether they are enforceable.[366]

SAMs have been imposed during pre-trial detention in a number of international terrorism cases. While awaiting trial in the Embassy Bombings case, for example, Wadih el-Hage was held in solitary confinement for fifteen months—though he was later housed with a cellmate—and was not permitted contact with the general prison population. *See United States v. el-Hage*, 213 F.3d 74, 78, 82 (2d Cir. 2000). Defendants in the Eastern District of Virginia, including Zacarias Moussaoui, John Walker Lindh, and Ahmed Omar Abu Ali, were subject to similar pre-trial restrictions, including restricted access to the mail, visitors, and the telephone. *See, e.g., Ali*, 396 F. Supp. 2d at 704, 710. In the case of attempted shoe-bomber Richard Reid, the court approved SAMs precluding defense counsel from disseminating any information or documents received from Reid except to "each other and third parties who are engaged in the preparation of Mr. Reid's defense or providing information which is necessary and helpful to that defense" and only "for the sole purpose of preparing Mr. Reid's defense." *Reid*, 214 F. Supp. 2d at 91.

The government also has imposed highly restrictive SAMs on inmates after their conviction for serious terrorism crimes. For example, Ramzi Yousef has been housed in a sound-proofed, solitary cell and subjected to SAMs that "restricted [his] access to mail, telephone, media, and visitors and limited his carrying of religious materials, recreation, and exercise time." *Yousef v. Reno*, 254 F.3d 1214, 1216 (10th Cir. 2001).

Mohamed Daoud al-'Owhali, one of the defendants in the Embassy Bombings case, has been subjected to similar restrictions while serving his life sentence. *See al-'Owhali v. Ashcroft*, 279 F. Supp. 2d 13, 17 (D.D.C. 2003). Perhaps most famously, Sheikh Abdel Rahman has been subjected to SAMs that "prohibited him from ... passing or receiving communications from third persons with few exceptions." *United States v. Sattar*, 395 F. Supp. 2d 79, 84 (S.D.N.Y. 2005). The SAMs applicable to Abdel Rahman permitted him to communicate only with his family members and his attorneys, and required that his correspondence be screened by the FBI to determine whether it contained messages regarding illegal activities. *See id.* Abdel Rahman's attorneys were forbidden to pass messages between Abdel Rahman and third parties, including the news media. *See id.* at 84-85.

Although SAMs can make it more difficult for pre-trial defendants to work with defense counsel in preparing for trial, courts generally have upheld such restrictions. The Second Circuit's analysis in *el-Hage* is representative. There, the court found that SAMs imposed on el-Hage during his pre-trial detention were reasonably related to the government's security concerns of "preventing El-Hage from communicating with his unconfined co-conspirators, and thereby from facilitating additional terrorist acts by those co-conspirators." *El-Hage*, 213 F.3d at 81-82. The court found "ample evidence of the defendant's extensive terrorist connections." *Id.* at 81; *accord United States v. Felipe*, 148 F.3d 101, 106-07, 109-12 (2d Cir. 1998) (upholding extraordinarily restrictive conditions of confinement for a notorious gang leader with history of directing murderous conspiracies from prison and an extensive network of co-conspirators inside and outside of prison).

At the same time, some courts have modified SAMs where a defendant's right to counsel is implicated—especially in the pre-trial context. In particular, some courts have excused defense counsel from complying with the government's demand that they sign affirmations pledging to abide by the SAMs. For instance, Judge Young held that requiring Richard Reid's attorneys to sign affirmations acknowledging their receipt of the SAMs imposed on Reid as a condition to meeting their client would "fundamentally and impermissibly intrude[] on the proper role of defense counsel." *Reid*, 214 F. Supp. 2d at 94.[367]

In a limited number of cases, courts have ordered other substantive changes in SAMs. For example, Earnest Ujaama, charged with conspiracy to provide material support to al Qaeda and using a firearm during a violent crime as a result of his efforts to organize an al Qaeda training camp in Oregon, *see* Indictment, *United States v. Ujaama*, No. 02-cr-00283 (W.D. Wash. Aug. 28, 2002) (Dkt. No. 1), initially was subject to SAMs that restricted his communications with his counsel and their assistants and required his attorneys to sign affirmations of receipt of the SAMs. *See* Mem. of Law in Support of Def.'s Mot. for Emergency Hr'g at Ex. A, *Ujaama* (W.D. Wash. Oct. 11, 2002) (Dkt. No. 17). His counsel challenged the restrictions, *see id.*, and, after negotiations between defense counsel and prosecutors with respect to a consent protective order, *see* Def.'s Pre-Hr'g Mem. Regarding Special Admin. Measures at 2-3, *Ujaama* (W.D. Wash. Dec. 6, 2002) (Dkt. No. 41), the court issued a protective order setting forth somewhat relaxed restrictions on Ujaama's ability to consult with his counsel. *See* Protective Order, *Ujaama*, (W.D. Wash. Dec. 12, 2002) (Dkt. No. 48). The protective order, inter alia, eliminated the requirement that Ujaama's counsel sign an affirmation acknowledging receipt of the SAMs—though it did require counsel to sign an affirmation acknowledging receipt of the protective order—and broadened the materials the defendant could review with counsel. *See id.* at 2, 5.

In another example, the District of Minnesota relaxed pre-trial SAMs imposed on Mohamed Abdullah Warsame, who initially was detained in early 2004 on charges of violating the material support statute and making false statements. After several years of pre-trial detention, Warsame moved to be released. *See* Order on Mot. for Release at 1-4, *United States v. Warsame*, No. 04-cr-00029 (D. Minn. Aug. 31, 2007) (Dkt. No. 120). The court declined to release Warsame from detention, but found that the SAMs imposed on him were "no longer necessary" and ordered that Warsame be transferred to a "more normal pretrial detention facility" that would permit him greater access to his family and lawyers. *Id.* at 10. In response, the government urged that the SAMs remained necessary to "limit the defendants' ability to communicate with and contact known and suspected terrorists," Mot. to Vacate at 4, *Warsame* (D. Minn. Sept. 21, 2007) (Dkt. No. 122), but nonetheless expressed willingness to discuss modifications of the SAMs with Warsame's defense counsel. *See id.* at 6-7. The court then stayed its order, *see* Order, *Warsame* (D. Minn. Sept. 28, 2007) (Dkt. No. 123), and, as of the writing of this White Paper, the government's motion to vacate the court's order was pending.

The government signaled just how serious it is about enforcing SAMs by prosecuting prominent defense attorney Lynne Stewart. Stewart, who had served for years as counsel for Sheikh Abdel Rahman, visited her client in prison in Minnesota on three occasions between 1999 and 2001. *See Sattar*, 395 F. Supp. 2d at 85-88. At the time, Abdel Rahman was serving a life sentence and, as noted above, was subject to restrictive SAMs that forbade him from passing messages to the news media and other third parties. *See id.* at 84-85. Before these visits, Stewart signed affirmations acknowledging that she was aware of the SAMs and that she and her staff would abide by them. *See id.* at 85-86, 88. At trial, however, the government demonstrated that Stewart had relayed messages and smuggled letters to Abdel Rahman from third parties regarding ongoing issues facing the Islamic Group, a designated foreign terrorist organization in Egypt with which Abdel Rahman was affiliated. *See id.* at 85-88. Stewart and a translator, who also was prosecuted and convicted, invited Abdel Rahman to respond to these letters, and Stewart, in direct violation of the SAMs, subsequently passed Abdel Rahman's messages to a news reporter. *See id.* at 85-88. Secret video recordings of the prison meetings showed that at one time Stewart "actively concealed the conversations between [the interpreter] and Abdel Rahman from the prison guards by, among other things, tapping a water bottle on the table while stating that she was 'just doing covering noises.'" *Id.* at 88.

The jury rejected Stewart's defense that she was merely representing her client in good faith and convicted her of serious felonies, including conspiracy to obstruct the enforcement of the SAMs; making false statements to the government; and providing material support to persons engaged in terrorist activities. *See id.* at 82. Upholding the verdict, the trial court found the evidence supported the conclusion that Stewart "employed the dishonest means of signing and submitting false affirmations in order to gain access to the prison" and used "dishonest means in order to take Abdel Rahman's messages out of prison in violation of the SAMs," *id.* at 89; falsely affirmed that she intended to abide by the SAMs, *see id.* at 90-92; and knew that she was supporting her co-conspirators' efforts to murder individuals outside of the United States and to engage in acts of terrorism by smuggling out and disseminating Abdel

Rahman's communications with his followers in the Islamic Group. *See id.* at 93-100. Stewart was sentenced to twenty-eight months' imprisonment and was disbarred. *See* Judgment, *United States v. Sattar*, No. 02-cr-00395 (S.D.N.Y. Oct. 26, 2006) (Dkt. No. 884); *Convicted Lawyer Is Disbarred*, N.Y. Times, Apr. 25, 2007, at B6.[368] Stewart's prosecution—and the government's use of recorded attorney-client communications—was controversial in some quarters. *See, e.g.*, Tamar R. Birckhead, *The Conviction of Lynne Stewart and the Uncertain Future of the Right to Defend*, 43 Am. Crim. L. Rev. 1, 9-12 (2006); *but see* Peter Margulies, *The Virtues and Vices of Solidarity: Regulating the Roles of Lawyers for Clients Accused of Terrorist Activity*, 62 Md. L. Rev. 173, 187 (2003) ("[T]he Government alleges that Stewart ended up facilitating the communication of more specific statements about violence, intended for action by members of the Islamic Group, including a directive to 'kill [Jews] wherever they are.' Such specificity risks transforming the lawyer into a collaborator in criminal activity.") (alteration in original). However, because of the case's notoriety, it likely will have an enormous influence on anyone dealing with prisoners subject to SAMs.

XV.
Conclusion

As we look ahead to the coming years, it is a grim and undeniable reality that our country is threatened by violent extremists, claiming to act in the name of religious piety and bent on attacking our country, killing our fellow citizens, and damaging or destroying important national symbols and institutions. Confronting this threat is among the greatest challenges that we face as a nation. After 9/11, it is incontestable that the government must pursue a multi-faceted counter-terrorism strategy involving the use of military, diplomatic, economic, cultural, and law-enforcement tools. No single response can serve as "the answer" to international terrorism.

However, as we strive for a vigorous and effective response to terrorism, we should not lose sight of the important tools that are already at our disposal, nor should we forget the costs and risks of seeking to "break new ground" by departing from established institutions and practices. As this White Paper shows, the existing criminal justice system is an established institution that has generally done a good job in handling international terrorism cases. It has become common, these days, for observers to point out the actual and perceived flaws in the criminal justice system and to argue that a new system should be created from scratch to handle international terrorism cases. Based on our research, however, we believe that the justice system generally deserves credit for the manner in which it has handled terrorism cases. Many of the purported criticisms of the justice system do not withstand scrutiny. Although the justice system is far from perfect, it has proved to be adaptable and has successfully handled a large number of important and challenging terrorism prosecutions over the past fifteen years without sacrificing national security interests or rigorous standards of fairness and due process.

As we move forward, we should confidently and judiciously make use of the criminal justice system—an existing and valuable resource that reflects many of the best aspects of our legal and cultural traditions—as one of the important tools in the campaign to eradicate international terrorism.

Appendices

A. Terrorism Prosecution Cases

1. United States v. Abdhir, No. 5:07-cr-00501-JF (N.D. Cal. Aug. 1, 2007)
2. United States v. Abdi, No. 1:01-cr-00404-TSE (E.D. Va. Oct. 23, 2001)
3. United States v. Abdi, No. 2:04-cr-00088-ALM (S.D. Ohio June 10, 2004)
4. United States v. Abdoulah, No. 3:01-cr-03240-TJW (S.D. Cal. Nov. 2, 2001)
5. United States v. Abdulah, No. 2:01-cr-00977-PGR (D. Ariz. Oct. 25, 2001) (related cases: No. 2:02-cr-00164-PGR (D. Ariz. Feb. 20, 2002) and No. 2:02-cr-00004-UA (C.D.Cal. Jan. 3, 2002))
6. United States v. Abu Ali, No. 1:05-cr-00053-GBL (E.D. Va. Feb. 3, 2005)
7. United States v. Abuali, No. 2:01-cr-686-WHW (D.N.J. Oct. 25, 2001)
8. United States v. Abu-Jihaad, No. 3:07-cr-00057-MRK (D. Conn. Mar. 21, 2007)
9. United States v. Afshari, No. 2:01-cr-00209-RMT (C.D. Cal. Feb. 26, 2001)
10. United States v. Ahmad, No. 3:04-cr-00301-MRK (D. Conn. Oct. 6, 2004)
11. United States v. Ahmed, No. 1:06-cr-00147-CC-GGB (N.D. Ga. Mar. 23, 2006)
12. United States v. Ahsan, No. 3:06-cr-00194-JCH (D. Conn. June 28, 2006)
13. United States v. Akhdar, No. 2:03-cr-80079-GCS (E.D. Mich. Feb. 3, 2003)
14. United States v. al-Draibi, No. 1:01-cr-00393-TSE (E.D. Va. Oct. 10, 2001)
15. United States v. Alamoudi, No. 1:03-cr-00513-CMH (E.D. Va. Oct. 10, 2003)
16. United States v. al-Arian, No. 8:03-cr-00077-JSM-TBM (M.D. Fla. Feb. 19, 2003)
17. United States v. Alfauri, No. 1:02-cr-00147-TSE (E.D. Va. Apr. 10, 2002)
18. United States v. al-Hussayen, No. 3:03-cr-00048-EJL (D. Idaho Feb. 13, 2003)
19. United States v. Alishtari, No. 1:07-cr-00115-AKH (S.D.N.Y. Feb. 14, 2007)
20. United States v. al-Marri, No. 1:03-cr-10044-MMM (C.D. Ill. May 22, 2003) (related cases: No. 1:02-cr-00147-VM (S.D.N.Y. Feb. 6, 2002) and No. 1:03-cr-00094-VM (S.D.N.Y. Jan. 22, 2003))
21. United States v. al-Moayad, No. 1:03-cr-01322-SJ (E.D.N.Y. Dec. 15, 2003)
22. United States v. al-Mughassil, No. 1:01-cr-00228-CMH (E.D. Va. June 21, 2001)
23. United States v. Alrababah, No. 1:02-cr-00096-GBL (E.D.Va. Nov. 16, 2001)
24. United States v. al-Timimi, No. 1:04-cr-00385-LMB (E.D. Va. Sept. 23, 2004)
25. United States v. Amawi, No. 3:06-cr-00719-JGC (N.D. Ohio Feb. 16, 2006)
26. United States v. Aref, No. 1:04-cr-00402-TJM (N.D.N.Y. Aug. 6, 2004)
27. United States v. Arnaout, No. 1:02-cr-00892-SBC (N.D. Ill. Oct. 9, 2002) (related case: No. 1:02-cr-00414-JBG (N.D. Ill. May 29, 2002))
28. United States v. Assi, No. 2:98-cr-80695-GER (E.D. Mich. Aug. 4, 1998)
29. United States v. Awadallah, No. 1:01-cr-01026-SAS (S.D.N.Y. Oct. 31, 2001)
30. United States v. Awan, No. 1:06-cr-00154-CPS-VVP (S.D.N.Y. Mar. 10, 2006)
31. United States v. Azmath, No. 1:02-cr-00045-SAS (S.D.N.Y. Jan. 14, 2002)
32. United States v. Babar, No. 1:04-cr-00528-VM (S.D.N.Y. June 2, 2004)
33. United States v. Badri, No. 4:01-cr-0323-FJG (W.D. Mo. Nov. 14, 2001)
34. United States v. Batiste, No. 1:06-cr-20373-JAL (S.D. Fla. June 22, 2006) (the "Liberty City Seven" case)
35. United States v. Battle, No. 3:02-cr-00399-JO (D. Or. Oct. 3, 2002)
36. United States v. Benevolence International Foundation, No. 1:02-cr-00414-JBG (N.D. Ill. May 29, 2002)
37. United States v. Benkahla, No. 1:06-cr-00009-JCC (E.D. Va. Feb. 9, 2006)
38. United States v. Biheiri, No. 1:03-cr-00365-TSE (E.D. Va. Aug. 7, 2003)

39. United States v. Budiman, No. 1:02-cr-00074-GBL (E.D. Va. Feb. 21, 2002)
40. United States v. Chandia, No. 1:05-cr-00401-CMH (E.D. Va. Sep. 14, 2005)
41. United States v. Damrah, No. 1:03-cr-00484-JG (N.D. Ohio Dec. 16, 2003)
42. United States v. Defreitas, No. 1:07-cr-00543-DLI (E.D.N.Y. June 28, 2007)
43. United States v. Doha, No. 1:01-cr-00832-RWS (S.D.N.Y. Aug. 27, 2002)
44. United States v. Dumeisi, No. 1:03-cr-00664-SBC (N.D. Ill. July 16, 2003)
45. United States v. Elashi, No. 3:02-cr-00052-SAL (N.D. Tex. Feb. 20, 2002)
46. United States v. Elfgeeh, No. 1:03-cr-00133-SJ (E.D.N.Y. Feb. 3, 2003)
47. United States v. el-Gabrowny, No. 1:93-cr-00181-MBM (S.D.N.Y. Mar. 17, 1993) (the "Sheikh Abdel Rahman/Landmarks and Tunnels" case)
48. United States v. el-Hage, No. 1:98-cr-01023-KTD (S.D.N.Y. Sept. 21, 1998) (the "Embassy Bombings" case)
49. United States v. el-Jassem, No. 1:73-cr-00500-JBW (E.D.N.Y. Mar. 17, 1973) (related case: United States v. al-Jawary, No. 1:73-cr-00481-UA (S.D.N.Y. May 23, 1973))
50. United States v. Faris, No. 1:03-cr-00189-LMB (E.D. Va. Apr. 30, 2003)
51. United States v. Gadahn, No. 8:05-cr-00254-UA (C.D. Cal. Oct. 12, 2005)
52. United States v. Galicia, No. 1:01-cr-00411-LMB (E.D. Va. Oct. 25, 2001)
53. United States v. Goba, No. 1:02-cr-00214-WMS-HKS (W.D.N.Y. Oct. 21, 2002) (the "Lackawanna Six" case)
54. United States v. Grecula, No. 4:05-cr-00257-KPE (S.D. Tex. June 16, 2005)
55. United States v. Hamed, No. 1:02-cr-00082-JCC (E.D. Va. Feb. 26, 2002)
56. United States v. Hammoud, No. 3:00-cr-00147-GCM-CH (W.D.N.C. July 31, 2000)
57. United States v. Haouari, No. 1:00-cr-00015-JFK (S.D.N.Y. Jan. 19, 2000)
58. United States v. Hashmi, No. 1:06-cr-00442-LAP (S.D.N.Y. May 24, 2006)
59. United States v. Hassan, No. 1:03-cr-00171-SJ (E.D.N.Y. Feb. 13, 2003)
60. United States v. Hassoun, No. 0:04-cr-60001-MGC (S.D. Fla. Jan. 8, 2004) (the "Jose Padilla" case)
61. United States v. Hayat, No. 2:05-cr-00240-GEB (E.D. Cal. June 16, 2005)
62. United States v. Holy Land Foundation for Relief and Development, No. 3:04-cr-00240-JAS (N.D. Tex. July 26, 2004)
63. United States v. Hussain, No. 2:01-cr-01328-JS (E.D.N.Y. Dec. 4, 2001)
64. United States v. Hussein, No. 1:01-cr-10423-REK (D. Mass. Nov. 14, 2001)
65. United States v. Islamic American Relief Agency, No. 4:07-cr-00087-NKL (W.D. Mo. Mar. 6, 2007)
66. United States v. Idris, No. 1:02-cr-00306-CMH (E.D. Va. Mar. 21, 2002)
67. United States v. Iqbal, No. 1:06-cr-01054-RMB (S.D.N.Y. Nov. 15, 2006)
68. United States v. Isse, No. 1:02-cr-00142-JCC (E.D. Va. Apr. 3, 2002)
69. United States v. Jabarah, No. 1:02-cr-01560-BSJ (S.D.N.Y. Dec. 12, 2002)
70. United States v. Jaber, No. 5:05-cr-50030-JLH (W.D. Ark. Aug. 11, 2005)
71. United States v. James, No. 8:05-cr-00214-CJC (C.D. Cal. Aug. 31, 2005)
72. United States v. Janjalani, No. 1:02-cr-00068 (D.D.C. Feb. 12, 2002)
73. United States v. Khadr, No. 1:06-cr-10028-GAO (D. Mass. Feb. 28, 2006)
74. United States v. Lafi Khalil, No. 1:99-cr-01134-JBW (E.D.N.Y. Dec. 14, 1999)
75. United States v. Naji Khalil, No. 1:04-cr-00573-GBD (S.D.N.Y. June 17, 2004) (related case: No. 4:05-cr-00200-GH (E.D. Ark. July 26, 2005))
76. United States v. Khoury, No. 4:01-cr-00751-DH (S.D. Tex. Oct. 3, 2001)
77. United States v. Mustafa Kilfat, No. 2:01-cr-00792-AMW (D.N.J. Dec. 11, 2001)
78. United States v. Ahmad Kilfat, No. 2:01-cr-00793-AMW (D.N.J. Dec. 11, 2001)
79. United States v. Koubriti, No. 2:01-cr-80778-GER (E.D. Mich. Sept. 27, 2001) (the "Detroit Sleeper Cell" case)
80. United States v. Kourani, No. 2:03-cr-81030-RHC-RSW (E.D. Mich. Jan. 15, 2004)
81. United States v. Lakhani, No. 2:03-cr-00880-KSH (D.N.J. Dec. 18, 2003)
82. United States v. Lindh, No. 1:02-cr-00037-TSE (E.D. Va. Feb. 5, 2002)
83. United States v. Lopez-Flores, No. 1:01-cr-00430-GBL (E.D. Va. Oct. 24, 2001)
84. United States v. Maflahi, No. 1:03-cr-00412-NG (E.D.N.Y. Apr. 9, 2003)

85. United States v. Maldonado, No. 4:07-cr-00124-GHM (S.D. Tex. Apr. 2, 2007)
86. United States v. Mandhai, No. 0:02-cr-60096-WPD (S.D. Fla. May. 16, 2002)
87. United States v. Martinez-Flores, No. 1:01-cr-00412-TSE (E.D. Va. Oct. 25, 2001)
88. United States v. Marzook, No. 1:03-cr-00978 (N.D. Ill. Oct. 9, 2003)
89. United States v. Moussaoui, No. 1:01-cr-00455-LMB (E.D. Va. Dec. 11, 2001)
90. United States v. Mubayyid, No. 4:05-cr-40026-FDS (D. Mass. May 11, 2005)
91. United States v. Mustafa, No. 1:04-cr-00356-JFK (S.D.N.Y. Apr. 19, 2004)
92. United States v. Noman, No. 2:02-cr-00431-JWB (D.N.J. May 21, 2002)
93. United States v. Obeid, No. 3:05-cr-00149-TMR (S.D. Ohio Oct. 25, 2005)
94. United States v. Paracha, No. 1:03-cr-01197-SHS (S.D.N.Y. Oct. 8, 2003)
95. United States v. Paul, No. 2:07-cr-00087-GLF (S.D. Ohio Apr. 11, 2007)
96. United States v. Pervez, No. 1:02-cr-00174-JES (S.D.N.Y. Feb. 13, 2002)
97. United States v. Qureshi, No. 6:04-cr-60057-RFD-CMH (W.D. La. Oct. 13, 2004)
98. United States v. Raissi, No. 2:01-cr-00911-EHC (D. Ariz. Oct. 9, 2001) (related case: No. 2:01-cr-01075-SRB (D. Ariz. Nov. 27, 2001))
99. United States v. Ranjha, No. 1:07-cr-00239-MJG (D. Md. May 23, 2007)
100. United States v. Ranson, No. 3:05-cr-00016-TSL-JCS (D. Miss. Feb. 18, 2005)
101. United States v. Rashed, No. 1:87-cr-00308-RCL (D.D.C. July 14, 1987)
102. Unites States v. Ressam, No. 99-cr-00666-JCC (W.D. Wash. Dec. 22, 1999) (the "Millenium Bomber" case)
103. United States v. Reid, No. 1:02-cr-10013-WGY (D. Mass. Jan. 16, 2002) (the "Shoe Bomber" case)
104. United States v. Rezaq, No. 1:93-cr-00284-RCL (D.D.C. July 15, 1993)
105. United States v. Rizvi, No. 1:01-cr-00418-WDM (D. Colo. Nov. 28, 2001)
106. United States v. Royer, No. 1:03-cr-00296-LMB (E.D. Va. June 25, 2003) (the "Virginia Jihad Network" case)
107. United States v. Salameh, No. 1:93-cr-00180-KTD (S.D.N.Y. Mar. 17, 1993) (the "World Trade Center I" and "Bojinka Plot" case)
108. United States v. Salim, No. 1:01-cr-00002-DAB (S.D.N.Y. Jan. 3, 2001)
109. United States v. Sattar, No. 1:02-cr-00395-JGK (S.D.N.Y. Apr. 9, 2002) (the "Lynne Stewart" case)
110. United States v. Serif Mohamed, No. 8:07-cr-00342-SDM-MAP (M.D. Fla. Aug. 29, 2007)
111. United States v. Tarik Shah, No. 1:05-cr-00673-LAP (S.D.N.Y. June 27, 2005)
112. United States v. Syed Shah, No. 3:02-cr-02912-MJL (S.D. Cal. Oct. 30, 2002)
113. United States v. Shannaq, No. 1:02-cr-00319-AMD (D. Md. July 2, 2002)
114. United States v. Shnewer, No. 1:07-cr-00459-RBK (D.N.J. June 5, 2007) (the "Fort Dix Plot" case)
115. United States v. Siraj, No. 1:05-cr-00104-NG (S.D.N.Y. Feb. 9, 2005)
116. United States v. Subeh, No. 6:04-cr-06077-CJS-MWP (W.D.N.Y. Apr. 22, 2004)
117. United States v. Tabatabai, No. 2:99-cr-00225-CAS (C.D. Cal. Mar. 10, 1999)
118. United States v. Taleb-Jedi, No. 1:06-cr-00652-BMC (E.D.N.Y. Sept. 29, 2006)
119. United States v. Ujaama, No. 2:02-cr-00283-BJR (W.D. Wash. Aug. 28, 2002)
120. United States v. Villalobos, No. 1:01-cr-00399-GBL (E.D. Va. Oct. 17, 2001)
121. United States v. Walker, No. 3:04-cr-02701-DB (W.D. Tex. Dec. 8, 2004)
122. United States v. Warsame, No. 0:04-cr-00029-JRT-FLN (D. Minn. Jan. 20, 2004)
123. United States v. Yunis, No. 1:87-cr-00377 (D.D.C. Sept. 15, 1987)

B. Historical Timeline of Significant Terrorism Statutes Enacted by Congress

Treason, U.S. Constitution, Article 3, section 3 (1787)

Alien Friends Act, ch. 58, 1 Stat. 570 (June 25, 1798)

Alien Enemies Act, ch. 66, 1 Stat. 577 (July 6, 1798)

Sedition Acts, ch. 73, 1 Stat. 596 (July 14, 1798); ch. 75, 40 Stat. 533 (May 16, 1918)

Conspiracies Act (Civil War), ch. 33, 12 Stat. 284 (July 31, 1861)

Smith Act of 1940, ch. 439, 54 Stat. 670, 671 (June 28, 1940)

Atomic Energy Act, ch. 724, 60 Stat. 755 (Aug. 1, 1946)
Substantive offenses codified as amended at:

42 U.S.C. § 2122	Prohibitions governing Atomic Weapons
42 U.S.C. § 2131	License Required
42 U.S.C. § 2138	Suspension of Licenses During War or National Emergency
42 U.S.C. §§ 2272-2284	Enforcement of Chapter 23 Offenses

Immigration and Nationality Act, ch. 477, 66 Stat. 163 (June 27, 1952)
Sections relating to terrorism codified as amended at:

8 U.S.C. § 1158	Asylum
8 U.S.C. § 1182	Inadmissible Aliens
8 U.S.C. § 1184	Admission of nonimmigrants
8 U.S.C. § 1202	Application for Visas
8 U.S.C. § 1227	Deportable Aliens

Espionage and Sabotage Act of 1954, ch. 1261, 68 Stat. 1216 (Sept. 3, 1954)
Substantive offenses codified as amended at:

18 U.S.C. § 794	Gathering or Delivering Defense Information to Aid a Foreign Government
18 U.S.C. §§ 2151, 2153-56	Sabotage

Organized Crime Control Act of 1970, Pub. L. No. 91-452, 84 Stat. 922 (Oct. 15, 1970)
Substantive offenses codified as amended at:

18 U.S.C. §§ 842-844	Relating to Importation, Manufacture, Distribution, and Storage of Explosive Materials

Act for the Protection of Foreign Officials and Official Guests of the United States, Pub. L. No. 92-539, 86 Stat. 1070 (Oct. 24, 1972)
Substantive offenses codified as amended at:

18 U.S.C. § 112	Protection of Foreign Officials, Official Guests, and Internationally Protected Persons
18 U.S.C. § 1116	Murder or Manslaughter of Foreign Officials, Official Guests, or Internationally Protected Persons

18 U.S.C. § 1117	Conspiracy to Murder
18 U.S.C. § 1201	Kidnapping

Antihijacking Act of 1974, Pub. L. No. 93-366, 88 Stat. 409 (Aug. 5, 1974)[369]

Substantive offenses codified as renumbered, amended and supplemented at:

49 U.S.C. § 46502	Aircraft Piracy
49 U.S.C. § 46504	Interference with Flight Crew Members and Attendants
49 U.S.C. § 46505	Carrying a Weapon or Explosive on an Aircraft
49 U.S.C. § 46506	Application of Certain Criminal Laws to Acts on Aircraft
49 U.S.C. § 46507	False Information and Threats

International Security Assistance and Arms Export Control Act of 1976, Pub. L. No. 94-329, 90 Stat. 729, 744 (June 30, 1976)

Sections relating to terrorism codified as amended at:

22 U.S.C. § 2778	Control of Arms Exports and Imports (*see* Title 22, Code of Federal Regulations, Part 127 for violations and penalties)
22 U.S.C. § 2779	Fees of Military Sales Agents (*see* Title 22, Code of Federal Regulations, Part 127 for violations and penalties)

Act for the Prevention and Punishment of Crimes Against Internationally Protected Persons, Pub. L. No. 94-467, 90 Stat. 1997 (Oct. 8, 1976)

Substantive offenses codified as amended at:

18. U.S.C. § 878	Threats and Extortion Against Foreign Officials, Official Guests, or Internationally Protected Persons

International Emergency Economic Powers Act (IEEPA), Pub. L. No. 95-223, 91 Stat. 1626 (Dec. 28, 1977)

Substantive offenses codified as amended at:

50 U.S.C. § 1705	Penalties for violating any license, order, or regulation issued pursuant to IEEPA

Convention on the Physical Protection of Nuclear Material Implementation Act of 1982, Pub. L. No. 97-351, 96 Stat. 1663 (Oct. 18, 1982)[370]

Substantive offense codified as amended at:

18 U.S.C. § 831	Prohibited Transactions Involving Nuclear Materials

Continuing Appropriations, 1985 (Comprehensive Crime Control Act of 1984), Pub. L. No. 98-473, 98 Stat. 1837, 2186-2187 (Oct. 12, 1984)

Substantive offenses codified as amended at:

8 U.S.C. § 3583(j)	Supervised Release Terms for Terrorism Predicates
18 U.S.C. § 1203[371]	Hostage Taking
18 U.S.C. § 32[372]	Destruction of Aircraft or Aircraft Facilities

The Omnibus Diplomatic Security and Antiterrorism Act of 1986, Public L. No. 99-399, 100 Stat. 853 (Aug. 27, 1986)

Substantive offense codified as renumbered and amended at:

18 U.S.C. § 2332	Criminal Penalties Relating to Terrorist Acts Abroad Against United States Nationals
22 U.S.C. § 2780	Transactions with Countries Supporting Acts of International Terrorism

Genocide Convention Implementation Act of 1987 (The Proxmire Act), Pub. L. No. 100-606, 102 Stat. 3045 (Nov. 4, 1988)[373]

Substantive offense codified as amended at:

18 U.S.C. § 1091	Genocide

Biological Weapons and Anti-Terrorism Act of 1989, Pub L. No. 101-298, 104 Stat. 201 (May 22, 1990)[374]

Substantive offense codified as amended at:

18 U.S.C. § 175	Prohibitions with Respect to Biological Weapons

Violent Crime Control and Law Enforcement Act of 1994, Pub L. No. 103-322, 108 Stat. 1796 (Sept. 13, 1994)

Substantive offenses codified as amended at:

18 U.S.C. § 1119	Foreign Murder of United States Nationals
18 U.S.C. § 930	Possession of Firearms and Dangerous Weapons in Federal Facilities
18 U.S.C. § 1121	Killing Persons Aiding Federal Investigations or State Correctional Officers
18 U.S.C. §§ 1541 et seq.	Crimes Facilitated by Unlawful Passports and Visas (originally enacted June 25, 1948, Foreign Relations and Intercourse Act)
18 U.S.C. § 2280[375]	Violence Against Maritime Navigation
18 U.S.C. § 2281[376]	Violence Against Maritime Fixed Platforms
18 U.S.C. § 37[377]	Violence at International Airports
18 U.S.C. § 2332a	Use of Certain Weapons of Mass Destruction
18 U.S.C. § 2339A	Providing Material Support to Terrorists

Foreign Relations Authorization Act for Fiscal Years 1994 and 1995, Pub. L. No. 103-236, 108 Stat. 382, 463 (Apr. 30, 1994)

Substantive offense codified as amended at:

18 U.S.C. § 2340A[378]	Torture

Antiterrorism and Effective Death Penalty Act of 1996, Pub. L. No. 104-132, 110 Stat. 1214 (Apr. 24, 1996)

Substantive offenses codified as amended at:

8 U.S.C. § 1189	Designation of Foreign Terrorist Organizations
8 U.S.C. § 1255	Adjustment of Status of nonimmigrant to that of Person Admitted for Permanent Residence
8 U.S.C. § 1531 et. seq.	Alien Terrorist Removal Procedures
18 U.S.C. § 2339B	Providing Material Support or Resources to Designated Foreign Terrorist Organizations
18 U.S.C. § 2332d	Financial Transactions
18 U.S.C. § 2339A	Providing Material Support to Terrorists
18 U.S.C. §§ 842, 844[379]	Unlawful Acts and Penalties Relating to Importation, Manufacture, Distribution and Storage of Explosive Materials
18 U.S.C. § 2332b	Acts of Terrorism Transcending National Boundaries
18 U.S.C. § 956	Conspiracy to Kill, Kidnap, Maim, or Injure Persons or Damage Property in a Foreign Country
18 U.S.C. § 1114	Protection of Officers and Employees of the United States
18 U.S.C. § 1956(c)(7)	Addition of terrorism offenses to money laundering statute term "specified unlawful activity"

War Crimes Act of 1996, Pub L. No. 104-192, 110 Stat. 2104 (Aug. 21, 1996)[380]

Substantive offense codified as renumbered and amended at:

18 U.S.C. § 2441	War Crimes

Omnibus Consolidated and Emergency Supplemental Appropriations Act, 1999 (Chemical Weapons Convention Implementation Act of 1988), Pub. L. No. 105-277, 112 Stat. 2681-866 (Oct. 21, 1998)

Substantive offense codified as amended at:

18 U.S.C. § 229	Prohibited Activities concerning Chemical Weapons
18 U.S.C. § 229A	Penalties

USA PATRIOT Act, Pub. L. No. 107-56, 115 Stat. 272 (Oct. 26, 2001)

Substantive offenses codified as amended at:

8 U.S.C. § 1226a	Mandatory Detention of Suspected Terrorists; Habeas Corpus; Judicial Review
18 U.S.C. § 175b	Biological Weapons; Possession by Restricted Persons
18 U.S.C. § 1961	Amended RICO statute by including "acts of terrorism" as racketeering activity
18 U.S.C. § 1993	Terrorist Attacks and Other Acts of Violence Against Mass Transportation Systems (repealed by the PATRIOT Improvement and Reauthorization Act of 2005, Pub. L. 109-177, Title I, § 110(a), Mar. 9, 2006, 120 Stat. 205)
18 U.S.C. § 2339	Harboring or Concealing Terrorists
18 U.S.C. § 5332	Bulk cash smuggling into or out of the United States

Terrorist Bombings Convention Implementation Act of 2002, Pub. L. No. 107-197, 116 Stat 721 (June 25, 2002)[381]

Substantive offense codified as amended at:

18 U.S.C. § 2332f	Bombing of Places of Public Use, Government Facilities, Public Transportation Systems and Infrastructure Facilities

Suppression of the Financing of Terrorism Convention Implementation Act of 2002, Pub. L. No. 107-197, 116 Stat. 724 (June 25, 2002)[382]

Substantive offense codified as amended at:

18 U.S.C. § 2339C	Prohibitions Against the Financing of Terrorism

Intelligence Reform and Terrorism Prevention Act of 2004, Pub. L. No. 108-458, 118 Stat. 3638 (Dec. 17, 2004)

Substantive offense codified as amended at:

18 U.S.C. § 175c	Variola Virus
18 U.S.C. § 832	Participation in Nuclear and Weapons of Mass Destruction Threats to the United States
18 U.S.C. § 1038	False Information and Hoaxes
18 U.S.C. § 2332g	Missile Systems Designed to Destroy Aircraft
18 U.S.C. § 2332h	Radiological Dispersal Devices
18 U.S.C. § 2339D	Receiving Military-Type Training from a Foreign Terrorist Organization

USA PATRIOT Improvement and Reauthorization Act of 2005, Pub. L. No. 109-177, 120 Stat. 192 (Mar. 9, 2006)

Substantive offense codified as amended at

18 U.S.C. § 226	Bribery Affecting Port Security
18 U.S.C. § 554	Smuggling Goods from the United States
18 U.S.C. § 1036	Entry by False Pretenses to any Real Property, Vessel or Aircraft of the United States or Secure Area of any Airport or Seaport
18 U.S.C. § 1510(e)	Obstruction of Criminal Investigations; Violations of Nondisclosure Provisions of National Security Letters
18 U.S.C. § 1956	Laundering of Monetary Instruments
18 U.S.C. § 1992	Terrorist Attacks and other Violence against Railroad Carriers and Against Mass Transportation Systems on Land, on Water, or Through the Air
18 U.S.C. § 2237	Criminal Sanctions for Failure to Heave to, Obstruction of Boarding, or Providing False Information
18 U.S.C. § 2282A	Devices or Dangerous Substances in Waters of the United States Likely to Destroy or Damage Ships or to Interfere with Maritime Commerce
18 U.S.C. § 2282B	Violence Against Aids to Maritime Navigation
18 U.S.C. § 2283	Transportation of Explosive, Biological, Chemical, or Radioactive or Nuclear Materials
18 U.S.C. § 2284	Transportation of Terrorists
18 U.S.C. § 2291	Destruction of Vessel of Maritime Facility

18 U.S.C. § 2292	Imparting or Conveying False Information
18 U.S.C. § 2312	Transportation of Stolen Vehicles
18 U.S.C. § 2313	Sale or Receipt of Stolen Vehicles
21 U.S.C. § 960a	Foreign Terrorist Organization, Terrorist Persons, and Groups

Endnotes

1. In this Paper we use terms such as "jihad" and "Islamic"—terms that are frequently used by terrorist groups themselves and employed by others who have analyzed terrorism and terrorist organizations. Throughout the Paper we have qualified these terms (e.g., "self-described jihadist") to make clear that they are intended to be descriptive. In no way are any of these words intended to imply that what self-described jihadists or Islamist extremist groups say or do is consistent with Islam. *See also 'Jihadist' Booted from Government Lexicon*, Associated Press, Apr. 24, 2008, *available at* http://ap.google.com/article/ALeqM5i3X6Gha4z-MCq9pU0vC4FWqDCXrwD908CUG00 (describing memo distributed within several federal agencies advising against use of terms such as "jihad" and "Islamic terrorist"). For example, in this Paper our use of the term "jihad" is not meant to imply that the correct meaning of this word, or the principle behind it, condones terrorism. Commentators have offered differing views on the proper meaning of "jihad," and we do not take any position on this complex question. Similarly, references to Muslim clerics or madrassas in this Paper merely describe the specific instances in which clerics or madrassas have been involved in terrorism. None of these terms inherently connotes terrorism, and nothing in this Paper is intended to denigrate the religion of Islam or its teachings.

2. *See, e.g.*, Ass'n of the Bar of the City of N.Y., Comm. on Fed. Courts, *The Indefinite Detention of "Enemy Combatants": Balancing Due Process and National Security in the Context of the War on Terror* (Feb. 6. 2004), *available at* http://www.abcny.org/pdf/1C_WL06!.pdf; Wesley K. Clark & Kal Raustiala, Op-Ed., *Why Terrorists Aren't Soldiers*, N.Y. Times, Aug. 8, 2007, at A19, *available at* http://www.nytimes.com/2007/08/08/opinion/08clark.html; John C. Coughenour, Op-Ed., *How to Try a Terrorist*, N.Y. Times, Nov. 1, 2007, at A27, *available at* http://www.nytimes.com/2007/11/01/opinion/01coughenour.html; John Farmer, Op-Ed., *A Terror Threat in the Courts*, N.Y. Times, Jan. 13, 2008, at § 4, p. 14, *available at* http://www.nytimes.com/2008/01/13/opinion/13farmer.html; Jack L. Goldsmith, *The Laws in Wartime: Boost Trust, Close Guantánamo, and Establish a National Security Court*, Slate.com, Apr. 2, 2008, http://www.slate.com/id/2187870/; Jack L. Goldsmith & Neal Katyal, Op-Ed., *The Terrorists' Court*, N.Y. Times, July 11, 2007, at A19, *available at* http://www.nytimes.com/2007/07/11/opinion/11katyal.html; Jack L. Goldsmith & Eric A. Posner, Op-Ed., *A Better Way on Detainees*, Wash. Post, Aug. 4, 2006, at A17, *available at* http://www.washingtonpost.com/wp-dyn/content/article/2006/08/03/AR2006080301257.html; Amos N. Guiora & John T. Parry, *Light at the End of the Pipeline?: Choosing a Forum for Suspected Terrorists*, 156 U. Pa. L. Rev. 356 (2008); Amos N. Guiora, *Where Are the Terrorists to Be Tried: A Comparative Analysis of Rights Granted to Suspected Terrorists*, 56 Cath. U. L. Rev. 805 (2007); David H. Laufman, *Terror Trials Work: Yes, Mr. Mukasey, Courts Can Handle National Security Cases*, Legal Times, Nov. 5, 2007, at 58-59; Andrew C. McCarthy & Alykhan Velshi, *We Need A National Security Court* (July 16, 2007) (unpublished manuscript, on file with the Foundation for Defense of Democracies), *available at* http://www.defenddemocracy.org/usr_doc/Court.doc; Kelly Moore, *The Role of Federal Criminal Prosecutions in the War on Terrorism*, 11 Lewis & Clark L. Rev. 837 (2007); Kelly Anne Moore, Op-Ed., *Take Al Qaeda to Court*, N.Y. Times, Aug. 21, 2007, at 19, *available at* http://www.nytimes.com/2007/08/21/opinion/21moore.html; Michael B. Mukasey, Op-Ed., *Jose Padilla Makes Bad Law*, Wall St. J., Aug. 22, 2007, at A15, *available at* http://opinionjournal.com/extra/?id=110010505; David B. Rivkin, Jr. & Lee A. Casey, Op-Ed., *Judges v. Jihadis*, Wall St. J., Nov. 8, 2007, at A23, *available at* http://online.wsj.com/article/SB119447456220685713.html; Kenneth Roth, *After Guantánamo: The Case Against Preventive Detention*, 87 Foreign Affairs 9 (May/June 2008), *available at* http://www.foreignaffairs.org/20080501facomment87302/kennethroth/after-guant-namo.html; Glenn M. Sulmasy, *Momentum for a National Security Court*, Jurist Forum, July 13, 2007, http://jurist.law.pitt.edu/forumny/2007/07/momentum-for-national-security-court.php; Glenn M. Sulmasy, *The National Security Court: A Natural Evolution*, Jurist Forum, May 10, 2006, http://jurist.law.pitt.edu/forumny/2006/05/national-security-court-natural.php; Glenn M. Sulmasy, *The Legal Landscape After Hamdan: The Creation of Homeland Security Courts*, 13 New Eng. J. Int'l & Comp. L. 1 (2006); Stuart Taylor, Jr., *Terrorism Suspects and the Law*, Nat'l J., May 12, 2007, at 17, *online version available at* http://www.theatlantic.com/doc/200705u/detainees; Stuart Taylor, Jr., *Rights, Liberties and Security: Recalibrating the Balance After September 11*, Brookings Inst. (Winter 2003), *available at* http://www.brookings.edu/articles/2003/winter_terrorism_jr.aspx?p=1; Serrin Turner & Stephen J. Schulhofer, Brennan Center for Justice at N.Y.U. Sch. of L., *The Secrecy Problem in Terrorism Trials* (2005), *available at* http://brennan.3cdn.net/6a0e5de414927df95e_lbm6iy66c.pdf; Mark D. Villaverde, *Structuring the Prosecutor's Duty to Search the Intelligence Community for Brady Material*, 88 Cornell L. Rev. 1471, 1478 (2003); Stephen I. Vladeck, *Due Process and Terrorism: A Post-Workshop Report*, Am. Bar Ass'n Standing Comm. on Law and Nat'l Security (Nov. 2007), *available at* http://www.abanet.org/natsecurity/Due_Process_and_Terrorism_Dec_2007.pdf; Ruth Wedgwood & Kenneth Roth, *Combatants or Criminals? How Washington Should Handle Criminals*, 83 Foreign Affairs 126 (May/June 2004), *available at* http://www.foreignaffairs.org/20040501faresponse83312/ruth-wedgwood-kenneth-roth/combatants-or-criminals-how-washington-should-handle-terrorists.html; Ruth Wedgwood, *Al Qaeda, Terrorism, and Military Commissions*, 96 Am. J. Int'l L. 328 (2002); Ruth Wedgwood, *After September 11th*, 36 New Eng. L. Rev. 725 (2002); Editorial, *Justice Demands a Legitimate Process*, Miami Herald, Apr. 17, 2008, at A22,

available at http://miamiherald.com/opinion/editorials/story/498929.html; *see also Special Issue: Law In the Age of Terror*, A.B.A. J. (Sept. 2007); Ass'n of the Bar of the City of N.Y., *The Role of the Judiciary in the War on Terror* (transcript of program on June 7, 2005) (on file with the authors); Ari Shapiro, *Mukasey Backs Special Courts for Terror Suspects,* Nat'l Pub. Radio, Oct. 12, 2007, *available at* http://www.npr.org/templates/story/story.php?storyId=15083453.

3   *See, e.g.,* McCarthy & Velshi, *We Need A National Security Court*; Sulmasy, *The Legal Landscape After Hamdan*; Goldsmith & Katyal, *The Terrorists' Court;* Mukasey, *Jose Padilla Makes Bad Law*. The proposals by McCarthy and Velshi and Sulmasy envision an entirely new court system to handle terrorism prosecutions, while the Goldsmith-Katyal proposal is aimed at the more limited, but still significant, issue of preventive detention.

4   Although we discuss sentencing of terrorism defendants at some length, we do not undertake a discussion of death-penalty procedures in such cases due to the highly specialized and intricate nature of those procedures.

5   There are many knowledgeable people with valuable information about and perspectives on the issues addressed in this White Paper. While we have undertaken to interview only a relatively small group of experts, our interviews have yielded a number of insights that we have attempted to incorporate into this White Paper. We interviewed James B. Comey, Joshua L. Dratel, Patrick J. Fitzgerald, Kenneth M. Karas, David N. Kelley, Andrew C. McCarthy, Kelly Anne Moore, Andrew G. Patel, David Raskin, Sam A. Schmidt, and Mary Jo White, as well as others not expressly acknowledged here. All of these individuals spoke with us in their individual capacities and not on behalf of any governmental or private-sector entity with which they are now affiliated or with which they were affiliated in the past. Furthermore, we wish to emphasize that the opinions and conclusions in this White Paper are ours alone and are not necessarily shared by any of the persons we interviewed. Finally, we wish to express our sincere appreciation to all the persons we interviewed for the time and care that they devoted and for the helpful insights they shared.

6   *See, e.g.,* Jess Bravin, *Political Sway at Guantánamo?*, Wall St. J., Oct. 27, 2007, at A4, *available at* http://online.wsj.com/public/article_print/SB119344235879773491.html; Morris D. Davis, Op-Ed., *AWOL Military Justice*, L.A. Times, Dec. 10, 2007, *available at* http://www.latimes.com/news/opinion/la-oe-davis10dec10,0,2446661.story. One Guantánamo detainee, David Hicks, pled guilty to charges that had been filed before a military commission. See William Glaberson, *Plea of Guilty from Detainee in Guantánamo*, N.Y. Times, Mar. 27, 2007, at A1, *available at* http://www.nytimes.com/2007/03/27/washington/27gitmo.html. Hicks was subsequently returned to his home country of Australia where he served a nine-month sentence and was released in December 2007. *See* Raymond Bonner, *Australian Terrorism Detainee Leaves Prison*, N.Y. Times, Dec. 29, 2007, at A7, *available at* http://www.nytimes.com/2007/12/29/world/asia/ 29hicks.html.

7   *See* Richard Baker, *Bomb Rocks Capitol, in 200 Notable Days: Senate Stories, 1787 to 2002* 112, 206 (2006), *available at* http://www.senate.gov/artandhistory/history/minute/Bomb_Rocks_Capitol.htm; Philip Shenon, *U.S. Charges 7 in the Bombing at U.S. Capitol*, N.Y. Times, May 12, 1988, at A20, *available at* http://query.nytimes.com/gst/ fullpage.html?res= 940DE5DD133DF931A 25756C0A96E948260.

8   *See* Nathan Ward, *The Fire Last Time: When Terrorists First Struck New York's Financial District*, Am. Heritage Mag. 46 (Nov. 1, 2001), *available at* http://www.americanheritage.com/articles/magazine/ah/2001/8/2001_8_46.shtml.

9   *See Monumental Plot*, Time, Feb. 26, 1965, at 22, *available at* http://www.time.com/time/magazine/article/0,9171,833472,00.html.

10 For reasons addressed elsewhere in this paper, the subsequent discussion excludes attacks using terrorist tactics by domestic groups such as the Ku Klux Klan in the 1940s, 50s and 60s, or the Black Panthers and Black Liberation Army in the 1970s, or by lone individuals like the Unabomber.

11 Black September, the group behind the 1972 Munich Olympics attack, was formed in reaction to Jordan's military action against and expulsion of Palestinian terrorist groups after the 1970 Dawson Field hijackings and targeted, among others, Jordanian politicians for assassinations. *See* Simon Reeve, *One Day in September: The Full Story of the 1972 Munich Olympics Massacre and the Israeli Revenge Operation "Wrath of God"* 20-35 (2000). Egyptian Islamist extremists assassinated President Anwar Sadat in 1981 and attempted to assassinate his successor, Hosni Mubarak. *See* Lawrence Wright, *The Looming Tower, Al-Qaeda and the Road to 9/11* ("*The Looming Tower*") 58-59, 242-43 (2006).

12 *See generally Can the Hijackers Be Halted?*, Time, Sept. 12, 1969, at 32, *available at* http://www.time.com/time/magazine/article/0,9171,901398,00.html; Pub. Broad. Serv., Timeline: Conflict in the Middle East, 1947-2000, *The American Experience; Hijacked*, http://www.pbs.org/wgbh/amex/hijacked/timeline/index.html.

13 *See* Siobhan O'Neil, Congressional Research Service, *Terrorist Precursor Crimes: Issues and Options for Congress* 5-6 (2007).

14 *See* Capt. Daniel Helmer, *Hezbollah's Employment of Suicide Bombing During the 1980s: The Theological, Political and Operational Development of a New Tactic*, July-Aug. Mil. Rev. 71, 71-72 (2006), *available at* http://usacac.army.mil/CAC/milreview/English/ JulAug06/Helmer.pdf.

15 *See Dammarell v. Islamic Republic of Iran*, 281 F. Supp. 2d 105, 111-13 (D.D.C. 2003) (describing sixty-three deaths and over one hundred other casualties from April 18, 1983, suicide truck bombing of the U.S. Embassy in Beirut); *Peterson v. Islamic Republic of Iran*, 264 F. Supp. 2d 46, 47-48 (D.D.C. 2003) (describing 241 American deaths from the October 23, 1983, suicide truck bombing of the U.S. Marines barracks in Beirut); *20 Years Later, Lebanon Bombing Haunts*, CNN.com, Oct. 23, 2003, http://www.cnn.com/2003/WORLD/meast/10/21/lebanon.anniv.ap (noting 241 and 58 French military deaths from October 23, 1983,

suicide truck bombing); Borzou Daragahi, *Victims of 1983 Bombing of U.S. Embassy in Beruit Remembered*, L.A. Times, Apr. 19, 2008, at 3, *available at* http://www.latimes.com/news/nationworld/world/la-fg-embassy19apr19,1,7837044.story (noting twenty-four deaths from September 20, 1984, bombing of U.S. Embassy annex in Beirut).

16 *See, e.g.*, Wright, *The Looming Tower*, at 197; Nat'l Comm'n on Terrorist Attacks Upon the U.S., *The 9/11 Commission Report* 96-97 (2004) (hereafter *"9/11 Commission Report"*).

17 The Italian court acquitted four and convicted two of lesser charges. *See Rome Court Acquits 6 in Anti-American Plot*, N.Y. Times, Oct. 18, 1985, at A11, *available at* http://select.nytimes.com/search/restricted/article?res=F00C11F9355D0C7B8DDDA90994DD484D81.

18 *See 9/11 Commission Report*, at 55-56; Wright, *The Looming Tower*, at 109-64.

19 *See 9/11 Commission Report*, at 55-57; Wright, *The Looming Tower*, at 208-10, 215-17, 284, 294-96, 380.

20 *See 9/11 Commission Report*, at 69-70; Wright, *The Looming Tower*, at 162-63, 237-39, 264-66, 278-80, 294-96, 341.

21 This discussion is drawn principally from the following sources: *United States v. Yousef*, 327 F.3d 56, 79 (2d Cir. 2003); *United States v. Rahman*, 189 F.3d 88 (2d Cir. 1999); *United States v. Salameh*, 152 F.3d 88 (2d Cir. 1998); *9/11 Commission Report*, at 71-73; Andrew McCarthy, *The Sudan Connection: The Missing Link in U.S. Terrorism Policy*, Weekly Standard, Nov. 2, 1998, at 26; Wright, *The Looming Tower*, at 200-03.

22 Once returned to the United States, Yousef and two other defendants were also tried and convicted for their failed conspiracy to execute a coordinated bombing of twelve commercial airliners departing from Manila. *See Yousef*, 327 F.3d at 79-80.

23 This discussion is drawn principally from the following sources: Rebecca Grant, *Khobar Towers*, 81 Air Force Mag., June 1, 1998, at 41, *available at* http://www.afa.org/magazine/june1998/0698khobar.asp; *U.S. Deports Saudi in Airmen's Bombing Deaths*, N.Y. Times, Oct. 12, 1999, at A4, *available at* http://query.nytimes.com/gst/fullpage.html? res=9F05E1DD1730F931A25753C1A96F958260; Press Release, Fed. Bureau of Investigation (June 21, 2001), *available at* http://www.fbi.gov/pressrel/pressrel01/khobar.htm; Wright, *The Looming Tower*, at 269-72.

24 *See Minute Entry, United States v. al-Mughassil*, No. 01-cr-00228 (E.D. Va. July 2, 2001) (continuing matter pending apprehension of defendants).

25 This discussion is drawn principally from the following sources: *9/11 Commission Report*, at 68-70; Transcript of Opening Statements, *United States v. el-Hage*, No. 98-cr-01023 (S.D.N.Y. Feb. 5, 2001) (Dkt. No. 602); Wright, *The Looming Tower*, at 306-24.

26 *See 9/11 Commission Report*, at 116-17; Wright, *The Looming Tower*, at 319-22.

27 Mamdouh Mahmud Salim was convicted of stabbing a prison guard while awaiting trial on charges relating to the embassy bombings. *See* Paul Hirschkorn, *Bin Laden Aide Sentenced to 32 Years in Prison for Jail Stabbing*, CNN.com, May 4, 2004, http://edition.cnn.com/2004/LAW/05/03/attacks.prison.stabbing/index.html. Ahmed Khalfan Ghailani is currently in custody at Guantánamo. *See* Office of the Dir. of Nat'l Intelligence, Biographies of High Value Terrorist Detainees Transferred to the U.S. Naval Base at Guantánamo Bay (Sept. 6, 2006), *available at* http://www.odni.gov/announcements/content/DetaineeBiographies.pdf.

28 Khalid al-Fawwaz, Ingrahim Eidarous and Adel Abdel Bary each were arrested in the United Kingdom in 1999, and since then have been subject to extradition proceedings. *See* Warren Hoge, *Court Approves Extraditions in Bombings of U.S. Embassies*, N.Y. Times, Dec. 18, 2001, at B6, *available at* http://query.nytimes.com/gst/fullpage.html?res=9E06EEDC143EF93BA25751C1A9679C8B63; *see also* Sean O'Neill, *Bin Laden's London Man May Finally Be Sent to U.S. After 7 Years*, Times (London), Aug. 31, 2005, at Home news 9, *available at* http://www.timesonline.co.uk/tol/news/uk/article560718.ece.

29 This discussion is drawn principally from the following sources: Hal Burton, Mike Carter, David Heath & James Neff, *The Terrorist Within* (Special Report, prologue, chs. 1-17 & epilogue), Seattle Times, June 23–July 7, 2002, *available at* http://seattletimes.nwsource.com/news/nation-world/terrorist within/; Wright, *The Looming Tower*, at 336-38.

30 Ressam's cooperation was described by Special Agent Frederick Humphries at Ressam's sentencing hearing. *See* Transcript of Sentencing Hearing at 17-68, *United States v. Ressam*, No. 99-cr-00666 (W.D. Wash. Apr. 27, 2005) (Dkt. No. 377).

31 *See* Judgment, *Ressam* (W.D. Wash. July 27, 2005) (Dkt. No. 383).

32 This discussion is drawn principally from the following sources: *9/11 Commission Report*, at 152, 190; Wright, *The Looming Tower*, at 338-39, 350, 360-61, 371-74.

33 *See* Press Release, U.S. Navy, USS *Cole* Rejoins the Fleet (Apr. 19, 2002), *available at* http://www.news.navy.mil/search/display.asp?story_id=1415.

34 *See 9/11 Commission Report*, at 146, 153, 488 n.2. Several other participants were arrested and convicted in Yemen. In what began an unusual series of events, many of these men escaped from prison and were later re-captured. *See* Henry Schuster, *Yemen: Eight Jail Tunnel Escapees Now in Custody*, CNN.com, Apr. 27, 2007, http://www.cnn.com/2006/WORLD/meast/04/27/yemen.escapees/index.html. Following re-capture, Yemeni authorities allowed Jamal al-Badawi to remain at liberty after he purportedly renounced terrorism and swore an oath to the Yemeni president, although they quickly put al-Bawadi back in prison after the United States threatened to withdraw aid. *See* Terry Frieden & Kelli Arena, *Justice Department 'Dismayed' Over Release of USS Cole Bombing Leader*, CNN.com, Oct. 26, 2007, http://www.cnn.com/2007/US/10/26/uss.cole/index.html; Robert F. Worth, *Wanted by F.B.I., but Walking Out of a Yemen Hearing*, N.Y.

Times, Mar. 1, 2008, at A3, *available at* http://www.nytimes.com/2008/03/01/world/middleeast/01yemen.html. Both al-Bawadi and Fahd al-Quso, a co-conspirator in the U.S.S. *Cole* attack, have been indicted in the Southern District of New York. *See* Twelfth Superseding Indictment, *el-Hage* (S.D.N.Y. May 12, 2003) (Dkt. No. 686).

35 *See, e.g., 9/11 Commission Report*, at 215-338; Wright, *The Looming Tower*, at 347-50, 402-421.

36 *See* Office of the Dir. of Nat'l Intelligence, Biographies of High Value Terrorist Detainees Transferred to the U.S. Naval Base at Guantánamo Bay.

37 *See* William Glaberson, *Hurdles Seen as Capital Charges Are Filed in 9/11 Case*, N.Y. Times, Feb. 12, 2008, at A14, *available at* http://www.nytimes.com/2008/02/12/washington/12gitmo.html.

38 *See United States v. Rashed*, No. 87-cr-00308 (D.D.C. July 14, 1987); *United States v. Yunis*, No. 87-cr-00377 (D.D.C. Sept. 15, 1987); *United States v. Rezaq*, No. 93-cr-00284 (D.D.C. July 15, 1993). Mohammed Rashed, a member of the Palestinian Liberation Organization, placed a bomb on a Pan Am flight from Tokyo to Honolulu on August 11, 1982. The bomb exploded while the plane was in transit, killing one passenger and wounding fifteen. Rashed was arrested by Greek authorities in 1988. Greece denied the U.S. extradition request and tried Rashed for homicide. He was sentenced to fifteen years' imprisonment but released in December 1996. The FBI subsequently captured Rashed and brought him to the United States, where he pled guilty to first and second degree murder and explosives charges. His sentence has a mandatory release date of March 20, 2013. *See United States v. Rashed*, 234 F.3d 1280, 1281 (D.C. Cir. 2000); Plea Agreement, *Rashed* (D.D.C. Dec. 17, 2002) (Dkt. No. 142); Judgment, *Rashed* (D.D.C. May 1, 2006) (Dkt. No. 172); *see also* Press Release, U.S. Dep't Justice, Jordanian Man Sentenced In 1982 Bombing Of Pan Am Flight From Tokyo To Honolulu (Mar. 24, 2006), *available at* http://washingtondc.fbi.gov/dojpressrel/pressrel06/wfo032406usa.htm.

Fawaz Yunis was one of five members of the Amal Militia who hijacked Royal Jordanian Airlines flight 402 from Beirut to Tunis, forcing it to fly to Cyprus and Sicily and then back to Beirut. The FBI used a cooperating informant to lure Yunis to a yacht in international waters off Cyprus, where he was apprehended and transported to the United States to be tried for hostage-taking. He was convicted by a jury and sentenced to thirty years' imprisonment. *United States v. Yunis*, 859 F.2d 953, 955-57 (D.C. Cir. 1988) ("*Yunis I*"); Judgment, *Yunis* (D.D.C. Oct. 4, 1989).

Omar Mohammed Ali Rezaq, a Palestinian and member of the ANO, hijacked an Egypt Air flight on November 23, 1985, along with two other members of the ANO. The flight was rerouted to Malta, where the hijackers began executing hostages. Egyptian commandos stormed the plane and captured Rezaq, who was tried and convicted in Malta. Although sentenced to twenty-five years' imprisonment, he was released after seven. While en route to Sudan after his release from Maltese custody, Rezaq was apprehended by Nigerian authorities and turned over to the FBI, which flew Rezaq to the United States to stand trial for aircraft piracy. He was convicted and sentenced to life imprisonment. *See United States v. Rezaq*, 899 F. Supp. 697, 700-01 (D.D.C. 1995) ("*Rezaq I*"); Judgment, *Rezaq* (D.D.C. Oct. 29, 1996) (Dkt. No. 303).

39 *See Yunis I*, 859 F.3d at 957-67 (defendant contended that interrogation while he was in transit to the United States violated his Fifth and Sixth Amendment rights); *United States v. Yunis*, 924 F.2d 1086, 1092-93 (D.C. Cir. 1991) ("*Yunis III*") (defendant contended that his apprehension involved outrageous governmental conduct); *Yunis III*, 924 F.2d at 1093-94 (defendant contended that U.S. Navy involvement in his apprehension violated the Posse Comitatus Act, 18 U.S.C. § 1385); *United States v. Rezaq*, 908 F. Supp. 6, 7-8 (D.D.C. 1995) ("*Rezaq II*") (defendant contended that government manufactured jurisdiction by forcibly and involuntarily removing him to the United States).

40 *See Yunis III*, 924 F.2d at 1090-92 (scope of Hostage Taking Act, 18 U.S.C. § 1203, and Anti-Hijacking Act, 18 U.S.C. § 1472(n)); *Rezaq I*, 899 F. Supp. at 709-10 (Anti-Hijacking Act).

41 *See United States v. Yunis*, 867 F.2d 617, 621-25 (D.C. Cir. 1989) ("*Yunis II*"); *Yunis III*, 924 F.2d at 1094-95; *Rezaq I*, 899 F. Supp. at 707-09; Order Directing Court Security Officer to Seek Appropriate Clearance for Defense Expert, *Rashed* (D.D.C. Dec. 6, 2001) (Dkt. No. 128).

42 *See* Order that an Anonymous Jury Will Be Selected in the Case, *United States v. el-Gabrowny*, No. 93-cr-00181 (S.D.N.Y. Nov. 21, 1994) (Dkt. No. 367).

43 *See United States v. Rahman*, 870 F. Supp. 47, 49-53 (S.D.N.Y. 1994).

44 *See United States v. Rahman*, 861 F. Supp. 247, 249-53 (S.D.N.Y. 1994).

45 *See Yousef*, 327 F.3d at 129-30.

46 *See id.* at 86-114.

47 *See id.* at 122-28.

48 *See Rahman*, 189 F.3d at 134-38.

49 *9/11 Commission Report,* at 72.

50 *See* Wright, *The Looming Tower*, at 310.

51 *See United States v. Bin Laden*, 132 F. Supp. 2d 168, 172-81, 189-198 (S.D.N.Y. 2001). Certain statements by al-'Owalhi in Kenya prior to his being fully apprised regarding his right to have a lawyer present during questioning were suppressed, but statements he made after this deficiency was cured were ruled admissible. *See id.* at 192-94.

52 *See* Judgment as to Wadih el-Hage, *el-Hage* (S.D.N.Y. Oct. 22, 2001) (Dkt. No. 637); Judgment as to Khalfan Khamis Mohamed, *el-Hage* (S.D.N.Y. Oct. 22, 2001) (Dkt. No. 638); Judgment as to Mohamed Rashed Daoud al-'Owahli, *el-Hage* (S.D.N.Y. Oct. 22, 2001) (Dkt. No. 640); Judgment as to Mohamed Sadeek Odeh, *el-Hage* (S.D.N.Y. Oct. 22, 2001) (Dkt. No. 641).

53 See Judgment, *United States v. Salim*, 01-cr-00002 (S.D.N.Y. May 5, 2004) (Dkt. No. 90).

54 See Judgment, *el-Hage* (S.D.N.Y. Feb. 21, 2003) (Dkt. No. 681) (121-month sentence for Mohamed Suleiman al-Nalfi after entry of guilty plea); Benjamin Weiser, *Terror Suspect Held Secretly For 4 Months*, N.Y. Times, Mar. 22, 2001, at B4, *available at* http://query.nytimes.com/gst/fullpage.html?res=9B03E1D7163CF931A15750C0A9679C8B63; *see also* Change of Plea Hearing as to Ali Mohamed, *el-Hage* (S.D.N.Y. Oct. 20, 2000); Judy Aita, U.S. Dep't of State, *Ali Mohamed: The Defendant Who Did Not Go To Trial*, May 15, 2001, *available at* http://usinfo.state.gov/is/Archive_Index/Ali_Mohamed.html.

55 See Press Release, U.S. Dep't of Defense, Charges Sworn Against Detainee Ghailani (Mar. 31, 2008), *available at* http://www.defenselink.mil/Releases/Release.aspx?ReleaseID=11795.

56 See U.S. Dep't of State, *Trial of Accused U.S. Embassy Bombers Begins*, Jan. 3, 2001, *available at* http://usinfo.state.gov/is/Archive_Index/Trial_of_Accused_U.S._Embassy_Bombers_Begins.html; Benjamin Weiser, *Going on Trial: U.S. Accusations Of a Global Plot; In Embassy Bombings Case, The Specter of a Mastermind*, N.Y. Times, Feb. 4, 2001, at 27, *available at* http://query.nytimes.com/gst/fullpage.html?res=9B03E1DC103EF937A35751C0A9679C8B63&scp=2.

57 See *United States v. Bin Laden*, No. 98-cr-01023, 2001 WL 66393 (S.D.N.Y. Jan 25, 2001) (discussing CIPA issues); *United States v. Bin Laden*, 58 F. Supp. 2d 113 (S.D.N.Y. 1999) (same); *United States v. Bin Laden*, No. 98-cr-01023, 2001 WL 30061 (S.D.N.Y. Jan. 2, 2001) (denying defendants' motion to suppress evidence gathered abroad, including wiretaps); *United States v. Bin Laden*, 126 F. Supp. 264 (S.D.N.Y. 2000) (same).

58 See *9/11 Commission Report*, at 247.

59 See *id.* at 247, 273.

60 See Second Superseding Indictment, *United States v. Moussaoui*, No. 01-cr-00455 (E.D. Va. July 16, 2002) (Dkt. No. 340).

61 See *United States v. Moussaoui*, No. 01-cr-00455, 2003 WL 21263699, at *6 (E.D. Va. Mar. 10, 2003).

62 See *United States v. Moussaoui*, 382 F.3d 453, 478-82 (4th Cir. 2004).

63 See Minute Entry, Change of Plea Hearing, *Moussaoui* (E.D. Va. Apr. 22, 2005).

64 See Jury Verdict, *Moussaoui* (E.D. Va. May 3, 2006) (Dkt. No. 1852).

65 See *United States v. Goba*, No. 02-cr-00214 (W.D.N.Y. Oct. 21, 2002).

66 *See generally* Matthew Purdy & Lowell Bergman, *Where the Trail Led: Between Evidence and Suspicion; Unclear Danger: Inside the Lackawanna Terror Case*, N.Y. Times, Oct. 12, 2003, § 1, at 1, *available at* http://query.nytimes.com/gst/fullpage.html?res=9E0CE1DF133FF931A25753C1A9659C8B63.

67 See Plea Agreement as to Faysal Galab, *Goba* (W.D.N.Y. Jan. 10, 2003) (Dkt. No. 79); Plea Agreement as to Shafal Mosed, *Goba* (W.D.N.Y. Mar. 24, 2003) (Dkt. No. 112); Plea Agreement as to Yahya Goba, *Goba* (W.D.N.Y. Mar. 25, 2003) (Dkt. No. 113); Plea Agreement as to Salim Alwan, *Goba* (W.D.N.Y. Apr. 8, 2003) (Dkt. No. 120); Plea Agreement as to Yasein Taher, *Goba* (W.D.N.Y. May 12, 2003) (Dkt. No. 128); Plea Agreement as to Mukhtar al-Bakri, *Goba* (W.D.N.Y. May 19, 2003) (Dkt. No. 132).

68 See Indictment, *United States v. Ujaama*, No. 02-cr-00283 (W.D. Wash. Aug. 28, 2002) (Dkt. No. 1).

69 See Plea Agreement (Redacted), *Ujaama* (W.D. Wash. Apr. 14, 2003) (Dkt. No. 75).

70 See Alan Feuer, *Swedish Man to Face Charges in U.S. of Aiding Terrorists*, N.Y. Times, Sep. 26, 2007, at A6, *available at* http://www.nytimes.com/2007/09/26/world/europe/26camp.html; Superseding Indictment, *United States v. Kassir*, No. 04-cr-00356 (S.D.N.Y. Feb. 6, 2006) (Dkt. No. 6).

71 See Superseding Indictment, *United States v. Royer*, No. 03-cr-00296 (E.D. Va. Sept. 25, 2003) (Dkt. No. 167).

72 See Court Verdict as to Masoud Ahmad Khan, *Royer* (E.D. Va. Mar. 4, 2004) (Dkt. No. 469); Court Verdict as to Seifullah Chapman, *Royer* (E.D. Va. Mar. 4, 2004) (Dkt. No. 470); Court Verdict as to Hammad Abdur-Raheem, *Royer* (E.D. Va. Mar. 4, 2004) (Dkt. No. 471).

73 See Order, *Royer* (E.D. Va. Feb. 20, 2004) (Dkt. No. 454) (granting motion for judgment of acquittal as to Caliph Ibn Abdur-Raheem); Judgment of Acquittal as to Sabri Benkahla, *Royer* (E.D. Va. Mar. 9, 2004) (Dkt. No. 481).

74 See Superseding Indictment, *United States v. Benkahla*, No. 06-cr-00009 (E.D. Va. July 13, 2006) (Dkt. No. 49).

75 See Indictment, *United States v. Shnewer*, No. 07-cr-00459 (D.N.J. June 5, 2007) (Dkt. No. 18).

76 See *id.*

77 See Plea Agreement as to Agron Abdullahu, *Shnewer* (D.N.J. Oct. 31, 2007) (Dkt. No. 89); Judgment as to Agron Abdullah, *Shnewer* (D.N.J. Mar. 31, 2008) (Dkt. No. 151).

78 See Order, *Shnewer* (D.N.J. Jan. 18, 2008) (Dkt. No. 136).

79 See Minute Entry, Plea Agreement Hearing as to Iyman Haris, *United States v. Faris*, No. 03-cr-00189 (E.D. Va. May 1, 2003). Faris was also implicated in a conspiracy to attack a mall in Columbus, Ohio, with Nuradin Abdi. *See United States v. Abdi*, 463 F.3d 547, 550-53 (6th Cir. 2006).

80 See Superseding Indictment, *United States v. Siraj*, 05-cr-00104 (E.D.N.Y. Mar. 14, 2006) (Dkt. No. 94); Jury Verdict, *Siraj* (E.D.N.Y. May 24, 2006) (Dkt. No. 166).

81 See Indictment, *United States v. Defreitas*, No. 07-cr-00543 (E.D.N.Y. June 28, 2007) (Dkt. No. 10).

82 Prior Beharry, *Brooklyn: Hearing in Airport Plot Case*, N.Y. Times, Dec. 10, 2007, at B2, *available at* http://query.nytimes.com/gst/fullpage.html?res=9802E0D71638F933A25751C1A9619C8B63.

83 See Second Superseding Indictment, *United States v. Koubriti*, No. 01-cr-80778 (E.D. Mich. Aug. 28, 2002) (Dkt. No. 152).

84 See *United States v. Koubriti*, 336 F. Supp. 2d 676, 682 (E.D. Mich. 2004).

85 See Fourth Superseding Indictment, *Koubriti* (E.D. Mich. Dec. 15, 2004) (Dkt. No. 580).

86 See Jury Verdict as to Lyglenson Lemorin, *United States v. Batiste*, No. 06-cr-20373 (S.D. Fla. Dec. 13, 2007) (Dkt. No. 706); Minute Entry, *Batiste* (S.D. Fla. Dec. 13, 2007) (Dkt. No. 704). Lyglenson Lemorin was subsequently charged by federal immigration officials with nearly identical offenses to those he faced in the criminal trial and is now facing removal proceedings. *See Ex-Terror Suspect is Charged Anew*, N.Y. Times, Feb. 7, 2008, at A23, *available at* http://www.nytimes.com/2008/02/07/us/07miami.html.

87 See Carmen Gentile, *Six Suspects Will be Tried a Third Time in Sears Plot*, N.Y. Times, Apr. 24, 2008, at A18, *available at* http://www.nytimes.com/2008/04/24/us/24miami.html. Prosecutors have announced that they will pursue a third trial against the six men. *See id.*

88 See Plea Agreement by Enaam Arnaout, *United States v. Arnaout*, No. 02-cr-00892 (N.D. Ill. Feb. 10, 2003) (Dkt. No. 178); Judgment as to Enaam Arnaout, *Arnaout* (N.D. Ill. Aug. 18, 2003) (Dkt. No. 213).

89 See Jury Verdict as to Holy Land Foundation for Relief and Development, *United States v. Holy Land Foundation*, No. 04-cr-00240 (N.D. Tex. Oct. 22, 2007) (Dkt. No. 863); Jury Verdict as to Shukri Abu Baker, *Holy Land Foundation* (N.D. Tex. Oct. 22, 2007) (Dkt. No. 864); Jury Verdict as to Mohammad el-Mezain, *Holy Land* (N.D. Tex. Oct. 22, 2007) (Dkt. No. 865); Jury Verdict as to Ghassan Elashi, *Holy Land Foundation* (N.D. Tex. Oct. 22, 2007) (Dkt. No. 866); Jury Verdict as to Mufid Abdulqader, *Holy Land Foundation* (N.D. Tex. Oct. 22, 2007) (Dkt. No. 867); Jury Verdict as to Abdulrahman Oden, *Holy Land Foundation* (N.D. Tex. Oct. 22, 2007) (Dkt. No. 868); Minute Entry, *Holy Land Foundation* (N.D. Tex. Oct. 22, 2007); Order, *Holy Land Foundation* (N.D. Tex. Oct. 22, 2007) (Dkt. No. 872).

90 "The theology of jihad requires a fatwa—a religious ruling—in order to consecrate actions that would otherwise be considered criminal." Wright, *The Looming Tower*, at 66.

91 Indictment at 4, *United States v. Sattar*, No. 02-cr-00395 (S.D.N.Y. Apr. 8, 2002) (Dkt. No. 1).

92 *Rahman*, 189 F.3d at 124.

93 *See id.* at 124-26.

94 See Jury Verdict as to al-Timimi, *United States v. al-Timimi*, No. 04-cr-00385 (E.D. Va. Apr. 26, 2005) (Dkt. No. 107); Judgment, *al-Timimi* (E.D. Va. July 13, 2005) (Dkt. No. 132).

95 See *Royer* (E.D. Va. June 25, 2003).

96 See Eric Lichtblau, *Scholar Is Given Life Sentence in 'Virginia Jihad' Case*, N.Y. Times, July 14, 2005, at A21, *available at* http://www.nytimes.com/2005/07/14/national/14cleric.html.

97 See Superseding Indictment, *United States v. Mustafa*, No. 04-cr-00356 (S.D.N.Y. Sept. 12, 2005) (Dkt. No. 5).

98 See *Britain: Cleric Can Be Tried in U.S., Judge Rules*, N.Y. Times, Nov. 16, 2007, at A12, *available at* http://www.nytimes.com/2007/11/16/world/europe/16briefs-cleric.html.

99 See *Rumsfeld v. Padilla*, 542 U.S. 426, 430-31 (2004).

100 See *Padilla v. Rumsfeld*, No. 02-cv-04445 (S.D.N.Y. June 12, 2002).

101 See *Padilla v. Rumsfeld*, 352 F.3d 695 (2d Cir. 2003); *Padilla v. Hanft*, 423 F.3d 386 (4th Cir. 2005).

102 See *Rumsfeld v. Padilla*, 542 U.S. 426 (2004).

103 See *Padilla v. Hanft*, 432 F.3d 582 (4th Cir. 2005); *Hanft v. Padilla*, 546 U.S. 1084 (2006).

104 See Jury Verdict, *United States v. Padilla*, No. 04-cr-60001 (S.D. Fla. Aug. 16, 2007) (Dkt. No. 1193).

105 See *al-Marri v. Wright*, 487 F.3d 160, 164 (4th Cir. 2007). The court in the Southern District of New York dismissed the first indictment in New York for lack of venue. *See id.* Al-Marri was then re-indicted in Illinois. *See id.*

106 *See id.* at 164-65.

107 *See id.* at 166, 195.

108 See Court Order, *al-Marri v. Wright*, No. 06-7427 (4th Cir. Aug. 22, 2007) (Dkt. No. 170) (granting motion for rehearing en banc).

109 See U.S. Dep't of Justice, Executive Office for U.S. Att'ys, *U.S. Attorneys' Annual Statistical Report: Fiscal Year 2002* 21 (2002), *available at* http://www.usdoj.gov/usao/reading_room/reports/asr2002/02_stat_book.pdf; U.S. Dep't of Justice, Executive Office for U.S. Att'ys, *U.S. Attorneys' Annual Statistical Report: Fiscal Year 2003* 21 (2003), *available at* http://www.usdoj.gov/usao/reading_room/

reports/asr2003/03_STAT_Report.pdf; U.S. Dep't of Justice, Executive Office for U.S. Att'ys, *U.S. Attorneys' Annual Statistical Report: Fiscal Year 2004* 19 (2004), *available at* http://www.usdoj.gov/usao/reading_room/reports/asr2004/asr2004.pdf; U.S. Dep't of Justice, Executive Office for U.S. Att'ys, *U.S. Attorneys' Annual Statistical Report: Fiscal Year 2005* 19 (2005), *available at* http://www.usdoj.gov/usao/reading_room/reports/asr2005/05statrpt.pdf; U.S. Dep't of Justice, Executive Office for U.S. Att'ys, *U.S. Attorneys' Annual Statistical Report: Fiscal Year 2006* 21 (2006), *available at* http://www.usdoj.gov/usao/reading_room/reports/asr2006/06statrpt.pdf.

[110] *See* Admin. Office of the U.S. Courts, *Judicial Business of the U.S. Courts 2006* Table D.2, *available at* http://www.uscourts.gov/judbus2006/contents.html.

[111] Michael B. Mukasey, Op-Ed., *Jose Padilla Makes Bad Law*, Wall St. J., Aug. 22, 2007, at A15, *available at* http://opinionjournal.com/extra/?id=110010505.

[112] U.S. Dep't of Justice, Counterterrorism Section, *Counterterrorism White Paper Update* 10-11 (2007) (hereafter *"DOJ Counterterrorism White Paper Update"*); *see also* U.S. Dep't of Justice, Counterterrorism Section, *Counterterrorism White Paper* 13-14 (2006) (hereafter *"DOJ Counterterrorism White Paper"*), *available at* http://trac.syr.edu/tracreports/terrorism/169/include/terrorism.whitepaper.pdf.

[113] For an overview of difficulties of classifying terrorism cases that have arisen in the context of the EOUSA's and FBI's classification systems, *see* Robert M. Chesney, *Federal Prosecution of Terrorism-Related Offenses: Conviction and Sentencing Data in Light of the "Soft-Sentence" and "Data-Reliability" Critiques*, 11 Lewis & Clark L. Rev. 851 (2007).

[114] *See* U.S. Dep't of Justice, *U.S. Attorneys' Annual Statistical Report: Fiscal Year 2006* at 21; *see also* Ex. E to Decl. of Susan Long at A-49-50, *Long v. U.S. Dep't of Justice*, No. 02-cv-02467 (D.D.C. May 16, 2003) (Dkt. No. 12) (LIONS User's Manual, Appendix A – LIONS Codes).

[115] *See* U.S. Dep't of Justice, Office of the Inspector Gen., Audit Div., *The Department of Justice's Internal Controls Over Terrorism Reporting* 38 (2007), *available at* http://www.usdoj.gov/oig/reports/plus/a0720/final.pdf.

[116] *See, e.g.*, Dir. of Nat'l Intelligence, *The 2006 Annual Report of the U.S. Intelligence Cmty.* 9-11 (2007), *available at* http://www.fas.org/irp/dni/2006annual.pdf (framing the terrorist threat as "jihadi-inspired terror"); Dir. of Nat'l Intelligence, *Nat'l Intelligence Estimate: The Terrorist Threat to the U.S. Homeland* 6 (2007), *available at* http://www.dni.gov/press_releases/20070717_release.pdf ("The main [terrorist] threat comes from Islamic terrorist groups and cells, especially al-Qa'ida, driven by their undiminished intent to attack the Homeland and a continued effort by these terrorist groups to adapt and improve their capabilities.").

[117] *See, e.g.*, William Yardley, *Radical Environmentalist Gets 9-Year Term*, N.Y. Times, May 26, 2007, at A9, *available at* http://www.nytimes.com/2007/05/26/us/26sentence.htm (discussing sentencing of members of the Environmental Liberation Front, who received terrorism enhancements for acts of arson); *Cyanide, Arsenal Stirs Domestic Terror Fear*, CNN.com, Jan. 30, 2004, http://www.cnn.com/2004/US/Southwest/01/30/cyanide.probe.ap/ (couple with militia ties plead guilty to charges relating to a stockpile of weapons found in Texas rental storage units); David Kocieniewski, *Six Animal Rights Advocates Are Convicted of Terrorism*, N.Y. Times, Mar. 3, 2006, at B3, *available at* http://www.nytimes.com/2006/03/03/nyregion/03animals.html (Stop Huntingdon Animal Cruelty, an animal rights group, and six of its members convicted of terrorism and Internet stalking); Christopher B. Daly, *Salvi Convicted of Murder in Shootings*, Wash. Post, March 19, 1996, at A01, *available at* http://www.washingtonpost.com/wp-srv/local/longterm/aron/salvi021996.htm (defendant described by prosecution as "anti-abortion terrorist" sentenced to life in prison for attacks on abortion clinics).

[118] For a list of Foreign Terrorist Organizations and descriptions, including LTTE and Mujahideen e-Khalq, *see* U.S. Dep't of State, Office of the Coordinator for Counterterrorism, Country Reports on Terrorism (Apr. 30, 2007), *available at* http://www.state.gov/s/ct/rls/crt/2006/82738.htm.

[119] *See generally* Mark P. Sullivan, *CRS Report for Congress, Latin America: Terrorism Issues* (2005); *see also* Indictment, *United States v. Barrera-De Amaris*, No. 03-cr-00182 (S.D. Tex. May 21, 2003) (Dkt. No. 1) (charging material support for the AUC under 18 U.S.C. § 2339B); Indictment, *United States v. Fuerzas Armadas Revolucionarias de Colombia*, No. 04-cr-00232 (D.D.C. May 13, 2004) (Dkt. No. 1) (charging FARC and one of its commanders with hostage-taking and material support in connection with kidnapping U.S. nationals in an attempt to coerce the Colombian government).

[120] A criminal docket was considered a terrorism case for purposes of this White Paper if the charging instruments or other evidence indicated a connection with al Qaeda, the Taliban, Hamas, Hezbollah or similar organizations. *See, e.g.*, U.N. Sec. Council, U.N. Sec. Council Comm. Established Pursuant to Resolution 1267 (1999) Concerning Al-Qaida and the Taliban and Associated Individuals and Entities, *The Consolidated List of the United Nations Security Council's al-Qaida and Taliban Sanctions Committee* (last updated Apr. 21, 2008), *available at* http://www.un.org/sc/committees/1267/pdf/consolidatedlist.pdf.

[121] *See generally Long v. U.S. Dep't of Justice*, 450 F. Supp. 2d 42 (2006) (discussing DOJ resistance to plaintiffs' FOIA requests).

[122] *See* Findlaw, http://news.findlaw.com/legalnews/us/terrorism/cases/index.html (last visited Apr. 25, 2008).

[123] *See 330 Suspects Charged*, Wash. Post, June 12, 2005, http://www.washingtonpost.com/wp-srv/nation/dojstats/full330.html.

[124] *See* N.Y.U. Sch. of Law, The Ctr. on Law and Sec., *Terrorist Trial Report Card: U.S. Ed.* (2006), *available at* http://www.lawandsecurity.org/publications/TTRCComplete.pdf.

125 Our searches targeted criminal cases charging violations of 18 U.S.C. §§ 175, 2332-2332h, 2339-2339d, 2381-2382, 2384, 2389-90, and 50 U.S.C. § 1705.

126 *See* cases filed after September 11, 2001 on Appendix A, Terrorism Prosecution Cases.

127 The fifteen defendants for whom all charges were resolved by acquittal or dismissal are the following: Abdullahi Jama Amir, *United States v. Abdoulah*, No. 01-cr-03240 (S.D. Cal.); Sameeh Taha Hammoudeh, *United States v. al-Arian*, No. 03-cr-00077 (M.D. Fla.); Ghassan Zayed Ballut, *United States v. al-Arian*, No. 03-cr-00077 (M.D. Fla.); Sami Omar al-Hussayen, *United States v. al-Hussayen*, No. 03-cr00048 (D. Idaho); Ali Saleh Kahlah al-Marri, *United States v. al-Marri*, No. 03-cr-10044 (C.D. Ill.); Benevolence International Foundation Inc., *United States v. Arnaout*, No. 02-cr-00892(N.D. Ill.) and *United States v. Benevolence International Foundation, Inc.*, No. 02-cr-00414 (N.D. Ill.); Osama Awadallah, *United States v. Awadallah*, No. 01-cr-01026 (S.D.N.Y.); Lygelson Lemorin, *United States v. Batiste*, No. 06-cr-20373 (S.D. Fla.); Habis Abdulla al-Saoub, *United States v. Battle*, No. 02-cr-00399 (D. Or.); Enaam Arnaout, *United States v. Benevolence International Foundation, Inc.*, No. 02-cr-00414 (N.D. Ill.); Farouk Ali-Haimoud, *United States v. Koubriti*, No. 01-cr-00778 (E.D. Mich.); Abdel Ilah Elmardoudi, *United States v. Koubriti*, No. 01-cr-80778 (E.D. Mich.); Sabri Benkahla, *United States v. Royer*, No. 03-cr-00296 (E.D. Va.); and Caliph Basha Ibn Abdur-Raheem, *United States v. Royer*, No. 03-cr-00296 (E.D. Va.).

128 Human Rights First defines terrorism as "any action or threat of action by individuals or groups acting outside the framework of state authority intended to cause death or serious bodily harm to civilians or non-combatants, or the taking of hostages, in order to intimidate a population or compel a government or an international organization to do or to abstain from doing any act. This definition applies under any circumstances, in peacetime or war, irrespective of the motivations of the perpetrator(s)."

129 We have included an historical timeline of significant statutes that have been enacted to address terrorism-related offenses at Appendix B.

130 Courts have held that individual plaintiffs may sue for and receive monetary damages, in civil actions under 18 U.S.C. § 2333, for acts that would constitute violations of §§ 2339A and 2339B. *See Boim v. Quranic Literacy Inst*, 291 F.3d 1000, 1012-16 (7th Cir. 2002). The plaintiffs' theory in *Boim* was that the defendant organizations aided and abetted Hamas, in violation of §§ 2339A and 2339B, by raising and funneling money to Hamas through a complicated web of front organizations. *See id.* at 1024. In a landmark decision in 2004, a jury awarded $156 million to the family of teenager David Boim, a U.S. citizen shot by Hamas in the West Bank. *See Boim v. Quranic Literacy Inst.*, No. 00-cr-02905, 2004 WL 2931337, at *2 (N.D. Ill. Dec. 14, 2004).

131 In response to the 9/11 attacks, President George W. Bush issued Executive Order 13224. *See* Exec. Order No. 13,224, 66 Fed. Reg. 49,079 (Sept. 23, 2001), *available at* http://www.ustreas.gov/offices/enforcement/ofac/programs/terror/terror.pdf. This Order, the purpose of which is similar to that of the material support statutes, prohibits financial transactions with persons who commit, threaten to commit, or support terrorism, among other things. *See id.* Executive Order 13224 was issued, in part, under the authority of the International Emergency Economic Powers Act (the "IEEPA"), 50 U.S.C. §§ 1701 et seq., which authorizes the President to investigate, regulate, or prohibit certain financial activity during a declared state of emergency. *See* 50 U.S.C. §§ 1701-02. Section 1705 provides for criminal penalties, including a maximum ten-year prison sentence, for violations of any order issued under the authority of the IEEPA. *See id.* § 1705(b).

Generally, Executive Order 13224 "provides a means by which to disrupt the financial support network for terrorists and terrorist organizations by authorizing the U.S. government to designate and block the assets of foreign individuals and entities that commit, or pose a significant risk of committing, acts of terrorism. In addition, because of the pervasiveness of the financial foundations of foreign terrorists, the Order authorizes the U.S. government to block the assets of individuals and entities that provide support, services, or assistance to, or otherwise associate with, terrorists and terrorist organizations designated under the Order, as well as their subsidiaries, front organizations, agents, and associates." U.S. Dep't of State, Office of the Coordinator for Counterterrorism, Fact Sheet for Executive Order 13224 (Dec. 20, 2002), *available at* http://www.state.gov/s/ct/rls/fs/2002/16181.htm. The list of terrorist groups identified under Executive Order 13224 is determined by either the Secretary of State, in consultation with the Secretary of the Treasury and the Attorney General, or the Secretary of the Treasury, in consultation with the Secretary of State and the Attorney General, based on criteria outlined in the Order. *See* Exec. Order No. 13,224; U.S. Dep't of State, Fact Sheet for Executive Order 13224. The current list of terrorists and groups identified under Executive Order 13224 is available at http://www.ustreas.gov/offices/enforcement/ofac/programs/terror/terror.pdf. In cases where the government has charged criminal violations of 50 U.S.C. § 1705 of the IEEPA and Executive Order 13224, it has often done so alongside material support charges under §§ 2339A and/or 2339B.

132 Prohibitions against some of these categories of "material support" have been struck down on vagueness grounds in a recent Ninth Circuit decision. *See Humanitarian Law Project v. Mukasey*, 509 F.3d 1122 (9th Cir. 2007). For example, § 2339A counts as material support the provision of "training," which it defines as "instruction or teaching designed to impart a specific skill, as opposed to general knowledge"; the Ninth Circuit found this definition impermissibly vague because it could not discern the distinction between imparting "a specific skill" versus "general knowledge." *Id.* at 1134-35. Similarly, § 2339A's inclusion of "expert advice or assistance"—imparting "scientific, technical or other specialized knowledge"—has been deemed unconstitutionally ill-defined because "other specialized knowledge" could cover "every conceivable subject." *Id.* at 1135-36. Indeed, even the government admitted at oral argument that "filing an amicus brief in support of a foreign terrorist organization" would constitute providing material support. *Id.* Finally, the Ninth Circuit held that § 2339A's undefined prohibition against providing "service" was vague. *See id.* at 1136. Like other courts, however, the Ninth Circuit *did* uphold the material support statute's definition of "personnel." *See id.*

133 Stewart raised a First Amendment challenge to the application of the material support statute in her case, claiming that she merely provided Abdel Rahman's speech to his adherents and that the speech should be protected by the First Amendment. *See Sattar*, 395 F. Supp. 2d at

101. The court rejected this argument, citing extensive evidence to support the jury verdict that Stewart and Abdel Rahman had in fact joined a conspiracy to provide material support to the Islamic Group. *See id.* In this regard, the court quoted the Second Circuit's holding in Abdel Rahman's earlier appeal that "'one is not immunized from prosecution for such speech-based offenses merely because one commits them through the medium of political speech or religious preaching.'" *Id.* (quoting *Rahman*, 189 F. 3d at 117).

[134] Although the *Shah* court was dealing with a prosecution under § 2339B, that section uses the same definition of "material support" as § 2339A. *See Shah*, 474 F. Supp. 2d at 496.

[135] *See also* Telephone Interview with Joshua L. Dratel, defense counsel (Jan. 24, 2008). Mr. Dratel observed that the material support statutes are susceptible to abuse because they do not necessarily distinguish between criminal conduct and conduct that is protected by the First Amendment, and also because they permit prosecution of conduct that is even more inchoate than in traditional conspiracy cases.

[136] *See* Chesney, *Beyond Conspiracy?*, at 487-88; *see also* Amy Waldman, *Prophetic Justice*, Atlantic Monthly, Oct. 2006, at 82-93. In addition to claiming that he had traveled to Pakistan for an arranged marriage, Hayat argued that his confession was improperly obtained and unreliable. *See* Chesney, *Beyond Conspiracy?*, at 488-89. The government, however, offered evidence corroborating Hayat's confession. For example, the prosecution corroborated Hayat's presence at a jihadi training camp by offering "his possession of a jihadi supplication; his multiple recorded conversations with [a co-defendant] related to his belief in jihad and desire to attend a jihadi camp; testimony regarding the existence of camps in Pakistan [from government experts]; Hayat's self-made jihadi scrapbook; and Hayat's possession of numerous well-known jihadi publications." *United States v. Hayat*, No. 05-cr-00240, 2007 WL 1454280, at *12 (E.D. Cal. May 17, 2007). The government also used the "jihadi supplication" to corroborate Hayat's criminal intent. *See id.* at *11. By itself, however, this evidence would not have proved that Hayat actually attended a jihadi training camp, because even the government's experts would only give "a sixty to seventy percent probability estimation that a training camp existed in Balakot, Pakistan," the city in which Hayat allegedly attended the camp. *Id.* at *10.

[137] Indeed, dissenting views in the legislative history of the bill raised concerns over the mens rea requirement by stating that the statute would limit the ability of citizens to associate with and support the lawful and humanitarian components of many groups labeled as foreign terrorist organizations. The dissenters noted that "because many 'controversial' political groups also have a large humanitarian component, the bill's restrictions on fundraising are likely to have a significant adverse impact on relief efforts in troubled parts of the world." H.R. Rep. No. 104-383 at 178-79.

[138] Supporting those courts' analyses, Congress explicitly disavowed any attempt to criminalize membership or association with any group: "This provision does not attempt to restrict a person's right to join an organization. Rather, the restriction only affects one's contribution of financial or material resources to a foreign organization that has been designated as a threat to the national security of the United States. The prohibition is on the act of donation. There is no proscription on one's right to think, speak, or opine in concert with, or on behalf of, such an organization." H.R. Rep. No. 104-383 at 44.

[139] Some commentators have asserted that § 2339B has been used in a significant majority of terrorist prosecutions after 9/11. *See, e.g.,* Tom Stacey, *The "Material Support" Offense: The Use of Strict Liability in the War Against Terror*, 14 Kan. J.L. & Pub. Pol'y 461, 461 (2005); *see also* David Henrik Pendle, Comment, *Charity of the Heart and Sword: The Material Support Offense and Personal Guilt*, 30 Seattle U. L. Rev. 777, 777 (2007).

[140] *Available at* http://www.washingtonpost.com/wp-dyn/content/article/2006/04/17/AR2006041701485.html.

[141] *Available at* http://www.sptimes.com/2006/05/02/Tampabay/Judge_sentences_Al_Ar.shtml. Al-Arian's guilty plea followed a lengthy, inconclusive trial. In December 2005, after a decade-long investigation and a six-month trial, the jury found al-Arian not guilty on eight of seventeen charges relating to his alleged support for Palestinian Islamic Jihad. *See* Jury Verdict, *al-Arian* (M.D. Fla. Dec. 7, 2005) (Dkt. No. 1463); *see also* Meg Laughlin, *Al-Arian Associate Gets Prison*, St. Petersburg Times, July 26, 2006, at 1B, *online version available at* http://www.sptimes.com/2006/07/25/Tampabay/Al_Arian_associate_se.shtml; *see generally Sami Al-Arian Trial Coverage*, St. Petersburg Times (various dates), *available at* http://www.sptimes.com/2005/webspecials05/al-arian/. The judge declared a mistrial on the nine remaining counts against al-Arian. *See* Declaration of Mistrial, *al-Arian* (M.D. Fla. Dec. 7, 2005) (Dkt. No. 1464). Co-defendant Fariz was acquitted on twenty-five of thirty-three charges, with the jury deadlocking on the remainder. *See* Jury Verdict, *al-Arian* (M.D. Fla. Dec. 7, 2005) (Dkt. No. 1467). He subsequently pled guilty and was sentenced to thirty-seven months, the low end of the sentencing guideline range for his offenses. *See* Revised Plea Agreement, *al-Arian* (M.D. Fla. July 26, 2006) (Dkt. No. 1627); Judgment, *al-Arian* (M.D. Fla. July 26, 2005) (Dkt. No. 1632); Transcript of Sentencing, *al-Arian* (M.D. Fla. Aug. 11, 2006) (Dkt. No. 1638). Co-defendants Hammodudeh and Ballut were acquitted on all charges against them. *See* Jury Verdicts, *al-Arian* (M.D. Fla. Dec. 7, 2005) (Dkt. Nos. 1465, 1466). "In the end, not a single guilty verdict was returned after a six-month trial that included more than 80 witnesses and 400 transcripts and intercepted phone conversations and faxes." Meg Laughlin, Jennifer Liberto & Justin George, *8 Times, Al-Arian Hears 'Not Guilty'*, St. Petersburg Times, Dec. 7, 2005, at 1A, *available at* http://www.sptimes.com/2005/12/07/Tampabay/8_times__Al_Arian_hea.shtml.

Al-Arian subsequently pled guilty to a single charge of conspiracy to provide support to the Islamic Jihad. *See* Plea Agreement at 1, *al-Arian* (M.D. Fla. Apr. 14, 2006) (Dkt. No. 1563). At sentencing, Judge James S. Moody exceeded the recommendations of prosecutors and defense counsel by sentencing al-Arian to fifty-seven months in prison. *See* Minute Entry, *al-Arian* (M.D. Fla. May 1, 2006) (Dkt. No. 1569); Transcript, *al-Arian* (M.D. Fla. May 1, 2006) (Dkt. No. 1594); *see also* Meg Laughlin, *In his Plea Deal, What Did Sami Al-Arian Admit To?*, St. Petersburg Times, Apr. 23, 2006, at 1B, *available at* http://www.sptimes.com/2006/04/23/Hillsborough/In_his_plea_deal__wha.shtml; Meg Laughlin, *Al-Arian Appeals Prison Term*, St. Petersburg Times, May 11, 2006, at 8B, *online version available at* http://www.sptimes.com/2006/05/10/Tampabay/Al_Arian_appeals_sent.shtml; Meg Laughlin, *Judge Sentences Al-Arian to Limit*, St. Petersburg Times, May 2, 2006, at 1A, *available at* http://www.sptimes.com/2006/05/02/Tampabay/Judge_sentences_Al_Ar.shtml. Subsequently, al-Arian was held in contempt and confined for an additional eighteen months because he refused to testify before a Virginia grand jury in a federal investigation of several Islamic charities suspected of aiding terrorist organizations. *See* Order, *al-Arian* (M.D. Fla. Nov. 9, 2006) (Dkt. No. 1666); Meg Laughlin, *Al-Arian Gets More Prison Time*, St. Petersburg Times, Nov. 17, 2006, at 4B, *available at* http://www.sptimes.com/2006/11/17/Tampabay/Al_Arian_gets_more_pr.shtml; David Guidi & Brad Bautista, *Al-Arian Ends Hunger Strike*, Univ. of S. Fla. Oracle, Mar. 26, 2007, at 1-2, *available at* http://media.www.usforacle.com/media/storage/paper880/news/2007/03/26/News/AlArian.Ends.Hunger.Strike-2791081.shtml. Upon being sentenced to that additional term of confinement, al-Arian went on a hunger strike to protest his terrorism-related charges. *See* Meg Laughlin, *Gaunt Al-Arian Shocks Family*, St. Petersburg Times, Mar. 20, 2007, at 3B, *available at* http://www.sptimes.com/2007/03/20/ Hillsborough/Gaunt_Al_Arian_shocks.shtml. On the afternoon of the day al-Arian ended his hunger strike, the Fourth Circuit affirmed the Virginia contempt ruling. *See* Guidi & Bautista, *Al-Arian Ends Hunger Strike*.

142 http://edition.cnn.com/2005/LAW/07/28/sheikh.sentence/index.html.

143 *Available at* http://www.washingtonpost.com/wp-dyn/content/article/2007/10/22/AR2007102200731.html.

144 *Available at* http://seattletimes.nwsource.com/html/localnews/2002097570_sami22m.html.

145 *Online version available at* http://www.dallasnews.com/sharedcontent/dws/news/localnews/stories/081007dnmetholyland.2dac4a9.html.

146 Section 2339C also imposes a civil penalty upon any legal entity if any person responsible for the management or control of that legal entity has, in such capacity, violated § 2339C, whether or not such person has been convicted of such offense. *See* 18 U.S.C. § 2339C(f). The civil prong of the statute has been invoked a handful of times as a basis for civil liability under § 2333(a). *See Weiss v. Nat'l Westminster Bank, PLC*, 453 F. Supp. 2d 609, 628-31 (E.D.N.Y. 2006); *Strauss v. Credit Lyonnais, S.A.*, No. 06-cv-00702, 2006 WL 2862704, at *15-17 (E.D.N.Y. Oct. 5, 2006); *Linde v. Arab Bank, PLC*, 384 F. Supp. 2d 571, 588 (E.D.N.Y. 2005). Even this limited use of § 2339C, however, has caused some in the media to complain that the statute is having a chilling effect on charitable giving in the United States, particularly among the Muslim population. *See generally* Nina J. Crimm, *High Alert: The Government's War on the Financing of Terrorism and Its Implications for Donors, Domestic Charitable Organizations, and Global Philanthropy*, 45 Wm. & Mary L. Rev. 1341 (2004).

147 Section 2339B carries a maximum penalty of fifteen years' imprisonment or life imprisonment if the death of any person results from the provision of material support; § 2339D carries a penalty of no more than ten years in prison. *Compare* 18 U.S.C. § 2339B(a)(1) *with* § 2339D(a).

148 Murder constitutes "the unlawful killing of a human being with malice aforethought." 18 U.S.C. § 1111(a) (incorporated by reference in 18 U.S.C. § 2332(a)(1)). "[M]anslaughter is the unlawful killing of a human being without malice. It is of two kinds: Voluntary—Upon a sudden quarrel or heat of passion. Involuntary—In the commission of an unlawful act not amounting to a felony, or in the commission in an unlawful manner, or without due caution and circumspection, of a lawful act which might produce death." *Id.* § 1112(a) (incorporated by reference in 18 U.S.C. §§ 2332(a)(2)–(3)). Under § 2332, murder of a national abroad carries a potential penalty of death or life imprisonment; voluntary manslaughter of a U.S. national abroad carries a potential penalty of ten years' imprisonment; and involuntary manslaughter of a U.S. national abroad carries a potential penalty of three years' imprisonment. *See id.* §§ 2332(a)(1)–(3). Convictions for an attempt to murder a U.S. national carry a maximum penalty of twenty years' imprisonment, while participation in a conspiracy to murder a U.S. national abroad carries a potential term of life imprisonment. *See id.* §§ 2332(b)(1)–(2).

149 A defendant convicted for engaging in physical violence with either the intent to, or resulting in, serious bodily injury of a U.S. national is subject to a potential ten-year term of imprisonment. *See* 18 U.S.C. § 2332(c). The "physical violence" provisions reach not only violence to persons, but also to property as long as the violence is intended or has the result of inflicting serious bodily injury on a U.S. national. *See* H.R. Rep. No. 99-783, at 87 (1986) (Conf. Rep.), *reprinted at* 1986 U.S.C.C.A.N. 1926, 1960 (noting that "Paragraph (c)… is designed to provide jurisdiction over violent attacks against property, including but not limited to bombings and arson, as well as violent attacks against persons. In any case, the attack must be one that is intended to, or does, result in serious bodily injury to a U.S. national.").

150 Congress stated its understanding that "'civilian population' includes a general population as well as other specific identifiable segments of society such as the membership of a religious faith or of a particular nationality, to give but two examples. Neither the targeted government nor civilian population, or segment thereof, has to be that of the United States." H.R. Rep. No. 99-783 at 88.

151 As originally enacted, § 2332a applied only to the use, conspiracy to use, or attempted use of weapons of mass destruction. *See* Pub. L. No. 103-322, § 60023(a), 108 Stat. 1796, 1980. The 1996 amendments broadened the statute to provide for prosecution of those who *threaten* to use weapons of mass destruction against a person within the United States. *See* Pub. L. No. 104-132, § 725, 110 Stat. 1214, 1300.

152 With respect to the "threat" element, the Fifth Circuit has held that a defendant's statement need not include an expression of intent to act in the future. *See United States v. Reynolds*, 381 F.3d 404, 406 (5th Cir. 2004); *accord United States v. Guevara*, 408 F.3d 252, 256-58 (5th Cir. 2005). In *Reynolds*, the defendant told a customer service representative at Countrywide Mortgage that he had "just dumped anthrax in your air conditioner." 381 F.3d at 405. Looking to precedent interpreting the term "threat" as a communication that "would have a reasonable tendency to create apprehension that its originator will act according to its tenor," the Fifth Circuit held that the evidence was sufficient to sustain Reynolds' conviction. *Id.* at 406 (relying on *United States v. Myers*, 104 F.3d 76, 79 (5th Cir. 1997)). In *Guevara*, the

defendant committed an anthrax hoax by sending a letter containing white powder to a federal judge, with a note stating "I am sick and tired of your games[.] All [A]mericans will die as well as you. You have been now been [sic] exposure [sic] to anthrax. Mohammed Abdullah." 408 F.3d at 255. Looking to *Reynolds*, the Fifth Circuit held that a "threat" under § 2332a did not require an intent to commit future conduct, and thus defendant Guevara's note constituted sufficient evidence of a threat. *See id.* at 257. Further, the Fifth Circuit held that the government is not required to prove that the defendant actually intended or was able to carry out his threat. *See id.*

With respect to attempt prosecutions under § 2332a, in *United States v. Polk* the evidence showed that the defendant participated in an organization dedicated to restoring the United States to its "common law roots," and organized and planned a "massive offensive" against the federal government, including a plan to destroy several Internal Revenue Service buildings throughout the country. 118 F.3d 286, 289-91 (5th Cir. 1997). Noting that a substantial step beyond mere preparation is all that is required for commission of the crime of attempt, the *Polk* court found that because the defendant sought assistance from others to carry out his plans, took photographs of IRS buildings and studied them to determine where bombs should be placed, and participated in meetings where he ordered materials necessary to carry out a bombing, a reasonable jury could have concluded that even though the defendant lacked the funds to carry out his plans, his other conduct constituted an attempt under § 2332a. *See id.* at 292.

Another interesting feature of § 2332a is the fact that the military may, in exceptional cases, be called upon to investigate violations of the statute. An exception to the Posse Comitatus Act of 1878, 18 U.S.C. § 1385, which outlaws the use of the military in law enforcement activities, the Attorney General can request military support from the Secretary of Defense to enforce § 2332a in an emergency situation involving weapons of mass destruction. *See* 18 U.S.C. § 2332e. Similar exceptions to the Posse Comitatus Act exist when civilian law enforcement is incapable of handling emergencies related to biological or chemical weapons, *see* 10 U.S.C. § 382, and nuclear weapons, *see* 18 U.S.C. § 831. These provisions can be invoked when the Attorney General and Secretary of Defense jointly determine that an emergency exists and that military preparedness would not be adversely affected. *See* 10 U.S.C. § 382 (cited in 18 U.S.C. § 2332e). An "emergency situation" is defined as one where a weapon of mass destruction poses a serious threat to the interests of the United States, and in which "(A) civilian expertise and capabilities are not readily available to provide the required assistance to counter the threat immediately posed by the weapon involved; (B) special capabilities and expertise of the Department of Defense are necessary and critical to counter the threat posed by the weapon involved; and (C) the enforcement of [18 U.S.C. § 2332e] would be seriously impaired if the Department of Defense assistance were not provided." 10 U.S.C. § 382(b).

[153] For example, while § 2332b had no applicability to the Oklahoma City bombings, which were carried out completely domestically, the statute did apply to the World Trade Center bombings, which were planned and instigated abroad.

[154] *Available at* http://seattletimes.nwsource.com/html/ localnews/2002406378_ressam27m.html.

[155] On appeal, the Ninth Circuit reversed Ressam's conviction on count nine—carrying an explosive during the commission of a felony in violation of 18 U.S.C. § 844(h)(2)—which has a ten-year mandatory minimum sentence. *Ressam*, 474 F.3d at 604. The Ninth Circuit vacated Ressam's sentence and remanded for resentencing in light of its decision because "[t]he district court articulated no basis upon which [the Ninth Circuit] could infer whether its sentence would be the same, or different, without a conviction on [count nine]." *Id.* at 604. As of May 2008, the district court had not yet resentenced Ressam. *See generally* Docket, *Ressam*, No. 99-cr-00666 (W.D. Wash.).

[156] *Available at* http://www.nytimes.com/2008/01/19/world/americas/19qaeda.html.

[157] Other statutes that look to the categories of conduct considered federal crimes of terrorism under § 2332b(g)(5) include the Attorney General's reward authority in terrorism cases, the availability of civil redress for terrorist acts, and the availability of sentencing enhancements. *See* H.R. Rep. No. 104-383 at 39. Further, as part of the USA Patriot Act, § 2332b(f) was added to provide the Attorney General with "investigative responsibility" over any act defined as a Federal crime of terrorism. Pub. L. No. 107-56, § 808, 115 Stat. 272, 378-79 (2001). Through this amendment, the Attorney General and the FBI assumed primary authority over terrorism investigations. In furtherance of this authority, and in recognition of the transnational scope of international terrorism, the Justice Department regularly investigates terrorism outside the geographic boundaries of the United States. *See "DOJ Oversight: Preserving Our Freedoms While Defending Against Terrorism": Hearing Before the S. Comm. on the Judiciary*, 107th Cong. 310 (Dec. 6, 2001) (statement of John Ashcroft, Att'y Gen. of the United States), *available at* http://judiciary.senate.gov/testimony.cfm?id=121&wit_id=42; John W. Whitehead & Steven H. Aden, *Forfeiting "Enduring Freedom" for "Homeland Security": A Constitutional Analysis of the USA PATRIOT Act and the Justice Department's Anti-Terrorism Initiatives*, 51 Am. U. L. Rev. 1081, 1088-89 (2002).

[158] Section 2332d was enacted as part of the AEDPA. *See* Pub. Law No. 104-132, § 321, 110 Stat. 1214, 1254.

[159] *Available at* http://www.state.gov/s/ct/c14151.htm. A country is designated as a supporter of terrorism pursuant to § 6(j) of the Export Administration Act of 1979. *See* 50 U.S.C. app. § 2405(j).

[160] Not all financial transactions with countries designated as supporters of terrorism are subject to penalty. The statute specifically exempts transactions that comply with "regulations issued by the Secretary of the Treasury, in consultation with the Secretary of State." 18 U.S.C. § 2332d(a). The Secretary of the Treasury issues regulations governing permissible and prohibited financial transactions for each country designated as a supporter of international terrorism. The regulations set forth the prohibited financial transactions and, in some cases, provide exemptions to the general prohibitions. *See, e.g.*, 31 C.F.R. §§ 538.211(b), (f) (with regard to Sudan, exempting humanitarian and journalistic transactions from penalty). The regulations may also permit certain transactions if licensed or authorized by the government. *See id.* § 501.801 (setting forth the procedures for applying for permission to engage in otherwise prohibited transactions from the Office of Foreign Assets Control, United States Treasury).

161 In *Chalmers*, the government charged a Bahamian company with a violation of § 2332d for engaging in prohibited transactions with Iraq under the Oil-for-Food Program. *See* 474 F. Supp. 2d at 564. In analyzing the application of § 2332d to foreign corporations, the court observed that "the Supreme Court, in considering the reach of a federal statute imposing economic sanctions on Burma, has interpreted 'United States persons' as excluding foreign corporations." *Id.* at 565 (citing *Crosby v. Nat'l Foreign Trade Council*, 530 U.S. 363, 379 (2000)). Moreover, it found that Congress crafted other federal regulations and statutes prohibiting transactions with hostile countries so as to clearly reach foreign entities. *See id.* As an example, the Cuban Assets Control Regulations proscribe certain transactions between Cuba and "any person subject to the jurisdiction of the United States" or "any person within the United States." *Id.* (citing 31 C.F.R. § 515, et seq.). Both categories of persons specifically include corporations, "wherever organized or doing business," that are owned or controlled by U.S. citizens or residents. *Id.* (citing §§ 515.329(d), 515.330(a)(4)). Because Congress did not explicitly include foreign corporations in defining "United States persons" in § 2332d(b)(2), the *Chalmers* court refused to read such breadth into the statute.

162 The scienter requirement of § 2332d has not been interpreted by the courts. However, the list of countries supporting international terrorism is short and reasonably well-publicized in government publications as well as the popular press. *See, e.g.,* U.S. Dept. of State, *State Sponsors of Terrorism* (Feb. 2008), *available at* http://www.state.gov/s/ct/c14151.htm; Bomi Lim, *N. Korea Says It Will Be Taken Off U.S. Terror List*, Bloomberg, Sept. 3, 2007, http://www.bloomberg.com/apps/news?pid=20601087&sid=aOU6rY7.fZll&refer=home.

163 A demand for payment of money would likely be construed as an attempt to compel another state or the United States to perform an act. *See United States v. Carrion-Caliz*, 944 F.2d 220, 223, 225 (5th Cir. 1991) (interpreting similar language under the Hostage Taking Act, 18 U.S.C. § 1203(a)). Demands for political concessions are also considered attempts to compel another state or the United States to act. *See Vine v. Republic of Iraq*, 459 F. Supp. 2d 10, 19 (D.D.C. 2006) (same). While federal or state criminal laws in existence at the time of passage covered the conduct prohibited by the Convention within the United States, subsection (b)(1) ensured jurisdiction where there is a unique federal interest. *See* 148 Cong. Rec. S5569, 5571 (daily ed. June 14, 2002) (statement of Sen. Patrick Leahy). Subsection 2332f(b) also enacts a "crucial element of the Convention" which requires all parties to the treaty to either extradite or prosecute offenders who are found within the jurisdiction of a signatory country. H.R. Rep. No. 107-307 at 11 .

164 In determining whether the act resulted in, or was likely to result in major economic loss, Congress directed the courts to consider the physical damage to the targeted facility, as well as other types of economic loss. These include the monetary loss or other adverse effects resulting from the interruption of its activities, the adverse effects on non-targeted entities and individuals, and even the adverse effects on the economy and the government. *See* H.R. Rep. No. 107-307 at 10-11.

165 Siraj was also charged and convicted of conspiracy to damage or destroy by means of an explosive, any building or other real property used in interstate commerce, in violation of 18 U.S.C. §§ 844(i), (n); conspiracy to wreck, derail, set fire to, or disable a public transportation vehicle, in violation of 18 U.S.C. §§ 1993(a)(1), (a)(8); and conspiracy to place a destructive device in a facility used in the operation of a public transportation vehicle without previously obtaining the permission of the public transportation provider, in violation of 18 U.S.C. §§ 1993(a)(3), (a)(8). *Siraj*, 468 F. Supp. 2d at 414.

166 *Available at* http://www.usdoj.gov/siraj_pr.pdf.

167 Siraj was also sentenced to twenty years' imprisonment on each of three other counts of conviction. At trial, the defense argued that Siraj had been entrapped and that the government's informant had in fact manufactured the crime. After the conviction, the defendant moved for a new trial on grounds of entrapment. *See Siraj*, 468 F. Supp. 2d at 414. He argued that: (a) there was evidence that the confidential informant induced him into taking steps to engage in violent conduct; (b) there was no evidence of defendant's predisposition to engage in violent conduct; and (c) the government's rebuttal evidence, testimony by an undercover officer, was insufficient to prove predisposition beyond a reasonable doubt. *See id.* The court found that testimony by a confidential informant about the defendant's interest in committing revenge bombings, his active participation in planning to bomb a Staten Island bridge, and his eventual decision to bomb the subway station instead of the bridge provided more than enough evidence to show that the defendant was predisposed to engaging in violent conduct. *See id.* at 415.

168 *Available at* http://trac.syr.edu/tracreports/terrorism/169/include/terrorism.whitepaper.pdf.

169 We are aware of one other case in which the government has charged a conspiracy to violate of § 2332g. *See generally* Indictment, *United States v. Kassar*, No. 07-cr-00354 (S.D.N.Y. May 29, 2007) (Dkt. No. 1) (alleging conspiracy to import and use anti-aircraft missiles).

170 In other contexts, courts have not interpreted "reasonable grounds to suspect" and "reasonable grounds to believe" as distinct mens rea elements. *See, e.g., Ybarra v. Illinois*, 444 U.S. 85, 93-94 (1979) (finding no Fourth Amendment violation where police officer has a "reasonable belief or suspicion" that a person is armed).

171 Senator Leahy described a number of concerns over the breadth of the President's initial proposal for what eventually became the USA Patriot Act. *See* 147 Cong. Rec. at 10996. In the context of describing the difference between "reasonable grounds to believe" and "reasonable grounds to suspect" Senator Leahy noted the importance of narrowing the crime to apply only to individuals who are "harboring people who have committed, or are about to commit, the most serious of Federal terrorism-related crimes." *Id.* at 10997.

172 Gadahn's life story has been chronicled elsewhere. *See* Raffi Khatchadourian, *Azzam the American: The Making of an Al Qaeda Homegrown*, New Yorker, Jan. 22, 2007, at 50. While that story cannot be recounted here in full detail, a few of the more interesting facts bear mentioning. Gadahn was born in Oregon and grew up in rural California. *See id.* His father, born Philip Pearlman, had experienced a religious epiphany and subsequently changed his name to Phil Gadahn (after the Hebrew name of the Biblical warrior Gideon, or Gid'on). *See id.* at

52. According to Khatchadourian's account, the child Adam "was shy, bookish, and by all accounts exceptionally bright." *Id.* at 53. Adam cultivated an intense interest in the "death metal" music genre, which in turn led him to the Internet, through which he tried to cultivate his knowledge of the music and connect with other aficionados. *See id.* at 52, 56, 58. It was through the Internet that Adam began learning about Islam, and he converted in November 1995 at the Islamic Society of Orange County. *See id.* at 56. Military campaigns in Bosnia and Chechnya, in which Gadahn considered Muslims to be the victims, as well as military clashes involving Islamists in Afghanistan, Algeria, and Tajikistan were followed by what Gadahn perceived as an outbreak of anti-Muslim vitriol following the Oklahoma City bombing, which, at first, was incorrectly attributed by popular belief to Muslim extremists. *See id.* at 57. All of these events in the 1990s led Gadahn to believe that Muslims were being persecuted and unfairly branded by Western society. *See id.* at 58. His interpretation of Islam became consistently more radical, and he began to gravitate toward more extreme Muslim colleagues. *See id.* at 60. Gadahn's trajectory eventually brought him to prominence within the ranks of al Qaeda's leadership—to the point where on an al Qaeda video Ayman al-Zawahiri says Gadahn's words and example must be followed—and Gadahn is now on the FBI's list of "Most Wanted Terrorists." *See id.* at 61, 62.

173 An even less utilized statute is misprision of treason, codified at 18 U.S.C. § 2382. This statute, which has not been used at all in recent years, provides that "Whoever, owing allegiance to the United States and having knowledge of the commission of any treason against them, conceals and does not, disclose and make known the same to the President or to some judge of the United States, or to the governor or to some judge or justice of a particular State, is guilty of misprision of treason and shall be fined under this title or imprisoned not more than seven years, or both." 18 U.S.C. § 2382. The person with knowledge of treason must report it "as soon as possible" in order to avoid a misprision charge. *See Charge to Grand Jury—Treason*, 30 F. Cas. 1032, 1034 (C.C.S.D.N.Y. 1861) (No. 18,270). The requirement that the report of treason must be made to the President, a governor, or a judge or justice appears odd; it is not clear why a person could not simply report treason to law enforcement. Because this statute has so rarely been invoked, however, the reporting requirement does not appear to have been examined, let alone challenged.

Like the treason statute, the misprision statute applies on its face only to those "owing allegiance" to the United States. Besides serving its facial purpose of requiring people to report acts of treason, the misprision statute could also be used against potential treason defendants whose level of involvement in a treasonous scheme or treasonous intent is questionable. For example, a profiteer who sells arms to a band of traitors might or might not have the intent required for treason because he is selling arms for personal gain rather than opposition to the U.S. government, but by failing to report the traitors he would be guilty of misprision. *See Hanauer v. Doane*, 79 U.S. (12 Wall.) 342, 347 (1870) ("He who, being bound by his allegiance to a government, sells goods to the agent of an armed combination to overthrow that government, knowing that the purchaser buys them for that treasonable purpose, is himself guilty of treason or a misprision thereof"). In the end, however, the misprision statute is necessarily constrained by the limitations on use of the treason statute: while the government need not actually convict anyone for treason, it must nonetheless prove at the misprision defendant's trial that an act of treason actually occurred. *Cf. United States v. Davila*, 698 F.2d 715, 717-21 (5th Cir. 1983) (misprision of felony statute, codified at 18 U.S.C. § 4, requires government to prove that underlying felony was committed, although it does not require that the underlying felons actually be convicted).

174 In part, the paucity of treason prosecutions may reflect that "[t]he framers of the Constitution were reluctant to facilitate such prosecutions because they were well aware of abuses, and they themselves were traitors in the eyes of England." *United States v. Rodriguez*, 803 F.2d 318, 320 (7th Cir. 1986); *accord United States v. Thompson*, No. 06-cr-00020, 2006 WL 1518968, at *9 (E.D. Wis. May 30, 2006). The framers were especially concerned with two particular risks of treason prosecutions: "(1) Perversion by established authority to repress political opposition; and (2) conviction of the innocent as a result of perjury, passion, or inadequate evidence." *Cramer*, 325 U.S. at 27; *see also* Lewis, *An Old Means to a Different End*, at 1220-21 ("Prior to 1787 the charge of treason had been used to oppress political dissent").

175 This difficulty in proving intent applies more to the "levying war" prong of treason; a stronger argument can be made that Lindh intended to give aid and comfort to a U.S. enemy, even if he did not intend to oppose the United States specifically, because he knew that the Taliban was a U.S. enemy. *See Chandler v. United States*, 171 F.2d 921, 942-44 (1st Cir. 1949) (intent to aid enemy enough for treason even if defendant believed that aid would benefit United States in long term).

176 It appears that a resident alien owes allegiance to the United States even if he resides in a U.S. territory temporarily outside of the United States' de facto control. *See Green's Case*, 8 Ct. Cl. 412 (1872) (alien residing in Confederate territory during Civil War still owed allegiance to United States). This rule would only be relevant if terrorists had somehow gained sustained control of a portion of U.S. territory large enough to domicile somebody, a factual context that will hopefully never present itself.

177 While it is well-established that conspiracy to commit treason is not itself treason, the *Bollman* court explained that conspiracy to commit treason would still be a "flagitious" crime, albeit a separate one. *See* 8 U.S. at 126. This "flagitious" crime was codified during the Civil War as the seditious conspiracy statute.

178 Other terrorist organizations that did not participate in the 9/11 attacks, however, would not fall under the AUMF and therefore would be less certain to qualify as "enemies" under the treason statute.

179 One who gives aid and comfort to the enemy "prompted solely by the expectation of pecuniary gain," however, is liable for treason. *Ohio Grand Jury Charge*, 30 F. Cas. at 1037.

180 Although post-World War II treason cases relied on an employment relationship (which the government has not alleged in the *Gadahn* indictment) to satisfy this element, *see Chandler*, 171 F.2d at 937-39; *Gillars*, 182 F.2d at 970-71, Gadahn is a spokesperson for al Qaeda and "a member of Al Qaeda's 'media committee,' and his responsiblities are thought to include those of translator, video producer, and

cultural interpreter." Khatchadourian, *Azzam the American*, at 50. Accordingly, Gadahn's relationship with al Qaeda appears sufficiently close to constitute "adherence" for purposes of treason.

[181] Because, as noted above, a conspiracy to commit treason is not punishable as treason itself, at least one court has hailed the "necessity of the [seditious conspiracy] statute … to meet the case of a treasonable conspiracy." *Ohio Grand Jury Charge*, 30 F. Cas. at 1038. Indeed, the *Ohio Grand Jury Charge* court lamented the fact that the seditious conspiracy statute was not passed simultaneously with the treason statute, because seditious conspiracy prosecutions might have preempted the machinations that led to the Civil War: "And it is perhaps to be regretted that this provision had not been a part of the act of 1790. With such a provision of law, properly enforced, there is reason to believe many persons who have been prominent in our national affairs, and once high in the confidence of the people, would have been the subjects of its penalties; and thus the great rebellion now in progress may have been prevented." 30 F. Cas. at 1038.

[182] *See also Albizu v. United States*, 88 F.2d 138, 141-42 (1st Cir. 1937) (upholding conviction of Puerto Rican separatist party leader for exhorting armed resistance to U.S. occupation of Puerto Rico); *United States v. Lebron*, 222 F.2d 531, 533-34 (2d Cir. 1955) (upholding seditious conspiracy conviction where alleged conspirators "had abandoned hope of achieving Puerto Rican independence through legitimate political processes in favor of overthrowing American authority in that commonwealth by force of arms and by violence").

[183] The term "levying war" carries the same definition as when that term is used in the treason statute. *See Bryant v. United States*, 257 F. 378, 386-87 (5th Cir. 1919) (conspiracy to prevent enforcement of a statute is conspiracy to levy war); *see also Anderson v. United States*, 273 F. 20, 26-27 (8th Cir. 1921) (no seditious conspiracy because intent was not to oppose government, but to oppose private corporate interests).

[184] Most saliently, courts have held that the offenses have different elements: only the seditious conspiracy statute requires an actual conspiracy (i.e., an agreement between two or more persons), while only the treason statute has the allegiance requirement. *See Rahman*, 189 F.3d at 113-14; *Rodriguez*, 803 F.2d at 320. Moreover, the consequences of a treason conviction are harsher than one for seditious conspiracy, not only because treason alone is punishable by death, but also because "[i]n the late colonial period, as today, the charge of treason carried a peculiar intimidation and stigma with considerable potentialities as a political epithet." *Rahman*, 189 F.3d at 113 (internal quotations omitted); *see also id.* ("The Framers may have intended to limit the applicability of the most severe penalties—or simply the applicability of capital punishment for alleged subversion—to instances of levying war against, or adhering to enemies of, the United States").

[185] *Available at* http://query.nytimes.com/gst/fullpage.html?res=9F0CE7D71730F93BA1575BC0A965958260.

[186] *Available at* http://query.nytimes.com/gst/fullpage.html?res=990CEFD91239F931A35753C1A963958260.

[187] *Available at* http://www.usdoj.gov/opa/pr/2005/August/05_crm_453.html.

[188] *Available at* http://news.lp.findlaw.com/hdocs/docs/terrorism/usbattle101603plea.pdf.

[189] *Available at* http://www.usdoj.gov/opa/pr/2003/October/03_crm_577.htm.

[190] *Available at* http://www.nytimes.com/2007/12/15/us/15brfs-GUILTYPLEASI_BRF.html.

[191] *Available at* http://www.nytimes.com/2007/12/14/us/nationalspecial3/14liberty.html.

[192] *Available at* http://www.nytimes.com/2008/04/24/us/24miami.html. Prosecutors have announced that they will pursue a third trial against the six men. *See* Gentile, *Six Suspects Will Be Tried a Third Time in Sears Plot*.

[193] The prosecution of a dangerous individual on an alternative, more readily provable charge is sometimes referred to by commentators as the "Al Capone approach," alluding to the notorious Chicago gangster who was prosecuted on federal criminal tax evasion charges, rather than on the many other racketeering crimes associated with him. *See* Daniel C. Richman & William J. Stuntz, *Al Capone's Revenge, An Essay on the Political Economy of Pretextual Prosecution*, 105 Colum. L. Rev. 583 (2005); Harry Litman, *Pretextual Prosecution*, 92 Geo. L.J. 1135 (2004).

[194] Each of these fraudulent representations could be the basis for criminal prosecution under numerous statutes including, among others, 18 U.S.C. § 1546 (fraudulently obtaining travel documents), 18 U.S.C. § 1425 (immigration violations); 18 U.S.C. § 1001 (making misrepresentations to federal investigators); 18 U.S.C. § 1015(a) (providing false information in a naturalization application); 18 U.S.C. § 1542 (providing false information in an application for a U.S. passport); 42 U.S.C. § 408(a)(7)(b) (use of a false social security number).

[195] The FBI agent who worked with the INS on the arrest of Moussaoui feared that Moussaoui was planning to hijack a plane. *See 9/11 Commission Report*, at 273. The FBI debated whether to arrest Moussaoui immediately or surveille him for additional information. *See id.* The decision to arrest demonstrated the FBI's desire—even pre-9/11—to prevent an incident even if it jeopardized a potential criminal prosecution.

[196] After 9/11, Ahmed Ressam, the Millennium Bomber, who was cooperating with U.S. authorities in 2001, identified Moussaoui as having been at the Afghan terror camps. *See 9/11 Commission Report*, at 275-76. Had Ressam made that connection immediately after Moussaoui's arrest in August 2001, the government might have uncovered the 9/11 plot ahead of time. *See id.* While those connections could have been made without arresting Moussaoui as well, had a search of his belongings yielded key information, his arrest would have been an enormous preventive success. Unfortunately, neither a criminal search warrant nor a FISA warrant was obtained to search Moussaoui's computer or his belongings at the time of his arrest, although there is reason to believe that a warrant could have been obtained. *See id.* at 273 n.94, 274.

197 In one case, Bihieri was sentenced to twelve months' imprisonment; in the other he was sentenced to thirteen months and one day in prison. See Judgment, *United States v. Biheiri*, No. 03-cr-00365 (E.D. Va. Jan. 12, 2004) (Dkt. No. 47); Judgment, *United States v. Biheiri*, No. 04-cr-00201 (E.D. Va. Jan. 14, 2005) (Dkt. No. 89).

198 *Available at* http://query.nytimes.com/gst/fullpage.html?res=9807E1D9133DF93AA25751C0A9629C8B63.

199 *Available at* http://fas.org/sgp/crs/terror/RL34014.pdf. The increase in precursor criminal activity has been attributed to four factors: the decline in state sponsorship which limits the availability of documents and money; the amateurization and decentralization of terror which means smaller groups may need to self-finance; enhanced counterterrorism measures; and changing terrorist demographics. *See* O'Neil, *Terrorist Precursor Crimes,* at 2.

200 One reason why some statutes, such as the material support statute, might have their own conspiracy provisions instead of relying on the general conspiracy statute is that individual conspiracy provisions, unlike § 371, do not necessarily require proof of overt acts. *See United States v. Shabani*, 513 U.S. 10, 11-14 (1994) (conspiracy provisions using language similar to § 371 require proof of overt acts, while provisions using different language do not require such proof); *accord Whitfield v. United States*, 543 U.S. 209, 214 (2005).

201 *Available at* http://www.nytimes.com/2006/01/08/magazine/08yemen.html.

202 *Available at* http://www.nytimes.com/2005/09/30/politics/30delay.html.

203 *Available at* http://www.sfgate.com/cgi-bin/article.cgi?f=/c/a/2003/03/06/MN192957.DTL.

204 Additional procedural advantages conferred by a conspiracy charge upon prosecutors include the abilities to select as venue for a trial any district in which any act in furtherance of a conspiracy took place, even for defendants who never set foot near that district, and to show juries a complete alleged criminal organization in one trial. Rosenberg, *Several Problems in Criminal Conspiracy Laws*, at 445-47.

205 *Available at* http://www.usdoj.gov/opa/pr/2007/August/07_nsd_624.html. In fact, the availability of conspiracy prosecutions could be a significant advantage of trying suspected terrorists in the criminal justice system, rather than military tribunals, as it is questionable whether a conspiracy charge can be brought under the laws of war. *See Hamdan v. Rumsfeld*, 126 S. Ct. 2749, 2785 (2006) (plurality opinion stating that "the Government has failed even to offer a merely colorable case for inclusion of conspiracy among those offenses cognizable by law-of-war military commission"); *see also id.* at 2809 (concurring opinion of Kennedy, J.) (declining to join either plurality opinion that military commissions cannot charge conspiracy or dissenting opinion to the contrary); Mahler, *The Bush Administration vs. Salim Hamdan*, at 51, 81 (quoting explanation from Hamdan's civilian counsel, Neal Katyal, that conspiracy can only be charged under a legal system with the U.S. criminal justice system's "'unique set of vibrant protections,'" which are not present in military commissions).

206 "Biological agent" means "any microorganism (including, but not limited to, bacteria, viruses, fungi, rickettsiae or protozoa), or infectious substance, or any naturally occurring, bioengineered or synthesized component of any such microorganism or infectious substance, capable of causing (A) death, disease, or other biological malfunction in a human, an animal, a plant, or another living organism; (B) deterioration of food, water, equipment, supplies, or material of any kind; or (C) deleterious alteration of the environment." 18 U.S.C. § 178(1).

"Toxin" means "the toxic material or product of plants, animals, microorganisms (including, but not limited to, bacteria, viruses, fungi, rickettsiae or protozoa), or infectious substances, or a recombinant or synthesized molecule, whatever their origin and method of production, and includes (A) any poisonous substance or biological product that may be engineered as a result of biotechnology produced by a living organism; or (B) any poisonous isomer or biological product, homolog, or derivative of such a substance." 18 U.S.C. § 178(2).

"Delivery system" means "(A) any apparatus, equipment, device, or means of delivery specifically designed to deliver or disseminate a biological agent, toxin, or vector; or (B) any vector," where "vector" is defined as "a living organism, or molecule, including a recombinant or synthesized molecule, capable of carrying a biological agent or toxin to a host." 18 U.S.C. §§ 178(3), (4).

207 The addition of § 175(b) complemented a ruling from the Eighth Circuit, which held that intent to use a biological agent as a weapon can be established simply by the defendant's possession of biological agents that are "extremely toxic, deadly in extremely small quantities, ... very difficult to detect, [with] no known antidote, and [that have] been popularized in various publications as a method to kill people." *United States v. Baker*, 98 F.3d 330, 338 (8th Cir. 1996) (holding that defendant's possession of ricin was sufficient to establish requisite intent for a § 175(a) prosecution). Section 175(b) does not render § 175(a) superfluous because § 175(b) carries a maximum penalty of ten years in prison, while § 175(a) carries a potential life sentence. *See* 18 U.S.C. § 175.

208 Finally, Congress's enhanced concern about the variola virus is reflected in a twenty-five-year minimum prison sentence for violation of § 175c, thirty years if the defendant uses, attempts to use, or possesses and threatens to use the virus. *See* 18 U.S.C. § 175c(c). In addition to these criminal penalties, Congress has authorized the Attorney General to seize materials regulated by chapter 10, which are then subject to forfeiture to the government. *See* 18 U.S.C. § 176. Congress has also authorized the government to seek civil injunctions against the conduct prohibited in chapter 10. *See* 18 U.S.C. § 177.

209 Another form of speech that can be relevant to terrorism, not addressed in this Paper, is knowledge-based speech. This is usually speech that conveys highly technical or scientific information that could be used by terrorists to the detriment of national security. *See, e.g.*, Laura K. Donohue, *Terrorist Speech and the Future of Free Expression*, 27 Cardozo L. Rev. 233, 271 (2005). Such speech may frequently be restricted pursuant to statutes intended to prevent dangerous individuals from obtaining sensitive information about biological or nuclear research. The concern over such speech has heightened since the 9/11 attacks and the raft of anthrax mailings in the United States that same year. *See id.* at 272-73.

210 The earliest decision to impose limits on the Smith Act, *Dennis*, tried to weigh the need to protect speech against the government's ability to preempt dangerous activity. Specifically, the *Dennis* plurality dismissed the idea that "before the Government may act, it must wait until the putsch is about to be executed, the plans have been laid and the signal is awaited." 341 U.S. at 509. "If Government is aware that a group aiming at its overthrow is attempting to indoctrinate its members and to commit them to a course whereby they will strike when the leaders feel the circumstances permit," the *Dennis* plurality reasoned, "action by the Government is required." *Id.* Thus, the Smith Act appears to have foreshadowed a preventive approach to prosecution against terrorism—the approach that animates the government's current use of, inter alia, the material support statutes.

Pursuant to this preventive logic, the *Dennis* plurality adopted a sliding scale test in which a court reviewing a Smith Act conviction asked "whether the gravity of the evil, discounted by its improbability, justifies such invasion of free speech as is necessary to avoid the danger." *Id.* at 510 (internal quotations omitted). Notably, under this formulation, if the "evil" advocated was severe enough and accompanied by an intent "to overthrow the Government by force and violence," the improbability of its accomplishment would not serve as a defense against prosecution. *Id.* at 499, 509 ("Certainly an attempt to overthrow the Government by force, even though doomed from the outset because of inadequate numbers or power of the revolutionists, is a sufficient evil for Congress to prevent"). The *Dennis* plurality used this test to affirm the convictions of individuals in the upper echelons of the U.S. Communist Party on the grounds that these individuals formed "a highly organized conspiracy, with rigidly disciplined members subject to call when the leaders ... felt that the time had come for action, coupled with the inflammable nature of world conditions, similar uprisings in other countries, and the touch-and-go nature of our relations with countries with whom [the defendants] were in the very least ideologically attuned." *Id.* at 511. The *Dennis* plurality also rejected a vagueness challenge to the statute because it only proscribed advocacy that created a "clear and present danger." *Id.* at 515-16 (internal quotations omitted).

The Supreme Court moved in a direction more protective of speech in *Yates v. United States*, 354 U.S. 298 (1957), *overruled in part on other grounds by Burks v. United States*, 437 U.S. 1 (1978). First, the *Yates* court clarified that the Smith Act does not prohibit "advocacy and teaching of forcible overthrow as an abstract principle, divorced from any effort to instigate action to that end, so long as such advocacy or teaching is engaged in with evil intent." 354 U.S. at 318. In overturning a conviction, the *Yates* court noted that the trial court had "been led astray by the holding in *Dennis* that advocacy of violent action to be taken at some future time was enough" to conclude that "advocacy, irrespective of its tendency to generate action, is punishable, provided only that it is uttered with a specific intent to accomplish overthrow." *Id.* at 320. The *Yates* court held that abstract advocacy of overthrowing the U.S. government, "even though uttered with the hope that it may ultimately lead to violent revolution, is too remote from concrete action" to be prosecutable. *Id.* at 321; *accord Silverman*, 248 F.2d at 681; *United States v. Kuzma*, 249 F.2d 619, 622 (3d Cir. 1957).

The *Yates* court's requirement that proscribed advocacy call for "concrete action" was amplified in *Noto v. United States*, 367 U.S. 290 (1961). The *Noto* court reiterated that a Smith Act conviction requires present advocacy of the "violent overthrow of the Government now or in the future." *Id.* at 298. *Noto* went beyond *Yates*, however, in emphasizing the need for present advocacy. *Id.* It was not enough that "the leadership of the Party was preparing the way for a situation in which future acts of sabotage might be facilitated ... it is present advocacy, and not an intent to advocate in the future or a conspiracy to advocate in the future once a groundwork has been laid," which violates the Smith Act. *Id.*

211 The first element originally incorporated the *Yates* standard to define unlawful advocacy. *See, e.g.*, *Scales*, 367 U.S. at 221. Presumably, the *Brandenburg* test would be used for this element now.

212 Some federal Courts of Appeals require that any extraterritorial legislation comport with principles of international law. *See, e.g.*, *United States v. MacAllister*, 160 F.3d 1304, 1308 (11th Cir. 1998); *United States v. Rezaq*, 134 F.3d 1121, 1133 (D.C. Cir. 1998) ("International law imposes limits on a state's ... ability to render its law applicable to persons or activities outside its borders"); *United States v. Dawn*, 129 F.3d 878, 882 (7th Cir. 1997). Other circuits have rejected such a requirement, ruling that the only limits on extraterritorial criminal statutes are the personal jurisdiction limits set by the Due Process Clause. *See, e.g.*, *United States v. Yousef*, 327 F.3d 56, 86 (2d Cir. 2003) ("If [Congress] chooses to do so, it may legislate with respect to conduct outside the United States, in excess of the limits posed by international law") (internal quotations omitted); *French*, 440 F.3d at 151; *United States v. Villanueva*, 408 F.3d 193, 197-99 (5th Cir. 2005) (stating that "the crux of [the extraterritoriality] issue is whether Congress intended [a given statute] to apply to extraterritorial conduct" and not discussing limits imposed by international law at all). Still other circuits are internally conflicted. *Compare, e.g.*, *United States v. Hill*, 279 F.3d 731, 739 (9th Cir. 2002) (extraterritoriality analysis includes examination of "compliance with principles of international law") *with United States v. Davis*, 905 F.2d 245, 248 (9th Cir. 1990) ("compliance with international law does not determine whether the United States may apply" a statute extraterritorially); *United States v. Harvey*, 2 F.3d 1318, 1328 (3d Cir. 1993) ("any exercise of extraterritorial criminal jurisdiction must comply with international law") *with Asplundh Tree Export Co. v. N.L.R.B.*, 365 F.3d 168, 173 (3d Cir. 2004) (stating that "Congress undoubtedly has the authority to enforce its laws beyond the territorial boundaries of the United States" and not discussing limits imposed by international law at all) (internal quotations and citations omitted).

Concerning the kind of criminal incitement at issue here, however, the disputes within and among the circuits should be moot, as extraterritorial application of the Smith Act and § 373 to foreign inciters of violence against the U.S. government should be upheld by U.S. courts as concordant with international law. Specifically, international law allows for extraterritorial legislation if the extraterritorial nature is justified by at least one of the following five principles: (1) "territorial," under which the offense occurs or has effects in the United States; (2) "protective," under which the offense "may impinge on the territorial integrity, security, or political independence of the United States"; (3) "national," under which the offender is a U.S. national; (4) "universal," dealing with crimes globally regarded as heinous; or (5) "passive personality," under which the victim is a U.S. national. *See United States v. Vasquez-Velasco*, 15 F.3d 833, 840, 840 n.5 (9th Cir. 1994).

Extraterritorial application of the Smith Act and § 373 for the purposes of stopping criminal incitement could reasonably be justified under at least the protective, territorial or passive personality principles.

213 The ability of the United States to succeed in having such an individual extradited, however, would still depend on whether the extraditing jurisdiction recognized a Smith Act violation or criminal solicitation equivalent to one of its own crimes under the doctrine of "dual criminality." *See, e.g., Gallo-Chamorro v. United States*, 233 F.3d 1298, 1306 (11th Cir. 2000) (dual criminality doctrine "mandates that a prisoner be extradited only for conduct that constitutes a serious offense in both the requesting and surrendering country"); *accord Ordinola v. Hackman*, 478 F.3d 588, 594 n.7 (4th Cir. 2007); *United States v. Anderson*, 472 F.3d 662, 665 n.1 (9th Cir. 2006); *Murphy v. United States*, 199 F.3d 599, 602 (2d Cir. 1999).

214 *Accord United States v. Matta-Ballesteros*, 71 F.3d 754, 761-62 (9th Cir. 1995) (defendant was forcibly abducted from his home in Honduras and immediately handed over to U.S. Marshals, who transported him to the United States within twenty-four hours; court rejected defendant's jurisdictional challenge, reasoning that "where the terms of an extradition treaty do not specifically prohibit the forcible abduction of foreign nationals, the treaty does not divest federal courts of jurisdiction over the foreign national"); *United States v. Mejia*, 448 F.3d 436, 439, 442-43 (D.C. Cir. 2006) (defendants in narcotics case were arrested by Panamanian authorities in Panama and then immediately handed over to DEA agents, who promptly transported defendants to United States; court held that these procedures were not expressly prohibited by the extradition treaty between the United States and Panama). As a practical matter, it is unlikely that a future defendant will be able to prevail on this theory, since many of the United States' extradition treaties follow a standard pattern and do not contain language expressly prohibiting forcible abduction. *See, e.g.*, Extradition Treaty with Great Britain and Northern Ireland, U.S.-Gr. Brit.-N. Ir., Mar. 31, 2003, S. Treaty Doc. No. 108-23 (2003); Extradition Treaty Between the United States of America and France, U.S.-Fr., Apr. 23, 1996, S. Treaty Doc. No. 105-13 (1996); Extradition Treaty with Jordan, U.S.-Jordan, Mar. 28, 1995, S. Treaty Doc. No. 104-3 (1995); Extradition Treaty with the Philippines, U.S.-Phil., Nov. 13, 1994, S. Treaty Doc. No. 104-16 (1994).

215 The Second Circuit itself subsequently made clear that its reasoning in *Toscanino* only encompassed cases involving "torture, brutality, and similar outrageous conduct" and did not apply to abductions free of such violent abuse. *United States ex rel. Lujan v. Gengler*, 510 F.2d 62, 65-66 (2d Cir. 1975) (rejecting due process argument because defendant did not allege "that complex of shocking governmental conduct sufficient to convert an abduction which is simply illegal into one which sinks to a violation of due process").

216 Although we are not aware of any case law to this effect, it might be the case that a defendant could obtain some relief if, as a result of prolonged detention or forcible treatment, his ability to defend himself became compromised. In the *Padilla* case, for example, defense counsel sought an order declaring that their client was not competent to stand trial due to his "experiences during his detention and interrogation" and "prolonged isolation" while in military confinement. *See* Def.'s Mot. for Order of Competency to Stand Trial at 2, *United States v. Padilla*, No. 04-cr-60001 (S.D. Fla. Dec. 13, 2006) (Dkt. No. 716). After an independent psychiatric examination, however, the trial court found that Padilla was competent to stand trial and his case went forward. *See* Order granting Mot. for Order of Competency to Stand Trial, *Padilla* (S.D. Fla. Mar. 1, 2007) (Dkt. No. 889).

217 In an earlier case, *United States v. Rashed*, the defendant's motion to dismiss for outrageous government conduct was also denied; because the underlying motion papers and the court's decision are sealed, however, the exact circumstances of the defendant's capture are unknown. It is known that after being prosecuted and convicted in Greece—for placing a bomb on a 1982 Pan Am flight from Tokyo to Honolulu that killed one passenger—and serving eight years in custody, Rashed left Greece, was apprehended, and was ultimately turned over to the FBI. *See United States v. Rashed*, 234 F.3d 1280, 1281 (D.C. Cir. 2000). Despite the tangled series of events, the court found the circumstances insufficient to dismiss the indictment. Rashed ultimately pled guilty to serious charges in the United States and was sentenced to fifteen years' imprisonment. *See* Judgment, *United States v. Rashed*, No. 87-cr-00308 (D.D.C. May 1, 2006) (Dkt. No. 172).

218 *Available at* http://www.nytimes.com/2008/01/23/us/23padilla.html.

219 A discussion of the scope of military detention is beyond the focus of this White Paper. Over the years, however, the Supreme Court has decided important cases in this area. *See, e.g., Johnson v. Eisentrager*, 339 U.S. 763 (1950) (no habeas corpus jurisdiction over German partisans who were captured during World War II in China, convicted by a U.S. military commission in China, and then repatriated to Germany to serve their sentences); *Hamdi v. Rumsfeld*, 542 U.S. 507, 533 (2004) (U.S. citizen captured on battlefield in Afghanistan and detained inside the United States must be provided with notice of the factual basis for his detention as well as an opportunity to rebut the government's showing before a neutral decision maker); *Rasul v. Bush*, 542 U.S. 466 (2004) (recognizing statutory habeas corpus jurisdiction over Guantánamo detainees). Currently on the Court's docket is *Boumediene v. Bush*, No. 06-1195, which presents the question whether the Military Commissions Act of 2006 validly stripped federal courts of jurisdiction to entertain habeas corpus jurisdiction over Guantánamo detainees.

220 *See* Kent Roach, *Must We Trade Rights for Security? The Choice Between Smart, Harsh, or Proportionate Security Strategies in Canada and Britain*, 27 Cardozo L. Rev. 2151, 2221 n.218 (2006) ("Maximum periods of detention without charge are one hundred sixty-eight hours in Australia, seventy-two hours in Canada, ninety-six hours in France, forty-eight hours in Norway, and one hundred twenty hours in Spain, with longer detention periods for those arrested and presumably charged in France, Germany, or Greece.") (*citing* Sec'y of State for Foreign and Commonwealth Affairs, *Counter-Terrorism Legislation and Practice: A Survey of Selected Countries* (2005) (discussing detention periods in various countries); Canada Criminal Code, R.S.C., ch. C-46, § 83.3 (1985), as amended by 2001 S.C., ch. 41 (providing for preventive arrest and detention for up to seventy-two hours on the basis of reasonable suspicion that arrest is necessary to prevent the detainee from carrying out a terrorist activity)). Israel has a thorough body of law on the detention of enemy combatants and, despite the constant terrorist threat of

terrorism, its laws ensure that suspected enemy combatants have substantial rights, including the right to judicial review of the basis for their detention within no more than fourteen days of their seizure. See Brief for Specialists in Israeli Military Law and Constitutional Law as Amici Curiae Supporting Petitioners, *Boumediene v Bush*, 2007 WL 2441592 (Aug. 24, 2007) (Nos. 06-1195, 06-1196).

221 *Available at* http://www.nytimes.com/2007/07/11/opinion/11katyal.html.

222 *Available at* http://www.washingtonpost.com/wp-dyn/content/article/2006/08/03/AR2006080301257.html.

223 The constitutional foundation of this authority is well-established. As the Supreme Court has noted, Congress has broad authority over naturalization and immigration and "regularly makes rules that would be unacceptable if applied to citizens." *See Denmore v. Kim*, 538 U.S. 510, 521 (2003) (quoting *Mathews v. Diaz*, 426 U.S. 67, 79-80 (1976)); *Wong Wing v. United States*, 163 U.S. 228, 235 (1896) ("We think it clear that detention, or temporary confinement, as part of the means necessary to give effect to the provisions for the exclusion or expulsion of aliens, would be valid.").

224 Under sections 411 and 412 of the USA PATRIOT Act, Congress authorized the arrest and detention of aliens believed to be connected to terrorism where no charges have been filed, but the statute requires the government to commence removal proceedings or to file criminal charges within seven days after arrest. *See* 8 U.S.C. §§ 1226a(a)(3), 1226a(a)(5). After an order of removal, such individuals may be detained for successive six-month periods "if the release of the alien will threaten the national security of the United States or the safety of the community or any person." 8 U.S.C. § 1226a(a)(6). The enforceability of this latter provision in light of *Zadvydas* has not been directly tested in court. However, Justice O'Connor implicitly approved its use in her concurring opinion in *Clark v. Martinez*, and at least one other court has cited the provision without questioning its enforceability or validity. *See* 543 U.S. 371, 387 (2005) (O'Connor, J., concurring); *Nadarajah v. Gonzalez*, 443 F.3d 1069, 1079 (9th Cir. 2006).

225 *Available at* http://www.usdoj.gov/oig/special/0306/index.htm.

226 *Available at* http://www.usdoj.gov/oig/special/0312/final.pdf.

227 In many cases, the decision about whether to charge individuals criminally or keep them detained in immigration custody was not clear-cut. Michael Chertoff, the Assistant Attorney General for the Criminal Division at the time, said that within days of the attacks it became evident that some aliens encountered in connection with the investigation were "out of status" in violation of the law. U.S. Dep't of Justice, *OIG September 11 Detainees Report*, at 13. This would have fallen within the civil jurisdiction of the immigration authorities. *Id*. The Department's policy was to "use whatever means [were] legally available" to detain a person who might present a terrorist threat and to insure that no one else was killed. *Id*. Chertoff noted that this could mean detaining aliens on immigration charges and in other cases on criminal charges. *Id*. Chertoff said he did not believe that the Department had a blanket policy to pursue one or the other, if both were possible, but that the most "efficacious" charge would be used. *Id*. He stated that he was involved in meetings with the Attorney General, the Deputy Attorney General, and the FBI Director at which this philosophy was discussed. *Id*.

228 Since October 2004, the court has allowed discovery to proceed on the plaintiffs' claims regarding their conditions of confinement and excessive force. *See, e.g.*, Order Setting Discovery Schedule, *Turkmen v. Ashcroft*, No. 02-cv-02307 (E.D.N.Y. Nov. 17, 2002) (Dkt. No. 134); Center for Constitutional Rights, Current Cases, *Turkmen v. Ashcroft*, http://ccrjustice.org/ourcases/current-cases/turkmen-v.-ashcroft. The plaintiffs have appealed the court's decision dismissing the claims that challenged plaintiffs' prolonged detention. *See Turkmen v. Ashcroft*, No. 02-cv-02307, 2006 WL 1662663 (E.D.N.Y. June 14, 2006), *appeal docketed*, No. 06-3745-cv(L) (2d Cir. March 26, 2007). Even absent discovery, there appear to have been valid concerns regarding the conditions of confinement experienced by some of the detainees, including, among other things, access to legal counsel, allegations of physical and verbal abuse, medical care and lighting conditions. *See* U.S. Dep't of Justice, *OIG September 11 Detainees Report*, at 111-84 (reviewing and comparing conditions of confinement at two prisons in which detainees were housed, the Metropolitan Detention Center in Brooklyn, New York and Passaic County Jail in Patterson, New Jersey).

229 *Available at* http://brennan.3cdn.net/6a0e5de414927df95e_lbm6iy66c.pdf.

230 *Available at* http://www.aclu.org/iclr/malhotra.pdf

231 *Available at* http://hrw.org/reports/ 2005/us0605/us0605.pdf. Another commentator recites estimates of more than forty detentions under the material witness statute after 9/11. *See* Roberto Iraola, *Terrorism, Grand Juries, and the Federal Material Witness Statute*, 34 St. Mary's L.J. 401, 402 (2003).

232 According to the Human Rights Watch and ACLU report, the conditions of arrest and confinement for those individuals arrested under material witness warrants were harsh: "…the witnesses were often arrested at gunpoint in front of families and neighbors and transported to jail in handcuffs. They typically were held around-the-clock in solitary confinement and subjected to the harsh and degrading high-security conditions typically reserved for prisoners accused or convicted of the most dangerous crimes. They were taken to court in shackles and chains." Human Rights Watch & ACLU, *Witness to Abuse*, at 3.

233 *Available at* http://www.washingtonpost.com/ac2/wp-dyn/A31438-2002Nov23.

234 Awadallah's first trial on the same charges resulted in a hung jury and was declared a mistrial. *See* Minute Entry, *United States v. Awadallah*, No. 01-cr-01026 (S.D.N.Y. May 4, 2006).

235 *Available at* http://www.nacdl.org/public.nsf/01cle7698280d20385256d0b00789923/9090373de4fa9c7d85256f3300551e42?OpenDocument.

236 *Available at* http://www.washingtonpost.com/wp-dyn/content/article/2006/11/29/AR2006112901179.html.

237 http://www.washingtonpost.com/wp-dyn/content/article/2006/11/29/AR2006112901155.html.

238 According to the government, the Federal Sentencing Guidelines range for Padilla was 360 months to life in prison; and the government argued for a life sentence—and against any downward departure—for Padilla. See Sentencing Memorandum by U.S.A. at 44-48, *Padilla* (S.D. Fla. Nov. 29, 2007) (Dkt. No. 1280). Padilla, relying in large part on his conditions of confinement at the Naval Brig, sought a reduced sentence. See Sentencing Memorandum by Jose Padilla at 14-21, *Padilla* (S.D. Fla. Nov. 29, 2007) (Dkt. No. 1279) (detailing allegations of torture and conditions of confinement at the Naval Brig).

239 *Available at* http://www.nytimes.com/2008/01/23/us/23padilla.html.

240 While acknowledging the government's expertise in conducting intelligence gathering, Judge Mukasey rejected this argument as speculative based on the record that was presented to him. See *Padilla*, 243 F. Supp. 2d at 51-52. Indeed, Judge Mukasey noted the competing scenario that counsel might play a constructive role in helping Padilla to cooperate with the government. See *id.* at 52, n.7 (noting that the experience of the federal courts under the Sentencing Guidelines "suggests that those facing the near certain prospect of custody have a fine appreciation of how to cut their losses"). We believe that as a general matter Judge Mukasey's observation is sound; defense counsel can often play a valuable role in working with their clients to explain the potential benefits of cooperation and to facilitate cooperation by assessing the evidence, developing a dialogue with the government, and preparing their clients to proffer truthfully to the government in an effort to cooperate.

241 For further discussion of FISA in the terrorism context, see Valerie Caproni, *Surveillance and Transparency*, 11 Lewis & Clark L. Rev. 1087 (2007); William Funk, *Electronic Surveillance of Terrorism: The Intelligence/Law Enforcement Dilemma—A History*, 11 Lewis & Clark L. Rev. 1099 (2007).

242 For a discussion of the history of FISA, *see* William C. Banks, *The Death of FISA*, 91 Minn. L. Rev. 1209, 1234 (2007). The pre-FISA debate over the Fourth Amendment issues is illustrated by *Zweibon v. Mitchell*. See 516 F.2d 594, 613-14 (D.C. Cir. 1975) ("Although we believe that an analysis of the policies implicated by foreign intelligence surveillance indicates that, absent exigent circumstances, all warrantless electronic surveillance is unreasonable and therefore unconstitutional, our holding need not sweep that broadly."); *United States v. Brown*, 484 F.2d 418, 426-27 (5th Cir. 1973) (President's authority to conduct foreign affairs includes ability to conduct foreign intelligence surveillance without a warrant); *United States v. Butenko*, 494 F.2d 593, 605 (3d Cir. 1974) (same). The Fourth Circuit, in a post-FISA decision regarding pre-FISA surveillance, held that the executive branch may conduct warrantless surveillance if the "primary purpose" is collecting foreign intelligence information. See *United States v. Truong Dinh Hung*, 629 F.2d 908, 915-16 (4th Cir. 1980).

243 *See* Intelligence Authorization Act for Fiscal Year 1995, Pub.L. No. 103-359, 108 Stat. 3443 (1994) (codified as amended at 50 U.S.C. § 1821 et seq.). In 1998, Congress further amended FISA to create slightly different procedures for authorizing the use of pen registers and trap and trace devices for foreign intelligence information, *see* Intelligence Authorization Act for Fiscal Year 1999, Pub.L. No. 105-272, 112 Stat. 2405 (1998) (codified as amended at 50 U.S.C. § 1841 et seq.), and to allow the executive branch access to business records for foreign intelligence and international terrorism investigations. See 18 U.S.C. §§ 1861-63.

244 In addition, Professor Viet Dinh of Georgetown Law School, who served in a senior position in the Department of Justice from 2001 through 2003, cites several examples where FISA evidence contributed to successful counterterrorism efforts. See Viet Dinh & Wendy J. Keefer, *FISA and The Patriot Act: A Look Back and a Look Forward*, 35 Geo. L.J. Ann. Rev. Crim. Proc. iii at xxvi (2006) (citing *USA Patriot Act: A Review for the Purpose of Its Reauthorization: Oversight Hearing Before H. Committee on the Judiciary*, 109th Cong. (2005) (statement of U.S. Att'y Gen. Alberto R. Gonzales)). Professor Dinh cites the following cases: the successful prosecutions of individuals involved in an al Qaeda drugs-for-weapons plot in San Diego, California; the prosecution of individuals such as Ali al-Timimi and others involved with the terrorist group Lashkar-e-Taiba, which is linked to al Qaeda; the prosecution and conviction of Mohammed Ali Hasan al-Moayad and Mohsehn Yahya Zayed for conspiring to provide material support to al Qaeda and the terrorist group Hamas; and the guilty plea of Enaam Arnout for diverting charitable funds to Osama bin Laden.

245 *Available at* http://www.usdoj.gov/archive/ag/speeches/2003/021003agenaamaranouttranscripthtm.htm.

246 *Available at* http://online.wsj.com/article/SB104311308659604224.html?mod=article-outset-box.

247 *Online version available at* http://www.law.com/jsp/article.jsp? id=1088138434813.

248 *Available at* http://www.washingtonpost.com/wp-dyn/content/article/2007/10/22/ AR2007102200731.html.

249 The FISC consists of eleven district court judges selected by the Chief Justice from at least seven judicial circuits and serving staggered seven year terms. See 50 U.S.C. § 1803(a). At least three of the FISC's judges must reside within twenty miles of Washington, D.C. *Id.* In the event that a FISA application is denied by a judge of the FISC, the government may seek review of such denial in the Foreign Intelligence Surveillance Court of Review ("FISCR"), and if necessary, in the Supreme Court. See 50 U.S.C. § 1803(b).

250 FISA includes a narrow exception authorizing surveillance outside the FISA process for up to one year when it is directed solely at "communications transmitted by means of communications used exclusively between or among foreign powers," and there is "no substantial likelihood" that communication involving a U.S. person will be acquired. 50 U.S.C. § 1802(a)(1). Because this exception is allowed only for direct foreign government communications, it does not allow surveillance outside the FISA process when foreign powers use public communications networks.

Congress has also adopted two other exceptions to the exclusivity of the FISA process for gathering foreign intelligence. One exception permits surveillance outside FISA for up to fifteen days following a declaration of war. 50 U.S.C. § 1811. The other permits the Attorney General to certify that "an emergency situation exists" that requires electronic surveillance before an order from the FISC can be obtained. *Id*. § 1805(f)(1). The emergency authority may be exercised for up to seventy-two hours from the time authorization is made by the Attorney General, until the information sought is obtained, or until the FISC denies the application for surveillance, whichever is earlier. *Id*. § 1805(f). The emergency procedures still demand an application to a judge, but it is not required until seventy-two hours after the emergency authorization. *Id*.

[251] *See* 50 U.S.C. §§ 1804(a) and 1823(a) for a detailed list of the required contents of a FISA application.

[252] *See* 50 U.S.C. §§ 1805(a), 1823(a). In addition to these probable cause findings, the FISC judge must also find that: (1) the President has authorized the Attorney General to approve applications for electronic surveillance or physical searches for foreign intelligence information; (2) the application has been made by a federal officer and approved by the Attorney General; (3) the proposed minimization procedures meet the respective definitions of minimization procedures for electronic surveillance and physical searches; and (4) the application contains all statements and certifications required by § 1804 for electronic surveillance and § 1823 for physical searches and, if the target is a U.S. person, the certification or certifications are not clearly erroneous on the basis of the statement made under §§ 1804(a)(7)(E) and 1823(a)(7)(E) of title 50 and any other information furnished under §§ 1804(d) and 1823(c) of title 50. *See* 50 U.S.C. §§ 1805(a), 1823(a).

[253] *Available at* http://judiciary.house.gov/media/pdfs/kris042805.pdf.

[254] OIPR was assigned to represent the government before the FISC and to ensure institutional responsibility for FISA compliance, allowing FISA expertise to develop inside the Department. *See* Banks, *The Death of FISA*, at 1234-35. When OIPR delivered applications to the FISC, the Department of Justice could represent that it sought electronic surveillance in pursuit of a "foreign intelligence" purpose, not to spy on political enemies or to end-run the statutory and constitutional protections in a criminal case. *See id*. Gradually, the insistence of OIPR and the FISC on fulsome FISA applications resulted in more elaborate procedures, including those that separated law enforcement and intelligence agents and activities. *See id*.

Meanwhile, in the mid-1990s, Deputy Attorney General Jamie Gorelick convened a working group to reconcile emerging differences of opinion between OIPR, the Criminal Division, and FBI over "wall" issues. *See 9/11 Commission Report*, at 79. After receiving OLC's views on the "primary purpose" issue, the working group made recommendations to Deputy Attorney General Gorelick, who in turn submitted them to Attorney General Reno. *See id*. In March 1995, Gorelick wrote a memorandum regarding "Instructions on Separation of Certain Counterintelligence and Criminal Investigations" that prescribed special "wall" procedures for two pending cases, including the 1993 World Trade Center bombing prosecution. *See* Mem. from Jamie S. Gorelick, Deputy Att'y Gen., to Mary Jo White, U.S. Attorney, S.D.N.Y., et al. 1-4 (Mar. 1995), *available at* http://www.usdoj.gov/ag/testimony/2004/1995_gorelick_memo.pdf. The memorandum instructed that the intelligence investigation in the New York case would go forward "without any direction or control" by the U.S. Attorney's office or the Criminal Division, and it required FBI headquarters or OIPR approval to share some portions of intelligence investigative memoranda with law enforcement agents. *Id*. at 3. In addition to these "wall" procedures, the March 1995 memorandum also encouraged cooperation and coordination between the intelligence and law enforcement personnel in a few particular ways. *See id*. at 2-3. According to a 2004 Office of the Inspector General report, the March 1995 memorandum from Gorelick was somehow misconstrued and its "wall" procedures were applied throughout the FBI for all FISA applications by 1997. *See* Banks, *Death of FISA*, at 1238.

In July 1995, Attorney General Janet Reno issued a set of secret internal guidelines to prescribe procedures for contacts among the Justice Department's Criminal Division, the FBI, and OIPR. *See* Mem. from Janet Reno, Att'y Gen., to Assistant Att'y Gen., Criminal Div., et al. (July 19, 1995) (regarding "Procedures for Contacts Between the FBI and the Criminal Division Concerning Foreign Intelligence and Foreign Counterintelligence Investigations"), *available at* http://www.fas.org/irp/agency/doj/fisa/1995procs.html. Contacts between the prosecutors and their investigators and intelligence officials were limited, logged, and noted to the OIPR. *See id*. These entities could exchange consultations and advice, but the contacts should "not inadvertently result in either the fact or the appearance of the Criminal Division's directing or controlling" an investigation. *Id*. The guidelines were not written to affect contacts and information-sharing between investigating agents, but instead were intended to apply only between investigators and prosecutors. *See 9/11 Commission Report*, at 79.

Under these procedures, a metaphorical "wall" between law enforcement and intelligence gathering developed whenever an intelligence investigation suggested some indication of criminal activity. *See id*. According to a later Office of Inspector General Report, the OIPR lawyers interpreted and applied the July 1995 Reno guidelines as containing the special procedures imposed in New York by the March 1995 Gorelick memorandum, thus interpreting FISA as essentially prohibiting contact between the law enforcement and intelligence sides of an investigation. See id. Coordination between law enforcement and intelligence officials that had occurred before 1995 fell off after issuance of the guidelines, and such contacts that did occur came so late in the process as to be practically useless. Banks, *Death of FISA*, at 1239.

OIPR maintained its gatekeeper role throughout this period—only through it would information pass to the Criminal Division. According to the 9/11 Commission, OIPR sustained its position in part by maintaining that it reflected the concerns of the chief judge of the FISC, and that "if it could not regulate the flow of information to criminal prosecutors, it would no longer present the FBI's warrant requests to the FISA Court." *9/11 Commission Report*, at 79. Although the OIPR FISA procedures were revised between 1995 and 2002 to permit consultation between the intelligence and prosecution sides of the FBI "aimed at preserving the option of criminal prosecution," the Criminal Division was not allowed to "direct or control the FISA investigation." *In re Sealed Case*, 310 F.3d at 729. During this period, the FISC approved the OIPR procedures and issued case-specific information screening walls. See *9/11 Commission Report*, at 539 n.83. These mechanisms varied with the complexity of the investigation, and sometimes the FISC served as the "wall" between the two sides. *See id.*

255 *Available at* http://www.eff.org/Censorship/Terrorism_militias/20010919_doj_ata_analysis.html.

256 Congress also added a provision permitting those who acquire foreign intelligence by conducting electronic surveillance to "consult with Federal law enforcement officers to coordinate efforts to investigate or protect against" terrorist activities by foreign powers or their agents. USA PATRIOT Act § 504(a), 115 Stat. 272, 364-65 (codified at 50 U.S.C. §§ 1806(k), 1825(k)). The Act states that such coordination "shall not preclude" the required FISA certification. *Id.*; *see also* 50 U.S.C. § 1804(a)(7)(B) (2000) (requiring certification that "a significant purpose" of the surveillance requested is to obtain foreign intelligence).

257 *Available at* http://fas.org/irp/agency/doj/fisa/ 2006rept.pdf. According to the Department of Justice, five of the 2,181 applications were withdrawn, and the government later re-submitted one of those five applications, which was approved. Thus, the FISC approved 2,176 applications. In addition, the FISC made substantive modifications to seventy-three applications and denied one application in part. *See* Letter from Richard A. Hertling, Acting Assistant Att'y Gen., to Hon. Nancy Pelosi.

258 Notably, at least two other district courts have rejected the reasoning in *Mayfield* and have found that the "significant purpose" standard does not violate the Fourth Amendment. *See United States v. Abu-Jihaad*, — F. Supp. 2d —, 2008 WL 219172 (D. Conn. Jan. 24, 2008); *United States v. Mubayyid*, 521 F. Supp. 2d 125, 137-38 (D. Mass. 2007).

259 First, the law clarifies that FISA warrants are not needed for "surveillance directed at a person reasonably believed to be located outside of the United States." Pub. L. No. 110-55, 121 Stat. 552. According to the White House, the new law clarifies that "FISA's definition of 'electronic surveillance' does not apply to activities directed at persons reasonably believed to be outside the United States, thereby restoring the statute to its original focus on appropriate protections for the rights of persons in the United States." Press Release, White House, Office of the Press Sec'y, Fact Sheet: FISA 101: Why FISA Modernization Amendments Must Be Made Permanent (Aug. 6, 2007), *available at* http://www.whitehouse.gov/news/releases/2007/09/20070919-1.html.

Second, the Act requires formal authorization of a program to conduct such monitoring and that the Director of National Intelligence and the Attorney General approve a program (for up to one year) reasonably designed to be limited to the monitoring of persons outside the United States. *See* Pub. L. No. 110-55, § 105(B). These procedures must be submitted to the FISA court, which then reviews whether the Executive's conclusion that the procedures are reasonably designed to only intercept the communications of people reasonably believed to be outside the United States is "clearly erroneous." *Id.* at § 105(C). If the conclusion is clearly erroneous, the court directs the Executive to submit new procedures within thirty days or cease any acquisitions under the program. *See id.* The government may appeal that determination to the FISCR and, if needed, the Supreme Court. *See id.*

Third, the Act permits the Director of National Intelligence and the Attorney General to direct a person, such as a communications service provider, to provide the information, facilities, and assistance necessary to conduct authorized foreign intelligence activities. *See id.* at § 105(B). In the event such a person fails to comply with a directive, the Attorney General may invoke the aid of the FISA Court to compel compliance with the directive. *See id.* The government is required to compensate a person for providing information, facilities, or assistance under the law. *See id.*

260 Well before CIPA's enactment, the Supreme Court recognized the need in criminal trials to "balanc[e] the public interest in protecting the flow of information against the individual's right to prepare his defense" and provided the general framework for a court to resolve questions involving sensitive information. *Roviaro v. United States*, 353 U.S. 53, 62 (1957). In *Roviaro*, the defendant, who was charged with selling heroin to a government informant, attempted to learn the identity of the informant, who was not called or identified at trial but was "the only witness in a position to amplify or contradict the testimony" of the lone government witness. *Id.* at 64. The prosecutor objected to disclosure of the informant's identity on the ground that it would prevent him from participating in future law enforcement operations. *See id.* at 65. The Supreme Court overturned the trial court's decision to withhold the informant's identity, holding that while there is "no fixed rule" in such circumstances, a court must perform a balancing test based on the specific facts of each case. *Id.* at 62. If the sensitive information at issue is "relevant and helpful to the defense of an accused, or is essential to a fair determination of a cause" then the government's interest in maintaining the secrecy of the sensitive information must "give way." *Id.* at 60-61.

261 For additional discussion of CIPA's procedures and its application in the context of terrorism trials, *see* Serrin Turner & Stephen J. Schulhofer, Brennan Ctr. for Justice at N.Y.U. Sch. of L., *The Secrecy Problem in Terrorism Trials* 17-25 (2005), *available at* http://brennan.3cdn.net/6a0e5de414927df95e_lbm6iy66c.pdf; Ass'n of the Bar of the City of N.Y., Comm. on Fed. Courts, *The Indefinite Detention of "Enemy Combatants": Balancing Due Process and National Security in the Context of the War on Terror* 135-46 (Feb. 6. 2004), *available at* http://www.abcny.org/pdf/1C_WL06!.pdf.

262 CIPA does not authorize courts to make determinations about whether information should be designated as classified; that determination is left to the executive branch agencies. *See United States v. Smith*, 750 F.2d 1215, 1217 (4th Cir. 1984) ("[T]he government... may determine what information is classified. A defendant cannot challenge this classification. A court cannot question it."); *United States v. Musa*, 833 F. Supp. 752, 755 (E.D. Mo. 1993) ("The determination whether to designate information as classified is a matter committed to the executive branch.").

263 *See also United States v. Smith*, 780 F.2d 1102, 1110 (4th Cir. 1985) (finding that under CIPA a "district court may order disclosure [of classified information] only when the information is at least 'essential to the defense,' 'necessary to the defense,' and neither merely

cumulative nor corroborative, nor speculative.") (internal citations omitted). In *United States v. Rahman*, Judge Mukasey applied the same standards as the D.C. Circuit in *Yunis* but outlined the steps in the process as follows: "determine (i) whether the information in question is properly deemed classified for purposes of the statute, then (ii) whether any of the classified information is discoverable under any otherwise applicable rule, then (iii) whether any of the classified information would be material or helpful to preparing the defense of any defendant, thereafter (iv) whether such information should be disclosed, and finally (v) if such classified information should be disclosed, whether it should be disclosed in some form other than the form in which it was submitted to the court." *Rahman*, 870 F. Supp. 47, 50 (S.D.N.Y. 1994).

[264] "The functions and duties of the Attorney General under [CIPA] may be exercised by the Deputy Attorney General, the Associate Attorney General, or by an Assistant Attorney General designated by the Attorney General for such purpose and may not be delegated to any other official." CIPA § 14.

[265] *Available at* http://query.nytimes.com/gst/fullpage.html?res=9405E1DD1439F935A25754C0A9649C8B63.

[266] *Available at* http://www.abcny.org/pdf/1C_WL06!.pdf.

[267] Courts have recognized the difficulties and issues raised by the rule and have rejected its use on a number of occasions. *See, e.g., United States v. Fernandez*, 913 F.2d 148, 162 (4th Cir. 1990) (rejecting use of code system by jurors to prevent disclosure of classified documents); *United States v. North*, No. 88-0080-02, 1988 WL 148481, at *3 (D.D.C. Dec. 12, 1988) (rejecting use of "silent witness rule" due to volume of classified material and possibility that extensive redactions and substitutions would hinder cross-examination and increase confusion, and a concern that it would be difficult to keep classified materials from public disclosure as testimony proceeded).

[268] *Available at* http://brennan.3cdn.net/6a0e5de414927df95e_lbm6iy66c.pdf.

[269] Courts in CIPA proceedings have also been able to balance the First Amendment concerns that favor public trials and disclosure of information against the requirement of ex parte hearings and sealed dockets. *See, e.g., United States v. Moussaoui*, 65 F. Appx. 881, 886 (4th Cir. May 13, 2003); *Abu Marzook*, 412 F. Supp. 2d at 926-27; *Ressam*, 221 F. Supp. 2d at 1264-65.

[270] Another critic has argued that CIPA unnecessarily "restrict[s] the type and quantity of information available to the public during the pre-trial and trial proceedings of those charged with acts of terror against the United States" in violation of the public's First Amendment rights. Cameron Stracher, *Eyes Tied Shut: Litigating for Access Under CIPA in the Government's "War on Terror"*, 48 N.Y.L. Sch. L. Rev. 173, 173 (2003/2004).

[271] *Available at* http://www.defenddemocracy.org/usr_doc/Court.doc.

[272] *Available at* http://opinionjournal.com/extra/?id=110010505.

[273] Although it seems well-established that the list reached Bin Laden, we are not aware of the basis for the claim that it did so within ten days. Andrew McCarthy, one of the trial prosecutors (and the author of the cover letter that transmitted the co-conspirator list to defense counsel) says the timing is uncertain. *See* Telephone Interview with Andrew McCarthy, former Assistant U.S. Att'y in the S.D.N.Y. (Dec. 7 & 10, 2007).

[274] Further, under current law, it is not clear that co-conspirator lists are required to be disclosed in all cases. *See, e.g., United States v. James*, No. 02-cv-00778, 2007 WL 914242, at *15 (E.D.N.Y. Mar. 21, 2007) ("Courts have required the government to provide a list of any unindicted co-conspirators or 'co-schemers' *if* the government intends to introduce evidence about those individuals at trial.") (emphasis added); *United States v. Jones*, No. 85-cr-01075, 1986 WL 275, at *3 (S.D.N.Y. May 28, 1986) ("If the Government expects to introduce evidence at trial concerning any unindicted co-conspirators or other individuals who may be considered 'co-schemers,' it must provide defendants promptly with the names and last known addresses of those individuals [] or, if their names are unknown, such other information concerning their identities as the Government may possess, unless the Government submits an ex parte affidavit showing that such disclosure might endanger the safety of prospective witnesses. Otherwise, the Government need not reveal any information concerning these individuals unless required to do so by Brady v. Maryland, 373 U.S. 83 (1983).").

[275] The 9/11 Commission Report pointed to a "leak" to *The Washington Times* and the ensuing article discussing Bin Laden's use of a satellite phone as the cause of Bin Laden abandoning the use of the phone, compromising U.S. intelligence efforts. *See* Nat'l Comm'n on Terrorist Attacks Upon the U.S., *The 9/11 Commission Report* 127 (2004) (hereafter "*9/11 Commission Report*") ("Worst of all, al Qaeda's senior leadership had stopped using a particular means of communication almost immediately after a leak to the *Washington Times*") & n. 105. The 9/11 Commission Report cites to an August 21, 1998 article in *The Washington Times* as the public disclosure of the leak and also cites to two interviews as support. While we have not had access to those interviews, it is highly unlikely that the article caused Bin Laden to cease using his phone. First, it had been reported since 1996 that Bin Laden used a satellite phone. *See* Glenn Kessler, *File the Bin Laden Phone Leak Under 'Urban Myths'*, Wash. Post, Dec. 22, 2005, at A02. Second, the United States had launched a cruise missile attack on Bin Laden the day before the article appeared and just missed him, reportedly, by hours. *See id.* This certainly would have caused him to be more circumspect about using the phone. *See generally id.* (discussing reasons why the August 21, 1998 article probably would not have been the cause of Bin Laden ceasing to use the phone).

[276] Al-Fawwaz was ultimately named as a defendant in the Embassy Bombings indictment, which charged him with setting up "a media information office in London, England … which was designed both to publicize the statements of USAMA BIN LADEN and to provide a cover in support of al Qaeda's 'military' activities, including … the procurement of necessary equipment (including satellite telephones).'" *See* Superseding Indictment at ¶ 9, *United States v. el-Hage*, No. 98-cr-01023 (S.D.N.Y. Mar. 12, 2001) (Dkt. No. 550). On March 26, 2001, during the Embassy Bombings trial, Detective Constable Paul Webber testified that on September 23, 1998, while he was assigned to work with the antiterrorism branch of New Scotland Yard in London, he participated in the search of a residence in London that he understood to

be the home of al-Fawwaz, during which New Scotland Yard recovered a large number of documents relating to Bin Laden and al Qaeda, including correspondence bearing names and telephone numbers. *See* Tr. of Record Proceedings at 3349- 73, *el-Hage* (S.D.N.Y. Mar. 26, 2001) (Dkt. No. 606) (trial testimony of Det. Constable Paul Webber).; *see also* Sean O'Neill, *The Worldwide Trail of Bloodshed that Leads to a Semi in Suburban London*, Daily Telegraph (U.K.), Sept. 19, 2001, at 3.

277 *See* Tr. of Record Proceedings at 3035 & Gov't Ex. 594, *el-Hage* (S.D.N.Y. Mar. 20, 2001) (Dkt. No. 605) (trial testimony of Marilyn Morelli of O'Gara Satellite Networks and exhibit establishing that the last activity for the satellite phone was October 9, 1998). The phone records reflect some 450 phone calls between January 1, 1998 and August 21, 1998, including seventy-seven calls between August 1, 1998 and August 21, 1998. *See id.* After August 21, 1998, however—which was the day after the cruise missile strikes against al Qaeda sites in Afghanistan and a pharmaceutical factory in Sudan, *see 9/11 Commission Report*, at 116-17, the phone went dead for the rest of the month of August. *See* Gov't Ex. 594, *el-Hage* (S.D.N.Y. Mar. 20, 2001) (Dkt. No. 605). Thereafter, the records show insignificant activity—a total of four calls in September 1998 and nine calls in October 1998. The last call was at 13:28 Greenwich Mean Time on October 9, 1998. *See id.*

278 *See* Tr. of Record Proceedings at 3035, *el-Hage* (S.D.N.Y. Mar. 20, 2001) (Dkt. No. 605) (trial testimony of Marilyn Morelli of O'Gara Satellite Networks).

279 The first defendant to be arrested in the Embassy Bombings case, Wadih el-Hage, was arrested on September 16, 1998. *See* Minute Entry, *el-Hage* (S.D.N.Y. Sept. 16, 1998). On October 7, 1998, just two days before the satellite phone went dead entirely, prosecutors and el-Hage's defense counsel appeared for an initial pretrial conference before Judge Sand and the government stated that it would need another month even to assess how long it would take to make discovery. *See* Minute Entry, *el-Hage* (S.D.N.Y. Oct. 7, 1998). Further, the protective order that governed discovery was not entered until December 17, 1998. *See* Protective Order, *el-Hage* (S.D.N.Y. Dec. 17, 1998) (Dkt. No. 27). Although the actual date of the government's first discovery production is not listed in the docket, based on our experience it is inconceivable that the government made discovery of the phone records within two days of the initial pretrial conference, especially when it had requested a month to even formulate an initial timetable for discovery and when the protective order governing discovery was not entered for more than two months after the initial pretrial conference.

280 We also understand that in the Embassy Bombings case, two defendants almost decided to represent themselves pro se but ultimately continued to be represented by their attorneys. Nevertheless, this indicates that the issue of pro se defendants and its interplay with classified information may recur. Indeed, we understand from prosecutors involved in the trials that both Sheikh Abdel Rahman and Ramzi Yousef, at certain points, sought to represent themselves pro se.

281 *Available at* http://trac.syr.edu/tracreports/terrorism/169/include/terrorism.whitepaper.pdf.

282 *See Porter v. White*, 483 F.3d 1294, 1303 n.4 (11th Cir. 2007) ("The right protected by the *Brady* rule is 'the defendant's right to a fair trial mandated by the Due Process Clause of the [Fourteenth] Amendment to the Constitution'") (quoting *United States v. Agurs*, 427 U.S. 97, 107 (1976)); *Grayson v. King*, 460 F.3d 1328, 1337 (11th Cir. 2006) ("The *Brady* rule is grounded in a defendant's right to a fair trial"). The right to a fair trial, in turn, stems from the procedural sphere of the Due Process Clause. *See Daniels v. Williams*, 474 U.S. 327, 337 (1986) (Stevens, J., concurring) (The Due Process Clause of the Fourteenth Amendment contains "a guarantee of fair procedure, sometimes referred to as 'procedural due process': the State may not ... imprison ... a defendant without giving him a fair trial").

283 *See, e.g., Youngblood v. West Virginia*, 547 U.S. 867, 126 S. Ct. 2188, 2190 (2006) (affirming *Brady*, holding that "[a] *Brady* violation occurs when the government fails to disclose evidence materially favorable to the accused" and that *Brady* obligations apply "to impeachment evidence as well as exculpatory evidence"); *Strickland v. Green*, 527 U.S. 263, 281-82 (1999) (a *Brady* violation requires a showing that: "[t]he evidence at issue must be favorable to the accused, either because it is exculpatory, or because it is impeaching; that evidence must have been suppressed by the State, either willfully or inadvertently; and prejudice must have ensued").

284 *Available at* http://news.corporate.findlaw.com/hdocs/docs/terrorism/uskoubriti83104g.pdf.

285 *Available at* http://www.nytimes.com/2004/09/01/national/01detroit.html.

286 *Available at* http://query.nytimes.com/gst/fullpage.html?res=9D02E7DA103BF933A1575AC0A9679C8B63.

287 *Available at* http://www.detnews.com/apps/pbcs.dll/article?AID=/20071208/METRO/710080371.

288 *Available at* http://www.nytimes.com/2006/03/29/national/29cnd-prosecutor.html.

289 *Available at* http://www.nytimes.com/2007/11/01/us/01detroit.html.

290 Although pre-trial depositions generally do not occur in federal criminal cases, Rule 15 of the Federal Rules of Criminal Procedure provides that the court may permit a deposition in lieu of trial testimony "because of exceptional circumstances and in the interest of justice." Fed. R. Crim. P. 15(a)(1). However, depositions are disfavored in criminal cases. *See, e.g., United States v. Ismaili*, 828 F.2d 153, 159 (3d Cir. 1987); *United States v. Wilson*, 601 F.2d 95, 97 (3d Cir. 1979). Indeed, the Advisory Committee that drafted the modern version of Rule 15 stated that it did "not want to encourage the use of depositions at trial, especially in view of the importance of having live testimony from a witness on the witness stand." Fed. R. Crim. P. 15 advisory committee's note (1975); *see also* 2 Charles Alan Wright, *Federal Practice and Procedure* § 241 (3d ed. 2000) (noting that "there is still a fear of 'trial by depositions,' and a strong preference for live testimony rather than depositions").

291 In this regard, the Fourth Circuit emphasized the limited scope of permissible additions by the government under Federal Rule of Evidence 106 and cautioned that the government would not be permitted to use "completeness" additions as a back-door method of offering incriminating evidence in violation of the Confrontation Clause. See *Moussaoui*, 382 F.3d at 481.

292 *See, e.g.*, Serrin Turner & Stephen J. Schulhofer, Brennan Ctr. for Justice at N.Y.U. Sch. of L., *The Secrecy Problem in Terrorism Trials* 44 (2005), *available at* http://brennan.3cdn.net/6a0e5de414927df95e_lbm6iy66c.pdf ("[B]oth the appeals court and trial court decisions [in *Moussaoui*] underscore the court's ability to adapt existing rights and procedures to fit novel problems. Neither decision treated the defendant's constitutional right to call witnesses as fixed or static; rather, both recognized the need to effectuate that right in a way that accommodated competing societal concerns. And both sought to do so by extending CIPA's 'substitution' concept into a new context. The case well illustrates that, where a workable balance between fairness and secrecy can be struck, the courts have the wherewithal to strike it.")

293 *Available at* http://brennan.3cdn.net/6a0e5de414927df95e_lbm6iy66c.pdf.

294 *See Lawfare: Terrorism & The Courts*, 33 Wm. Mitchell L. Rev. 1667, 1669 (2007) ("The Government rarely discloses these aspects of the intelligence community's operations and such information will almost always qualify for protection under CIPA. As an example, [United States District Court] Judge [Gerald] Rosen explained that the defense counsel in the Zacarias Moussaoui trial sought exculpatory statements from detainees held at the Guantánamo Bay facilities. The court denied that request and the Government was allowed to produce 'substitute evidence.'" Judge Rosen stated generally that substitute evidence often poses problems because, "like evidence produced for the privilege log, is not very helpful to defense counsel because it has been 'scrubbed' to a point that erases its utility." Continuing with his analysis of the substitute evidence used in *Moussaoui*, Judge Rosen stated that "one is left to question whether 'substitute information' violates the accused's constitutional right to a fair, public trial.")

295 In one extreme case, the government produced roughly twenty-three million pages of documents, with more documents continuing to pour in, in its prosecution of former KPMG partners on charges of conspiracy and tax evasion. Moreover, the government designated nearly seventy witnesses and approximately 2,000 exhibits for its case in chief. *See United States v. Stein*, 495 F. Supp. 2d 390, 418, 424 (S.D.N.Y. 2007). The estimated cost per defendant to defend the *Stein* case was between seven million and twenty-four million dollars. *Id.*

296 Undigested FISA information creates complications for the criminal justice system, but more importantly, if FISA intercepts are not being efficiently reviewed on a timely basis, it raises the question of whether important intelligence information is being lost. Efficient, timely review therefore is beneficial in every way.

297 Mr. Dratel has proposed amending CIPA to provide for the declassification of FISA interceptions of the defendant's own communications, subject to various provisions including continued classification upon a particularized demonstration of need by the government. *See* Dratel, *Sword or Shield?*, at 186-89.

298 Within the various approaches, courts apply the doctrines differently. For a thorough discussion of the different views that the courts take, *see* Mark D. Villaverde, *Structuring the Prosecutor's Duty to Search the Intelligence Community for Brady Material*, 88 Cornell L. Rev. 1471, 1493-1512 (2003).

299 For a thoughtful review of Miranda's application to suspected terrorists, *see* William J. Stuntz, *Local Policing After the Terror*, 111 Yale L.J. 2137, 2189 (2002) (discussing the implications of *Miranda* for terrorist suspects and stating, "[a] few months ago, *Miranda* seemed unshakeable. Now, it may be untenable"); *see also* Mark A. Godsey, *Miranda's Final Frontier—The International Arena: A Critical Analysis of United States v. Bin Laden, and a Proposal for a New Miranda Exception Abroad*, 51 Duke L.J. 1703 (2002) (analyzing and mapping out proposals for how to apply *Miranda* rights internationally); Michael R. Hartman, *A Critique of United States v. Bin Laden in Light of Chavez v. Martinez and the International War on Terror*, 43 Colum. J. Transnat'l L. 269, 269 (2004) (criticizing the *Bin Laden* court's holding as being "legally unsound" and arguing that the holding has "exacerbat[ed] existing tensions between the law enforcement community and the courts solely in order to extract very tenuous civil liberties gains"); Note, *Comparative Domestic Constitutionalism: Rethinking Criminal Procedure using the Administrative Constitution*, 119 Harv. L. Rev. 2530, 2538 (2006) ("Applying *Miranda's* strict conduct rules to terrorism cases, for example, yields untenable results (and doubtless discourages the government from bringing criminal charges in the first place). Sophisticated terror suspects can hide behind *Miranda's* protection, closing their lips around information vital to national security.")

300 In *Yousef*, the Second Circuit noted only two exceptions to the general rule that voluntary statements taken by foreign officials are admissible. The first exception, known as the "joint venture" doctrine, dictates that statements made during interrogation by foreign authorities may be suppressed if an American agent actively participated in the interrogation or utilized foreign authorities as agents in order to circumvent the requirements of *Miranda*. The second exception dictates that statements obtained by foreign officials under circumstances that "shock the judicial conscience" may be suppressed. *Yousef*, 327 F.3d at 145; *see also U.S. v. Yunis*, 859 F.2d 953 (D.C. Cir. 1988) (involuntary statements made to U.S. or foreign officers compels a declarant to be a witness against himself in violation of the Fifth Amendment).

301 Judge Sand also denied the motion to suppress filed by another defendant, Khalfan Khamis Mohamed, who was questioned by U.S. agents while in custody in South Africa. As Judge Sand held, although the FBI advice-of-rights form given to Mohamed was also deficient, he was affirmatively apprised of his right to counsel under South African law. *See Bin Laden*, 132 F. Supp. 2d at 194.

302 Judge Sand's ruling, along with a number of other issues raised by defendants, has been briefed and argued on appeal to the Second Circuit. *See United States v. el-Hage*, No. 01-cr-01535 (2d Cir. filed Oct. 19, 2001).

303 *See, e.g.*, Shawn Boyne, *The Future of Liberal Democracies in a Time of Terror: A Comparison of the Impact on Civil Liberties in the Federal Republic of Germany and the United States*, 11 Tulsa J. Comp. & Int'l L. 111, 143 (2003); Brian Haagensen II, Comment, *Federal Courts Versus Military Commissions: The Comedy of No Comity*, 32 Ohio N.U. L. Rev. 395 (2006).

304 The U.S. Army's Field Manual 27-10, The Law of Land Warfare ("Field Manual"), one of the major resources used for educating U.S. military personnel on the law of war, does not require a recitation of rights to be read to enemy fighters captured on the battlefield. In Chapter 3 (Prisoners of War) of the Field Manual, paragraph 93 (Interrogation) of Section IV presents the guidelines for questioning prisoners whose status qualify as prisoners of war (POWs). However, the rights of POWs vary from detainees who are designated as unlawful combatants or non-privileged combatants. Further discussion of this topic falls outside the scope of this White Paper.

305 Jeffrey S. Becker, *A Legal War on Terrorism: Extending New York v. Quarles and the Departure from Enemy Combatant Designations*, 53 DePaul L. Rev. 831 (2003); see also M.K.B. Darmer, *Beyond Bin Laden and Lindh: Confessions Law In An Age of Terrorism*, 12 Cornell J. L. & Pub. Pol'y 319 (2003); M.K.B. Darmer, *Lessons from the Lindh Case: Public Safety and the Fifth Amendment*, 68 Brook. L. Rev. 241 (2002); Godsey, *Miranda's Final Frontier—The International Arena*.

306 Lindh filed five motions to suppress his statements made after he had been captured and move into U.S. custody. See Mot. to Supress Statements for Violation of Fifth Amendment Rights (*Miranda* and *Edwards*), *Lindh* (E.D. Va. June 14, 2002) (Dkt. No. 224); Mot. to Supress Statements for Violation of Fed. R. Crim. Pro. 5(a) (*McNabb-Mallory*), *Lindh* (E.D. Va. June 17, 2002) (Dkt. No. 232); Mot. to Supress Involuntary Statements, *Lindh* (E.D. Va. June 17, 2002) (Dkt. No. 237); Mot. to Supress Statements Made on Dec. 1, 2001 to U.S. Special Forces & Robert Pelton, *Lindh* (E.D. Va. June 17, 2002) (Dkt. No. 240); Mot. to Supress the Interrogation by U.S. Agents at Qala-I-Janghi, *Lindh* (E.D. Va. June 17, 2002) (Dkt. No. 242). Only one motion to suppress pertained to violation of *Miranda*.

307 If this allegation is true, it provides an interesting window into the degree to which military personnel were thinking in terms of courtroom rules of evidence. The government, however, denied the assertion, claiming that after doctors declared the wound non-infectious, Lindh was given the choice whether to keep the bullet in his leg. See Gov't's Resp. to the Def.'s Proffer of Facts at 5-6, *Lindh* (E.D. Va. July 1, 2002) (Dkt. No. 273).

308 *Available at* http://www.defenselink.mil/speeches/speech.aspx?speechid=505.

309 Colonel Frederic L. Borch III, former chief prosecutor for the Department of Defense's Office of Military Commissions, complains: "[s]oldiers cannot be expected to complete a chain-of-custody document when under fire from an enemy combatant in a cave." Frederic L. Borch III, *Why Military Commissions Are the Proper Forum and Why Terrorists Will Have "Full and Fair" Trials: A Rebuttal to "Military Commissions: Trying American Justice,"* 2003 Army Law. 10, 13 (2003).

310 *See, e.g.*, Tung Yin, *Ending the War on Terrorism One Terrorist at a Time: A Noncriminal Detention Model for Holding and Releasing Guantánamo Bay Detainees*, 29 Harv. J.L. & Pub. Pol'y 149, 178 (2005). The author notes, "[w]hen soldiers gather physical evidence, however, criminal procedure is not their chief concern. First and foremost, any evidence-gathering by soldiers is incidental to their main purpose, which is to capture or kill enemies of the United States. There may not be time to process the physical evidence." *Id.* In a supporting footnote, the author speculates: "[w]eapons, for example, might be destroyed outright rather than collected and retained." *Id.* at n.138. The author adds the concern that "during operations outside the United States, it may not be practicable to seek a search warrant." *Id.* at 178. However, the author concedes that "[a]dmittedly, however, the Court has recognized this problem and held that an alien who has no voluntary connection with the United States has no Fourth Amendment rights relating to searches that take place outside the United States." *Id.* at n.139. Finally, the author raises the specter that "law enforcement personnel can reasonably expect to be called into court to testify in connection with their investigations, but military soldiers may well be unavailable to testify in criminal trials," speculating that "U.S. soldiers on active duty may still be posted overseas, or they may have been killed in subsequent military action." *Id.* at n.140.

311 Crona & Richardson, *Justice for War Criminals of Invisible Armies*, at 382-86. The authors cite the indictment in the Pan Am Flight 103 case, which details the alleged purchase of clothing by Libyan intelligence agent Abdel Bassett, for placement in the suitcase with the bomb to disguise the contents of the suitcase containing the bomb. See Indictment, *United States v. Abdel Basset Ali al-Megrahi*, No. 91-cr-00645 (D.D.C. Mar. 11, 1992) (Dkt. No. 3), "Under the rules of evidence applicable in U.S. District Court, the prosecution would have to produce in person the Maltese shopkeeper to identify Abdel Bassett as the man who allegedly purchased the clothing back in 1988, as opposed to producing the investigator who tracked down the shopkeeper and showed him a photograph of Abdel Bassett. Even if we assume that the shopkeeper could be located six years or more after the fact, we recognize that it is nearly impossible to secure involuntary testimony from a witness who is a citizen of a foreign country, especially one that historically has been less than sympathetic to the United States. The reach of a federal court subpoena simply does not extend to Malta.... . Assembling the proof in that case from numerous witnesses in several different countries, even if the witnesses were available and cooperative, would be logistically more difficult than reassembling the actual suitcase and the bomb. Part of the reason for the large cast of witnesses in the World Trade Center trial was to lay evidentiary foundations. This raises the question of whether U.S. prosecutors would be expected to fly into the United States every Scottish villager and investigator who recovered a shard of the suitcase, including fragments of the bomb and the garments used to conceal it, in order to lay a foundation for the admission of the items into evidence. The investigation of the Pan Am 103 flight has now covered 52 nations and 14,000 witnesses, with numerous forensic techniques used. The logistics of presenting the evidence in such a case under the rules of evidence for civilian trials seem overwhelming." Crona & Richardson, *Justice for War Criminals of Invisible Armies*, at 383-84.

In fact, the Lockerbie case, though tried in Scotland under Scottish rules of procedure, demonstrates the extent to which a civilian criminal justice system can accommodate the requirements of a terrorism case involving complex issues of evidence. See Symposium, *International*

Terrorism, Victim's Rights and the Lockerbie Criminal Trial, 29 Syracuse J. Int'l L. & Com. 1, 29 (2001). In the Lockerbie case, "[t]he Prosecution required to put in place arrangements to call 1160 witnesses, residents of a wide range of countries: the United Kingdom, the United States, Libya, Japan, Germany, Malta, Switzerland, Slovenia, Sweden, Czech Republic, India, France and Singapore." *Id.* at 29. The case also involved "10,000 pieces of debris which could be of evidential significance." *Id.* at 43. Ultimately, through negotiation between the prosecution and defense counsel, 230 witnesses were called from thirteen different countries, and the prosecution focused on a "mere" 300 pieces of debris. *Id.* at 29, 43.

312 *Available at* http://www.washingtonpost.com/wp-dyn/content/article/2007/05/18/AR2007051801758_pf.html.

313 *Available at* http://www.nytimes.com/2007/08/18/us/nationalspecial3/18legal.html.

314 *Available at* http://www.esquire.com/features/ESQ0307murphy?click=main_sr.

315 *See, e.g., United States v. el-Hage*, 213 F.3d 74, 79-81 (2d Cir. 2000) (thirty to thirty-three months of pre-trial detention, while extraordinary, does not violate defendant's due process rights given exceptional complexity of case and other factors); *United States v. el-Gabrowny*, 35 F.3d 63, 65 (2d Cir. 1994) (eighteen-month pre-trial detention, while unquestionably a long duration, does not violate due process, given importance and complexity of case, extensive evidence, including numerous tapes in Arabic); *United States v. Aref*, No. 04-cr-00402, 2006 WL 1650660, at *2 (N.D.N.Y. June 8, 2006) ("Given the complexity of this case ... no violation of Defendant's due process rights occurs by virtue of his pretrial detention of approximately one year"). In addition, convicted terrorists Mohammed Ali al-Moayad and Mohammed Mohsen Zayed were detained thirty-one months and thirty-five months, respectively, from their dates of arrest to the dates of their sentencing hearings. *See* Dep't of Justice, Press Release, Yemeni Citizens Arrested for Conspiring to Provide Support to Al Qaeda, Hamas, and Other Terrorist Groups (Mar. 4, 2003), *available at* http://www.usdoj.gov/opa/pr/2003/March/03_ag_134.htm (stating that al-Moayad and Zayed were arrested on January 10, 2003); Minute Entry of Sentencing Hearing for al-Moayad, *United States v. al-Moayad,* No. 03-cr-01322 (E.D.N.Y. July 28, 2005); Minute Entry of Sentencing Hearing for Zayed, *al-Moayad,*(E.D.N.Y. July 28, 2005).

316 *See United States v. Watford*, 468 F.3d 891, 901-05 (6th Cir. 2006) (holding that sixty-nine-month interval between indictment and arraignment did not violate defendant's Sixth Amendment right to a speedy trial in a narcotics trafficking case); *United States v. White*, 443 F.3d 582, 588-91 (7th Cir. 2006) (nine-month delay from defendant's arrest until the date of trial did not violate defendant's Sixth Amendment speedy trial right in prosecution for armed robbery); *United States v. Register*, 182 F.3d 820, 826-28 (11th Cir. 1999) (pre-trial delay of over thirty-eight months did not violate the defendants' speedy trial rights in a prosecution for various drug trafficking and firearms offenses); *United States v. Munoz-Franco*, 112 F. Supp. 2d 204, 207-22 (D.P.R. 2000) (pre-trial delays of over three and four years did not violate the defendants' speedy trial rights due to complex nature of conspiracy charges related to a large bank failure, the massive amounts of documents produced, and numerous motions made by defendants); *United States v. Twitty*, 107 F.3d 1482, 1487-91 (11th Cir. 1997) (pre-trial delay of over two years did not violate the defendant's speedy trial rights in a prosecution for bank fraud and conspiracy charges related to real estate development).

317 Under the *Barker* test, a court is to examine: (1) the length of the delay; (2) the reason for the delay; (3) whether and how the defendant asserted his right to a speedy trial; and (4) the prejudice to the defendant. *Barker*, 407 U.S. at 530-32. The Courts of Appeals regularly apply these factors in the context of complex criminal prosecutions. *See, e.g., United States v. Munoz-Franco*, 487 F.3d 25, 58-61 (1st Cir. 2007) (applying *Barker* factors in a case involving bank fraud, conspiracy, and misapplication of bank funds and holding that the five-year pre-trial delay between indictment and trial, while "troublesome," did not justify dismissal); *United States v. Brown*, 498 F.3d 523, 529-32 (6th Cir. 2007) (applying *Barker* factors in case involving kidnapping, transportation of a minor with intent to engage in criminal sexual activity, and sex trafficking of children, and holding that nine-month pre-trial delay did not violate defendant's Sixth Amendment rights); *United States v. Tchibassa*, 452 F.3d 918, 922-27 (D.C. Cir. 2006) (applying *Barker* factors in a case involving hostage-taking and conspiring to commit hostage-taking, based on defendant's participation in taking a United States citizen working in Angola hostage, the court held that the eleven-year pre-trial delay between indictment and trial did not justify dismissal due to the unique circumstances in the case).

318 *Available at* http://www.washingtonpost.com/wp-dyn/content/article/2007/03/23/AR2007032301673.html.

319 As this brief discussion makes clear, some terrorism defendants are potentially subject to the death penalty upon conviction. Due to the complexity of death-penalty procedures, those proceedings are outside the scope of this White Paper.

320 The Second Circuit has also held that where the terrorism enhancement "overrepresents the seriousness of defendant's past criminal conduct or the likelihood that defendant will commit other crimes," the sentencing court always has the discretion to make a downward departure under § 4A1.3 of the Guidelines. *See United States v. Meskini*, 319 F.3d 88, 92 (2d Cir. 2003); *see also United States v. Aref*, No. 04-cr-00402, 2007 WL 804814, at *2-3 (N.D.N.Y. Mar. 14, 2007) (applying terrorism enhancement to convictions for providing material support to a terrorist organization, money laundering, and other offenses, but reducing the criminal history category imposed by the enhancement).

321 Notably, the sentences received by many of Benkahla's former co-defendants were close to and in some cases less than 120 months, even though those individuals had been convicted of "significantly more severe, violent offenses," including conspiracy to contribute material support to a terrorist organization and the use and discharge of a firearm in relation to a crime of violence. *Benkahla*, 2007 WL 2254657, at *12.

322 Another issue provoking debate is the determination of the type of crime to which the Guidelines' terrorism enhancement should apply. In several cases, this powerful enhancement has been applied to the acts of domestic terrorism. Examples upheld on appeal include the

terrorism enhancement's application to a defendant who threw a Molotov cocktail into a municipal police department, purportedly to destroy evidence, *United States v. Harris*, 434 F.3d 767 (5th Cir. 2005), and a defendant who committed arson at an Internal Revenue Service office. *United States v. Dowell*, 430 F.3d 1100 (10th Cir. 2005).

In one recent case, a federal district court judge in Oregon permitted the application of the terrorism enhancement to certain crimes committed by a group of environmental and animal rights activists, each of whom had pled guilty to various counts in connection with a string of targeted arsons they committed to promote their views on environmental issues. *See United States v. Thurston*, No. 06-cr-00155, 2007 WL 1500176 (D. Or. May 21, 2007). One of the defendants, thirty-year old Chelsea Gerlach, who had promoted environmental causes since her teenage years, was sentenced to 108 months for her role in the crimes, which caused property damage, but no injuries. *See* William Yardley, *Radical Environmentalist Gets 9-Year Term for Actions Called 'Terrorist'*, N.Y. Times, May 26, 2007, at A9, *online version available at* http://www.nytimes.com/2007/05/26/us/26sentence.html. Without the terrorism enhancement, Gerlach would have faced a Sentencing Guidelines Range of sixty-three to seventy-eight months. *See id.* Another co-defendant, Stanislas Meyerhoff, was sentenced to 156 months after the application of the terrorism enhancement for his role in the crimes, which included setting fire to over thirty sport utility vehicles at an Oregon dealership. *See id.* In deciding that the terrorism enhancement could be applied, the court held that the application of the terrorism enhancement did not require a crime transcending national boundaries, nor did it require a substantial risk of injury. *See Thurston*, 2007 WL 1500176, at *12.

323 *See also* 28 U.S.C. § 994(n) (authorizing the Sentencing Guidelines Commission to reflect in the Guidelines a reduction in sentence in response to a defendant's substantial assistance to law enforcement).

324 In some districts, the defendant is required to plead guilty to all the crimes to which he admitted in the proffer sessions with the government, above and beyond simply the crimes for which he was initially charged. In many districts, this practice may vary case to case and according to the prosecutor. It may also depend on the strategic concerns of the government. For instance, if the government intends to arrest others for conduct for which the cooperating defendant has not been charged, it will frequently require the defendant to plead to such conduct so that he will not ultimately testify regarding conduct for which it appears he did not take responsibility.

325 In some districts, the government as a matter of policy does not recommend a sentence. In all districts, the ultimate authority to sentence the defendant rests with the judge and the defendant is given no assurances of the extent of leniency until the actual sentence is imposed.

326 If a defendant violates the terms of his cooperation agreement (for example, by being untruthful) prior to sentencing, the government may terminate the cooperation agreement, and the defendant is left to face sentencing without the potential benefit of a 5K1 letter from the government. Only in rare instances is a defendant permitted to withdraw his guilty plea even if the government voids his cooperation agreement and refuses to make a 5K1 motion.

327 http://www.lifeandliberty.gov/subs/a_terr.htm.

328 *Available at* http://www.usdoj.gov/opa/pr/2003/March/03_crm_178.htm.

329 Goba received a 120-month sentence—the maximum sentence under 18 U.S.C. § 2339B at the time of the conduct giving rise to the offense. *See* 18 U.S.C. § 2339B(a)(1) (2000). As part of the plea agreement the government did not prosecute Goba for the additional count with which he was originally charged—conspiracy to provide material support to a foreign terrorist organization. *See* Plea Agreement at 10, *Goba* (W.D.N.Y. Mar. 25, 2003) (Dkt. No. 113) ("At sentencing, the government will move to dismiss the open count of the Indictment in this action as to this defendant."). Had Goba pled guilty to both counts, the Guidelines range of 188 to 235 months would have been a relevant factor in the court's sentencing decision.

330 *Online version available at* http://www.nytimes.com/2005/03/02/nyregion/02sheik.html.

331 *Available at* http://www.washingtonpost.com/wp-dyn/content/article/2007/05/18/AR2007051801758_pf.html.

332 *Available at* http://www.usdoj.gov/opa/pr/2003/April/03_crm_237.htm.

333 During the period of supervised release, Ujaama breached his plea agreement by making false statements to a federal officer and leaving the United States without obtaining permission from the U.S. Attorney's office. *See* Order of Finding of Material Breach of Plea Agreement, *Ujaama* (W.D. Wash. Aug. 10, 2007) (Dkt. No. 128). As a result, his supervised release was revoked, he served twenty-four additional months in prison, and the government was released from its commitments under the plea agreement—allowing it to prosecute Ujaama for any and all federal crimes he has committed, including the previously dismissed charges. *See id.*; Judgment on Revocation of Probation/Supervised Release, *Ujaama* (W.D. Wash. Feb. 1, 2007) (Dkt. No. 126). Ujaama was subsequently transferred to the Southern District of New York where he pled guilty pursuant to a plea agreement to a four-count information charging him with two counts of conspiring to provide material support to terrorists, one count of providing material support to terrorists, and one count of unlawful flight to avoid giving testimony. *See* Information, *United States v. Ujaama*, No. 04-cr-00356 (S.D.N.Y. Aug. 13, 2007) (Dkt. No. 10); Minute Entry, *Ujaama* (S.D.N.Y. Aug. 13, 2007); *see also* U.S. Dep't of Justice, Counterterrorism Section, *Counterterrorism White Paper Update* 13 (2007). The combined statutory maximum sentence is thirty years, but Ujaama has not yet been sentenced.

334 *Available at* http://www.nytimes.com/2008/01/19/world/americas/19qaeda.html.

335 *Available at* http://www.nytimes.com/ 2005/07/28/national/28ressam.html.

336 Judge Leonie Brinkema, who presided over *Moussaoui, al-Timimi*, and other terrorism trials, echoed the same belief in an address given at a conference regarding the need for establishing a national security court. *See* Hon. Leonie Brinkema, Address at the Am. U. Washington

College of Law/Brookings Institution Conference: "Terrorists and Detainees: Do We Need A New National Security Court," (Feb. 1, 2008), *audio available at* http://www.wcl.american.edu/podcast/audio/20080201_WCL_TAD.mp3?rd=1.

[337] Judge Coughenour amplified these points in a *New York Times* op-ed piece published in November 2007. *See* John C. Coughenour, Op-Ed., *How to Try a Terrorist*, N.Y. Times, Nov. 1, 2007, at A27, *available at* http://www.nytimes.com/2007/11/01/opinion/01coughenour.html

[338] *Available at* http://seattletimes.nwsource.com/html/localnews/2002406378_ressam27m.html.

[339] *Available at* http://query.nytimes.com/gst/fullpage.html?res= 9906E2DB1F3BF930A15755C0A96F958260.

[340] *Available at* http://query.nytimes.com/gst/fullpage.html?res=9A07E6DB1539F936A35752C1A9669C8B63&sec=&spon=&pagewanted=1.

[341] http://edition.cnn.com/2004/ LAW/05/03/attacks. prison.stabbing/index.html.

[342] *Available at* http://www.senate.gov/~schumer/SchumerWebsite/pressroom/press_releases/2004/PR02733.peppe6070704.html.

[343] *Available at* http://query.nytimes.com/gst/fullpage.html?res=9C02E2D91038F935A35752C1A960958260.

[344] *Online version available at* http://www.nytimes.com/2005/03/11/national/11lefkow.htm.

[345] *Online version available at* http://www.nytimes.com/2005/03/20/national/20judges.html.

[346] Though an analysis of state courts is beyond the scope of this paper, there is reason to believe that violence may occur more frequently in state courts than federal courts, possibly due to weaker state court security measures. *See* Sontag, *In Courts, Threats Become Alarming Fact of Life*. In May 2005, for example, a defendant on trial for rape in state court in Atlanta shot and killed the judge presiding over the case, a court reporter, a sheriff's deputy, and a U.S. Customs agent. *See* Rhonda Cook & Bill Torpy, *Nichols Trial: Costly, Tedious, – Necessary*, Atlanta Journal-Constitution, Jan. 11, 2007, at A1.

[347] http://archives.cnn.com/2001/LAW/01/10/ embassy.bombings.security.crim/.

[348] *Available at* http://query.nytimes.com/gst/fullpage.html?res=9905E2DE103BF930A35752C0A9679C8B63.

[349] *Available at* http://query.nytimes.com/gst/fullpage.html?res=9401E6DF173EF934A25753C1A9679C8B63.

[350] *Available at* http://query.nytimes.com/gst/fullpage.html?res=9C0DE4DD133EF93AA25753C1A9679C8B63.

[351] *Available at* http://www.washingtonpost.com/wp-dyn/content/article/2006/03/01/AR2006030100760.html.

[352] *Available at* http://query.nytimes.com/gst/fullpage.html?res=9A06E2DD113AF936A35750C0A962958260.

[353] *Available at* http://query.nytimes.com/gst/fullpage.html?res=940DE3DB1239F932A25756C0A96E948260.

[354] *Available at* http://www.nytimes.com/2005/04/07/national/07hale.html.

[355] *Available at* http://www.usdoj.gov/oig/reports/USMS/e0710/final.pdf.

[356] *Available at* http://www.nytimes.com/2007/02/10/nyregion/10mcgriff.html.

[357] *Available at* http://www.nytimes.com/2006/11/27/nyregion/27trial.html.

[358] *Available at* http://query.nytimes.com/gst/fullpage.html?res=9400E0DD143EF935A35752C0A9659C8B63.

[359] *Available at* http://www.nytimes.com/2005/01/05/nyregion/05witness.html.

[360] *Available at* http://query.nytimes.com/gst/ fullpage.html?res=9C06E6DA103CF933A2575BC0A961958260.

[361] *Available at* http://query.nytimes.com/gst/fullpage.html?res=9E0CE7DF1F3AF93AA25756C0A964958260.

[362] *Available at* http://query.nytimes.com/gst/fullpage.html?res=9E0CE7D91F3FF930A35757C0A964958260.

[363] *Available at* http://www.usmarshals.gov/duties/factsheets/fugitive.pdf.

[364] U.S. Marshals Service protectees include federal judges, including U.S. Supreme Court Justices; U.S. Attorneys, Assistant U.S. Attorneys and their staffs; U.S. Probation Officers; Pre-trial Services Officers; Tax Court judges; clerks; Federal Public Defenders; U.S. Trustees; witnesses and jurors. *See* U.S. Dep't of Justice, *The United States Marshals Service Judicial Security Process*, at 2.

[365] The U.S. Marshals Service's threat assessment and management process generally is described at pages 14-19 of the OIG's report. *See* U.S. Dep't of Justice, *The United States Marshals Service Judicial Security Process*, at 14-19. Local Judicial Security Inspectors, who are senior-level Deputy Marshals, plan security for high-threat trials like terrorism trials. *See id.* at 12-13.

[366] On April 9, 20002 on the same date that the indictment of Lynne Stewart was announced, former Attorney General John Ashcroft disclosed that the government would be invoking SAMs under § 501.3(d), on a prospective basis, in order to monitor future communications between Sheikh Omar Abdel Rahman and his new attorneys. *See* Prepared Remarks of Attorney General John Ashcroft, Islamic Group Indictment/SAMs (Apr. 9, 2002), *available at* http://www.usdoj.gov/archive/ag/speeches/ 2002/040902agpreparedremarksislamicgroupindictments.htm. We are not aware of any ruling on the legality of these SAMs. In the different context of detainees held in military custody at the Guantánamo Bay Naval Base, however, where the SAMs regulations do not apply, courts have expressed qualms about government efforts to generally monitor attorney-client communications. *See, e.g., al-Odah v. United States*, 346 F. Supp. 2d 1, 12-13 (D.D.C. 2004) (finding that 28 C.F.R. § 501.3(d) does not provide a basis for monitoring attorney-client communications of detainees at Guantánamo Bay Naval Base). It should be noted that the government may monitor attorney-client communications in limited circumstances under other legal authority, such as Title III of the Omnibus Crime Control and Safe Streets Act of

1968, Pub. L. No. 90-351, 82 Stat. 212 (codified as amended at 18 U.S.C. §§ 2510-2522), or the Foreign Intelligence Surveillance Act of 1978 ("FISA"), Pub. L. No. 95-511, 92 Stat. 1783 (codified as amended at 50 U.S.C. §§ 1801-1862). *See, e.g.*, Mem. Op. & Order, *United States v. Sattar*, No. 02-cr-00395 (S.D.N.Y. Sept. 15, 2003) (Dkt. No. 215) ("The Court has conducted an ex parte, in camera review of the materials submitted by the government and finds that the FISA surveillance was lawfully authorized and executed."); *In re: Application of the United States*, 723 F.2d 1022 (1st Cir. 1983) (affirming trial court's denial of law firm's request to disclose wiretap recordings of communications at law offices, made pursuant to 18 U.S.C. § 2518); *cf. Nat'l City Trading Corp. v. United States*, 635 F.2d 1020 (2d Cir. 1980) (upholding search warrant executed on attorney's files where the lawyer permitted an allegedly criminal business operation to take place at his office).

[367] One commentator reports on compromises between the prosecution and defense counsel relating to attorney affirmations in other terrorism-related cases, including those of Ali Saleh Kahlah al-Marri and Mohammed Abdullah Warsame. See Tamar R. Birckhead, *The Conviction of Lynne Stewart and the Uncertain Future of the Right to Defend*, 43 Am. Crim. L. Rev. 1, 45-49 (2006).

[368] *Available at* http://query.nytimes.com/gst/fullpage.html?res=9E00E6D7143EF936A15757C0A9619C8B63.

[369] An Act to implement the "Convention for the Suppression of Unlawful Seizure of Aircraft" (signed at the Hague by United States on Dec. 16, 1970; ratified by the United States Senate, Sept. 14, 1971; entered into force Oct. 14, 1971).

[370] An Act to implement the "Convention on the Physical Protection of Nuclear Material" (signed by the United States, Mar. 3, 1980; ratified by the U.S. Senate, Dec. 13, 1982; entered into force Feb. 8, 1987).

[371] An Act to implement the "International Convention Against the Taking of Hostages" (signed by the United States, Dec. 21, 1979; ratified by the U.S. Senate, Dec. 7, 1984; entered into force for the United States Jan. 6, 1985).

[372] An Act to fully implement the "Convention for the Suppression of Unlawful Acts Against the Safety of Civil Aviation," and to expand the protection accorded to aircraft and related facilities (signed by the United States, Sept. 23, 1971; ratified by the U.S. Senate, Nov. 1, 1972; entered into force Jan. 26, 1973).

[373] An Act to implement the "Convention on the Prevention and Punishment of the Crime of Genocide" (signed by the United States, Dec. 11, 1948; ratified by the U.S. Senate, Nov. 25, 1988; entered into force for the United States Feb. 23, 1989).

[374] An Act to implement the "Convention on the Prohibition of the Development, Production, and Stockpiling of Bacteriological (Biological) and Toxin Weapons and Their Destruction." (signed by the United States, Apr. 10, 1972; ratified by the U.S. Senate, Mar. 26, 1975; entered into force Mar. 26, 1975).

[375] Implements the "Convention for the Suppression of Unlawful Acts Against the Safety of Maritime Navigation" (signed by the United States, Mar. 10, 1988; ratified by the U.S. Senate; entered into force Nov. 21, 1989).

[376] Implements the "Protocol for the Suppression of Unlawful Acts Against the Safety of Fixed Platforms Located on the Continental Shelf" (signed by the United States, Mar. 10, 1988; ratified by the U.S. Senate, Nov. 18, 1994; entered into force for the United States Mar. 6, 1995).

[377] Implements the "Protocol for the Suppression of Unlawful Acts of Violence at Airports Serving International Civil Aviation Supplementary to the Convention for the Suppression of Unlawful Acts Against the Safety of Civil Aviation" (signed by the United States, Feb. 24, 1988; ratified by the U.S. Senate, Oct. 19, 1994; entered into force for the United States Nov. 18, 1994).

[378] Implements the "Convention against Torture and Other Cruel, Inhuman or Degrading Treatment or Punishment" (signed by the United States, Apr. 18, 1988; ratified by the U.S. Senate, Oct. 21, 1994; entered into force for the United States Nov. 20, 1994).

[379] Fully implements the "Convention on the Marketing of Plastic Explosives for the Purpose of Detection" (signed by the United States, Mar. 1, 1991; ratified by the U.S. Senate, Apr. 9, 1997; entered into force June 21, 1998).

[380] An Act to amend Title 18 of the United States Code, to carry out the international obligations of the United States under the Geneva Conventions to provide criminal penalties for certain war crimes.

[381] This Act implements the "International Convention for the Suppression of Terrorist Bombings" (signed by the United States, Jan. 12, 1998; ratified by the U.S. Senate, June 26, 2002; entered into force for the United States July 22, 2002).

[382] This Act implements the "Convention for the Suppression of Financing of Terrorism" (signed by the United States, Jan. 10, 2000; ratified by the U.S. Senate, June 26, 2002; entered into force for the United States July 26, 2002).